You Stink!

You Stink!

MAJOR LEAGUE BASEBALL'S

Terrible Teams & Pathetic Players

Eric J. Wittenberg and
Michael Aubrecht

Foreword by Dave Raymond

Black Squirrel Books
Kent, Ohio

Black Squirrel Books
The Black Squirrel Books imprint includes new nonfiction for the general reader as well as reprints of valuable studies of Ohio and its people, including historical writings, literary studies, biographies, and literature.

© 2012 by The Kent State University Press, Kent, Ohio 44242

ISBN 978-1-60635-138-3

Manufactured in the United States of America
Cataloging information for this title is available at the Library of Congress.

16 15 14 13 12   5 4 3 2 1

For all the kids who struck out in the "big game."
You're not alone.

★ Contents

Dave Raymond, the "Founding Phanatic" (Dave Raymond)

> Ultimately what you get with *You Stink!* is the celebration
> of a sport that gives us more than wins and losses.
>
> —*Dave Raymond*

It's late December 2008. I am at my desk working on the business of *fun*. That's right . . . the second best job I have ever had. We sell fun in the form of animated characters and mascots. I learned all of the lessons of valuable fun by animating a 300-pound green furry Muppet called the *Phillie Phanatic,* the best job I have ever had. It was hard work trying to gain acceptance from the same fans who booed Santa Claus and the Easter Bunny, threw batteries at officials, and booed women for saying yes when they were proposed to on PhanaVision. But it was, without question, the greatest job on the planet.

As I was saying, I sell fun now, and it is all about memorable entertainment, positive messaging, and making sure to steer clear of the Funkillers.

I'm at my desk when an e-mail comes in with a subject line that says: "Request for foreword to baseball book." This is certainly different from what I am used to seeing, so I have some immediate interest. I open it and read the first few lines and here is what it said . . . "My name is Michael Aubrecht and I am an author and historian from Virginia. I am currently co-authoring a baseball book with fellow historian Eric Wittenberg titled *YOU STINK! Major League Baseball's Terrible Teams and Pathetic Players*."

As I read the rest of the e-mail I discover that they want me to write the foreword for this new book! Uh-oh, this sounds like a problem. Of course, I was flattered, but my Funkiller alarm was going off. After a quick search I found out why. Michael is an unabashed Yankees fan, and Eric is an attorney. Run away, run away . . . *funkillers!* Couple that with this thought . . . If I did write a foreword for *You Stink!* wouldn't I be supporting a book that poked fun at and took advantage of long-suffering baseball fans?

Of course, Philadelphia Phillies baseball history has had its share of "disappointments" and by association I would be piling on with a couple of funkillers. The Phillie Phanatic—an ultimate traitor to those same Philadelphia baseball fans who embraced him and even thought he was an improbable choice to rally behind. I typed a quick e-mail response to Michael saying that I was quite busy and would be happy to talk to them again in a month or so. There . . . throw it back on them.

Surely in a month or so they would find someone more appropriate and talented to write this foreword. Steve Bartman comes to mind. As it turned out, that didn't work, so here I am writing this foreword. It took some convincing, but I changed my mind. After talking to Eric and Michael, I discovered that I wasn't dealing with funkillers at all. To the contrary, what I found were two guys with the same passion for baseball that I had, and, with their persuasion, they convinced me that there was no one better to write the foreword. Then I read their book, and I was hooked.

I am, at the heart, one of those long-suffering Philadelphia Phillies fans. My father used to take me to Connie Mack Stadium when I was a young boy. During that time—the early 1960s—the Phillies were at times hapless losers (no less than nine Philadelphia baseball teams are listed in "worst major league baseball teams" category in *You Stink!* in the history of baseball) but that didn't matter to me. The 1961 Phillies are listed as one of the top "Terrible Teams" in *You Stink!,* but they were still my heroes. How about a roster, managed by Gene Mauch, that included Dallas Green, Tony Taylor, Johnny Callison, Ruben Amaro, Chris Short, Art Mahaffey, and Robin Roberts? These are storied names in Phillies history that include a Hall of

Famer and a World Series championship manager, and yet members of a Phillies team that went 47 and 107 and holds the distinction of the longest losing streak in baseball history—23 games!

Memories of those players, for me, were slices of all that was positive as a young baseball fan. Winning then was an icing-on-the-cake thing. I loved those guys and wanted to meet them, get their autographs, and watch them play. I pretended to be them when I was having a catch with Dad in the back yard and when they won it was special. No expectations, just the joy of saying that we beat someone! What surprised me most, when I read about those Phillies in this book, was that I had a sense of pride that they were my team, and I stuck with them through those losses. I was a Phillies fan and that experience was to become the heart and foundation of the Phanatic's personality. The embodiment of fun, tough, and knowledgeable Philadelphia baseball fans.

What was fun for me while reading *You Stink!* was looking at each of the rosters of "Terrible Teams" or "Hall of Shame" and recognizing how many great players are included in them. Michael and Eric did extensive research and used a statistical analysis approach for grading each dubious distinction. You will be armed with a ton of baseball trivia for the water cooler and dinner table after just skimming through this book. I found myself saying, at least a dozen times, "I never knew that" while reading the details and descriptions of the teams, players, and owners. You get the chance to review the great history of the game and to read about the history of our passion for baseball.

Ultimately what you get with *You Stink!* is the celebration of a sport that gives us more than wins and losses. It drives right to the heart of what all of us love about baseball. We bond with our teams and everyone who has had to suffer through slumps. Watching our heroes, at times, stumble through ineptitude, bonehead plays, and heartbreaking losses is part of what we celebrate when winning finally comes. What we have seen and felt in Philadelphia can be shared with baseball fans in Chicago, Boston, San Francisco, and, yes Michael, even in New York, "The Evil Empire!"

This is why we are baseball fans. Of course, we want to be champions but sometimes the hope from the eternal loser is stronger and more real than celebration of the perennial winners. So sit back and enjoy this celebration of the "most neglected topic in the annals of baseball history" and remember—it could be worse . . . you could be a Cubbies fan.

Dave Raymond
"The Phillie Phanatic"

Introduction
Monument to Mediocrity

> The one constant through all the years, Ray, has been
> baseball. America has rolled by like an army of steam-
> rollers. It has been erased like a blackboard, rebuilt, and
> erased again. But baseball has marked the time. This field,
> this game: it's a part of our past, Ray. It reminds of us of all
> that once was good, and it could be again.
>
> —*Terence Mann (James Earl Jones) in Field of Dreams*

I had the misfortune of being born into a family of Philadelphia sports
nuts. My father was a dedicated A's fan, until they moved to Kansas City,
that is. Up until then, he'd always turned up his nose at the Phillies, but
when the A's moved away, it left only the Phillies. And so, he reluctantly
became a Phillies fan. I was born in 1961, six years after the A's moved
away. By then, my father had been smitten. He was a suffering, diehard
Phillies fan, rooting for a bad baseball team. The 1961 Phillies went 47–107
and are generally considered to be one of the worst teams in the history
of major league baseball.

So, against, this backdrop, I was doomed. It was inevitable that I also
would be bitten by the Phillies bug, and I was. Some of my earliest memories arc of watching Dick "Don't Call Me Richie" Allen hit long home runs
clear out of old Connie Mack Stadium with my father. In 1964, when I was
three years old, the Phillies managed one of the greatest collapses in the
history of professional sports. In first place with 12 games to go, the Phils
lost 10 in a row and blew a six-game lead in the process. They finished
third. They would not come close again for twelve more long years.

Times were very bad for Philadelphia's professional sports teams. The
Eagles, who won the NFL championship in 1960 just a few months before I
was born, became one of the league's consistently worst teams. The 76'ers,
who won an NBA championship in 1967, posted a record of 9–73 in 1973,
the absolute worst record ever in the long history of professional sports.

Chicago White Sox Outfielder Al Smith in the 1959 World Series (Library of Congress)

Only the Flyers provided us with some hope, winning the Stanley Cup two years in a row in 1974 and 1975.

And then things changed. The Phils won the National League's Eastern Division in 1976, 1977, and 1978, losing in the divisional playoffs each time. They finished second in 1979, and then a miracle happened—they won the World Series in 1980, the first world championship in the 126 years of the team's existence. They won the Fall Classic again in 2008, ending a 28-year drought for the Phillies and an overall drought of 100 professional seasons for the City of Brotherly Love (25 years x 4 professional sports = 100 seasons; the last world championship was the 76'ers in 1983). That makes two championships in 126 years. They've also lost three more times in the Fall Classic, in 1983, 1993, and 2009. In 2007, they finally vanquished the ghosts of 1964 and won the National League East after an even more epic collapse by the New York Mets, who lost 11 of their last 15 games, while the Phils went 12–3 down the stretch, winning the division championship on the final day of the season. However, along the way, in July 2007, the Phillies became the only professional sports franchise in history to post 10,000 losses.

Therefore, as someone who has avidly rooted for the Phillies for half a century, I know losing. I understand losing. I know what it's like to suffer while watching epic loss after epic loss. I had long understood what it was like to find another team to root for during the postseason because my team hadn't made it there. And along the way, I came up with an idea.

In 1974, as a 13-year-old, I came up with the idea of doing a study of the worst teams in the history of major league baseball, which I wanted to call *The Losers*. I picked out some teams and thought it would be fun to do the research for a project like this. I even wrote a letter to Joe Garagiola, then a star announcer for NBC, asking for permission to quote from his book, *Baseball Is a Funny Game*. I still have his letter denying me that permission tucked inside an album full of sports autographs I've had since childhood.

I wanted my project to be a celebration of the very worst teams in the history of major league baseball, a lighthearted look at the worst that the National Pastime has had to offer. Narrowing down the list was a challenge. There have been many really terrible teams in the history of major league baseball. However, one entrant in that Hall of Shame was obvious. The all-time worst team in the history of major league baseball was the 1899 Cleveland Spiders. They went 20–134 and had to play their last 35 or so games on the road, because no National League team would come to their field to play due to a lack of attendance. The 1899 Spiders are the gold standard against which all other awful teams have to be measured.

Or then, there were the 1930 Phillies, who had a team batting average in excess of .310 and a team ERA well over 6.00, meaning that even with that kind of offense, they finished dead last in the National League, as they had one of the worst pitching staffs in the history of the game. Or Garagiola's Pittsburgh Pirates teams of the early 1950s, which were consistently atrocious. Or the 1962 New York Mets, the worst team of the modern era, who posted a record of 40–120 in their inaugural season. Or the 1969 Seattle

Pilots, who posted a record of 64–98, finishing 33 games out of first place in the only year of the franchise's existence. (This team has been called the Milwaukee Brewers since 1970.) My problem was that I was only 13 years old when I came up with this concept, and I had absolutely no idea what was involved in researching and writing a book like this.

Consequently, I stored this idea away years ago, never figuring I would ever get a chance to do anything about it. I just didn't have the resources or knowledge regarding how to do that sort of research, and I always had other projects. I continued to harbor the hope that I might someday find a way to bring the project to fruition, but with each passing year, the likelihood of doing so grew less and less.

I met Michael Aubrecht as a consequence of our mutual interest in the American Civil War. I knew that Michael had done a great deal of writing on baseball over the years for *Baseball-Almanac,* and I also knew that he was familiar with this sort of research. In the course of a few exchanges of e-mail, I mentioned my idea for a study of the worst that major league baseball had to offer to Michael, who fell in love with the concept once he learned more about it. That clinched it. After further discussion, we decided to find a way to bring my long-dormant dream to fruition. You are holding the results of that collaboration. I'm just thrilled that this idea that I came up with almost 40 years ago has finally come to fruition. We hope that you enjoy it as much as we have enjoyed telling these stories of monumental failure that have cried out to be told for too long.

Eric J. Wittenberg
Columbus, Ohio

Almost a decade ago, Sean Holtz, at *Baseball-Almanac (BA)*, gave me my first paid writing assignment and a shot at a second career. Over the years, I have provided *BA* with complete studies of the World Series, All-Star Games, regular and post seasons, player, team, and commissioner bios, as well as some totally biased editorial pieces on my personal favorites, the New York Yankees.

Since then, I have been privileged to write and publish hundreds of additional studies on the game, along with an online reference book and multiple magazine and newspaper articles. Although my books today focus almost entirely on the War Between the States, baseball remains a mainstay in my private and professional life. It is the source of my agony and my ecstasy.

As a lifelong baseball fan, I have always been fascinated with the legacy of America's National Pastime. Nothing pleases me more than digging through my library of books or surfing the Net and learning about teams and individuals who played this wonderful sport decades before my parents were even born. As I continue to study the game's past, I seem to have more respect for the players of yesterday and less for the players of today.

Ballplayers of the past were nothing like the modern athlete. These were men who played the game simply to escape the harsh realities of the steel mills or the coal mines. There were no agents, or endorsements, or trainers, or supplements. There was no drug testing, or labor disputes, or free agency, or no-trade clauses. They didn't need legal representation or negotiation and, more importantly, they didn't want it. Just give 'em a damn ball and a bat, and they'd play. And they'd be thankful for the opportunity and give you 110 percent. The concept was perfect.

But that was then and this is now. Frankly folks, far too many players today are spoiled rotten, and it's left me and many other diehards with a bad taste in our mouths. I'll put it this way. The players of the past played for the name on the *front* of the uniform. The players of today play for the name on the *back*.

As the state of baseball continues to rock back and forth between the owners and the league and the fans, I'd like to recommend that everyone spend a little time reading about the history of the game, its origins, and its originators. Learn about pitchers who would go for 12 complete innings and then pitch again, with no rest, during a doubleheader the following day. Or other players, who were injured—and even struck by lightning! And they always returned to finish the game, never whining, never complaining—just willing to give it all, for the privilege to play.

That's the difference between an "athlete" and a "player." I would take the player any day. They were grateful to play the game, and I'm grateful that their history is still available for us to review. That goes for both the winners and losers.

And that's why I was so pleased when Eric Wittenberg, a fellow historian for whom I have a great deal of respect and admiration, pitched the idea of working on a baseball book that would focus on *the* worst.

In a market that is oversaturated with inflated tales of glory, Eric's vision for a book that took the opposite approach to the norm was very inviting. My friend, renowned Civil War painter Mort Künstler, once told me that artists always try to be totally original in their work because there won't be anything else out there to compare them to. I agree.

The first half of this book is based on statistical data. The second half is based on our own personal opinions. Readers may or may not agree, and we welcome your feedback. We have labored, to the best of our abilities, to accurately research and present what we feel are the worst players, teams, moments, and performances in the history of baseball. You will note that we have chosen to address what we consider to be highly original and/or far-too-neglected subjects.

However, it is almost impossible to incorporate everything; therefore, we have included an extensive list of reference materials used in this project and recommend each and every one for those who are interested in reading additional information. For additional data, composite statistics, individual box scores, and more information on all things pertaining to baseball, visit Baseball-Almanac.com.

In closing, I would like to add that no portion of this project has been created in a mean-spirited manner. Even our "Hall of Shame" segments are intentionally presented in a quasi-tribute style.

We are, after all, fans and we hope that this book is received in the manner in which it was intended, as an interesting and highly original read.

Michael Aubrecht
Fredericksburg, Virginia

Terrible Teams

#1 | Not Louisville Sluggers
The 1889 Louisville Colonels (27–111)

> The '89 team just sucked lukewarm prune juice through
> a plastic straw, putting up a pythagorean win-loss mark
> of 37–101 and underperforming even that toxic waste
> pool by going 27–111 on the field. This wasn't just a last
> place team, it was a bad joke told by a bad comedian.
> —*Jeff Angus in* Management by Baseball

Louisville, Kentucky, will always be an integral part of major league baseball's story. As worldwide headquarters of the Hillerich & Bradsby Company, manufacturers of the Louisville Slugger, the town has produced beautifully crafted clubs for more than 120 years while becoming the gold standard for the bat manufacturing industry. Ever since the company pioneered a sports marketing concept by paying Hall of Fame hitter Honus Wagner to use his name on a bat, Hillerich & Bradsby has put lumber in the hands of baseball's legendary greats, from Ty Cobb and Babe Ruth to Cal Ripken and Tony Gwynn.

Louisville was also responsible for another milestone: baseball's inaugural "worst to first" franchise. Originally part of the American Association, the Louisville Colonels were purchased by Horace Phillips the owner/manager of the Pittsburgh Alleghenys (later called the Pirates). As happened with several of the other nineteenth-century franchises in this book, multiteam owners often shuffled their players from one team to another, hoping to secure a winning combination. As a result, many of the Colonels' standout players were transferred from Louisville to Pittsburgh's National League team at the insistence of its new owner.

Despite having their talent pool drained, Louisville's 1889 ball club still retained some quality members. These players included Pete "The Wooden Indian" Browning who dominated at the plate with a .341 average over 13 seasons, all-star caliber outfielder Chicken Wolf and right-handed pitching sensation Guy Becker. Another standout on the mound was a grizzled veteran named Toad Ramsey, who had tossed an astounding 588, 561, and 342 innings of strikeout ball.

1889 Louisville Colonels (Baseball Hall of Fame Library, Cooperstown, NY)

That was about it for bragging rights, as the rest of Louisville's rotation left much to be desired. Poor pitchers of note included Scott Stratton, John Ewing, and Red Ehret, who all put up deplorable numbers. Ehret, for instance, posted a 10–29 mark, while his teammate Ewing went 6–30.

The Colonels also suffered from a severe lack of leadership. Opening Day debuted a hot-tempered utility infielder-turned-skipper named Thomas J. "Dude" Esterbrook who logged time with seven different franchises over his journeyman career. In 1884, he had played magnificently for the New York Metropolitans, where he batted .314 and led the league in most hitting categories. That was the highlight of his career—it was all downhill from there. Unfortunately, Dude's skills on the diamond did not translate into the clubhouse.

Prior to the '89 season Esterbrook was named captain of the Colonels, but after winning 2 games in the first 10, he was terminated in favor of Jimmy "Chicken" Wolf. According to Society for American Baseball Research (SABR) baseball historian Bob Baily:

His one time in the spotlight for non-playing activities came in 1889. The Louisville Colonels that season were one of the worst teams in the history of major league baseball. They posted a 27–111 record while battling the team's owners and each other. The season opened with Dude Esterbrook as team captain. Esterbrook insisted on people doing things his way and began assessing fines on players who chose not to take his advice to heart. In late April, Esterbrook fined second baseman Dan Shannon ten dollars for failing to obey his instructions on how to throw the ball. A few days later Wolf and Esterbrook engaged in a heated argument over that fine. As the temperature and tempers rose, Esterbrook dropped a ten-dollar fine on Jimmy. More words were exchanged, the fine escalated to forty dollars, and Wolf was on his way to visit Mordecai Davidson, the team owner. Within a week Esterbrook was no longer captain, and the team selected Wolf as their new leader.

Unfortunately, this would not be the last transfer of power, as the Colonels cycled through four different managers over the course of the year.[1] Jack Chapman, who had led the team previously, was the last to take the helm, but even he could only muster a miserable 1–6 record. With a win-loss record of 27–111–2 (.196 winning percentage), the last-place Louisville Colonels set the historic distinction of recording the longest-ever losing streak of 26 games (May 22–June 22). Over the course of the '89 campaign Louisville scored 632 runs while surrendering 1,091 runs.

Amazingly, the 1890 Louisville Colonels rebounded to win the American Association's pennant with an incredibly improved 88–44 record. The title marked the greatest percentage of improvement (over consecutive seasons) in major league baseball history. This epic turnaround could be attributed in part to new owners and the fact that the Colonels' biggest competition had thinned out. The best team in the American Association,

Left-Handed Pitcher and "Clown-Prince" Nicholas Altrock (Library of Congress)

the Brooklyn Bridegrooms, and the fourth best, Cincinnati's Red Stockings, jumped to the National League.

Ironically, one of the greatest players ever to don a cap made his debut in a Colonels' uniform before moving on the Pirates. Honus Wagner was a gifted shortstop who played in the National League circuit from 1897 to 1917. In his first year in Louisville, he hit .338 in just 61 games. Following the 1899 season, the National League contracted from 12 to 8 teams, and the Colonels were one of the four teams eliminated. Wagner became one of Pittsburgh's greatest athletes. In 1936, the Baseball Hall of Fame inducted him as one of the first five members, receiving the second-highest vote total behind Ty Cobb and ahead of Babe Ruth.

Perhaps if Honus Wagner had broken into the major leagues a decade earlier, he may have prevented the 1889 Louisville franchise from making its mark as the first team in major-league history to lose more than 100 games in a season. Then again, maybe even the "The Flying Dutchman" could not have kept this team from crashing and burning.

1889 Louisville Colonels Schedule

GAME	DATE	OPPONENT	SCORE	DECISION	RECORD
1	04–17–1889	vs Kansas City Blues	4–7	L	0–1
2	04–18–1889	vs Kansas City Blues	6–8	L	0–2
3	04–19–1889	vs Kansas City Blues	5–7	L	0–3
4	04–20–1889	vs Kansas City Blues	9–14	L	0–4
5	04–21–1889	vs St. Louis Browns	10–12	L	0–5
6	04–22–1889	vs St. Louis Browns	6–13	L	0–6
7	04–23–1889	vs St. Louis Browns	17–7	W	1–6
8	04–25–1889	at Kansas City Blues	5–16	L	1–7
9	04–27–1889	at Kansas City Blues	5–4	W	2–7
10	04–28–1889	at Kansas City Blues	4–5	L	2–8
11-I	04–30–1889	at St. Louis Browns	2–3	L	2–9
12-II	04–30–1889	at St. Louis Browns	4–10	L	2–10
13	05–01–1889	at St. Louis Browns	1–9	L	2–11
14	05–02–1889	at St. Louis Browns	1–5	L	2–12
15	05–04–1889	at Cincinnati Red Stockings	8–2	W	3–12

1889 Louisville Colonels Schedule (cont.)

GAME	DATE	OPPONENT	SCORE	DECISION	RECORD
16	05–05–1889	at Cincinnati Red Stockings	5–12	L	3–13
17	05–06–1889	at Cincinnati Red Stockings	7–8	L	3–14
18	05–07–1889	vs Brooklyn Bridegrooms	3–13	L	3–15
19	05–08–1889	vs Brooklyn Bridegrooms	2–21	L	3–16
20	05–10–1889	vs Brooklyn Bridegrooms	6–10	L	3–17
21	05–11–1889	vs Philadelphia Athletics	5–1	W	4–17
22	05–12–1889	vs Philadelphia Athletics	0–2	L	4–18
23	05–13–1889	vs Philadelphia Athletics	2–1	W	5–18
24	05–16–1889	vs Columbus Colts	6–10	L	5–19
25	05–17–1889	vs Columbus Colts	1–9	L	5–20
26	05–18–1889	vs Columbus Colts	13–3	W	6–20
27	05–19–1889	vs Columbus Colts	4–1	W	7–20
28	05–21–1889	vs Baltimore Orioles	8–4	W	8–20
29	05–22–1889	vs Baltimore Orioles	2–11	L	8–21
30	05–23–1889	vs Baltimore Orioles	8–9	L	8–22
31-I	05–26–1889	at Cincinnati Red Stockings	7–8	L	8–23
32-II	05–26–1889	at Cincinnati Red Stockings	4–16	L	8–24
33	05–27–1889	at Cincinnati Red Stockings	9–10	L	8–25
34	05–28–1889	at Cincinnati Red Stockings	12–13	L	8–26
35	05–31–1889	at Columbus Colts	2–7	L	8–27
36	06–01–1889	at Columbus Colts	3–8	L	8–28
37-I	06–02–1889	at Columbus Colts	4–11	L	8–29
38-II	06–02–1889	at Columbus Colts	3–12	L	8–30
39	06–05–1889	at Philadelphia Athletics	10–11	L	8–31
40-I	06–06–1889	at Philadelphia Athletics	2–5	L	8–32
41-II	06–06–1889	at Philadelphia Athletics	3–16	L	8–33
42	06–07–1889	at Philadelphia Athletics	7–9	L	8–34
43	06–08–1889	at Brooklyn Bridegrooms	5–14	L	8–35

1889 Louisville Colonels Schedule (cont.)

GAME	DATE	OPPONENT	SCORE	DECISION	RECORD
44	06–09–1889	at Brooklyn Bridegrooms	2–12	L	8–36
45	06–10–1889	at Brooklyn Bridegrooms	5–7	L	8–37
46	06–11–1889	at Brooklyn Bridegrooms	2–4	L	8–38
47	06–13–1889	at Baltimore Orioles	2–4	L	8–39
48	06–15–1889	at Baltimore Orioles	2–4	L	8–40
49-I	06–17–1889	at Baltimore Orioles	6–10	L	8–41
50-II	06–17–1889	at Baltimore Orioles	0–10	L	8–42
51	06–18–1889	at Baltimore Orioles	7–17	L	8–43
52	06–21–1889	vs St. Louis Browns	3–7	L	8–44
53-I	06–22–1889	vs St. Louis Browns	6–7	L	8–45
54-II	06–22–1889	vs St. Louis Browns	2–3	L	8–46
55	06–23–1889	vs St. Louis Browns	7–3	W	9–46
56	06–26–1889	at Kansas City Blues	2–12	L	9–47
57	06–27–1889	at Kansas City Blues	6–5	W	10–47
58-I	06–28–1889	at Kansas City Blues	3–7	L	10–48
59-II	06–28–1889	at Kansas City Blues	3–9	L	10–49
60	06–29–1889	at St. Louis Browns	1–10	L	10–50
61	06–30–1889	at St. Louis Browns	7–12	L	10–51
62	07–01–1889	at St. Louis Browns	2–8	L	10–52
63-I	07–04–1889	vs Philadelphia Athletics	8–2	W	11–52
64-II	07–04–1889	vs Philadelphia Athletics	1–12	L	11–53
65	07–05–1889	vs Philadelphia Athletics	1–9	L	11–54
66	07–06–1889	vs Baltimore Orioles	5–6	L	11–55
67	07–07–1889	vs Baltimore Orioles	11–3	W	12–55
68	07–08–1889	vs Baltimore Orioles	5–2	W	13–55
69	07–10–1889	vs Brooklyn Bridegrooms	0–3	L	13–56
70-I	07–12–1889	vs Brooklyn Bridegrooms	4–3	W	14–56
71-II	07–12–1889	vs Brooklyn Bridegrooms	1–8	L	14–57
72	07–13–1889	vs Columbus Colts	5–3	W	15–57
73	07–15–1889	vs Columbus Colts	4–9	L	15–58
74	07–16–1889	vs Columbus Colts	8–9	L	15–59
75	07–18–1889	vs Kansas City Blues	5–1	W	16–59
76	07–21–1889	vs Kansas City Blues	3–1	W	17–59
77	07–23–1889	at Baltimore Orioles	3–6	L	17–60

1889 Louisville Colonels Schedule (cont.)

GAME	DATE	OPPONENT	SCORE	DECISION	RECORD
78	07–24–1889	at Baltimore Orioles	3–17	L	17–61
79	07–25–1889	at Baltimore Orioles	4–8	L	17–62
80	07–26–1889	at Columbus Colts	3–6	L	17–63
81	07–27–1889	at Columbus Colts	6–2	W	18–63
82	07–28–1889	at Columbus Colts	11–10	W	19–63
83-I	08–01–1889	at Brooklyn Bridegrooms	6 8	L	19–64
84-II	08–01–1889	at Brooklyn Bridegrooms	1–14	L	19–65
85	08–02–1889	at Philadelphia Athletics	1–8	L	19–66
86	08–03–1889	at Philadelphia Athletics	0–3	L	19–67
87	08–04–1889	at Philadelphia Athletics	7–0	W	20–67
88	08–07–1889	vs Cincinnati Red Stockings	4–5	L	20–68
89	08–08–1889	vs Cincinnati Red Stockings	3–4	L	20–69
90	08–09–1889	vs Cincinnati Red Stockings	8–15	L	20–70
91	08–10–1889	vs Philadelphia Athletics	9–11	L	20–71
92	08–11–1889	vs Philadelphia Athletics	3–12	L	20 72
93-I	08–12–1889	vs Philadelphia Athletics	3–9	L	20–73
94-II	08–12–1889	vs Philadelphia Athletics	5–10	L	20–74
95	08–13–1889	vs Baltimore Orioles	1–6	L	20–75
96	08–14–1889	vs Baltimore Orioles	3–8	L	20–76
97	08–15–1889	vs Baltimore Orioles	0–3	L	20–77
98	08–17–1889	vs Brooklyn Bridegrooms	0 10	L	20–70
99	08–18–1889	vs Brooklyn Bridegrooms	3–6	L	20–79
100	08–19–1889	vs Brooklyn Bridegrooms	8–9	L	20–80
101	08–20–1889	vs Brooklyn Bridegrooms	11–18	L	20–81
102	08–22–1889	vs Columbus Colts	14–6	W	21–81
103	08–24–1889	vs Columbus Colts	7–16	L	21–82
104	08–25–1889	vs Columbus Colts	8–5	W	22–82
105	08–26–1889	at Cincinnati Red Stockings	6–19	L	22–83

1889 Louisville Colonels Schedule (cont.)

GAME	DATE	OPPONENT	SCORE	DECISION	RECORD
106	08–27–1889	at Cincinnati Red Stockings	4–10	L	22–84
107	08–28–1889	at Cincinnati Red Stockings	4–6	L	22–85
108	08–30–1889	at Baltimore Orioles	4–3	W	23–85
109	08–31–1889	at Baltimore Orioles	3–12	L	23–86
110	09–02–1889	at Baltimore Orioles	2–10	L	23–87
111	09–03–1889	at Columbus Colts	3–7	L	23–88
112	09–04–1889	at Columbus Colts	0–6	L	23–89
113	09–06–1889	at Columbus Colts	3–7	L	23–90
114	09–07–1889	at Philadelphia Athletics	4–4	T	23–90–1
115	09–08–1889	at Philadelphia Athletics	6–7	L	23–91–1
116	09–09–1889	at Philadelphia Athletics	10–7	W	24–91–1
117-I	09–14–1889	at Brooklyn Bridegrooms	2–6	L	24–92–1
118-II	09–14–1889	at Brooklyn Bridegrooms	3–6	L	24–93–1
119-I	09–15–1889	at Brooklyn Bridegrooms	5–6	L	24–94–1
120-II	09–15–1889	at Brooklyn Bridegrooms	2–7	L	24–95–1
121	09–17–1889	vs Cincinnati Red Stockings	1–5	L	24–96–1
122	09–18–1889	vs Cincinnati Red Stockings	3–4	L	24–97–1
123	09–19–1889	vs Cincinnati Red Stockings	8–0	W	25–97–1
124	09–21–1889	at Kansas City Blues	7–5	W	26–97–1
125	09–22–1889	at Kansas City Blues	5–10	L	26–98–1
126	09–23–1889	at Kansas City Blues	4–6	L	26–99–1
127	09–26–1889	at St. Louis Browns	4–5	L	26–100–1
128	09–28–1889	at St. Louis Browns	2–2	T	26–100–2
129	09–30–1889	at St. Louis Browns	3–6	L	26–101–2
130	10–01–1889	at St. Louis Browns	4–7	L	26–102–2
131	10–03–1889	at Cincinnati Red Stockings	3–14	L	26–103–2
132	10–04–1889	at Cincinnati Red Stockings	2–9	L	26–104–2
133	10–05–1889	at Cincinnati Red Stockings	1–8	L	26–105–2

1889 Louisville Colonels Schedule (cont.)

GAME	DATE	OPPONENT	SCORE	DECISION	RECORD
134	10–07–1889	at Cincinnati Red Stockings	3–4	L	26–106–2
135	10–08–1889	vs St. Louis Browns	3–9	L	26–107–2
136	10–09–1889	vs St. Louis Browns	4–8	L	26–108–2
137	10–10–1889	vs St. Louis Browns	1–9	L	26–109–2
138	10–12–1889	vs Kansas City Blues	6–4	W	27–109–2
139	10–13–1889	vs Kansas City Blues	5–6	L	27–110–2
140	10–14–1889	vs Kansas City Blues	5–7	L	27–111–2

Data courtesy of Baseball-Almanac.com.

#2 | Bad News Brownies
The 1898 St. Louis Browns (39–111)

> During his lone season as manager, he led the Browns
> to just 39 wins, with 111 losses in 154 games.
>
> —*Wiki-bio of manager Tim Hurst*

The 1898 St. Louis Browns have a riches-to-rags story. In order to fully appreciate this historic franchise's rise and fall from grace, one must first examine the ball club's unlikely origins. Perhaps no other story in professional sports better personifies the "American Dream" than that of the team's founder Christian Friedrich Wilhelm von der Ahe.

After immigrating to the United States, Von der Ahe took a meager job as a grocery clerk and began stockpiling his accumulated revenues with plans to open his own business. The hard-working entrepreneur eventually bought out his employer and immediately expanded the premises to include a small saloon off the back of the store. Many of the bar's patrons arrived at the conclusion of local baseball games and Von der Ahe immediately recognized another business opportunity within the sport's growing popularity.

In 1882, he invested $1,800 of his own funds into the then-bankrupt St. Louis Brown Stockings, a fledging franchise whose reputation was mired in scandal and in rumors of mismanagement. In an effort to distance the team from its tarnished reputation, Von der Ahe immediately dropped Stockings from the name and entered the organization into the more respectable American Association (AA). He then hired Charles Comiskey as his first baseman and manager. Comiskey later became one of baseball's most prolific owners.

Despite an obvious lack of experience and knowledge of baseball, Von der Ahe took an active role in the team's day-to-day operations. With his thick German accent and enormously bushy mustache, the owner became one of the first celebrated off-the-field sports personalities of the day. A talented showman with an obvious love of attention, he called himself "Der boss president of der Prowns." The team also held an affection for their

1898 St. Louis Browns (Library of Congress)

eccentric leader and played with zeal early on. This zeal paid tremendous dividends, as the Browns dominated the AA League and won four consecutive championships starting in 1885. In just a few seasons, the St. Louis Browns became one of the first dynasties in sports.

Businesswise, the Browns were also one of the first ball clubs to generate mass revenues. Von der Ahe made more than $500,000 from the team alone and purposefully lowered ticket prices in order to sell more beer. As attendance at home games grew, so did the capacity of the Browns' ballpark, which was expanded multiple times to accommodate the swelling crowds. It has been suggested that Von der Ahe referred to people in the stands as "fanatics," which was later shortened to "fans," and that he was the first to sell hot dogs, although neither statement has ever been officially confirmed.

Always an entrepreneur, Von der Ahe can be credited with several major innovations to the game, some of which are still used today. He believed that talent could be developed from within, so he organized the first farm club, called the St. Louis Whites. He is also credited with initiating one of the first World Series—like championship tournaments.

In 1885, the American Association–leading Browns and National League champion Chicago White Stockings went head-to-head for six championship games (winning three each), resulting in a rare tie. Despite the forming of a special committee to determine a winner, both teams were declared champions and split the $1,000 purse.

That same year Von der Ahe shamelessly exhibited his ever-growing ego when he erected a larger-than-life statue of himself outside of Sportsman's Park. The local press lambasted him, and some beat writers accused the German of having a "Napoleon Complex." Two years later the Browns suffered a poor showing in the postseason and their owner, who was becoming more irate as time went on, threatened to withhold their earnings for lack of effort.

By 1891, Von der Ahe had expanded his operations and had become a majority owner in the Cincinnati Porkers, who also played in the American Association for part of one season. This conflict of interests caused a great deal of stress for the Browns, who felt that their founder had betrayed them. Comiskey himself lost patience with his employer and left to take a player/manager position with the Cincinnati Reds. After Comiskey's departure, the Browns sank to a last-place team.

Plagued with mounting legal problems and financial issues, Von der Ahe moved his franchise to a larger field that was surrounded by a city block of his own amusements and concessions. He relocated his team solely to recoup lost revenues as the Browns' profits dwindled. By compensating for the lack of ticket sales with an amusement park, a beer garden, and a horse track, Von der Ahe put his team's needs last. Additional business ventures came later, including a water flume ride and an ice-skating rink.

Despite the popularity of the carnival-like atmosphere that the general public enjoyed, the league vehemently disapproved of gambling on the grounds, and the sportswriters took Von der Ahe to task for ignoring the foundation of his enterprise in the name of the almighty dollar. One newspaper called the facility "Von der Ha Ha." Baseball seemed no longer all that important to the man, and he sold off many of his players' contracts to the Brooklyn Bridegrooms.

The Browns' 17th season set a new all-time low as the team went 39–111 and finished dead last (12th) in the National League. Despite a horrible overall showing, there were a few moments worth remembering during the tumultuous '98 campaign.

In late April, St. Louis ace Jim Hughey dominated his old team, the Pittsburgh Pirates, 13–1. A complete player, Hughey scattered 11 hits, started 2 double plays, and had a home run and triple at the plate. Unfortunately the Pirates got their revenge three days later by beating their former teammate by a whopping 21–2.

On June 3, left-handed catcher Jack Clements became the first player to catch 1,000 games. He also drove in the winning run in a 5–4 victory over Baltimore. Other than those isolated highlights, the 1898 season was a never-ending nightmare from beginning to end. With a roster full of disgruntled players, a depressed and distracted owner, and a total lack of fan support, the St. Louis Browns fell into a quicksand that swallowed the team for the entire year. In the end, they scored a measly 571 runs, while allowing 929.

1898 represented not only the worst year in St. Louis Browns' history, but also the worst year in Christian Friedrich Wilhelm von der Ahe's life. During a game against the Chicago Orphans, a fire broke out and destroyed an entire section of the ballpark. Forty patrons were injured as the crowd of 6,000 stampeded to escape. The Browns' new manager Tim Hurst and his players helped workers remove debris so that an April 17 day game could be played. This was the only recorded instance when Hurst was able to motivate his players. After mismanaging the Browns for one season, Hurst returned to the role of an on-again, off-again umpire in the National League from 1891 to 1903. He then moved to the American League and stayed there from 1905 to 1909. Despite his failure as a skipper, Hurst excelled as an official, and was among the first umpires named to a Roll of Honor by the Baseball Hall of Fame in 1946.

With no praise to bestow on his own miserable team, Hurst snubbed its memory when reminiscing in his golden years. He fondly recalled one of the Browns' earlier players in a piece titled "Baseball Reminiscences." He wrote:

Tom McCarthy, of the famous St. Louis Browns, and afterwards with the Bostons, is one of the players that one could never forget. He was full of tricks, and the most resourceful out-fielder that ever played the game. He had no end of nerve, and was never afraid to take a chance. He could make some of the alleged players of today open their eyes in wonder if they saw such a fielder who backed up every base, and it was nothing unusual for him to go behind the catcher when there was need. Throw? Well, I guess yes. He was very strong, quick and accurate and always had the situation gauged to a nicety. Think of an outfielder making two double plays in one game—off the same runner. I can testify to that, for I umpired the game in which it was done. Those who were so partisan that they could not appreciate that kind of a play, yelled, "Dirty ball," and this in Baltimore.

As the seemingly endless 1898 season finally neared its painful conclusion, things went from bad to worse for the Browns' owner. Von der Ahe's
second wife left him and his bondsman kidnapped him for not paying his
debts. With his entire empire crumbling all around him, the once wealthy
immigrant sold off most of his assets. Following a highly publicized investigation into the tragic fire, the unlucky German lost his once beloved
baseball team. Brothers Stanley and Frank Robison bought the Browns and
renamed them the St. Louis Perfectos, and later, the Cardinals.[1] (Note: The
American League team known as the St. Louis Browns from 1902 to 1953
had no connection to Von der Ahe's team aside from the name.)

Ironically, Von der Ahe eventually lost all of his amusement properties
and returned to working in the small saloon where his roller-coaster journey began. Charles Comiskey, now the owner of the White Sox, felt sorry
for his former boss and frequently sent money so that he could make ends
meet. Following his death in 1913, Von der Ahe's statue was used as the
marker adorning his grave.

1898 St. Louis Browns Statmaster: Hitting

NAME	POS	GAMES	AVG	SLG	AB	H	2B	3B	HR	AB/HR	R	RBI	BB	SO	SB
Lou Bierbauer	2B	4	.000	.000	9	0	0	0	0	0.0	0	0	1	-	0
John Callahan	P	2	.000	.000	4	0	0	0	0	0.0	0	0	0	-	0
Kid Carsey	P	38	.200	.248	105	21	0	1	1	105.0	8	10	10	-	3
Jack Clements	C	99	.257	.370	335	86	19	5	3	111.7	39	41	21	-	1
Jack Crooks	2B	72	.231	.280	225	52	4	2	1	225.0	33	20	40	-	3
Lave Cross	3B	151	.317	.405	602	191	28	8	3	200.7	71	79	28	-	14
Pete Daniels	P	10	.176	.235	17	3	1	0	0	0.0	1	1	3	-	0
George Decker	1B	76	.259	.304	286	74	10	0	1	286.0	26	45	20	-	4
Jim Donnelly	3B	1	1.000	1.000	1	1	0	0	0	0.0	0	0	0	-	0
Tommy Dowd	OF	139	.244	.297	586	143	17	7	0	0.0	70	32	30	-	16
Duke Esper	P	11	.370	.370	27	10	0	0	0	0.0	1	5	1	-	0
Joe Gannon	P	1	.000	.000	3	0	0	0	0	0.0	0	0	0	-	0
George Gillpatrick	P	7	.125	.125	16	2	0	0	0	0.0	1	1	0	-	0
Russ Hall	SS	39	.245	.273	143	35	2	1	0	0.0	13	10	7	-	1
Dick Harley	OF	142	.246	.275	549	135	6	5	0	0.0	74	42	34	-	13
Ducky Holmes	OF	23	.238	.267	101	24	1	1	0	0.0	9	0	2	-	4
Jim Hughey	P	35	.113	.165	97	11	0	1	1	97.0	6	6	10	-	1

1898 St. Louis Browns Statmaster: Hitting (cont.)

NAME	POS	GAMES	AVG	SLG	AB	H	2B	3B	HR	AB/HR	R	RBI	BB	SO	SB
Tom Kinslow	C	14	.283	.358	53	15	2	1	0	0.0	5	4	1	-	0
Mike Mahoney	1B	2	.000	.000	7	0	0	0	0	0.0	0	0	0	-	0
Harry Maupin	P	2	.429	.429	7	3	0	0	0	0.0	0	1	0	-	0
Joe Quinn	2B	103	.251	.304	375	94	10	5	0	0.0	35	36	24	-	13
Germany Smith	SS	51	.159	.204	157	25	2	1	1	157.0	16	9	24	-	1
Tom Smith	P	1	.500	.500	2	1	0	0	0	0.0	0	0	1	-	0
Jake Stenzel	OF	108	.282	.381	404	114	15	11	1	404.0	64	33	41	-	21
Willie Sudhoff	P	41	.158	.192	120	19	2	1	0	0.0	5	4	5	-	0
Joe Sugden	C	89	.253	.284	289	73	7	1	0	0.0	29	34	23	-	5
Suter Sullivan	SS	42	.222	.243	144	32	3	0	0	0.0	10	12	13	-	1
Jack Taylor	P	54	.242	.318	157	38	5	2	1	157.0	17	18	12	-	1
Tommy Tucker	1B	72	.238	.282	252	60	7	2	0	0.0	18	20	18	-	1
Tuck Turner	OF	35	.199	.255	141	28	8	0	0	0.0	20	7	14	-	1
TEAM TOTALS	-	-	.247	.305	5,214	1,290	149	55	13	401.1	571	470	383	-	104

Data courtesy of Baseball-Almanac.com.

1898 St. Louis Browns Statmaster: Pitching

NAME	GAMES	W	L	W%	ERA	GS	CG	IP	HA	BB	SO	SHU
John Callahan	2	0	2	.000	16.20	2	1	8.1	18	7	2	0
Kid Carsey	20	2	12	.143	6.33	13	10	123.2	177	37	10	0
Pete Daniels	10	1	6	.143	3.62	6	3	54.2	62	14	13	0
Duke Esper	10	3	5	.375	5.98	8	6	64.2	86	22	14	0
Joe Gannon	1	0	1	.000	11.00	1	1	9.0	13	5	2	0
George G Ilpatrick	7	0	2	.000	6.94	3	1	35.0	42	19	12	0
Jim Hughey	35	7	24	.226	3.93	33	31	283.2	325	71	74	0
Harry Maupin	2	0	2	.000	5.50	2	2	18.0	22	3	3	0
Tom Smith	1	0	1	.000	2.00	1	1	9.0	9	5	1	0
Willie Sudhoff	41	11	27	.289	4.34	38	35	315.0	355	102	65	0
Suter Sullivan	1	0	0	.000	1.50	0	0	6.0	10	4	3	0
Jack Taylor	50	15	29	.341	3.90	47	42	397.1	465	83	89	0
NAME	GAMES	W	L	W%	ERA	GS	CG	IP	HA	BB	SO	SHU
TEAM TOTALS		39	111	.250	4.53	154	133	1324.1	1,584	372	288	0

Data courtesy of Baseball-Almanac.com.

1898 St. Louis Browns Statmaster: Fielding

NAME	POS	GAMES	PO	A	E	DP	TC/G	FLD%
Lou Bierbauer	2B	2	0	3	4	0	3.5	.429
Lou Bierbauer	3B	1	0	0	0	0	0.0	.000
Lou Bierbauer	SS	1	3	7	0	0	10.0	1.000
John Callahan	P	2	0	2	0	0	1.0	1.000
Kid Carsey	P	20	4	39	3	2	2.3	.935
Kid Carsey	2B	10	19	25	8	1	5.2	.846
Kid Carsey	OF	8	6	1	2	0	1.1	.778
Jack Clements	C	86	287	81	11	8	4.4	.971
Jack Crooks	2B	66	192	209	17	23	6.3	.959
Jack Crooks	3B	3	1	7	0	0	2.7	1.000
Jack Crooks	SS	2	5	8	2	1	7.5	.867
Jack Crooks	OF	1	5	0	0	0	5.0	1.000
Lave Cross	3B	149	215	351	33	20	4.0	.945
Lave Cross	SS	2	3	7	2	2	6.0	.833
Pete Daniels	P	10	2	14	4	1	2.0	.800
George Decker	1B	75	772	17	16	31	10.7	.980
Jim Donnelly	3B	1	0	1	1	0	2.0	.500
Tommy Dowd	OF	129	208	11	19	3	1.8	.920
Tommy Dowd	2B	11	23	28	6	3	5.2	.895
Duke Esper	P	10	2	17	1	0	2.0	.950
Joe Gannon	P	1	0	2	0	0	2.0	1.000
George Gillpatrick	P	7	2	6	4	0	1.7	.667
Russ Hall	SS	35	50	102	30	12	5.2	.835
Russ Hall	3B	3	2	11	2	2	5.0	.867
Russ Hall	OF	1	1	1	0	0	2.0	1.000
Dick Harley	OF	141	311	26	27	3	2.6	.926
Ducky Holmes	OF	22	39	6	5	3	2.3	.900
Jim Hughey	P	35	8	67	11	2	2.5	.872
Tom Kinslow	C	14	44	18	5	4	4.8	.925
Mike Mahoney	1B	2	22	1	2	1	12.5	.920
Harry Maupin	P	2	0	1	0	0	0.5	1.000
Joe Quinn	2B	62	139	191	13	19	5.5	.962
Joe Quinn	SS	41	79	149	18	11	6.0	.927
Joe Quinn	OF	1	2	0	0	0	2.0	1.000
Germany Smith	SS	51	79	167	26	14	5.3	.904

1898 St. Louis Browns Statmaster: Fielding (cont.)

NAME	POS	GAMES	PO	A	E	DP	TC/G	FLD%
Tom Smith	P	1	0	3	0	0	3.0	1.000
Jake Stenzel	OF	108	257	8	16	2	2.6	.943
Willie Sudhoff	P	41	15	114	12	5	3.4	.915
Joe Sugden	C	60	181	88	18	8	4.8	.937
Joe Sugden	OF	15	17	0	2	1	1.3	.895
Joe Sugden	1B	8	74	3	1	4	9.8	.987
Suter Sullivan	SS	23	52	60	16	6	5.6	.875
Suter Sullivan	OF	10	9	3	0	0	1.2	1.000
Suter Sullivan	2B	6	14	15	3	1	5.3	.906
Suter Sullivan	1B	1	0	0	0	0	0.0	.000
Suter Sullivan	P	1	0	0	0	0	0.0	.000
Jack Taylor	P	50	18	144	22	2	3.7	.880
Jack Taylor	OF	2	1	0	0	0	0.5	1.000
Tommy Tucker	1B	72	755	36	22	40	11.3	.973
Tuck Turner	OF	34	50	2	4	1	1.6	.929
NAME	POS	GAMES	PO	A	E	DP	TC/G	FLD%
TEAM TOTALS			3,968	2,052	388	236	4.5	.939

Data courtesy of Baseball-Almanac.com.

#3 | Squashed Like a Bug
The 1899 Cleveland Spiders (20–134)

> The '99 Cleveland Spiders home/road splits for the regular season were 9–33 (0.214 winning percentage) at home and 11–101 (0.098 winning percentage) away.
>
> —Baseball-Almanac

As appalling as the 1898 Browns were, they were nothing compared to the '99 Spiders, the team widely considered by many historians to be the single worst major league baseball franchise of all time. Interestingly, both teams' legacies crossed, with Cleveland getting the shorter end of the stick. Fortunately, the Spiders' lifespan was mercifully short, only spanning 1887 to 1899. Part of the American Association, the Spiders began their professional career as a struggling franchise with little fan or player support.

All that changed, however, after the acquisition of one of the greatest pitchers ever to toe a pitcher's mound—future Hall of Fame charter member Cy Young. In retrospect, it seems hard to believe that one of baseball's most celebrated all-stars began his epic career with what became baseball's sorriest franchise. Perhaps Young's casual approach to the game kept him from falling under the Cleveland curse.

He once told a reporter, "I never warmed up 10, 15 minutes before a game like most pitchers do. I'd loosen up, three, four minutes. Five at the outside. And I never went to the bullpen. Oh, I'd relieve all right, plenty of times, but I went right from the bench to the box, and I'd take a few warm-up pitches and be ready. Then I had good control. I aimed to make the batter hit the ball, and I threw as few pitches as possible. That's why I was able to work every other day."

Almost immediately after signing the ace, things began to look up for the Spiders. In 1892, they finished with a respectable 93–56 record, finishing in second place. Second baseman Cupid Childs stepped up to the plate as a contender and led Cleveland's less-than-stellar offense, while pitching remained the biggest weapon in the team's arsenal. As Young became one

1899 Cleveland Spiders (Library of Congress)

of the National League's greatest hurlers of his time, rookie teammate Nig Cuppy pitched well in support. These two eventually combined to form one of the best one-two starting combinations in major league history.

At the conclusion of the 1892 regular season, Cleveland and the first-place Boston Beaneaters played a "World's Championship Series" exhibition. Unfortunately, the Spiders only managed one tie in six games, providing a glimpse of the futility that was yet to come. In 1895, the Spiders again finished second to the equally gritty Orioles.

This time, however, the Spiders finished the job and walked away with the newly christened "Temple Cup" after winning four out of five outings against Baltimore. The following year resulted in a rematch, with the Orioles sweeping their former adversaries in four games. Cleveland stayed in the hunt over the next two seasons but never finished higher than fifth in the standings. Young threw the first of his three no-hitters for the Spiders on September 18, 1897.

Then came the year that would live in infamy . . . 1899.

As stated in the previous chapter, Stanley and Frank Robison purchased the fledgling St. Louis Browns' franchise and, in 1899, changed the name to the St. Louis Perfectos. In an effort to breathe some life into what they thought would be a better investment, the brothers transferred most of the Spiders' talent, including future Baseball Hall of Famers Cy Young, Jesse Burkett, and Bobby Wallace from their old team to the new one.

The results of these self-defeating trades were disastrous, as Cleveland went 20–134 (.130), while losing 40 of their last 41 games of the season. The Spiders finished 84 games behind the pennant-winning Brooklyn Superbas and 35 games behind the next-to-last (11th) place Washington club in the worst single-season plummet in the history of major league baseball. On the road, the team tallied a shameful 11–109 record, while posting a 9–24 mark at home.

According to historian David Fleitz, in *The 1899 Cleveland Spiders: Baseball's Worst Team:*

> On July 15, 1899, the Spiders accomplished the rare feat of playing a doubleheader against the Orioles without scoring a run, losing 10–0 and 5–0. The Spiders allowed more than 8 runs per game while scoring only 3 per game themselves. Second baseman Joe Quinn, appointed manager after Cross' firing, batted .286 and led the league in fielding at his position, but other promising players were quickly shuttled to the Perfectos. The Spiders wound up the season losing a record 87 percent of their games.

The longest winning streak that the Spiders managed was two. The team's poor play was downright astonishing. Cleveland's opponents scored 10 or more runs 49 times over a span of 154 games. Statistically, the team posted a batting average of .253, which was 19 average points worse than the next closest team. They also averaged a meager 3.44 runs per game, 1.8 runs per game less than the overall league average. Even more telling, the Spiders lineup managed just 12 home runs the entire season.

Hitting was just one of the team's issues.[1] Cleveland's pitching rotation started poorly, finished poorly, and were absolutely awful in between. Skipper Lafayette Cross faced the impossible task of winning games with perhaps the worst pitching staff in history, which allowed a record 1,252 runs.

Pitcher Jim Hughey, who had been respectable in previous years, went 4–30. "Coldwater," as his teammates called him, tallied a 5.41 ERA, and allowed an astonishing 403 hits in 283 innings. Teammate Charles Knepper faired worse with a 4–22 mark. Harry Colliflower earned the dubious honor of being the worst of the bunch, going 1–11 with an 8.17 ERA. The team's ERA stood at an embarrassing 6.37, compared to a league average of 3.85.

Looking back, perhaps it was a blessing that the Spiders' gate sales plummeted dramatically, as only 6,088 fans (averaging just 179 people per game) bought tickets to witness their epic decline. Local sports writers struggled to cover the team, and some gave the unlovable losers new nicknames, including the "Wanderers," "Exiles," and "Waifs." One reporter with a sense of humor named Elmer Bates proclaimed the positive side to the Spiders' plight, wittingly writing:

Pros to the Cleveland Spider's season:
1. There is everything to hope for and nothing to fear.
2. Defeats do not disturb one's sleep.
3. An occasional victory is a surprise and a delight.
4. There is no danger of any club passing you.
5. You are not asked 50 times a day, 'What was the score?' (People know you lost.)

The '99 Spiders also set the major league record for most consecutive losses in a season (24, from July 26 to September 16), most losses in a month (27 losses in July), and had six double-digit losing streaks. The 1962 New York Mets (40–120) and 2003 Detroit Tigers (43–119) claim the modern-era worst records in their respective leagues, and thus draw frequent comparisons to the Spiders for futility.

It somehow seems fitting that in the final game of the season, the desperation, or perhaps resignation, of the team shone through. The Spiders invited amateur Eddie Kolb, who made his living as a cigar store clerk, to pitch against the Reds. The Cincinnati franchise "smoked" the unproven hurler 19–3 for Cleveland's 134th loss of the year, the most in major league history.

Following the Spiders' grand finale of failure, the players presented the team's traveling secretary George Muir with a jeweled locket containing an apologetic dedication as he "had the misfortune to watch us in all our games."

At the conclusion of the 1899 season, the National League contracted from 12 to 8 clubs. Understandably, the 12th-place Cleveland Spiders were one of the first to be disbanded, as they had mutated into an athletic and financial disaster. Baltimore, Louisville, and Washington followed soon after.

In 2004, mathematician Fred Worth of Henderson State University, a professor and member of the Society for American Baseball Research (SABR), presented a statistical paper that mathematically determined baseball's worst team. After evaluating a variety of contributing factors, including a statistical comparison of individual and team performances, he concluded: "For flat out pathetic baseball, it seems like the worst team has to be the

1899 Cleveland Spiders. They scored nearly two runs per game less than the league average and had an ERA over 2.5 runs worse than the average."

Perhaps the players themselves are not entirely to blame for the historic debacle of the 1899 Spiders. Poor moves by the front office, lack of media and fan support, and a lot of plain old "bad luck" created the perfect storm of ineptitude. Still, if not for their disastrous season, Cleveland's original ball club may have been forgotten altogether in the annals of baseball history. At the end of the day, perhaps it was best to be the worst?

1899 Cleveland Spiders Statmaster: Fielding

NAME	POS	GAMES	PO	A	E	DP	TC/G	FLD%
Frank Bates	P	20	10	38	8	1	2.8	.857
Frank Bates	OF	2	4	0	2	0	3.0	.667
George Bristow	OF	3	4	1	0	0	1.7	1.000
Kid Carsey	P	10	5	24	4	2	3.3	.879
Kid Carsey	SS	1	4	5	0	1	9.0	1.000
Jack Clements	C	4	8	7	1	0	4.0	.938
Harry Colliflower	P	14	1	26	4	2	2.2	.871
Harry Colliflower	OF	6	10	0	2	0	2.0	.833
Harry Colliflower	1B	4	25	0	2	1	6.8	.926
Lave Cross	3B	38	66	81	7	7	4.1	.955
Tommy Dowd	CF	147	341	10	17	2	2.5	.954
Jim Duncan	1B	17	164	6	5	13	10.3	.971
Jim Duncan	C	14	25	16	7	0	3.4	.854
Dick Harley	OF	142	299	27	27	7	2.5	.924
Jack Harper	P	5	1	7	0	0	1.6	1.000
Charlie Hemphill	RF	54	61	6	11	1	1.4	.859
Bill Hill	P	11	1	19	4	1	2.2	.833
Jim Hughey	P	36	9	48	12	3	1.9	.826
Charlie Knepper	P	27	8	49	6	2	2.3	.905
Eddie Kolb	P	1	0	0	1	0	1.0	.000
Otto Krueger	3B	9	12	17	9	2	4.2	.763
Otto Krueger	2B	2	6	6	1	1	6.5	.923
Otto Krueger	SS	2	4	4	0	1	4.0	1.000
Harry Lochhead	SS	146	319	490	81	54	6.1	.909
Harry Lochhead	P	1	0	0	0	0	0.0	.000
Harry Lochhead	2B	1	1	3	0	0	4.0	1.000
Harry Maupin	P	5	0	2	1	0	0.6	.667

1899 Cleveland Spiders Statmaster: Fielding (cont.)

NAME	POS	GAMES	PO	A	E	DP	TC/G	FLD%
Sport McAllister	OF	79	106	10	7	4	1.6	.943
Sport McAllister	C	17	36	20	9	2	3.8	.862
Sport McAllister	3B	7	15	14	7	3	5.1	.806
Sport McAllister	1B	6	43	2	3	2	8.0	.938
Sport McAllister	SS	3	16	8	1	0	8.3	.960
Sport McAllister	P	3	0	3	0	0	1.0	1.000
Sport McAllister	2B	1	2	2	1	0	5.0	.800
Joe Quinn	2B	147	350	440	31	61	5.6	.962
Crazy Schmit	P	20	7	43	6	0	2.8	.893
Crazy Schmit	OF	6	11	0	1	0	2.0	.917
Ossee Schreckengost	C	39	104	60	16	6	4.6	.911
Ossee Schreckengost	SS	1	0	0	0	0	0.0	.000
Ossee Schreckengost	RF	1	1	0	0	0	1.0	1.000
Ossee Schreckengost	1B	1	14	0	0	0	14.0	1.000
Louis Sockalexis	RF	5	7	2	2	1	2.2	.818
Jack Stivetts	P	7	2	16	0	0	2.6	1.000
Jack Stivetts	OF	7	11	1	0	0	1.7	1.000
Jack Stivetts	3B	1	0	1	0	0	1.0	1.000
Jack Stivetts	SS	1	1	2	1	0	4.0	.750
Willie Sudhoff	P	11	5	31	4	1	3.6	.900
Joe Sugden	C	66	196	108	21	11	4.9	.935
Joe Sugden	RF	4	3	0	0	0	0.8	1.000
Joe Sugden	1B	3	14	3	0	3	5.7	1.000
Joe Sugden	3B	1	0	0	2	0	2.0	.000
Suter Sullivan	3B	101	110	237	23	21	3.7	.938
Suter Sullivan	OF	20	27	1	5	0	1.7	.848
Suter Sullivan	1B	3	18	2	0	0	6.7	1.000
Suter Sullivan	SS	3	2	4	0	0	2.0	1.000
Suter Sullivan	2B	2	4	4	1	1	4.5	.889
Tommy Tucker	1B	127	1,229	58	30	71	10.4	.977
Highball Wilson	P	1	1	1	0	0	2.0	1.000
Charlie Ziegler	SS	1	1	2	1	0	4.0	.750
Charlie Ziegler	2B	1	1	3	0	0	4.0	1.000
Chief Zimmer	C	20	58	30	4	4	4.6	.957
TEAM TOTALS			3,783	2,000	388	292	4.3	.937

Data courtesy of Baseball-Almanac.com.

1899 Cleveland Spiders Statmaster: Pitching

NAME	GAMES	W	L	W%	ERA	GS	CG	IP	HA	BB	SO	SHU
Frank Bates	20	1	18	.053	7.24	19	17	153.0	239	105	13	0
Kid Carsey	10	1	8	.111	5.68	9	8	77.2	109	24	11	0
Harry Colliflower	14	1	11	.083	8.17	12	11	98.0	152	41	8	0
Jack Harper	5	1	4	.200	3.89	5	5	37.0	44	12	14	0
Bill Hill	11	3	6	.333	6.97	10	7	72.1	96	39	26	0
Jim Hughey	36	4	30	.118	5.41	34	32	283.0	403	88	54	0
Charlie Knepper	27	4	22	.154	5.78	26	26	219.2	307	77	43	0
Eddie Kolb	1	0	1	.000	10.13	1	1	8.0	18	5	1	0
Harry Lochhead	1	0	0	.000	0.00	0	0	3.2	4	2	0	0
Harry Maupin	5	0	3	.000	12.60	3	2	25.0	55	7	3	0
Sport McAllister	3	0	1	.000	9.56	1	1	16.0	29	10	2	0
Crazy Schmit	20	2	17	.105	5.86	19	16	138.1	197	62	24	0
Jack Stivetts	7	0	4	.000	5.68	4	3	38.0	48	25	5	0
Willie Sudhoff	11	3	8	.273	6.98	10	8	86.1	131	25	10	0
Highball Wilson	1	0	1	.000	9.00	1	1	8.0	12	5	1	0
TEAM TOTALS		20	134	.130	6.37	154	138	1264	1,844	527	215	0

Data courtesy of Baseball-Almanac.com.

1899 Cleveland Spiders Statmaster: Hitting

NAME	POS	GAMES	AVG	SLG	AB	H	2B	3B	HR	AB/HR	R	RBI	BB	SO	SB
Frank Bates	P	21	.215	.231	65	14	1	0	0	0.0	5	3	7	-	0
George Bristow	OF	3	.125	.250	8	1	1	0	0	0.0	0	0	0	-	0
Kid Carsey	P	11	.278	.278	36	10	0	0	0	0.0	5	4	3	-	0
Jack Clements	C	4	.250	.250	12	3	0	0	0	0.0	1	0	0	-	0
Harry Colliflower	P	23	.303	.355	76	23	4	0	0	0.0	5	9	2	-	0
Lave Cross	3B	38	.236	.338	154	44	5	0	1	154.0	15	20	8	-	2
Tommy Dowd	OF	147	.278	.336	605	163	17	6	2	302.5	81	35	48	-	28
Jim Duncan	1B	31	.229	.362	105	24	2	3	2	52.5	9	9	4	-	0
Dick Harley	OF	142	.250	.307	567	142	15	7	1	567.0	70	50	40	-	15
Jack Harper	P	5	.132	.182	11	2	0	0	0	0.0	2	1	4	-	0
Charlie Hemphill	OF	55	.277	.371	202	56	3	5	2	101.0	23	23	6	-	3
Bill Hill	P	11	.129	.129	31	4	0	0	0	0.0	2	0	1	-	0
Jim Hughey	P	36	.162	.171	111	18	1	0	0	0.0	9	5	5	-	0
Charlie Knepper	P	27	.135	.180	89	12	2	1	0	0.0	6	2	4	-	0
Eddie Kolb	P	1	.250	.250	4	1	0	0	0	0.0	1	0	0	-	0
Otto Krueger	3B	13	.227	.250	44	10	1	0	0	0.0	4	2	8	-	1
Harry Lochhead	SS	148	.238	.261	541	129	7	1	1	541.0	52	43	21	-	23
Harry Maupin	P	5	.000	.000	10	0	0	0	0	0.0	0	0	0	-	0
Sport McAllister	OF	113	.237	.297	418	99	6	8	1	418.0	29	31	19	-	5

1899 Cleveland Spiders Statmaster: Hitting (cont.)

NAME	POS	GAMES	AVG	SLG	AB	H	2B	3B	HR	AB/HR	R	RBI	BB	SO	SB
Joe Quinn	2B	147	.286	.345	615	176	24	6	0	0.0	73	72	21	-	22
Crazy Schmit	P	25	.157	.157	70	11	0	0	0	0.0	6	1	6	-	2
Ossee Schreckengost	C	43	.313	.407	150	47	8	3	0	0.0	15	10	6	-	4
Louis Sockalexis	OF	7	.273	.318	22	6	1	0	0	0.0	0	3	1	-	0
Jack Stivetts	OF	18	.205	.282	39	8	1	1	0	0.0	8	2	6	-	0
Willie Sudhoff	P	11	.065	.129	31	2	0	1	0	0.0	1	6	4	-	0
Joe Sugden	C	76	.276	.304	250	69	5	1	0	0.0	19	14	11	-	2
Suter Sullivan	3B	127	.245	.292	473	116	16	3	0	0.0	37	55	25	-	16
Tommy Tucker	1B	127	.241	.296	456	110	19	3	0	0.0	40	40	24	-	3
Highball Wilson	P	1	.333	.667	3	1	1	0	0	0.0	0	0	0	-	0
Charlie Ziegler	SS	2	.250	.250	8	2	0	0	0	0.0	2	0	0	-	0
Chief Zimmer	C	20	.342	.479	73	25	2	1	2	36.5	9	14	5	-	1
TEAM TOTALS			.253	.305	5,279	1,333	142	50	12	439.9	529	454	289	-	127

Data courtesy of Baseball-Almanac.com.

#4 | "Et Tu, Brute?"
The 1904 Washington Senators (38–114)

"For the Washington Senators, the worst time of year is
the baseball season."
—*Roger Kahn, author of* The Boys of Summer.

America has always loved baseball. In 1866, sports writer Charles A. Pever-
elly wrote, "The game of base ball has now become beyond question the
leading feature of the outdoor sports of the United States . . . It is a game
which is peculiarly suited to the American temperament and disposition; . . .
in short, the pastime suits the people, and the people suit the pastime."

It somehow seems fitting that the country's capital introduced some of
the game's most celebrated traditions. Now a nationally anticipated event,
Opening Day has become a political pitcher's arena for U.S. presidents to
show their "stuff." On April 14, 1910, the 27th President of the United States,
William Howard Taft, attended the home opener in Washington, D.C. Since
then, 11 sitting U.S. presidents have tossed out the season's ceremonial first
pitch. One standout, Harry S. Truman, showcased his ambidextrous talent
by throwing balls with both hands in 1950.

E. Lawrence Phillips became the first person to use a megaphone to an-
nounce starting lineups before a game at Washington's Griffith Stadium.
It was also the first ballpark with a team that issued a gold season pass.
President Theodore Roosevelt became the first recipient.

The seventh-inning stretch apparently debuted in "The District." The
popular theory gives sole credit to President Taft. One of America's less
memorable leaders, Taft was an obese man, tipping the scales at more than
300 pounds. He probably displayed more fervor regarding his favorite game
of baseball than he did toward running the country.

According to reports, as the game dragged on, the six-foot-two president
grew increasingly uncomfortable in the small wooden chair that was undoubtedly overtaxed by the weight of its presidential patron. By the middle

1904 Washington Senators (Library of Congress)

of the seventh inning, Taft could no longer bear the pain any longer and stood up to stretch his aching legs. In those days, the leader of the free world commanded a tremendous amount of reverence and when his fellow spectators noticed him rising, they followed his lead as a sign of respect. A few minutes later, Taft returned to his seat and the game resumed.

Another historical gem, courtesy of America's central city, was the Washington Senators. Originally established as a National League franchise in 1899, a new version of the team debuted under the American League banner in 1901. Ironically called the "Nationals," this inaugural franchise debuted with a 5–1 victory over the Philadelphia's Athletics on April 26, 1901. Unfortunately, the team never reached its potential in the first decade of its existence. The Senators finished last four times in their first nine seasons and didn't rise above sixth place until they finished second in 1912 and 1913.

Tragedy struck the team on July 2, 1903, when its most celebrated hitter, Ed Delahanty, died in an accidental fall from a train near Niagara Falls. Only in his second season with the team, Delahanty had posted an impressive .333 batting average at the plate after tallying .376 the previous year. With the catastrophic loss of the team's best offensive player, Washington finished last in the American League with an awful 43–94 record. Little did they know that their circumstances were going to change from bad to worse.

Even American League founder Ban Johnson empathized with the Senators' pathetic showing. After saving the team from financial ruin, he said, "I have promised the Washington people a good club for the coming season, and I will keep my word. Every club in the American League has from four to twelve extra men they cannot use, and if Washington needs additional players they will get the first call." Needless to say, Johnson's promise came up empty.

Anticipating a poor showing, only 3,000 "lukewarm" spectators showed up for Washington's 1904 opener. Little changed in the coming months; over the course of the major league season attendance climbed at virtually every ballpark except the Senators. Only slightly more than 132,000 people attended their games for the entire season, and the box office losses were staggering.

The Senators started the '04 campaign by losing their first 13 games. After 31 contests, they were 6–25. All in all, Washington managed to win 38 outings, while dropping 114. In the month of June, the team went 4 19. Over the course of the season, they scored 437 runs and allowed 743. This was the worst performance in the long history of a franchise that boasted of many terrible teams, as they finished a whopping 55.5 games out of first place. One writer later penned that Washington was "first in war, first in peace, and last in the American League."

The team's newest manager was a tough Irishman named Patrick Donovan, who was hired to replace Malachi Kittridge after the team's slow start.[1] Called "Patsy" by both the fans and the players, Donovan established himself early on as one of the game's most consistent players, but even his talents and work ethic could not keep the Senators' sinking ship afloat. SABR biographer David Jones wrote that:

Let go by the Cardinals, Donovan spent the rest of the decade managing some of the worst teams of the Deadball Era. After his 1904 Washington Senators managed to win only 38 games (the lowest total in the history of that unfortunate franchise), Donovan took a year off before accepting the manager's job with the Brooklyn Dodgers in 1906. Over three seasons in Brooklyn, Donovan failed to lift the team out of the second division and was let go after a 53–101, seventh-place finish in 1908. "I did as well as could be expected of any manager with the material at hand," he explained to Reds President Garry Herrman in a November 1908 letter inquiring about a managerial opening with that club. "Before leaving baseball I would like to have the opportunity of handling a club where I would have free rein and financial backing to secure talent."

A future Hall of Famer, Donovan's major league playing career spanned 17 years from the 1880s through the 1900s. He played for the Pittsburgh Pirates, the St. Louis Cardinals, the Washington Senators, the Brooklyn Dodgers, and the Boston Red Sox. For another 20 years, he served as a major league scout and minor league manager. Of all of his teams, whether as a player or a coach, the '04 Senators were by far the worst. "Finish what you start" was a favorite admonition of Donovan's, but this bunch seemed unable to start or finish anything.

For example, Happy Jack Townsend pitched his way to a shameful 5–26 record, while a promising rookie named Beanie Jacobson went 6–23. The rest of the rotation fared similarly. Tom Hughes, who was acquired from the New York Highlanders, went 2–13 in an ill-advised trade. Jacobson mustered a 12-inning shutout of Cleveland on July 29.

1904 proved to be a year of setting unwanted records by the Senators. On June 23, Kip Selbach tied a major league record by committing three outfield errors in one inning. The team collectively set a new twentieth-century record for losses when they hit the 113 mark. And one Washington player achieved the unique distinction of pitching for two of the worst teams in major league baseball (MLB) history. That unlucky individual was a right-handed hurler named Howard Paul "Highball" Wilson, who punched a timecard with both the 1899 Cleveland Spiders and the '04 Senators.

In *On a Clear Day They Could See Seventh Place,* author George Robinson outlined a series of miserable milestones achieved by Washington's '04 squad, including the following:

- New York's Jack Chesbro tallied 41 victories on the mound in 1904. The entire Senators team collectively won 38.
- They wound up 55½ games out of first place, 23½ games behind the seventh-place Detroit team.
- They dropped the season series with every other club in the league.
- They were last in fielding with a percentage of .951.
- They had two one-hit games pitched against them; six two-hit games pitched against them; and three three-hit games pitched against them.
- They were shut out 25 times (in contrast the N.Y. Highlanders were shut out only eight times).

- Their pitching staff, such as it was, boasted three 20-game losers: Albert ("Beany") Jacobson, 6–23, Case Patten, 14–23, and John Townsend, 5–26.
- John "Happy" Townsend's record of 5–26 was the worst record in the league.
- The team ERA was 3.62, almost a full run more than the seventh-place Detroit's 2.77 mark (the league ERA that year was 2.60).
- Senator pitchers gave up 1,487 hits, 142 more than the seventh-place Detroit team.
- They had a league batting average of .227, 17 points below the league average.
- The Senators did lead the league in one category—double plays—with 97. However, this makes complete sense because, when the 347 free passes issued by Washington pitchers are counted, more than 1,800 opposing players reached base that season, for an average of nearly 12 per game.
- They drew a mere 131,744 fans while the pennant-winning Boston club drew 623,295.

One player in particular personified the sorry state of the Washington Senators in '04. Jake Stahl, once a promising player, started the season by hitting a minuscule .088, which, as some fans pointed out, was just a few digits above the temperature. *The Sporting Life* (*TSL*) took Stahl to task on two occasions, but also reported his rare and unusual contributions to the game.

On April 15, *TSL* reported that he had set a major league record (that stood for 65 years) by being hit by pitchers three times in one game. A short time later, it recalled this highlight play:

A spectator who has closely followed the game for many years declared that the greatest catch he ever saw was Jake Stahl's capture of a foul fly close to the stand, in the fifth inning [against Boston]. Just as the fly, which was a cloud-scraper, was about to be gathered in, Stahl, who was still running, slipped in the mud and fell flat on his back. He kept his eye on the ball, which must have been caught when he was falling, and near the earth.

Perhaps the only bright light in the entire season of darkness came when Stahl ended his slump and hit .261, giving Washington loyalists a reason to hope for the future. His improvement over the course of the season, however, went virtually unnoticed in the league standings. So, too, did those of a 21-year-old shortstop named Joe Cassidy, who hit 19 triples and led all American League players in fielding runs with 34.

In 1904, a local sports writer humorously stated, "The Senators were not at bat long enough for their friends to recognize them, but when the visitors were up there were happenings and occurrences." Later in the season, he added, "The writer knows scores, if not hundreds, of fans here who would go to nearly all the games if a fairly good club was located here, and every one of them says that he knows 'hundreds' who feel the same way; but, as things are going now, they never attend the games." Perhaps it was a blessing that few Washingtonians witnessed the debacle of the team's miserable 1904 campaign.

Daily News sports writer Bill Madden summarized the Senators' legacy of losing in 2005 with a retrospective article titled "History hasn't been kind to baseball in Washington," declaring:

In the 70 years Washington was in the American League (1901–1971), the Senators finished last 14 times, were almost always an under-.500, second-division team and won only one world championship, in 1924. Before that, they made finishing last an art form in the National League as well. The earliest Washington team, in the NL from 1886–89, finished last three out of those four years, compiling an overall 163–337 record.

There was some silver lining to the dark cloud of the 1904 season. Within three short years, they introduced perhaps the greatest pitcher in the history of the game to the world. In 1907, a promising right-handed ace named Walter Johnson stepped atop the mound in a Senators' uniform.

Over the next 21 years, "The Big Train" dominated the American League. In 1912–1913, Johnson had perhaps the best back-to-back seasons any pitcher has ever had, and in so doing, he single-handedly pulled Washington into the first division for the first time. In 1912, he went 32–12, with a 1.39 ERA and 303 strikeouts. In 1913, he was a staggering 36–7, with a 1.09 ERA and 243 strikeouts in 346 innings.

To put things in perspective, Walter Johnson's stats as an individual topped many of the '04 numbers for the team. For instance, Johnson had 12 20-plus win seasons, including 10 in a row. The 1904 Washington Senators couldn't win more than three consecutive games in a row, and only managed that small feat once in a series over the equally dismal St. Louis Browns.

1904 Washington Senators Schedule

GAME	DATE	OPPONENT	SCORE	DECISION	RECORD
1	04–14–1904	vs Philadelphia Athletics	3–8	L	0–1
2	04–15–1904	vs Philadelphia Athletics	6–6	T	0–1–1
3	04–16–1904	vs Philadelphia Athletics	2–12	L	0–2–1
4	04–18–1904	at Boston Americans	0–5	L	0–3–1
5-I	04–19–1904	at Boston Americans	0–1	L	0–4–1
6-II	04–19–1904	at Boston Americans	2–3	L	0–5–1
7	04–22–1904	vs New York Highlanders	0–2	L	0–6–1
8	04–23–1904	vs New York Highlanders	3–4	L	0–7–1
9	04–25–1904	vs New York Highlanders	1–4	L	0–8–1
10	04–29–1904	vs Boston Americans	3–4	L	0–9–1
11	04–30–1904	vs Boston Americans	1–4	L	0–10–1
12	05–02–1904	at New York Highlanders	0–5	L	0–11–1
13	05–03–1904	at New York Highlanders	2–8	L	0–12–1
14	05–04–1904	at New York Highlanders	3–6	L	0–13–1
15	05–05–1904	at New York Highlanders	9–4	W	1–13–1
16	05–06–1904	at Philadelphia Athletics	6–16	L	1–14–1
17	05–07–1904	at Philadelphia Athletics	4–11	L	1–15–1
18	05–09–1904	at Philadelphia Athletics	3–6	L	1–16–1
19	05–11–1904	vs St. Louis Browns	7–3	W	2–16–1
20	05–12–1904	vs St. Louis Browns	7–8	L	2–17–1
21	05–13–1904	vs St. Louis Browns	3–2	W	3–17–1
22	05–16–1904	vs Chicago White Sox	4–3	W	4–17–1
23	05–17–1904	vs Chicago White Sox	5–9	L	4–18–1
24	05–19–1904	vs Chicago White Sox	0–5	L	4–19–1
25	05–20–1904	vs Detroit Tigers	3–0	W	5–19–1
26	05–21–1904	vs Detroit Tigers	0–0	T	5–19–2
27	05–23–1904	vs Detroit Tigers	4–2	W	6–19–2
28	05–24–1904	vs Cleveland Blues	6–10	L	6–20–2
29	05–25–1904	vs Cleveland Blues	3–7	L	6–21–2
30	05–26–1904	vs Cleveland Blues	3–7	L	6–22–2
31	05–27–1904	at Boston Americans	2–4	L	6–23–2
32	05–28–1904	at Boston Americans	2–3	L	6–24–2
33-I	05–30–1904	at Boston Americans	3–7	L	6–25–2
34-II	05–30–1904	at Boston Americans	2–8	L	6–26–2
35	06–01–1904	at Chicago White Sox	0–1	L	6–27–2

1904 Washington Senators Schedule (cont.)

GAME	DATE	OPPONENT	SCORE	DECISION	RECORD
36	06–02–1904	at Chicago White Sox	7–13	L	6–28–2
37	06–03–1904	at Chicago White Sox	1–5	L	6–29–2
38	06–04–1904	at Chicago White Sox	2–0	W	7–29–2
39	06–05–1904	at St. Louis Browns	5–6	L	7–30–2
40	06–06–1904	at St. Louis Browns	3–5	L	7–31–2
41	06–07–1904	at St. Louis Browns	3–6	L	7–32–2
42	06–08–1904	at St. Louis Browns	0–12	L	7–33–2
43	06–10–1904	at Detroit Tigers	4–1	W	8–33–2
44	06–11–1904	at Detroit Tigers	3–8	L	8–34–2
45	06–13–1904	at Detroit Tigers	0–3	L	8–35–2
46	06–14–1904	at Detroit Tigers	5–5	T	8–35–3
47	06–15–1904	at Cleveland Blues	0–8	L	8–36–3
48	06–16–1904	at Cleveland Blues	5–3	W	9–36–3
49	06–17–1904	at Cleveland Blues	2–10	L	9–37–3
50	06–18–1904	at Cleveland Blues	4–8	L	9–38–3
51	06–20–1904	at Philadelphia Athletics	3–11	L	9–39–3
52	06–21–1904	vs New York Highlanders	0–3	L	9–40–3
53	06–22–1904	vs New York Highlanders	6–11	L	9–41–3
54	06–23–1904	vs New York Highlanders	4–7	L	9–42–3
55	06–24–1904	vs New York Highlanders	3–5	L	9–43–3
56	06–25–1904	at Philadelphia Athletics	3–6	L	9–44–3
57	06–27–1904	vs Philadelphia Athletics	2–3	L	9–45–3
58	06–28–1904	vs Philadelphia Athletics	2–1	W	10–45–3
59	07–01–1904	at New York Highlanders	3–8	L	10–46–3
60-I	07–02–1904	at New York Highlanders	3–2	W	11–46–3
61-II	07–02–1904	at New York Highlanders	6–11	L	11–47–3
62-I	07–04–1904	vs Boston Americans	2–8	L	11–48–3
63-II	07–04–1904	vs Boston Americans	2–5	L	11–49–3
64	07–05–1904	vs Boston Americans	2–6	L	11–50–3
65	07–06–1904	vs Boston Americans	0–3	L	11–51–3
66	07–08–1904	at Philadelphia Athletics	1–2	L	11–52–3
67-I	07–09–1904	at Philadelphia Athletics	0–3	L	11–53–3
68-II	07–09–1904	at Philadelphia Athletics	11–3	W	12–53–3
69	07–11–1904	at Philadelphia Athletics	1–3	L	12–54–3
70	07–12–1904	vs St. Louis Browns	2–6	L	12–55–3

1904 Washington Senators Schedule (cont.)

GAME	DATE	OPPONENT	SCORE	DECISION	RECORD
71	07–13–1904	vs St. Louis Browns	9–4	W	13–55–3
72	07–14–1904	vs St. Louis Browns	5–2	W	14–55–3
73	07–15–1904	vs St. Louis Browns	2–7	L	14–56–3
74	07–16–1904	vs Chicago White Sox	0–3	L	14–57–3
75	07–18–1904	vs Chicago White Sox	1–12	L	14–58–3
76	07–19–1904	vs Chicago White Sox	1–5	L	14–59–3
77	07–20–1904	vs Chicago White Sox	0–8	L	14–60–3
78	07–21–1904	vs Detroit Tigers	11–5	W	15–60–3
79	07–22–1904	vs Detroit Tigers	0–0	T	15–60–4
80-I	07–23–1904	vs Detroit Tigers	3–2	W	16–60–4
81-II	07–23–1904	vs Detroit Tigers	2–3	L	16–61–4
82-I	07–27–1904	vs Cleveland Blues	3–2	W	17–61–4
83-II	07–27–1904	vs Cleveland Blues	0–7	L	17–62–4
84-I	07–29–1904	vs Cleveland Blues	1–0	W	18–62–4
85-II	07–29–1904	vs Cleveland Blues	2–6	L	18–63–4
86	07–30–1904	at Cleveland Blues	4–9	L	18–64–4
87	08–01–1904	at Chicago White Sox	2–4	L	18–65–4
88	08–02–1904	at Chicago White Sox	1–5	L	18–66–4
89	08–03–1904	at Chicago White Sox	2–3	L	18–67–4
90	08–04–1904	at Chicago White Sox	1–10	L	18–68–4
91	08–05–1904	at St. Louis Browns	4–5	L	18–69–4
92	08–06–1904	at St. Louis Browns	2–1	W	19–69–4
93	08–07–1904	at St. Louis Browns	7–2	W	20–69–4
94	08–08–1904	at St. Louis Browns	9–1	W	21–69–4
95	08–10–1904	at Detroit Tigers	1–4	L	21–70–4
96	08–11–1904	at Detroit Tigers	3–7	L	21–71–4
97	08–12–1904	at Detroit Tigers	2–3	L	21–72–4
98-I	08–13–1904	at Detroit Tigers	2–4	L	21–73–4
99-II	08–13–1904	at Detroit Tigers	2–1	W	22–73–4
100	08–15–1904	at Cleveland Blues	0–1	L	22–74–4
101	08–16–1904	at Cleveland Blues	1–7	L	22–75–4
102	08–17–1904	at Cleveland Blues	2–3	L	22–76–4
103	08–19–1904	vs Detroit Tigers	0–5	L	22–77–4
104-I	08–20–1904	vs Detroit Tigers	1–12	L	22–78–4
105-II	08–20–1904	vs Detroit Tigers	4–5	L	22–79–4

1904 Washington Senators Schedule (cont.)

GAME	DATE	OPPONENT	SCORE	DECISION	RECORD
106-I	08–23–1904	vs Detroit Tigers	7–2	W	23–79–4
107-II	08–23–1904	vs Detroit Tigers	2–5	L	23–80–4
108	08–24–1904	vs Cleveland Blues	2–1	W	24–80–4
109	08–25–1904	vs Cleveland Blues	4–8	L	24–81–4
110	08–26–1904	vs Cleveland Blues	0–1	L	24–82–4
111	08–27–1904	vs Cleveland Blues	0–1	L	24–83–4
112	08–29–1904	vs St. Louis Browns	7–2	W	25–83–4
113-I	08–30–1904	vs St. Louis Browns	2–3	L	25–84–4
114-II	08–30–1904	vs St. Louis Browns	4–1	W	26–84–4
115	08–31–1904	vs St. Louis Browns	1–2	L	26–85–4
116	09–01–1904	vs Chicago White Sox	1–0	W	27–85–4
117	09–02–1904	vs Chicago White Sox	2–5	L	27–86–4
118-I	09–03–1904	vs Chicago White Sox	1–6	L	27–87–4
119-II	09–03–1904	vs Chicago White Sox	5–4	W	28–87–4
120-I	09–05–1904	at Boston Americans	5–12	L	28–88–4
121-II	09–05–1904	at Boston Americans	3–8	L	28–89–4
122-I	09–06–1904	at Boston Americans	1–4	L	28–90–4
123-II	09–06–1904	at Boston Americans	6–3	W	29–90–4
124-I	09–07–1904	vs Boston Americans	3–8	L	29–91–4
125-II	09–07–1904	vs Boston Americans	6–1	W	30–91–4
126-I	09–08–1904	vs Boston Americans	2–8	L	30–92–4
127-II	09–08–1904	vs Boston Americans	1–3	L	30–93–4
128	09–09–1904	vs Boston Americans	0–7	L	30–94–4
129-I	09–10–1904	at New York Highlanders	3–2	W	31–94–4
130-II	09–10–1904	at New York Highlanders	5–6	L	31–95–4
131	09–12–1904	at New York Highlanders	2–4	L	31–96–4
132-I	09–15–1904	at Philadelphia Athletics	4–8	L	31–97–4
133-II	09–15–1904	at Philadelphia Athletics	3–4	L	31–98–4
134	09–16–1904	at Philadelphia Athletics	5–3	W	32–98–4
135	09–17–1904	at New York Highlanders	5–6	L	32–99–4
136	09–19–1904	vs New York Highlanders	3–4	L	32–100–4
137-I	09–20–1904	vs New York Highlanders	2–3	L	32–101–4
138-II	09–20–1904	vs New York Highlanders	1–5	L	32–102–4
139	09–21–1904	vs New York Highlanders	4–2	W	33–102–4
140-I	09–25–1904	at St. Louis Browns	1–0	W	34–102–4

1904 Washington Senators Schedule (cont.)

GAME	DATE	OPPONENT	SCORE	DECISION	RECORD
141-II	09–25–1904	at St. Louis Browns	0–1	L	34–103–4
142	09–26–1904	at St. Louis Browns	2–2	T	34–103–5
143	09–27–1904	at Chicago White Sox	1–2	L	34–104–5
144	09–28–1904	at Chicago White Sox	3–4	L	34–105–5
145	09–29–1904	at Chicago White Sox	0–3	L	34–106–5
146	09–30–1904	at Cleveland Blues	0–3	L	34–107–5
147-I	10–01–1904	at Cleveland Blues	0–4	L	34–108–5
148-II	10–01–1904	at Cleveland Blues	2–9	L	34–109–5
149	10–03–1904	at Detroit Tigers	2–3	L	34–110–5
150-I	10–05–1904	at Detroit Tigers	4–1	W	35–110–5
151-II	10–05–1904	at Detroit Tigers	1–1	T	35–110–6
152-I	10–07–1904	vs Philadelphia Athletics	2–3	L	35–111–6
153-II	10–07–1904	vs Philadelphia Athletics	3–2	W	36–111–6
154-I	10–08–1904	vs Philadelphia Athletics	12–5	W	37–111–6
155-II	10–08–1904	vs Philadelphia Athletics	0–2	L	37–112–6
156-I	10–10–1904	vs Philadelphia Athletics	6–7	L	37–113–6
157-II	10–10–1904	vs Philadelphia Athletics	4–3	W	38–113–6

Data courtesy of Baseball-Almanac.com.

#5	**The Curse Continues**
	The 1932 Boston Red Sox (43–111)

> In the beginning they were gods, a dynasty of sorts. Be-
> fore expansion, before Inter-league play, before the DH,
> they were the mighty Red Sox.
> —*Columnist Jason Perry, Baseball-Almanac.com*

The Boston Red Sox won 5 of the first 15 World Series, including the 1916 and 1918 series, in which star hurler George Herman "Babe" Ruth pitched for the Sox. The team also won the 1915 World Series in which Ruth appeared once as a pinch hitter. However, the owner of the team, Harry Frazee, sold Ruth to the New York Yankees on January 3, 1920, in order to finance a Broadway musical that he was producing. Thus was born the "Curse of the Bambino," which prevented the Red Sox from winning another World Series championship for 86 years (they finally won again in 2004, breaking the curse). Along the way, the Red Sox appeared in a number of Fall Classics, including one that is often considered the best ever played, 1975. For those 86 years, though, Red Sox fans knew nothing but frustration and pain.

Prior to obtaining Ruth, the Yankees had never won a World Series. After hiring Ruth the Yankee dynasty that dominated the next three decades was born. Along the way, Frazee gutted his franchise over the next few years by sending the Yankees Hall of Fame pitcher Herb Pennock, and solid players such as Joe Dugan, Everett Scott, George Pipgras, "Bullet" Joe Bush, and Sam Jones without receiving adequate compensation for the talent unloaded. It's not surprising that as the Yankees' fortunes improved, the fortunes of the Red Sox plummeted. Frazee sold the team to J. A. Robert Quinn in 1923 for $1.5 million. Bob Quinn was an experienced baseball man, and had served as the general manager of the St. Louis Browns for several years. He inherited a team saddled by serious financial problems and a devastated farm system.

The 1925 Red Sox went 47–105. The next year's team posted a nearly identical record of 46–107, and the team went 51–103 in 1927, the year that the Yankees fielded what many consider to be the greatest team in the his-

1932 Red Sox first baseman Dale Alexander (Library of Congress)

tory of major league baseball. The Red Sox improved slightly in 1928 and 1929, avoiding 100 losses with records of 57–96 and 58–96, respectively. In 1930, they went 52–102, and in 1931, they finished in sixth place with a record of 62–90. They finished dead last in the American League every year from 1922 to 1930, except for 1924, when they finished seventh. By 1932, Quinn was in serious financial trouble and was nearly out of money. Only 182,000 fans clicked the turnstiles at Fenway Park in 1932, for an average attendance of only 2,275 per game. Quinn had to borrow $500,000 from the American League just to keep his team afloat.

He had little to work with. His team had little talent, and the farm system offered little hope. As author Peter Golenbock described it in *Red Sox Nation: An Unexpurgated History of the Boston Red Sox*, his history of the Red Sox, "The typical Red Sox players of the Bob Quinn era were either untried kids, over-the-hill vets, problem players dumped by other teams, or players with one skill: hitting *or* fielding. Few became household names. Most were out there just doing their best, glad to have a paycheck or hoping to get traded to a better team."

John Francis "Shano" Collins, a former outfielder and first baseman for the Red Sox, had the unenviable task of managing the team, knowing he had almost no talent.[1] The year of 1932 would be his second season at the helm of the Red Sox—and he would have to do so without his team's best pitcher. "Big Ed" Morris, a lanky righty, had won 19 games with the 1928 Red Sox. He was a hard-thrower and had a lot of potential. In 1931, Morris went 5–7 in 37 appearances, and Collins expected a lot of him in 1932. However, on the eve of spring training in 1932, Morris' friends from home in Alabama threw him a going-away party, where one of his friends stabbed him. Morris jumped in the river that separates Alabama and Florida and swam to the other side. He got the chills, contracted pneumonia, and died in the hospital. His tragic death left the Red Sox without their pitching staff's leader, meaning that Collins started the season with a significant handicap.

The team's best player was second baseman Marty McManus. McManus was a 12-year veteran of the major leagues. He hit a triple in his first major league time at bat and spent most of the 1920s with the St. Louis Browns, where he excelled. Known for his speed and hitting, he had more than 90 RBIs three times, with a high of 109 in 1922. When Collins resigned as manager in June 1932 after 55 games, McManus was appointed player-manager. The team went a pathetic 11–44 under Collins, and 32–67 under McManus. The dual role as player and manager obviously took a toll on him. The 1932 season proved to be his worst, as he hit only .235 that year in 93 games, by far the lowest average of his fine career. He had only 5 homers and 24 RBIs in an unproductive and disappointing season.[2]

The Red Sox had a few legitimate offensive threats, led by outfielder Smead Jolley. Jolley, known as "Smudge," was a big, slow, and ponderous fielder who wielded a big left-handed stick. Defense was not his forte. Because he was 28 years old when he made his major league debut, his career lasted only five seasons. In 1932, he hit .309 with 18 homers and 99 RBIs, providing the offensive punch in the middle of the Red Sox lineup.

A teammate left the following description of Jolley's defensive deficiencies.

Smead Jolley was a big, strong, dumb guy who could hit the ball as far as Ruth. Smead played Duffy's Cliff. It was called that because Duffy Lewis was one of only three players who knew how to play it. The secret was, when the ball went out here, you had to be able to judge if it was catchable if you went up the cliff. If you got to the top and didn't catch it, the ball would hit the wall and bounce past you, and now you would have to run down and chase it halfway back to the infield. If you knew you couldn't catch it, you just turned and waited for it to come off, and the batter would get a single. Jolley could never do that. Sometimes he'd go up and the ball would go over his head, and as the ball would come back at him, he'd fall and roll and roll. "They taught me to climb up the damn hill, but not how to come down."

Twenty-nine-year-old speedy outfielder Roy Johnson was a fine hitter. He hit .300 or better four times in his career and finished with a career batting average of .296. In 1932, he hit .298 with 11 homers and 47 RBIs in 94 games. First baseman Dale Alexander, who was acquired from the Detroit Tigers after 23 games, hit an impressive .372 in 101 games with the Red Sox, with 8 homers and 56 RBIs. Third baseman Urbane Pickering hit .260 with no power production to speak of, and shortstop Warstler, a good fielder but an anemic hitter, managed a meager .211 in 115 games.

The Red Sox had a team batting average of .251, with 53 homers and only 529 RBIs. The players didn't score many runs, and they could not rely on pitching to win games for them. In fact, their pitching was the team's downfall. The pitching staff allowed a mind-boggling 1,574 hits in only 1,362 innings, with a bad team ERA of 5.02. It's no wonder that the Red Sox posted a record of 43-111 in 1932 and finished 64 games behind the pennant-winning New York Yankees. Forty-one different players shuttled in and out of Collins' and McManus' lineups that long season.

The Red Sox had one pitcher who posted a winning record in 1932. Ivy Andrews, a 6-foot, 1-inch, 200-pound righty from Alabama, posted an 8–6 record after being acquired from the Yankees during the season's second week. Andrews threw hard. "He is a strictly overhand pitcher whose fine winning record has been compiled by judicious use of a blazing fast ball, a good curve and a fair change of pace," wrote beat writer Clifford Blood-good in 1933. "They have proved to be all the assortment he needs." Andrews had a respectable 3.81 ERA in 141.2 innings and was by far the most effective pitcher for the Red Sox that year. It all went downhill from there.

Bob Kline, the erstwhile ace of the staff, posted an 11–13 record in 47 games. Kline was hit hard, giving up 203 hits in only 172 innings, with a 5.28 ERA. Lefty Bob Weiland notched a 6–16 record in 43 appearances, allowing 231 hits in 195.2 innings with an ERA of 4.51. Righty Wilcy Moore, who had won 19 games with the 1927 Yankees, was hit just as hard. Moore went 4–10 with a 5.23 ERA in 37 games, almost all of which were out of the bull pen. Righty Ed Durham went 6–13 with a respectable ERA of 3.80. All told, 18 different pitchers toiled for the Red Sox that long season.

Weiland, who came to the Red Sox from the St. Louis Cardinals, summed up the plight of the Red Sox players well. "In 1932, the team was 43 and 111. Can't you imagine? It's no fun playing on a loser. You try like hell, but nothing seems to go right for you. It seems like you get no breaks at all. A lot of times I pitched well and didn't get the win." After describing his hard-luck season, he concluded, "With the Cards, I had a good ball club behind me. Those guys could field ground balls and catch fly balls!" Another declared, "The Red Sox in those days were a lot like Stengel's Mets."

The 1932 Red Sox were probably the worst team fielded by Quinn during the 10 years that he owned the team. After the end of that long, miserable season, Quinn sold the Red Sox to Tom Yawkey, who started with a clean slate. After the 1935 season, Quinn became the president and general manager of the crosstown Boston Braves. The long decade of misery for Red Sox fans had finally ended, and better days lay ahead. Seven years later, in 1939, a skinny left-handed hitting outfielder from San Diego with a sweet swing named Ted Williams made his debut with the Sox.

However, not even the sale of the team to Yawkey could break the Curse of the Bambino. The Curse hung over the heads of the Sox faithful until the 2004 edition of the team finally vanquished it by winning the World Series. In 1932, though, the Curse was in full force and effect, and the few fans who made their way to Fenway Park to root for the Red Sox had little to look forward to each day.

1932 Boston Red Sox Statmaster: Fielding

NAME	POS	GAMES	PO	A	E	DP	TC/G	FLD%
Dale Alexander	1B	101	1,051	67	9	93	11.2	.992
Ivy Andrews	P	25	4	27	1	3	1.3	.969
Pete Appleton	P	11	5	19	0	0	2.2	1.000
Charlie Berry	C	10	28	6	2	3	3.6	.944
Larry Boerner	P	21	4	14	0	0	0.9	1.000
Ed Connolly	C	75	233	55	13	0	4.0	.957
Pete Donohue	P	4	1	5	0	0	1.5	1.000
Ed Durham	P	34	14	37	1	4	1.5	.981
Ed Gallagher	P	9	2	5	1	0	0.9	.875
Roy Johnson	OF	85	167	6	13	0	2.2	.930
Smead Jolley	OF	126	234	12	15	3	2.1	.943
Smead Jolley	C	5	21	2	0	0	4.6	1.000
Bob Kline	P	47	16	44	1	6	1.3	.984
Regis Leheny	P	2	0	2	0	0	1.0	1.000
Hod Lisenbee	P	19	2	12	1	0	0.8	.933
Danny MacFayden	P	12	4	17	2	3	1.9	.913
Jud McLaughlin	P	1	0	1	0	0	1.0	1.000
Marty McManus	2B	49	123	161	9	26	6.0	.969
Marty McManus	3B	30	24	66	8	2	3.3	.918
Marty McManus	SS	2	1	0	1	0	1.0	.500
Marty McManus	1B	1	3	1	0	0	4.0	1.000
Gordon McNaughton	P	6	2	6	0	1	1.3	1.000
John Michaels	P	28	5	24	3	1	1.1	.906
Wilcy Moore	P	37	3	30	1	3	0.9	.971
Tom Oliver	CF	116	328	12	6	4	3.0	.983
Marv Olson	2B	106	266	324	28	68	5.8	.955
Marv Olson	3B	1	0	3	0	0	3.0	1.000
Hank Patterson	C	1	0	0	0	0	0.0	.000
Urbane Pickering	3B	126	110	222	21	22	2.8	.941
Urbane Pickering	C	1	1	0	1	0	2.0	.500
Johnny Reder	1B	10	88	8	1	11	9.7	.990
Johnny Reder	3B	1	1	0	1	0	2.0	.500
Gordon Rhodes	P	12	6	15	1	0	1.8	.955
Hal Rhyne	SS	55	92	161	9	31	4.8	.966
Hal Rhyne	3B	4	6	6	0	0	3.0	1.000
Hal Rhyne	2B	1	1	1	1	0	3.0	.667
Jack Rothrock	LF	12	35	1	1	0	3.1	.973

1932 Boston Red Sox Statmaster: Fielding (cont.)

NAME	POS	GAMES	PO	A	E	DP	TC/G	FLD%
Jack Russell	P	11	2	10	1	0	1.2	.923
Andy Spognardi	2B	9	14	33	1	6	5.3	.979
Andy Spognardi	SS	3	0	4	0	0	1.3	1.000
Andy Spognardi	3B	2	0	1	0	0	0.5	1.000
Howie Storie	C	5	11	0	0	0	2.2	1.000
George Stumpf	OF	51	78	2	4	0	1.6	.952
Bennie Tate	C	76	244	50	8	7	4.0	.974
Al Van Camp	1B	25	249	18	4	20	10.8	.985
Rabbit Warstler	SS	107	254	373	41	84	6.2	.939
Johnny Watwood	OF	46	101	3	6	0	2.4	.945
Johnny Watwood	1B	18	149	16	7	17	9.6	.959
Earl Webb	RF	50	74	7	3	2	1.7	.964
Earl Webb	1B	2	14	1	1	2	8.0	.938
Bob Weiland	P	43	14	49	3	7	1.5	.955
Johnny Welch	P	20	1	17	1	0	1.0	.947
TEAM TOTALS			4,086	1,956	231	429	3.8	.963

Data courtesy of Baseball-Almanac.com.

1932 Boston Red Sox Statmaster: Hitting

NAME	POS	GAMES	AVG	SLG	AB	H	2B	3B	HR	AB/HR	R	RBI	BB	SO	SB
Dale Alexander	1B	101	.372	.524	376	140	27	3	8	47.0	58	56	55	19	4
Ivy Andrews	P	27	.137	.157	51	7	1	0	0	0.0	5	1	0	13	0
Pete Appleton	P	11	.176	.235	17	3	1	0	0	0.0	3	1	0	5	0
Charlie Berry	C	10	.188	.281	32	6	3	0	0	0.0	0	6	3	2	0
Larry Boerner	P	21	.000	.000	17	0	0	0	0	0.0	0	1	0	5	0
Ed Connolly	C	75	.225	.297	222	50	8	4	0	0.0	9	21	20	27	0
Pete Donohue	P	4	.000	.000	3	0	0	0	0	0.0	0	0	0	1	0
Ed Durham	P	35	.123	.123	57	7	0	0	0	0.0	2	1	4	16	0
Ed Gallagher	P	9	.000	.000	5	0	0	0	0	0.0	0	0	0	3	0
Roy Johnson	OF	94	.298	.484	349	104	24	4	11	31.7	70	47	44	41	13
Smead Jolley	OF	137	.309	.480	531	164	27	5	18	29.5	57	99	27	29	0
Bob Kline	P	47	.130	.185	54	7	1	1	0	0.0	0	1	0	13	0
Regis Leheny	P	2	.000	.000	1	0	0	0	0	0.0	0	0	0	0	0
Hod Lisenbee	P	19	.048	.048	21	1	0	0	0	0.0	0	0	2	7	0
Johnny Lucas	PH	1	.000	.000	1	0	0	0	0	0.0	0	0	0	0	0
Danny MacFayden	P	12	.120	.160	25	3	1	0	0	0.0	0	3	0	14	0
Jud McLaughlin	P	1	.000	.000	1	0	0	0	0	0.0	0	0	0	1	0
Marty McManus	2B	93	.235	.374	302	71	19	4	5	60.4	39	24	36	30	1
Gordon McNaughton	P	6	.250	.375	8	2	1	0	0	0.0	1	0	0	3	0
John Michaels	P	29	.143	.143	21	3	0	0	0	0.0	1	0	1	2	0
Otto Miller	PH	2	.000	.000	2	0	0	0	0	0.0	0	0	0	0	0
Wilcy Moore	P	37	.045	.045	22	1	0	0	0	0.0	1	0	1	11	0

1932 Boston Red Sox Statmaster: Hitting (cont.)

NAME	POS	GAMES	AVG	SLG	AB	H	2B	3B	HR	AB/HR	R	RBI	BB	SO	SB
Tom Oliver	OF	122	.264	.327	455	120	23	3	0	0.0	39	37	25	12	1
Marv Olson	2B	115	.248	.313	403	100	14	6	0	0.0	58	25	61	26	1
Hank Patterson	C	1	.000	.000	1	0	0	0	0	0.0	0	0	0	0	0
Urbane Pickering	3B	132	.260	.357	457	119	28	5	2	228.5	47	40	39	71	3
Johnny Reder	1B	17	.135	.162	37	5	1	0	0	0.0	4	3	6	6	0
Gordon Rhodes	P	12	.074	.148	27	2	0	1	0	0.0	2	1	0	10	0
Hal Rhyne	SS	71	.227	.333	207	47	12	5	0	0.0	26	14	23	14	3
Jack Rothrock	OF	12	.208	.229	48	10	1	0	0	0.0	3	0	5	5	3
Jack Russell	P	13	.091	.091	11	1	0	0	0	0.0	1	0	0	6	0
Andy Spognardi	2B	17	.294	.324	34	10	1	0	0	0.0	9	1	6	6	0
Howie Storie	C	6	.375	.375	8	3	0	0	0	0.0	0	0	0	0	0
George Stumpf	OF	79	.201	.254	169	34	2	2	1	169.0	18	18	18	21	1
Bennie Tate	C	81	.245	.348	273	67	12	5	2	136.5	21	26	20	6	0
Al Van Camp	1B	34	.223	.301	103	23	4	2	0	0.0	10	6	4	17	0
Rabbit Warstler	SS	115	.211	.276	388	82	15	5	0	0.0	26	34	22	43	9
Johnny Watwood	OF	95	.248	.289	266	66	11	0	0	0.0	26	30	20	11	7
Earl Webb	OF	52	.281	.417	192	54	9	1	5	38.4	23	27	25	15	0
Bob Weiland	P	43	.148	.262	61	9	5	1	0	0.0	2	3	3	17	0
Johnny Welch	P	23	.250	.389	36	9	2	0	1	36.0	5	3	0	9	0
TEAM TOTALS			.251	.351	5,294	1,330	253	57	53	99.9	566	529	470	537	46

Data courtesy of Baseball-Almanac.com.

1932 Boston Red Sox Statmaster: Pitching

NAME	GAMES	W	L	W%	ERA	GS	CG	IP	HA	BB	SO	SHU
Ivy Andrews	25	8	6	.571	3.81	19	8	141.2	144	53	30	0
Pete Appleton	11	0	3	.000	4.11	3	0	46.0	49	26	15	0
Larry Boerner	21	0	4	.000	5.02	5	0	61.0	71	37	19	0
Pete Donohue	4	0	1	.000	7.82	2	0	12.2	18	6	1	0
Ed Durham	34	6	13	.316	3.80	22	4	175.1	187	49	52	0
Ed Gallagher	9	0	3	.000	12.55	3	0	23.2	30	28	6	0
Bob Kline	47	11	13	.458	5.28	19	4	172.0	203	76	31	1
Regis Leheny	2	0	0	.000	16.87	0	0	2.2	5	3	1	0
Hod Lisenbee	19	0	4	.000	5.65	6	3	73.1	87	25	13	0
Danny MacFayden	12	1	10	.091	5.10	11	6	77.2	91	33	29	0
Jud McLaughlin	1	0	0	.000	15.00	0	0	3.0	5	4	0	0
Gordon McNaughton	6	0	1	.000	5.43	2	0	21.0	21	22	6	0
John Michaels	28	1	6	.143	5.13	8	2	80.2	101	27	16	0
Wilcy Moore	37	4	10	.286	5.23	2	0	84.1	98	42	28	0
Gordon Rhodes	12	1	8	.111	5.11	11	4	79.1	79	31	22	0
Jack Russell	11	1	7	.125	6.81	6	1	39.2	61	15	7	0
Bob Weiland	43	6	16	.273	4.51	27	7	195.2	231	97	63	0
Johnny Welch	20	4	6	.400	5.23	8	3	72.1	93	38	26	1
TEAM TOTALS		43	111	.279	5.02	154	42	1362	1,574	612	365	2

Data courtesy of Baseball-Almanac.com.

#6 | Even the Babe Couldn't Save This One
The 1935 Boston Braves (38–115)

Yesterday's home runs don't win today's games.

—*George Herman Ruth*

The National League franchise that played in Boston—and which now plays in Atlanta—is the oldest ongoing franchise in professional baseball, tracing its roots to the Boston Red Caps, a team formed in 1876. Over the next 37 years, the team operated under various names, including the Beaneaters, Doves, and Rustlers before the team was renamed the Braves in 1912. The team had a long history of wretchedness. From 1903 to 1912, the team finished 32, 51, 54, 66, 47, 36, 55, 50, 54, and 52 games out of first place.

Somehow, the 1914 Braves managed to win 34 out of their last 44 games to win the National League pennant, and then the "Miracle Braves" beat Connie Mack's mighty Philadelphia Athletics in the World Series. However, 1914 was an anomaly. Before long, the Braves were back in the basement. They lost 100 games per season in 1922, 1923, and 1924, and then lost 103 games in each of the 1928 and 1929 seasons, setting a gold standard for being terrible. However, the worst was yet to come.

Led by a genuine superstar—lanky blonde outfielder Wally Berger—the Braves improved a bit in 1933 and 1934, finishing fourth both years. The franchise actually made money for the years 1930 through 1934. However, Judge Emil Fuchs, the team's owner, was having dire financial trouble and was known for spending every dollar that came in the door. All of those years of awful teams meant that the Braves filled few seats in their stands, and the team had major cash-flow problems. The team's future was much in doubt. Desperate for cash flow, Fuchs threatened to operate a dog racetrack in his team's stadium, Braves Field, while the Braves played their home games in Fenway Park. Judge Fuchs had a $200,000 note coming due in August 1935, and had only his ball club with which to pay it.

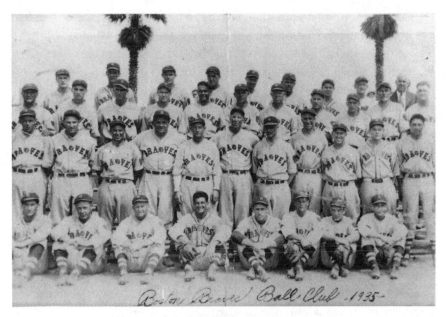

1935 Boston Braves (Baseball Hall of Fame Library, Cooperstown, NY)

In the meantime, Col. Jacob Ruppert, the owner of the New York Yankees, had had just about enough of George Herman "Babe" Ruth's shenanigans. Ruth, who lived by the motto, "I swing big, with everything I've got. I hit big or I miss big. I like to live as big as I can," was true to his belief. He lived hard and had grown old prematurely as a result. By 1934, his legendary baseball skills had deteriorated significantly, and the Babe had made it clear that he expected to be the next manager of the Yankees if his playing days were over. Ruppert was happy with his current manager, Joe McCarthy, so he went looking for a team that would take the troublesome Ruth off his hands. He found a willing taker in Judge Fuchs, who hoped that the Babe's star power would fill seats in Braves Field. In February 1935, Ruppert assigned Ruth's contract to the Braves.

Ruth signed a $25,000 contract on February 27, 1935, and became player, assistant manager, and second vice president of the team. "I will take full charge of the Braves on the field next year," declared Ruth. "My main ambition still is to manage a big-league club, and I am going to Boston with the full understanding that it will be fulfilled."

Player/Manager Babe Ruth (Library of Congress)

That announcement undoubtedly came as unwelcome news to the present Braves manager, Bill McKechnie. McKechnie, who was headed for the Hall of Fame, had already won a World Series title with the 1925 Pittsburgh Pirates and another National League pennant with the 1928 St. Louis Cardinals. McKechnie ranked as the fourth winningest manager in major league history when he retired, and he was the first manager to win World Series titles with two teams and pennants with three. (He also won a World Series title with the 1940 Cincinnati Reds.) A quiet man who sang in his church choir, the manager was known as Deacon. His personality could not have been more diametrically opposed to that of the flamboyant Ruth. He managed the Braves to their fourth-place finishes in 1933 and 1934 "with teams that should have been eighth," as Lee Allen, historian of the National League, later put it. The Braves were fortunate to have such an accomplished manager, and the addition of an ambitious putative manager such as Babe Ruth caused problems almost immediately.

Center fielder Wally Berger was a bona fide superstar. Berger hit 38 home runs in his rookie season of 1930, a record for rookies that stood until Mark McGwire shattered it in 1987. Berger batted .310 that season and drove in 119 runs, another rookie record. In 1933, Berger finished second in the Most Valuable Player balloting after slugging 27 homers to finish second in the National League. In an 11-season career Berger posted a .300 batting average with 242 home runs and 898 RBIs in 1,350 games played. He hit 199 of those homers with the Braves, a team record that stood until Eddie Matthews came along in the 1950s. Berger was precisely the sort of player that a manager could use to build a winning team.

The 1935 Braves also featured another future Hall of Famer facing the end of a long and productive career. Forty-four-year-old shortstop Walter James Vincent "Rabbit" Maranville, who earned his nickname for his blazing speed and small stature, was about to start his record 23rd major league season (a mark that he held until Pete Rose broke the record in 1986). He was the only member of the 1914 Miracle Braves still playing in the major leagues. He had badly broken a leg the previous season and was determined to return to the major leagues. Rabbit was known as one of "baseball's most famous clowns" because of his practical jokes and lack of inhibitions, traits that did not serve him well when he tried his hand at being a player-manager with the Chicago Cubs in the 1920s. "There is much less drinking now than there was before 1927," declared Maranville in 1928, "because I quit drinking on May 24, 1927." Not surprisingly, the Rabbit and the Babe were friendly, having bent an elbow together a time or two over the years. Maranville retired during the 1935 season with a .258 batting average, 1,255 runs scored, a meager 28 homers, 884 RBIs, and 291 stolen bases. He set a record for his position with 5,139 putouts, and was named to the Hall of Fame in 1954.

With Ruth and Maranville both at the ends of their long careers, McKechnie faced challenges about how to coax one last productive season out of the old stars. He also faced a more significant problem: The presence of the Babe, combined with his special deal with Judge Fuchs, made it all but impossible for the manager to enforce discipline. The combination of Ruth's huge salary and the outfielder's special dispensation to live apart from the rest of the team on the road handcuffed McKechnie's attempts to enforce discipline on his team. And it showed. The 1935 Braves finished with a record of 38–115, finishing dead last in the National League.

Ruth lasted only 28 games, batting an atrocious .181 in his last appearances in the major leagues. On opening day, he faced New York Giants ace screwballer Carl Hubbell and hit a home run and a double that day. He also made a nice running catch in the outfield, but it was clear that this was no longer the great Babe of old. He was slow and ponderous. He hit another couple of homers before catching a bad cold, which drove him from the lineup for several days. When he recovered, he showed one final flash of greatness against the Pirates on May 25 by slugging three homers in one game for only the second time in his long career. One of those homers, the 714th and final of his storied career, carried nearly 600 feet, clearing the right field roof. He also had a single and six RBIs that day before taking himself out of a game that the Braves still managed to lose 11–7. Pitcher Guy Bush, who suffered this fusillade, commented of the Babe's single, "If he'd ever lifted that one it would have been a homerun, too. He really laid the wood on it." The next day in Cincinnati, he went 0–4 with three strikeouts, and then grounded out against the Phillies on Memorial Day in his last major league at bat. Although he could still swing the bat, his abused legs could no longer carry his bloated body. On June 2, he called a meeting with the New York and Boston writers and announced his retirement, claiming that Judge Fuchs was playing games with him. It was a sad end to one of the greatest careers the game has ever seen.

In Donald Honig's *Baseball America,* Braves rookie first baseman Elbie Fletcher left a poignant description of the elderly Babe.

> He couldn't run. He could hardly bend down for a ball, and he couldn't hit the way he used to. It was sad watching those great skills fading

away. One of the saddest things of all is when an athlete begins to lose it. A ball goes past you that you would have been on top of a few years before. And then, being a left-handed hitter, you begin to realize that most of your good shots are going to center and left-center, and you know you've lost just that fraction of a second and can't always pull the ball the way you used to. And to see it happening to Babe Ruth, to see Babe Ruth struggling on a ball field, well, then you realize we're all mortal and nothing lasts forever.

Maranville didn't fare much better. His swan song lasted 23 games. He had only 10 hits in 67 at bats, for an anemic batting average of .149, although he managed to drive in five runs. His defensive skills had also deteriorated; the once slick fielder made 3 errors in only 81 chances. Seeing the handwriting on the wall, and following Ruth's lead, the Rabbit also retired early in the season, leaving a second hole in the Braves' roster. At season's end, the organization offered him a job managing the team's minor league affiliate in Allentown, Pennsylvania. "Where the hell is Allentown?" snarled the Rabbit. Instead, he took a job managing the Elmira team in the New York-Pennsylvania League for the kingly sum of $4,000. He hit .323 in 123 games as a player-manager.

By August 1, Judge Fuchs had completely run out of money and could not pay the $200,000 note that came due.[1] Consequently, his creditors and minority shareholders assumed control of the team, forcing him to step down as president. All of the chaos took its toll on the team. The Braves fell into last place on May 22 and never emerged from the cellar. They lost 15 games in a row, all on the road. And then things got worse. From August 18 to September 14, the Braves went 2–30 and finished a staggering 61.5 games out of first place. The team hit .263, but had only 75 homeruns. Only 232,754 attended Braves' games for the entire season, meaning that he had no way to pay the note when it came due.

As bad as the rest of the Braves were, Wally Berger had the finest season of his career that long summer. Berger hit .295 with 34 homers, 39 doubles, 130 RBIs, and a slugging percentage of .548. Considering that the Braves hit a total of 75 homers the entire season, Berger had nearly half of them in his stellar season. Remarkably, Ruth's 6 homers in 28 games put him in second place among Braves for 1936.

Third baseman Pinky Whitney, formerly of the Phillies, hit .273 with 4 homers and 60 RBIs. First baseman Buck Jordan hit .279 with 5 homers and 35 RBI's. Jordan found his way into the record books by banging out eight hits in a single doubleheader on August 25. Slick-fielding outfielder Hal Lee hit .303 but didn't hit a single homer and drove in only 39 runs. Second baseman Les Mallon hit .274 with 2 homers and an anemic 25 RBIs. Outfielders Randy Moore and Tommy Thompson, who split playing time, hit .275 and .273 respectively, combining for 8 homers and 72 RBIs. Other than Berger, the team simply had no offensive punch.

The pitching staff was not much better. Thirty-four-year-old righty Ben Cantwell won 20 games for the Braves in 1933, when they finished fourth in the National League. However, Cantwell posted a miserable 4–25 record in 1935, with an ERA of 4.81, surrendering 235 hits (including 15 homers) in 210.2 innings pitched. At one point, he lost 13 consecutive starts. His .138 winning percentage has to be close to the worst in the history of major league baseball. He was baseball's last 25-game loser, a dubious distinction at best.

Righty Fred Frankhouse, who went 17–9 in 1934, was the staff ace, posting an 11–15 record with a 4.76 ERA. Another right-hander, Bob Smith, posted an 8–18 record with a respectable ERA of 3.94 in 203.1 innings. Hard-throwing lefty Big Ed Brandt rounded out the starting pitching with a 5–19 record and a hefty ERA of 5.00. He won 16 games in 1934 and 18 in 1933. The pitching staff combined for a team ERA of 4.93, giving up 1,645 hits in only 1,330 innings, and posting a meager 355 strikeouts. Unfortunately, all of the team's starting pitchers were over the age of 30, and the relievers were even older. Many of these hurlers had lost a foot or two off their fastballs. Consequently, the team's pitching staff was horrible, and when it was combined with the lack of discipline and the lack of offensive punch, there's no surprise that the Braves posted a miserable 38–115 record in 1935.

McKechnie did everything he could. He juggled lineups. He brought up players from the minor leagues. He moved men in and out of the lineup, so that only a handful played in more than 100 games. No matter what he tried, nothing worked. The Braves just kept on losing. On top of all of it, he ended up serving as the team's acting president after Fuchs turned the team over to majority shareholder Charles Francis Adams at the beginning of August.[2]

The Braves had such a terrible season in 1935 that the team's name was changed once more after the season. They played from 1936 to 1940 as the Boston Bees before again taking on the Braves moniker for good. However, with new management in place, the team actually improved significantly in 1936. The Braves finished sixth and went 71–83, meaning that they won twice as many games in just a year.

What makes the 1935 Braves so remarkable is that their collapse was completely unforeseen and completely unpredictable. After two solid years of finishing in fourth place in 1933 and 1934, with solid pitching, it looked like the addition of Ruth and the return of Maranville might make the Braves a contender. Instead, the lack of discipline, the sideshow created by Ruth's pathetic performance, and the breakdown of the pitching doomed the 1935 Braves to become the laughingstock of the National League. Luckily, the collapse lasted only that one miserable season, as the team returned to respectability a year later.

1935 Boston Braves Statmaster: Fielding

NAME	POS	GAMES	PO	A	E	DP	TC/G	FLD%
Larry Benton	P	29	2	12	0	1	0.5	1.000
Wally Berger	CF	149	458	8	17	1	3.2	.965
Huck Betts	P	44	3	40	1	0	1.0	.977
Al Blanche	P	6	0	4	0	0	0.7	1.000
Ed Brandt	P	29	7	42	3	1	1.8	.942
Bob Brown	P	15	4	8	1	0	0.9	.923
Ben Cantwell	P	39	12	54	1	4	1.7	.985
Joe Coscarart	3B	41	28	74	4	5	2.6	.962
Joe Coscarart	SS	27	61	66	8	10	5.0	.941
Joe Coscarart	2B	15	26	37	2	5	4.3	.969
Art Doll	C	3	11	2	2	0	5.0	.867
Elbie Fletcher	1B	39	353	27	1	22	9.8	.997
Fred Frankhouse	P	40	15	63	2	2	2.0	.975
Shanty Hogan	C	56	175	25	2	2	3.6	.990
Buck Jordan	1B	95	857	66	16	59	9.9	.983
Buck Jordan	3B	8	13	13	1	1	3.4	.963
Buck Jordan	RF	2	6	0	0	0	3.0	1.000
Hal Lee	OF	110	273	7	11	0	2.6	.962
Bill Lewis	C	1	0	0	0	0	0.0	.000
Danny MacFayden	P	28	5	42	2	1	1.8	.959
Les Mallon	2B	73	166	219	10	31	5.4	.975
Les Mallon	3B	36	34	62	8	3	2.9	.923
Les Mallon	RF	1	1	0	0	0	1.0	1.000
Leo Mangum	P	3	0	1	0	0	0.3	1.000
Rabbit Maranville	2B	20	32	46	3	10	4.1	.963
Randy Moore	OF	78	161	10	9	3	2.3	.950
Randy Moore	1B	21	209	10	4	11	10.6	.982

1935 Boston Braves Statmaster: Fielding (cont.)

NAME	POS	GAMES	PO	A	E	DP	TC/G	FLD%
Ed Moriarty	2B	8	11	25	3	0	4.9	.923
Joe Mowry	OF	45	62	3	2	0	1.5	.970
Ray Mueller	C	40	64	27	2	6	2.3	.978
Flint Rhem	P	10	1	10	0	0	1.1	1.000
Babe Ruth	OF	26	39	1	2	0	1.6	.952
Bob Smith	P	46	10	39	1	1	1.1	.980
Al Spohrer	C	90	230	45	12	4	3.2	.958
Tommy Thompson	OF	85	184	9	7	3	2.4	.965
Johnnie Tyler	LF	11	24	1	3	0	2.5	.893
Billy Urbanski	SS	129	258	356	40	52	5.1	.939
Pinky Whitney	3B	74	83	144	10	8	3.2	.958
Pinky Whitney	2B	49	113	161	7	17	5.7	.975
TEAM TOTALS			3,991	1,759	197	263	3.7	.967

Data courtesy of Baseball-Almanac.com.

1935 Boston Braves Statmaster: Hitting

NAME	POS	GAMES	AVG	SLG	AB	H	2B	3B	HR	AB/HR	R	RBI	BB	SO	SB
Larry Benton	P	29	.200	.250	20	4	1	0	0	0.0	1	1	1	4	0
Wally Berger	OF	150	.295	.548	589	174	39	4	34	17.3	91	130	50	80	3
Huck Betts	P	44	.159	.159	44	7	0	0	0	0.0	1	1	3	5	0
Al Blanche	P	6	.167	.167	6	1	0	0	0	0.0	0	0	0	0	0
Ed Brandt	P	31	.210	.210	62	13	0	0	0	0.0	5	2	1	3	0
Bob Brown	P	16	.105	.105	19	2	0	0	0	0.0	1	0	0	2	0
Ben Cantwell	P	41	.284	.299	67	19	1	0	0	0.0	4	2	2	8	0
Joe Coscarart	3B	86	.236	.299	284	67	11	2	1	284.0	30	29	16	28	2
Art Doll	C	3	.100	.100	10	1	0	0	0	0.0	0	0	1	1	0
Elbie Fletcher	1B	39	.236	.318	148	35	7	1	1	148.0	12	9	7	13	1
Fred Frankhouse	P	40	.263	.316	76	20	4	0	0	0.0	10	7	9	9	0
Shanty Hogan	C	59	.301	.387	163	49	8	0	2	81.5	9	25	21	8	0
Buck Jordan	1B	130	.279	.383	470	131	24	5	5	94.0	62	35	19	17	3
Hal Lee	OF	112	.303	.374	422	128	18	6	0	0.0	49	39	18	25	0
Bill Lewis	C	6	.000	.000	4	0	0	0	0	0.0	1	0	1	1	0
Danny MacFayden	P	28	.157	.216	51	8	3	0	0	0.0	2	3	0	15	0
Les Mallon	2B	116	.274	.357	412	113	24	2	2	206.0	48	25	28	37	3
Leo Mangum	P	3	.000	.000	0	0	0	0	0	0.0	0	0	0	0	0
Rabbit Maranville	2B	23	.149	.179	67	10	2	0	0	0.0	3	5	3	3	0
Randy Moore	OF	125	.275	.373	407	112	20	4	4	101.8	42	42	26	16	1

1935 Boston Braves Statmaster: Hitting (cont.)

NAME	POS	GAMES	AVG	SLG	AB	H	2B	3B	HR	AB/HR	R	RBI	BB	SO	SB
Ed Moriarty	2B	8	.324	.529	34	11	2	1	1	34.0	4	1	0	6	0
Joe Mowry	OF	81	.265	.360	136	36	8	1	1	136.0	17	13	11	13	0
Ray Mueller	C	42	.227	.371	97	22	5	0	3	32.3	10	11	3	11	0
Flint Rhem	P	10	.000	.000	10	0	0	0	0	0.0	0	1	0	2	0
Babe Ruth	OF	28	.181	.431	72	13	0	0	6	12.0	13	12	20	24	0
Bob Smith	P	47	.270	.270	63	17	0	0	0	0.0	3	4	1	5	0
Al Spohrer	C	92	.242	.288	260	63	7	1	1	260.0	22	16	9	12	0
Tommy Thompson	OF	112	.273	.343	297	81	7	1	4	74.3	34	30	36	17	2
Johnnie Tyler	OF	13	.340	.553	47	16	2	1	2	23.5	7	11	4	3	0
Billy Urbanski	SS	132	.230	.286	514	118	17	0	4	128.5	53	30	40	32	3
Pinky Whitney	3B	126	.273	.367	458	125	23	4	4	114.5	41	60	24	36	2
TEAM TOTALS			.263	.362	5,309	1,396	233	33	75	70.8	575	544	353	436	20

Data courtesy of Baseball-Almanac.com.

1935 Boston Braves Statmaster: Pitching

NAME	GAMES	W	L	W%	ERA	GS	CG	IP	HA	BB	SO	SHU
Larry Benton	29	2	3	.400	6.88	0	0	72.0	103	24	21	0
Huck Betts	44	2	9	.182	5.47	19	2	159.2	213	40	40	1
Al Blanche	6	0	0	.000	1.56	0	0	17.1	14	5	4	0
Ed Brandt	29	5	19	.208	5.00	25	12	174.2	224	66	61	0
Bob Brown	15	1	8	.111	6.37	10	2	65.0	79	36	17	1
Ben Cantwell	39	4	25	.138	4.61	24	13	210.2	235	44	34	0
Fred Frankhouse	40	11	15	.423	4.76	29	10	230.2	278	81	64	1
Danny MacFayden	28	5	13	.278	5.10	20	7	151.2	200	34	46	1
Leo Mangum	3	0	0	.000	3.86	0	0	4.2	6	2	0	0
Flint Rhem	10	0	5	.000	5.36	6	0	40.1	61	11	10	0
Bob Smith	46	8	18	.308	3.94	20	8	203.1	232	61	58	2
TEAM TOTALS		38	115	.248	4.93	153	54	1330	1,645	404	355	6

Data courtesy of Baseball-Almanac.com.

You can't win them all.

— *Connie Mack, manager of the 1916 Athletics*

The American League was formed in 1901. The Shibe family of Philadelphia, which was in the sporting goods business, received one of its original franchises. The team was called the Athletics. Connie Mack, a catcher who played major league baseball before the turn of the century, became the general manager of the team's operations. Mack was known as an astute judge of baseball talent, and he led his team to five World Series championships and nine American League flags. The team won its first American League pennant in 1902 and repeated in 1905, losing the World Series to John J. McGraw's New York Giants, who were led by the great hurler Christy Matthewson.

The Philadelphia team moved into Shibe Park at 21st and Lehigh in the city's north end in 1909 and began its dynastic run, winning world championships in 1910, 1911, and 1913, including revenge over McGraw and the Giants in 1911. The Athletics relied on the combined prowess of the so-called $100,000 infield of Stuffy McInnis, Eddie Collins, Jack Barry, and Frank "Home Run" Baker. Collins and Baker ended up in the Hall of Fame as the "Mackmen" and established baseball's first true dynasty. Those Athletics teams are still considered to be some of the greatest teams to ever put on spikes.

In 1912, Mack purchased a 50 percent interest in the team from owner Ben Shibe. Connie Mack was a good man: he was considerate of his players, gentle, restrained, and religious. "Connie Mack. There was a wonderful person. A truly religious man. I mean *really* religious," said Rube Bressler, one of his former players, Rube Bressler. "Not a hypocrite, like some are. He really respected his fellow man. If you made a mistake, Connie never bawled you out on the bench or in front of anybody else. He'd get you alone

1916 Philadelphia Athletics (Baseball Hall of Fame Library, Cooperstown, NY)

a few days later, and then he'd say something like, 'Don't you think it would have been better if you'd made the play this way?'" Mack set a record for longevity as manager of the Athletics that remains intact today by leading his team for more than 50 years.

The Athletics won another American League pennant in 1914, but were swept out by the "Miracle Braves" in the World Series. "I really am glad that in losing we were beaten four straight games," cryptically declared Mack in one of the Philadelphia newspapers after the World Series. "It is the best thing that could have happened in baseball. It proves the honesty of the game, which comes before everything else."

That same year, an "outlaw" league called the Federal League began operations, and it stocked its rosters by raiding players from existing major league teams. The next year, the Athletics played second fiddle to their crosstown rivals, the Phillies, as the Phils won their first National League flag in 1915, losing to the Boston Red Sox in the World Series.

However, the Athletics had lost money in 1914 when attendance dropped, meaning that when the owner of the cash-strapped Baltimore Orioles called to offer to sell Mack his prize prospect, a young left-handed pitcher named George Herman "Babe" Ruth for $23,000, Mack had to say no. Ruth instead went to the Boston Red Sox and eventually to the New York Yankees, where he became one of the game's greatest players. It also meant that the cash-strapped Athletics could not compete in bidding wars with the upstart Federal League. After learning that three of his players were considering signing with the new league, Mack unloaded his best pitchers—

"Gettysburg Eddie" Plank, Chief Bender, and Jack Coombs—giving them their unconditional releases. That December, he sold future Hall of Famer Eddie Collins to the Chicago White Sox for $50,000 to avoid having to pay Collins his 1915 salary of $14,000.

When Baker asked for a raise after the 1914 season and Mack would not give him the desired increase, Baker sat out the entire 1915 season. In June 1915, Mack sold pitcher Herb Pennock and shortstop Barry to the Boston Red Sox for cash. Pitcher Bob Shawkey went to the Yankees for $18,000, and outfielder Eddie Murphy went to Chicago for $13,500. The team's batting average plummeted from .272 to .237 while total run production dropped by 172. The 1915 Athletics posted a record of 34–109, drawing only 146,223 while the crosstown Phillies won the National League pennant.

Things did not bode well for the 1916 edition of the Mackmen. In January of that year, Mack sold off the disgruntled Baker to the Yankees for $37,500 and catcher Jack Lapp to the White Sox. Several other veterans were also unloaded, meaning that the Athletics' great dynasty had ended by its owner's own hand. Only a couple of the mainstays from the championship seasons remained, and they were not enough to make a difference for what was obviously going to be an absolutely atrocious team made up of sandlotters and kids just out of school. Mack evidently believed that if he gave enough youngsters a chance, sooner or later he would find some with real talent, so many players came and went that long season. Mack used a then-record 50 players over the course of that long, nightmarish season.

Six of the American League's eight teams finished with winning records that year, and the seventh-place Washington Senators finished only one game under .500. However, the Athletics opened the season by reeling off six straight losses and finished the season at 36–117. They were, without question, one of the very worst teams in the history of major league baseball. Their 117 losses set an American League record for wretchedness that stood for years. They finished 54½ games out of first place, and 40 games behind the seventh-place Senators. At one point, the Athletics lost 20 straight games, setting an American League record for frustration. Their run production was 87 below the next lowest-scoring team, and they gave up 155 more runs than the next most generous team. The team committed 66 more errors than any other team in the league, and the terrible pitching staff led the league in most walks, hits, and runs given up. Only 184,471 turned out to watch the team that year.

The Athletics were shut out a staggering 14 times over the course of the 1916 season, and they were blown out 39 times. They posted a horrendous

2–28 record in July, including the 20 game-losing streak. They posted as many as seven wins against another team only against the Yankees. Against Chicago, Cleveland, and Detroit, they put up matching 4–18 records. When asked about his terrible team, the laconic Mack, accustomed to success, responded simply, "You can't win them all."

Second baseman Napoleon "Larry" Lajoie, who was a star on the 1902 pennant-winning team, returned to the Athletics to end his career. Now 40, old, slow, and lumbering, Lajoie's best days were long behind him. Lajoie hit .246 in 113 games before an injury ended his Hall of Fame career on August 22. There were also a few other holdovers from the dynastic teams. Reliable first baseman Stuffy McInnis hit .295 and had 60 RBIs. Outfielder Amos Strunk hit .316 and stole 21 bases. Outfielder/catcher Wally Schang hit .266 and clubbed 7 of the team's 19 homeruns for the season.

Charlie Grimm, a 17-year-old outfielder, made his major league debut that year. Grimm hit only .091 in 22 games, beginning what would be an outstanding 20-year career in the major leagues, including two trips to the World Series as a player-manager with the Chicago Cubs. Grimm, however, was the exception and not the rule. The vast majority of these youngsters never appeared in another major league game after their tryouts with the 1916 Athletics.

If anything, Mack's pitching staff was even less effective. Hard-throwing righty "Bullet Joe" Bush was the ace of the pitching staff, with a 15–24 record, a decent earned run average of 2.57, and eight shutouts. Bush worked more than 286 innings that long year. Twenty-two-year-old right-hander Elmer Myers, of York Spring, Pennsylvania, posted a 14–23 record with a respectable 3.66 ERA in 315 innings worked. It only got worse after the two workhorses of the staff.

Twenty-two-year-old righty Tom Sheehan, in his second year with the Athletics, posted an atrocious 1–16 record for 1916. Sheehan threw 188 innings in 38 appearances, and posted a 3.69 ERA. Sheehan did not appear in a major league uniform again until 1921, when he pitched in 12 games for the New York Yankees. He then dropped from sight again until 1924, when he appeared in 36 games for the Cincinnati Reds, posting a 9–11 record. By 1926, his career was over. Sheehan posted a 17–39 record in his undistinguished major league career.

However, Sheehan's record was not the worst on Mack's pitching staff that year. That honor fell to 28-year-old right-hander Jack Nabors, of Montevallo, Alabama, who was in his first full season in the major leagues. Nabors had what may well be *the* worst record of any major league pitcher in history in 1916, going 1–20 in 40 appearances. Nabors posted an almost unbelievable .048 winning percentage that year but still had a decent ERA of 3.47. One quote by Nabors summed up the entire season for the 1916 Athletics. After wild pitching in the losing run in the ninth inning of a 1–1 game, Nabors said, "If they think I'd stand there in that sun and pitch another nine innings waiting for our bums to make another run, they're crazy." Nabors appeared in only two games in 1917 and then ended his short stint in the major leagues with a 1–25 career record.

Marsh Williams had a 48-day major league career in 1916. Williams, a 23-year-old right-handed pitcher from North Carolina, appeared in 10 games in July and August, posting a record of 0–6. He gave up 71 hits and 45 earned runs in 51 innings, for an ERA of 7.89. He never appeared in another major league baseball game. Or, there was 22-year-old Jack Richardson, who gave up three earned runs in two-thirds of an inning that year, for a staggering 40.48 ERA. Richardson was one five pitchers who appeared in only one game for the Mackmen that year. Of the 20 hurlers to toe the rubber for the Athletics in 1916, 14 of them appeared in 10 games or less.

Fortunately, Connie Mack's legendary eye for talent served him well. Although the Athletics again finished last in 1917 with a 55–98 record, they were much improved. In 1918, with the season shortened by the entry of the United States into World War I, the Mackmen went 52–76, and the last of the players from the dynastic years were traded or sold. By 1923, the Athletics were competitive again, and in 1924, having added several all-time greats in Al Simmons, Lefty Grove, and Jimmie Foxx, the Athletics won 71 games. By 1928, they won 98 games and finished a mere 2½ games behind the mighty New York Yankees. The Mackmen then won three straight American League flags in 1929, 1930, and 1931, including two World Series championships. Those Athletics teams are considered some of the very best to ever take the field of play. Ironically, Mack, who was always strapped for cash, dismantled his second dynasty just as he dismantled the first, by selling off his best players. He never recaptured the magic a third time, though. The Athletics labored in mediocrity until Mack finally retired in 1950 after five decades at the helm. The team was sold and moved to Kansas City after the 1954 season, ending the team's long run in the City of Brotherly Love.

However, the glory of the superb Athletics teams of 1910–1914 and 1928–1931 was not even a glimmer of hope over the long, hot, miserable summer of 1916. Instead, Connie Mack presided over what might well be the worst team in the history of the American League. With their 20 straight losses and 117 defeats for the season, the 1916 Athletics deserve a prominent place in the pantheon of major league baseball's very worst teams.

1916 Philadelphia Athletics Schedule

GAME	DATE	OPPONENT	SCORE	DECISION	RECORD
1	04–12–1916	at Boston Red Sox	1–2	L	0–1
2	04–13–1916	at Boston Red Sox	2–8	L	0–2
3	04–15–1916	at Boston Red Sox	1–2	L	0–3
4	04–18–1916	at New York Yankees	2–4	L	0–4
5	04–19–1916	at New York Yankees	1–2	L	0–5
6	04–20–1916	vs Boston Red Sox	1–7	L	0–6
7	04–21–1916	vs Boston Red Sox	3–1	W	1–6
8	04–22–1916	vs Boston Red Sox	6–2	W	2–6
9	04–24–1916	vs Boston Red Sox	0–4	L	2–7
10	04–26–1916	at Washington Senators	3–2	W	3–7
11	04–27–1916	at Washington Senators	2–4	L	3–8
12	04–28–1916	at Washington Senators	6–7	L	3–9
13	04–29–1916	vs New York Yankees	2–4	L	3–10
14	05–01–1916	vs New York Yankees	4–2	W	4–10
15	05–02–1916	vs New York Yankees	4–9	L	4–11
16	05–03–1916	vs New York Yankees	3–2	W	5–11
17	05–04–1916	vs Washington Senators	1–5	L	5–12
18	05–06–1916	vs Washington Senators	4–1	W	6–12
19	05–08–1916	vs Washington Senators	4–2	W	7–12
20	05–09–1916	vs Detroit Tigers	2–16	L	7–13
21	05–10–1916	vs Detroit Tigers	3–9	L	7–14
22	05–11–1916	vs Detroit Tigers	3–2	W	8–14
23	05–12–1916	vs Detroit Tigers	6–8	L	8–15
24	05–13–1916	vs St. Louis Browns	4–3	W	9–15
25	05–15–1916	vs St. Louis Browns	5–4	W	10–15
26	05–17–1916	vs St. Louis Browns	4–7	L	10–16
27	05–18–1916	vs Chicago White Sox	5–1	W	11–16
28	05–19–1916	vs Chicago White Sox	1–0	W	12–16
29	05–20–1916	vs Chicago White Sox	0–11	L	12–17
30	05–22–1916	vs Cleveland Indians	10–8	W	13–17
31	05–24–1916	vs Cleveland Indians	4–5	L	13–18
32	05–26–1916	at Washington Senators	1–2	L	13–19
33-I	05–27–1916	at Washington Senators	3–5	L	13–20
34-II	05–27–1916	at Washington Senators	1–3	L	13–21
35	05–29–1916	at Washington Senators	5–5	T	13–21–1
36-I	05–30–1916	at New York Yankees	2–7	L	13–22–1
37-II	05–30–1916	at New York Yankees	1–0	W	14–22–1
38-I	05–31–1916	at New York Yankees	7–8	L	14–23–1
39-II	05–31–1916	at New York Yankees	5–9	L	14–24–1

1916 Philadelphia Athletics Schedule (cont.)

GAME	DATE	OPPONENT	SCORE	DECISION	RECORD
40	06–01–1916	at New York Yankees	5–0	W	15–24–1
41	06–03–1916	at St. Louis Browns	2–3	L	15–25–1
42	06–04–1916	at St. Louis Browns	3–4	L	15–26–1
43	06–10–1916	at Cleveland Indians	1–10	L	15–27–1
44	06–11–1916	at Cleveland Indians	2–7	L	15–28–1
45	06–12–1916	at Cleveland Indians	1–3	L	15–29–1
46	06–13–1916	at Cleveland Indians	2–11	L	15–30–1
47	06–15–1916	at Detroit Tigers	1–5	L	15–31–1
48	06–16–1916	at Detroit Tigers	3–4	L	15–32–1
49	06–17–1916	at Detroit Tigers	3–7	L	15–33–1
50	06–18–1916	at Detroit Tigers	2–8	L	15–34–1
51	06–20–1916	vs Washington Senators	1–2	L	15–35–1
52-I	06–22–1916	vs Washington Senators	4–2	W	16–35–1
53-II	06–22–1916	vs Washington Senators	1–6	L	16–36–1
54	06–23–1916	at Boston Red Sox	0–1	L	16–37–1
55-I	06–24–1916	at Boston Red Sox	2–3	L	16–38–1
56-II	06–24–1916	at Boston Red Sox	3–7	L	16–39–1
57	06–26–1916	at Boston Red Sox	8–5	W	17–39–1
58	06–27–1916	at Boston Red Sox	2–7	L	17–40–1
59	06–28–1916	vs New York Yankees	7–9	L	17–41–1
60	06–29–1916	vs New York Yankees	0–5	L	17–42–1
61	06–30–1916	vs New York Yankees	0–7	L	17–43–1
62	07–01–1916	vs New York Yankees	4–5	L	17–44–1
63	07–03–1916	vs Boston Red Sox	4–6	L	17–45–1
64-I	07–04–1916	vs Boston Red Sox	2–11	L	17–46–1
65-II	07–04–1916	vs Boston Red Sox	2–5	L	17–47–1
66	07–06–1916	vs Detroit Tigers	4–9	L	17–48–1
67	07–07–1916	vs Detroit Tigers	2–9	L	17–49–1
68	07–08–1916	vs Detroit Tigers	2–3	L	17–50–1
69-I	07–11–1916	vs St. Louis Browns	3–8	L	17–51–1
70-II	07–11–1916	vs St. Louis Browns	3–0	W	18–51–1
71-I	07–12–1916	vs St. Louis Browns	3–8	L	18–52–1
72-II	07–12–1916	vs St. Louis Browns	1–2	L	18–53–1
73	07–13–1916	vs St. Louis Browns	3–7	L	18–54–1
74-I	07–15–1916	vs Chicago White Sox	1–4	L	18–55–1
75-II	07–15–1916	vs Chicago White Sox	0–1	L	18–56–1
76-I	07–18–1916	vs Chicago White Sox	2–9	L	18–57–1
77-II	07–18–1916	vs Chicago White Sox	2–3	L	18–58–1
78	07–19–1916	vs Cleveland Indians	5–12	L	18–59–1

1916 Philadelphia Athletics Schedule (cont.)

GAME	DATE	OPPONENT	SCORE	DECISION	RECORD
79-I	07–20–1916	vs Cleveland Indians	2–4	L	18–60–1
80-II	07–20–1916	vs Cleveland Indians	2–0	W	19–60–1
81	07–21–1916	vs Cleveland Indians	2–7	L	19–61–1
82	07–25–1916	at St. Louis Browns	3–8	L	19–62–1
83-I	07–26–1916	at St. Louis Browns	0–5	L	19–63–1
84-II	07–26–1916	at St. Louis Browns	1–5	L	19–64–1
85	07–27–1916	at St. Louis Browns	2–3	L	19–65–1
86	07–28–1916	at St. Louis Browns	6–8	L	19–66–1
87-I	07–29–1916	at Chicago White Sox	1–6	L	19–67–1
88-II	07–29–1916	at Chicago White Sox	4–6	L	19–68–1
89-I	07–30–1916	at Chicago White Sox	1–10	L	19–69–1
90-II	07–30–1916	at Chicago White Sox	0–7	L	19–70–1
91	07–31–1916	at Chicago White Sox	3–4	L	19–71–1
92-I	08–01–1916	at Chicago White Sox	0–3	L	19–72–1
93-II	08–01–1916	at Chicago White Sox	2–3	L	19–73–1
94	08–02–1916	at Chicago White Sox	2–8	L	19–74–1
95	08–03–1916	at Cleveland Indians	1–3	L	19–75–1
96	08–04–1916	at Cleveland Indians	2–5	L	19–76–1
97	08–05–1916	at Cleveland Indians	3–12	L	19–77–1
98	08–06–1916	at Cleveland Indians	2–5	L	19–78–1
99	08–07–1916	at Detroit Tigers	2–4	L	19–79–1
100	08–08–1916	at Detroit Tigers	0–9	L	19–80–1
101	08–09–1916	at Detroit Tigers	7–1	W	20–80–1
102	08–10–1916	at Detroit Tigers	4–10	L	20–81–1
103-I	08–12–1916	at New York Yankees	9–3	W	21–81–1
104-II	08–12–1916	at New York Yankees	2–0	W	22–81–1
105	08–14–1916	at New York Yankees	3–4	L	22–82–1
106	08–15–1916	at New York Yankees	2–6	L	22–83–1
107-I	08–17–1916	vs St. Louis Browns	4–3	W	23–83–1
108-II	08–17–1916	vs St. Louis Browns	2–3	L	23–84–1
109	08–18–1916	vs St. Louis Browns	3–4	L	23–85–1
110	08–19–1916	vs Detroit Tigers	2–6	L	23–86–1
111	08–21–1916	vs Detroit Tigers	1–7	L	23–87–1
112	08–22–1916	vs Detroit Tigers	1–0	W	24–87–1
113	08–23–1916	vs Detroit Tigers	3–10	L	24–88–1
114-I	08–24–1916	vs Cleveland Indians	6–5	W	25–88–1
115-II	08–24–1916	vs Cleveland Indians	2–4	L	25–89–1
116-I	08–25–1916	vs Cleveland Indians	9–13	L	25–90–1
117-II	08–25–1916	vs Cleveland Indians	2–10	L	25–91–1

1916 Philadelphia Athletics Schedule (cont.)

GAME	DATE	OPPONENT	SCORE	DECISION	RECORD
118	08–26–1916	vs Cleveland Indians	5–0	W	26–91–1
119	08–28–1916	vs Chicago White Sox	0–1	L	26–92–1
120	08–29–1916	vs Chicago White Sox	9–2	W	27–92–1
121	08–30–1916	vs Chicago White Sox	3–7	L	27–93–1
122	08–31–1916	vs Chicago White Sox	1–7	L	27–94–1
123-I	09–01–1916	at Washington Senators	1–3	L	27–95–1
124-II	09–01–1916	at Washington Senators	4–1	W	28–95–1
125	09–02–1916	at Washington Senators	6–7	L	28–96–1
126-I	09–04–1916	at Washington Senators	0–2	L	28–97–1
127-II	09–04–1916	at Washington Senators	1–3	L	28–98–1
128-I	09–05–1916	vs Boston Red Sox	5–2	W	29–98–1
129-II	09–05–1916	vs Boston Red Sox	1–7	L	29–99–1
130	09–06–1916	vs Boston Red Sox	2–5	L	29–100–1
131	09–07–1916	vs Boston Red Sox	0–2	L	29–101–1
132	09–08–1916	vs New York Yankees	8–2	W	30–101–1
133-I	09–09–1916	vs New York Yankees	1–4	L	30–102–1
134-II	09–09–1916	vs New York Yankees	0–4	L	30–103–1
135	09–13–1916	at Cleveland Indians	4–8	L	30–104–1
136	09–14–1916	at Cleveland Indians	1–9	L	30–105–1
137	09–15–1916	at Cleveland Indians	2–3	L	30–106–1
138	09–16–1916	at Detroit Tigers	3–4	L	30–107–1
139	09–17–1916	at Detroit Tigers	5–6	L	30–108–1
140	09–18–1916	at Detroit Tigers	2–0	W	31–108–1
141	09–19–1916	at Chicago White Sox	4–5	L	31–109–1
142	09–20–1916	at Chicago White Sox	7–8	L	31–110–1
143	09–21–1916	at Chicago White Sox	8–0	W	32–110–1
144	09–22–1916	at St. Louis Browns	3–6	L	32–111–1
145	09–23–1916	at St. Louis Browns	2–4	L	32–112–1
146-I	09–24–1916	at St. Louis Browns	2–0	W	33–112–1
147-II	09–24–1916	at St. Louis Browns	2–3	L	33–113–1
148	09–27–1916	vs Washington Senators	3–13	L	33–114–1
149	09–28–1916	vs Washington Senators	1–4	L	33–115–1
150-I	09–30–1916	vs Washington Senators	6–8	L	33–116–1
151-II	09–30–1916	vs Washington Senators	10–9	W	34–116–1
152	10–02–1916	at Boston Red Sox	2–4	L	34–117–1
153-I	10–03–1916	at Boston Red Sox	5–3	W	35–117–1
154-II	10–03–1916	at Boston Red Sox	7–5	W	36–117–1

Data courtesy of Baseball-Almanac.com.

#8 | Tie: '42 and '61 Phillies

62.5 Games Out of First Place
The 1942 Philadelphia Phillies (55–99)

> They [Pirates] never thought he could possibly make the
> team 'cause Lloyd only weighed about 130 pounds then. He
> was only twenty years old, and was even smaller than me.
> —*Paul Waner on his brother*
> *who went on to join the '42 Phils*

1941 was one of the greatest years in the history of major league baseball. Ted Williams of the Boston Red Sox, the Splendid Splinter, as he was known, hit an eye-popping .406 for the season. Joe DiMaggio, the graceful, elegant center fielder for the New York Yankees, had a 56-game hitting streak that still stands as a major league record. Forty-one-year-old Red Sox pitcher Lefty Grove won the 300th game of a magnificent career and promptly retired after winning nine ERA titles and after leading the American League in strikeouts seven times. The Yankees won the pennant by 17 games.

In the National League, the Brooklyn Dodgers, led by most valuable player (MVP) first baseman Dolph Camilli and aggressive rookie center fielder Pete Reiser, won the pennant after a tight race with the St. Louis Cardinals. Interestingly, the Dodger lineup was filled with former Cardinal players, including manager Leo Durocher.

The Yankees took a 2–1 lead in the crosstown World Series, but it looked like the Dodgers were going to win game four, taking a 4–3 lead into the ninth inning. With tough Hugh Casey on the mound, it looked good for the Dodgers. Tommy Henrich, the fine Yankee right fielder, came up with two outs and nobody on base. Henrich struck out, seemingly ending the game. However, catcher Mickey Owen committed one of the great blunders of World Series history, allowing a passed ball that permitted Henrich to reach first base safely. DiMaggio then singled, left fielder Charlie "King Kong" Keller doubled, catcher Bill Dickey walked, and second basemen Joe Gordon doubled to win the game 7–4. The Yankees clinched the next day.

After a season like that, fans eagerly looked forward to the 1942 season and a possible World Series rematch. However, fate intervened. On Decem-

1942 Philadelphia Phillies (Baseball Hall of Fame Library, Cooperstown, NY)

ber 7, 1941, the Japanese launched a sneak attack on the U.S. Navy base at Pearl Harbor, Hawaii. The Japanese sank four U.S. battleships and damaged four more. They also sank three cruisers, three destroyers, a minelayer, and they destroyed 188 aircraft—2,402 U.S. servicemen died, and another 1,282 were wounded. The next day, calling it "a day of infamy," President Franklin Roosevelt asked Congress to declare war on the Japanese and their allies, Germany and Italy.

Hollywood stars and sports heroes flocked to enlist to fight the Axis. Williams enlisted and became a Navy fighter pilot, and proved to be almost as good a pilot as he was a hitter. Hank Greenberg, the Hall of Fame first baseman of the Detroit Tigers also enlisted, as did the American League's best pitcher, Bob Feller of the Cleveland Indians. Other stars who enlisted included DiMaggio, Johnny Mize, Johnny Pesky, Gil Hodges, Phil Rizzuto, and Bill Dickey.

With its ranks decimated, what would happen to major league baseball in 1942? Minor league teams shut down their operations due to lack of players. However, when President Roosevelt was asked whether baseball should continue to be played during the war, he wrote a letter to Commissioner Kennesaw Mountain Landis saying, "I honestly feel that it would be best for the country to keep baseball going." And so the game continued.

With their rosters filled with minor leaguers, 4-Fs, and a few holdover major leaguers, the quality of play was watered down. One-armed outfielder Pete Gray, who lost an arm in a childhood accident, made it to the major leagues for the 1945 season. Other players who never would have had a chance to make the big time got their shot because of the war. It may not have been the caliber of play that the public was used to, but it was professional baseball.

Against this backdrop, it should come as no surprise that some of those teams were truly atrocious. Unquestionably, the worst of them was the 1942 Philadelphia Phillies. The Phightin' Phillies had been riding a long wave of misery. They had not had a winning team in more than two decades. They were coming off four especially terrible years, winning only 45 games in 1938 and 1939, 50 games in 1940, and only 43 games in 1941. The team's owner, Gerald P. Nugent, was nearly bankrupt, and the National League had to advance him operating funds just to meet payroll in 1942.

The team's name was changed for the 1942 season. Although they had been called the Phillies since their inception, a cigar company had introduced a product line named "Phillies," but Nugent did not have the funds to pursue a trademark infringement claim. Instead, he meekly changed the team's name to the Phils. Fortunately, the change only lasted a single season. However, with this sort of start to the season, there was no reason to expect good results.

Culminating an unprecedented five-year run of awfulness, the 1942 Phils posted an atrocious 42–109 record, for a winning percentage of just .278.[1] By contrast, two teams—the Cardinals and Dodgers—finished with more than 100 wins (106 and 104, respectively), and the Giants won 85. The Phils finished 18½ games behind the seventh place Boston Braves and a staggering 62.5 games out of first place. They drew only 230,000 fans the entire season, and only 393 people turned out to see the Phils lose to Cincinnati on September 11. With average attendance of less than 3,000 per game, Shibe Park was usually more empty than filled that wretched season.

They lost their first three games of the season to Boston and then the next game to the Dodgers. Things only got worse from there. The Phils won 10 games in a month only once the entire season (May, when they posted a 10–20 record). They were shut out 16 times and blown out 32 times. They won no more than eight games against any opponent (they went 8–14 against both the Cubs and Braves). Their manager, 60-year-old Hans Lobert, acidly complained about the lack of talent and lack of talent displayed by his players. His team lost 3 of its last 4 games and mercifully ended the season on September 27 after only 151 games.

Their offense was impotent at best. The team hit only .232 with 44 home runs and a mere 37 stolen bases. The team's slugging percentage was a weak .306, and they scored only 394 runs for the entire season, for an average of only 2.6 runs per game.

The Phils had only one player who had a good year. Left fielder Danny Litwhiler posted a .271 average with a team-leading 9 home runs and 56 RBIs. He also set a major league record by not committing a single error in 151 games. However, Lobert was not impressed. "Danny Litwhiler's perfect fielding record was not a true indication of his fielding ability," he grumbled. "I can remember many an afternoon when I would have given Litwhiler a dozen errors for some of the plays he made, or didn't make, in left field."

Shortstop Bobby Bragan hit a wretched .218, and second baseman Al Glossop hit .225, meaning that they made one of the least offensively productive double-play combinations in baseball history. Weak-hitting third baseman Pinky May hit .238 without a single homer in 345 at bats. Catchers Mickey Livingston and Bennie Warren split time behind the plate, hitting .205 in 89 games and .209 in 90 games. First baseman Nick Etten hit a decent .264, smacked 8 long balls and drove in 41. He was one of the more productive members of the team's anemic offense.

Future Hall of Fame outfielder Chuck Klein, now 38 years old and nearing the end of his storied career, hit an anemic .071 in just 14 miserable games. Klein played in 12 games in 1943 and in 4 more in 1944 and then wisely called it a career. Another future Hall of Fame outfielder, Lloyd "Little Poison" Waner, was 36 years old and well past his prime; 1942 was the last time he had as many as 287 at bats. Waner hit a respectable .260 in 101 games, but that was only a shadow of his career batting average of .316. Waner retired in 1945 after playing in only 47 more major league games over three seasons.

The Phils pitching was no better. The staff combined for a team ERA of 4.12, and allowed 1,328 hits and 605 walks in 1,341 innings. They accounted for two shutouts. The team earned run average was the worst in the National League. However, its relatively low number reflected the lack of overall offense in a league depleted by the departure of so many everyday players for military service.

The ace of the pitching staff was 22-year-old hard-throwing right-hander Tommy Hughes, who notched a 12–18 record and a respectable ERA of 3.06 in 253 innings spread over 31 starts. Philadelphia sportswriter Stan Baumgartner called Hughes "just about the best young pitcher in the National League." He deserved a better team, and he deserved a better fate. Instead, Hughes was drafted and went off to serve his country. He did not pitch in the majors again until 1946, when he posted a 6–9 record. His career was over by 1948.

Twenty-five-year-old righty Rube Melton, who stood an imposing 6-foot 5-inches tall, posted a terrible 9–20 record, but had a decent ERA of 3.70.

Fourteen-year veteran Silas "Si" Johnson, a right-hander, was 8–19 with a 3.69 ERA. Frank "Lefty" Hoerst, a 24-year-old Philadelphia native, put up 4–16 record with a 5.20 ERA, and bespectacled 22-year-old righty Johnny Podganji went 6–14 with a 3.91 ERA. "Subway Sam" Nahem, a 26-year-old Jewish relief pitcher from Brooklyn, went 1–3 but finished 16 games. Nahem twirled 74.2 innings in 1942 before enlisting in the military. He did not pitch in the major leagues again until 1948, when he returned to the Phillies for a final season.

By the end of the season, Gerry Nugent was bankrupt, and the National League had had enough. Needing money to operate the team, Nugent sold pitcher Melton to the Dodgers for $30,000 and first baseman Etten to the Yankees for $15,000. However, the team owed more than $300,000, meaning that these sums, for which Nugent had mortgaged whatever future his franchise had, did not come close to satisfying the team's cash needs.

After the World Series, the National League's owners met to discuss Nugent's plight. Determined not to advance Nugent any more funds, the league realized that a sale of the team was the only solution to the problem. On February 9, 1943, the National League purchased all of Nugent's shares in the team at a price of $10 per share for all 2,600 shares and an agreement to assume the team's debt. Eleven days later, on February 20, the league sold the Phillies to a syndicate headed by William D. Cox, 33-year-old Yale-educated lumber broker who outbid prominent Philadelphia brick contractor Jack Kelly, father of actress and future Princess of Monaco, Grace Kelly. Cox's group purchased the team for $250,000 and held out the hope of turning things around for the woebegone franchise.

Indeed, attendance increased dramatically in 1943, more than doubling the 1942 figure as a result of a fast start by the Phillies. However, after a controversy involving new manager Bucky Harris and shortstop Danny Murtaugh, the team's fortunes sank, and the Phils finished the season in seventh place, but at least out of the National League's cellar for the first time in years.

Unfortunately, during the off-season, Cox was banned from baseball permanently after admitting that he had placed numerous bets on the Phillies during the 1943 season. The team was then sold to Robert R. M. Carpenter, a vice president of E. I. duPont de Nemours, the giant chemical conglomerate headquartered in Wilmington, Delaware. Carpenter was married to a duPont daughter and brought the wealth of the chemical industry to the table. Finally, the Phillies had adequate working capital to fund their operations without having to sell every marginally talented player they had.

The Carpenter family retained ownership of the team until 1981, seeing the Phillies go to the World Series twice, and winning the Fall Classic for the first time in 1980.

It is difficult to imagine a much worse five-year run of wretchedness by any team than that experienced by the Phillies from 1938 to1942, climaxed by the atrocious 1942 club, which finished a mind-boggling 62.5 games behind the pennant-winning Cardinals, who notched 106 wins that year. Offensively anemic, bad in the field, without speed, and featuring inconsistent pitching, the 1942 Phils have to be considered one of the very worst teams in the history of Major League Baseball.

1942 Philadelphia Phillies Statmaster: Fielding

NAME	POS	GAMES	PO	A	E	DP	TC/G	FLD%
Boom-Boom Beck	P	26	3	9	1	2	0.5	.923
Stan Benjamin	OF	45	75	7	2	1	1.9	.976
Stan Benjamin	1B	15	99	6	3	11	7.2	.972
Cy Blanton	P	6	1	4	0	0	0.8	1.000
Bobby Bragan	SS	78	161	238	26	49	5.4	.939
Bobby Bragan	C	22	68	15	1	4	3.8	.988
Bobby Bragan	2B	4	13	10	0	2	5.8	1.000
Bobby Bragan	3B	3	0	0	0	0	0.0	.000
Bill Burich	SS	19	44	44	8	6	5.1	.917
Bill Burich	3B	3	5	5	0	0	3.3	1.000
Benny Culp	C	1	1	0	1	0	2.0	.500
Nick Etten	1B	135	1,152	83	19	99	9.3	.985
Hilly Flitcraft	P	3	0	1	0	0	0.3	1.000
Ed Freed	OF	11	13	2	0	0	1.4	1.000
Al Glossop	2B	118	322	351	27	79	5.9	.961
Al Glossop	3B	1	0	0	0	0	0.0	.000
George Hennessey	P	5	1	2	0	0	0.6	1.000
Bert Hodge	3B	2	1	2	0	0	1.5	1.000
Lefty Hoerst	P	33	11	40	2	2	1.6	.962
Tommy Hughes	P	40	9	69	2	3	2.0	.975
Si Johnson	P	39	3	30	0	2	0.8	1.000
Ernie Koy	OF	78	149	4	3	1	2.0	.981
Gene Lambert	P	1	0	1	0	0	1.0	1.000

1942 Philadelphia Phillies Statmaster: Fielding (cont.)

NAME	POS	GAMES	PO	A	E	DP	TC/G	FLD%
Andy Lapihuska	P	3	1	5	0	0	2.0	1.000
Danny Litwhiler	OF	151	308	9	0	0	2.1	1.000
Mickey Livingston	C	78	275	36	4	8	4.0	.987
Mickey Livingston	1B	6	59	1	1	5	10.2	.984
Harry Marnie	2B	11	14	20	1	5	3.2	.971
Harry Marnie	SS	7	16	12	3	4	4.4	.903
Harry Marnie	3B	1	0	0	0	0	0.0	.000
Paul Masterson	P	4	0	2	0	0	0.5	1.000
Pinky May	3B	107	109	227	13	23	3.3	.963
Rube Melton	P	42	8	33	1	2	1.0	.976
Ed Murphy	1B	8	69	3	0	7	9.0	1.000
Danny Murtaugh	SS	60	132	176	20	32	5.5	.939
Danny Murtaugh	3B	53	84	103	15	14	3.8	.926
Danny Murtaugh	2B	32	86	98	8	15	6.0	.958
Sam Nahem	P	35	6	19	1	2	0.7	.962
Earl Naylor	OF	34	59	1	1	0	1.8	.984
Earl Naylor	P	20	7	10	0	0	0.9	1.000
Ron Northey	OF	109	206	12	11	2	2.1	.952
Ike Pearson	P	35	2	17	0	2	0.5	1.000
Bill Peterman	C	1	0	0	0	0	0.0	.000
Johnny Podgajny	P	43	6	39	3	2	1.1	.938
Lloyd Waner	OF	75	170	6	6	0	2.4	.967
Bennie Warren	C	78	264	50	9	4	4.1	.972
Bennie Warren	1B	1	3	1	1	0	5.0	.800
TEAM TOTALS			4,015	1,803	193	388	3.6	.968

Data courtesy of Baseball-Almanac.com.

1942 Philadelphia Phillies Statmaster: Hitting

NAME	POS	GAMES	AVG	SLG	AB	H	2B	3B	HR	AB/HR	R	RBI	BB	SO	SB
Boom-Boom Beck	P	27	.333	.417	12	4	1	0	0	0.0	2	3	0	0	0
Stan Benjamin	OF	78	.224	.319	210	47	8	3	2	105.0	24	8	10	27	5
Cy Blanton	P	6	.125	.125	8	1	0	0	0	0.0	0	0	0	1	0
Bobby Bragan	SS	109	.218	.284	335	73	12	2	2	167.5	17	15	20	21	0
Bill Burich	SS	25	.288	.300	80	23	1	0	0	0.0	3	7	6	13	2
Benny Culp	C	1	.000	.000	0	0	0	0	0	0.0	0	0	0	0	0
Nick Etten	1B	139	.264	.375	459	121	21	3	8	57.4	37	41	67	26	3
Hilly Flitcraft	P	3	.000	.000	0	0	0	0	0	0.0	0	0	0	0	0
Ed Freed	OF	13	.303	.455	33	10	3	1	0	0.0	3	1	4	3	1
Al Glossop	2B	121	.225	.289	454	102	15	1	4	113.5	33	40	29	35	3
George Hennessey	P	5	.000	.000	5	0	0	0	0	0.0	0	0	0	1	0
Bert Hodge	3B	8	.182	.182	11	2	0	0	0	0.0	0	0	1	0	0
Lefty Hoerst	P	33	.152	.174	46	7	1	0	0	0.0	1	0	3	8	0
Tommy Hughes	P	42	.100	.100	80	8	0	0	0	0.0	1	0	0	20	0
Si Johnson	P	35	.103	.103	58	6	0	0	0	0.0	3	0	0	16	0
Chuck Klein	PH	14	.071	.071	14	1	0	0	0	0.0	0	0	0	2	0
Ernie Koy	OF	91	.244	.349	258	63	9	3	4	64.5	21	26	14	50	0
Gene Lambert	P	1	.000	.000	0	0	0	0	0	0.0	0	0	0	0	0
Andy Lapihuska	P	3	.286	.286	7	2	0	0	0	0.0	0	0	0	0	0
Danny Litwhiler	OF	151	.271	.389	591	160	25	9	9	65.7	59	56	27	42	2
Mickey Livingston	C	89	.205	.264	239	49	6	1	2	119.5	20	22	25	20	0
Harry Marnie	2B	24	.167	.167	30	5	0	0	0	0.0	3	0	1	2	1
Paul Masterson	P	4	.000	.000	0	0	0	0	0	0.0	0	0	0	0	0

1942 Philadelphia Phillies Statmaster: Hitting (cont.)

NAME	POS	GAMES	AVG	SLG	AB	H	2B	3B	HR	AB/HR	R	RBI	BB	SO	SB
Pinky May	3B	115	.238	.281	345	82	15	0	0	0.0	25	18	51	17	3
Rube Melton	P	42	.123	.215	65	8	3	0	1	65.0	3	7	2	26	0
Ed Murphy	1B	13	.250	.321	28	7	2	0	0	0.0	2	4	2	4	0
Danny Murtaugh	SS	144	.241	.289	506	122	16	4	0	0.0	48	27	49	39	13
Sam Nahem	P	35	.100	.100	20	2	0	0	0	0.0	1	1	1	1	0
Earl Naylor	OF	76	.196	.232	168	33	4	1	0	0.0	9	14	11	18	1
Ron Northey	OF	127	.251	.331	402	101	13	2	5	80.4	31	31	28	33	2
Ike Pearson	P	35	.043	.043	23	1	0	0	0	0.0	1	0	1	5	0
Bill Peterman	C	1	1.000	1.000	1	1	0	0	0	0.0	0	0	0	0	0
Johnny Podgajny	P	44	.183	.217	60	11	0	1	0	0.0	5	5	0	15	0
Lloyd Waner	OF	101	.261	.307	287	75	7	3	0	0.0	23	10	16	6	1
Bennie Warren	C	90	.209	.356	225	47	6	3	7	32.1	19	20	24	36	0
TEAM TOTALS			.232	.306	5,060	1,174	168	37	44	115.0	394	356	392	487	37

Data courtesy of Baseball-Almanac.com.

1942 Philadelphia Phillies Statmaster: Pitching

NAME	GAMES	W	L	W%	ERA	GS	CG	IP	HA	BB	SO	SHU
Boom-Boom Beck	26	0	1	.000	4.75	1	0	53.0	69	17	10	0
Cy Blanton	6	0	4	.000	5.64	3	0	22.1	30	13	15	0
Hilly Flitcraft	3	0	0	.000	8.10	0	0	3.1	6	2	1	0
George Hennessey	5	1	1	.500	2.65	1	0	17.0	11	10	2	0
Lefty Hoerst	33	4	16	.200	5.20	22	5	150.2	162	78	52	0
Tommy Hughes	40	12	18	.400	3.06	31	19	253.0	224	99	77	0
Si Johnson	39	8	19	.296	3.69	26	10	195.1	198	72	78	1
Gene Lambert	1	0	0	.000	9.00	0	0	1.0	3	0	1	0
Andy Lapihuska	3	0	2	.000	5.23	2	0	20.2	17	13	8	0
Paul Masterson	4	0	0	.000	6.48	0	0	8.1	10	5	3	0
Rube Melton	42	9	20	.310	3.70	29	10	209.1	180	114	107	1
Sam Nahem	35	1	3	.250	4.94	2	0	74.2	72	40	38	0
Earl Naylor	20	0	5	.000	6.12	4	1	60.1	68	29	19	0
Ike Pearson	35	1	6	.143	4.54	7	0	85.1	87	50	21	0
Johnny Podgajny	43	6	14	.300	3.91	23	6	186.2	191	63	40	0
TEAM TOTALS		42	109	.278	4.12	151	51	1341	1,328	605	472	2

Data courtesy of Baseball-Almanac.com.

A Major League Record: 23 Straight Losses
The 1961 Philadelphia Phillies (47–107)

> In 1961, the Phillies lost 23 games in a row. But you didn't
> hear Phillies fans complain, not exactly. Complaining was
> for other towns. No, Philadelphians were like their fighter,
> Joe Frazier.
>
> —*McClatchy Tribune News*

Like 1941, 1961 was a watershed year for major league baseball. The American League expanded for the first time, as the Washington Senators relocated to Minnesota, and a new Senators franchise launched. The Los Angeles Angels also made their debut that year. The National League followed suit and added new teams in New York and Houston the next year. Thus, 1961 marked the last time that the National League featured only its original eight teams.

1961 was also a watershed year on the field. Roger Maris and Mickey Mantle of the New York Yankees played out their epic duel to see which one of them could eclipse Babe Ruth's 1927 record of 60 home runs in a single season. Mantle hit 56 but had his season shortened by an abscess on his leg that landed him in the hospital. Maris broke the record by hitting his 61st homer on the final day of the season, but the feat was downplayed when an asterisk was placed by his name in the record books because he had not broken Ruth's record in 154 games. Norm Cash of the Detroit Tigers, a strapping first baseman with a big stick, led the American League with a .361 average. The Yankees won 109 games and won the pennant over a good Tiger team that also won more than 100 games.

In the National League, future Hall of Fame right fielder Roberto Clemente of the Pittsburgh Pirates won the batting title at .351. Orlando Cepeda of the San Francisco Giants clouted 46 homers and drove in 142 runs. Warren Spahn, the superb left-handed ace of the Milwaukee Braves, posted 25 wins, 21 complete games, and led the league with a 3.02 ERA. Another future Hall of Fame southpaw, Sandy Koufax of the Los Angeles Dodgers, notched 269 strikeouts, and Roy Face of the Pirates and Stu Miller of the Giants both had 17 saves to pace the league. The Cincinnati Reds won the pennant, losing to the Yankees in the Fall Classic.

The Philadelphia Phillies, perennial doormats of the National League, had what might have been the worst of many truly awful seasons in 1961.

Phillies manager Gene Mauch
(Library of Congress)

The Phils went 47–107, finishing 46 games out of first place and 17 games behind the seventh-place Cubs. They also found eternal infamy by reeling off 23 straight losses in July and August, setting a record for futility that may never fall. In a history marked by a lot of really bad teams, the 1961 edition of the Phightin' Phils just might have been the worst of the lot.

Eleven years earlier, the Phils broke a 35-year drought and won the National League pennant. The New York Yankees shattered their dreams, sweeping the Whiz Kids, as the young Phillies were known, in the World Series

From 1951 through 1957, the Phillies were competitive, but never again made a serious run at the flag, featuring future Hall of Famers Richie Ashburn in center field and Robin Roberts on the mound. However, by 1959, the Whiz Kids had been dispersed, and none of them continued to wear the pinstripes. The Phillies were back in the cellar. A new general manager, John Quinn, came on board in 1959 with the task of rebuilding the team. He faced a difficult task.

For many years, the Phillies shared Shibe Park with the American League Athletics. The A's were mired in their own seemingly endless streak of frustrating years of losing. Team owner Connie Mack had built and then dismantled two dynasties, but was unable to capture lightning in a jar a third time. The A's had not been competitive since the 1930s, and the popularity of the Phillies drove them out of Philadelphia and on to Kansas City after the 1954 season. For the first time in the history of the franchise, the Phillies had the City of Brotherly Love to themselves. Quinn faced the task of filling Shibe Park and keeping it filled.

Eddie Sawyer, who managed the 1950 team to the World Series, was still the helm. However, after losing the 1960 opener, Sawyer suddenly and unexpectedly quit. "I'm 49 years old," he declared, "and I want to live to be 50." Quinn replaced Sawyer with Gene Mauch, a scrappy 34-year-old former infielder from the Dodger system. Mauch didn't have much talent, but he had a lot of moxie and he was smart. The Little General, as Mauch was known, was hired from Minneapolis of the American Association, where he was generally considered to be the brightest young manager in the minor leagues. His "small ball" style of play emphasized good defense, speed and stolen bases, and base-to-base tactics on offense rather than power hitting. His style drew praise for its focus on fundamentals of game play as well as criticism for its low scoring. The 1960 edition of the Phillies finished 59–95, just a game behind the Cubs for seventh place. Things seemed to be moving in the right direction.

The team, in the midst of a rebuilding program that came within a whisker of bringing the 1964 pennant to Philadelphia, had some talented young players and some not very talented ones. In 1959, Quinn had traded for a highly regarded young outfielder with movie star good looks named Johnny Callison, who was the nucleus of the Phillies offense. Callison hit .266 with 9 homers and 47 RBIs. Three years later, he hit 31 homers and drove in 104. The young outfielder's star was rising.

Outfielder Don Demeter hit 20 homers and drove in 68 runs, while speedy Cuban-born center fielder Tony Gonzalez hit a solid .277 with 12 homers and 15 stolen bases, all the while playing solid defense. Slick fielding short-stop Ruben Amaro hit a respectable .257 while playing spectacular defense. Catcher Clay Dalrymple brought solid defense and consistency behind the plate, hitting only .220. Bobby Malkmus and Tony Taylor, who enjoyed a long and productive career with the Phillies, hit .231 and .250 respectively. Third baseman Charley Smith hit .248 with nine homers and played solid defense. Mid-season acquisition, outfielder Wes Covington, had a lot of trouble with left-handed pitching, but he hit righties hard. Covington hit .303 with 7 homers and 26 RBIs in only 57 games with the Phils.

The young Phillies hit .243 as a team, with 103 home runs and 56 stolen bases. Their pitching showed similar trends. Future Hall of Famer Roberts, the sole remaining member of the 1950 World Series team, was now 35 and on the down slope of a great career, prompting Mauch to describe the once-great hurler as "throwing like Dolley Madison." He posted a 1–10 record with an awful 5.85 ERA and was sold to the Yankees on October 16. Art Mahaffey, a promising 23-year-old righty who won 19 games in 1962, notched an 11–19 record with a 4.10 ERA in his first full season in the major leagues. He set a team record with 17 strikeouts against the Chicago Cubs on April 23.

Twenty-six-year-old right-hander John Buzhardt went 6–18 with a 4.49 ERA, and Frank Sullivan, acquired in a mid-season trade with the Red Sox, went 3–16 with a 4.29 ERA. "I am in the twilight of a mediocre career," declared the 31-year-old Sullivan that summer, demonstrating remarkable self-awareness. A number of other pitchers also contributed to that long season, including a talented 23-year-old southpaw named Chris Short, from nearby Medford, Delaware, who became a mainstay of the Phillies' pitching staff for the entire decade of the 1960s, winning 20 games in 1966. In 1961, Short went 6–12, with an ugly 5.94 ERA. He was still learning to pitch, and had the misfortune of having to do so on a bad team.

Jack Baldschun anchored the bull pen. Baldschun, a hard-throwing 23-year-old right-hander from Ohio, led the National League with 65 appearances in 1961. He notched a 5–3 record with three saves and a respectable 3.88 ERA. He had several more good seasons for the Phillies before blowing out his arm.

Along the way, the Phillies set a record for futility by losing 23 consecutive games. "That 23-game losing streak wasn't too nice to go through," said pitcher Chris Short. "I lost the 23rd game, but John Buzhardt won the second game, 7–4. Sometimes you have to go through things like that, but it molded us into a better ball club."

In May, they reeled off 10 straight losses, giving a preview of wretchedness yet to come. On July 28, they won the second game of a doubleheader in San Francisco by a score of 4–3. John Buzhardt was the winning pitcher. They did not win again until August 20, when Buzhardt went the distance to beat the Braves in the second game of a doubleheader, 7–4. Remarkably, they won four games in a row before reverting to their losing ways.

The record-shattering losing streak went like this:

1961 Philadelphia Phillies Losing Streak

GAME	DATE	OPPONENT	SCORE	DECISION	RECORD
96	07–29–1961	vs San Francisco Giants	3–4	L	30–65–1
97	07–30–1961	vs San Francisco Giants	2–5	L	30–66–1
98-I	08–02–1961	at Cincinnati Reds	2–4	L	30–67–1
99-II	08–02–1961	at Cincinnati Reds	2–3	L	30–68–1
100	08–03–1961	at Cincinnati Reds	1–7	L	30–69–1
101	08–04–1961	at St. Louis Cardinals	8–9	L	30–70–1
102	08–05–1961	at St. Louis Cardinals	0–7	L	30–71–1
103-I	08–06–1961	at St. Louis Cardinals	1–3	L	30–72–1
104-II	08–06–1961	at St. Louis Cardinals	2–3	L	30–73–1

GAME	DATE	OPPONENT	SCORE	DECISION	RECORD
105	08–07–1961	vs Pittsburgh Pirates	1–3	L	30–74–1
106-I	08–08–1961	vs Pittsburgh Pirates	2–10	L	30–75–1
107-II	08–08–1961	vs Pittsburgh Pirates	2–3	L	30–76–1
108	08–09–1961	vs Cincinnati Reds	0–5	L	30–77–1
109	08–11–1961	at Pittsburgh Pirates	0–6	L	30–78–1
110	08–12–1961	at Pittsburgh Pirates	0–4	L	30–79–1
111	08–13–1961	at Pittsburgh Pirates	4–13	L	30–80–1
112	08–14–1961	at Chicago Cubs	2–9	L	30–81–1
113	08–15–1961	at Chicago Cubs	5–6	L	30–82–1
114	08–16–1961	at Chicago Cubs	5–9	L	30–83–1
115	08–17–1961	at Milwaukee Braves	6–7	L	30–84–1
116	08–18–1961	at Milwaukee Braves	1–4	L	30–85–1
117	08–19–1961	at Milwaukee Braves	3–4	L	30–86–1
118-I	08–20–1961	at Milwaukee Braves	2–5	L	30–87–1

Data courtesy of Baseball-Almanac.com.

The Phillies lost close games and they got blown out during the streak. They lost at home and on the road. They lost to six of the seven other teams in the National League during their run, missing only the Los Angeles Dodgers along the way. The record for futility set by the 1961 Phillies still stands as the gold standard for losing in the major leagues to this day.

However, Mauch was laying the groundwork for things to come. The 1962 edition of the Phillies finished a game over .500 and came out of the cellar to finish in seventh place. By 1964, the talented young team had a 6-game lead with 12 left to play and looked like a shoo-in to win the National League pennant. However, Mauch was forced to use Short and future Hall of Famer Jim Bunning, acquired from the Tigers after the 1963 season, every other day when Mahaffey's arm went dead and Mauch lost confidence in his other pitchers. Wearing out his two aces at the height of the pennant race, the Phillies lost 10 in a row before winning their last two games and finished third with a record of 92–70. However, the turnaround from their woes of 1961 was both complete and remarkable. The Little General helmed the Phillies for eight years, from 1960 through the 1968 season, when he was fired.

Gene Mauch managed in the major leagues for nearly 4,000 games, ranking fourth in total games managed. He won 1,902 games, ranked eighth among all managers, but never won a pennant. He was, by far, the winningest major league manager to never experience the World Series, although he came close several times, he never came closer than he did with the Phillies in 1964.

Better days lay ahead for the Phillies, but it was difficult to see that in the fog of the record-shattering losing streak of 1961.

1961 Philadelphia Phillies Statmaster: Fielding

NAME	POS	GAMES	PO	A	E	DP	TC/G	FLD%	GS
Ruben Amaro	SS	132	243	379	19	91	4.9	.970	-
Ruben Amaro	1B	3	11	0	0	1	3.7	1.000	-
Ruben Amaro	2B	1	0	1	0	0	1.0	1.000	-
Jack Baldschun	P	65	9	18	0	0	0.4	1.000	0
Paul Brown	P	5	0	2	0	0	0.4	1.000	1
John Buzhardt	P	41	20	34	3	4	1.4	.947	27
Johnny Callison	OF	124	227	10	8	2	2.0	.967	-
Jimmie Coker	C	11	59	1	1	0	5.5	.984	-
Choo Choo Coleman	C	14	38	4	1	1	3.1	.977	-
Wes Covington	OF	45	53	4	3	1	1.3	.950	-
Tony Curry	LF	8	8	2	2	0	1.5	.833	-
Clay Dalrymple	C	122	551	86	14	10	5.3	.978	-
Bobby Del Greco	OF	32	80	1	0	0	2.5	1.000	-
Bobby Del Greco	3B	1	0	0	0	0	0.0	.000	-
Bobby Del Greco	2B	1	0	0	0	0	0.0	.000	-
Don Demeter	OF	79	173	9	1	3	2.3	.995	-
Don Demeter	1B	22	148	15	2	22	7.5	.988	-
Turk Farrell	P	5	0	0	0	0	0.0	.000	0
Don Ferrarese	P	42	8	12	1	1	0.5	.952	14
Don Ferrarese	CF	1	0	0	0	0	0.0	.000	-
Tony Gonzalez	OF	118	246	7	4	4	2.2	.984	-
Dallas Green	P	42	14	22	1	2	0.9	.973	10
Pancho Herrera	1B	115	1,003	96	8	104	9.6	.993	-
Darrell Johnson	C	21	99	13	2	2	5.4	.982	-
Al Kenders	C	10	27	3	0	1	3.0	1.000	-
Joe Koppe	SS	5	2	2	1	1	1.0	.800	-
Ken Lehman	P	41	6	16	0	1	0.5	1.000	2
Art Mahaffey	P	36	14	28	3	2	1.3	.933	32
Bobby Malkmus	2B	58	146	180	4	52	5.7	.988	-
Bobby Malkmus	SS	34	48	81	7	12	4.0	.949	-

1961 Philadelphia Phillies Statmaster: Fielding (cont.)

NAME	POS	GAMES	PO	A	E	DP	TC/G	FLD%	GS
Bobby Malkmus	3B	25	16	38	1	3	2.2	.982	-
Jack Meyer	P	1	0	0	0	0	0.0	.000	0
Cal Neeman	C	19	63	5	1	0	3.6	.986	-
Jim Owens	P	20	4	13	2	3	1.0	.895	17
Jim Owens	RF	1	0	0	0	0	0.0	.000	-
Robin Roberts	P	26	6	15	0	1	0.8	1.000	18
Bob Sadowski	3B	14	10	23	1	3	2.4	.971	-
Chris Short	P	39	6	20	1	1	0.7	.963	16
Chris Short	C	1	0	0	0	0	0.0	.000	-
Bobby Gene Smith	OF	47	91	8	3	1	2.2	.971	-
Charley Smith	3B	94	75	194	22	19	3.1	.924	-
Charley Smith	SS	14	25	28	5	8	4.1	.914	-
Frank Sullivan	P	49	10	34	2	0	0.9	.957	18
Tony Taylor	2B	91	231	270	10	74	5.6	.980	-
Tony Taylor	3B	3	2	9	0	0	3.7	1.000	-
Elmer Valo	RF	1	0	0	0	0	0.0	.000	-
Lee Walls	1B	28	202	19	3	29	8.0	.987	-
Lee Walls	3B	26	22	39	5	3	2.5	.924	-
Lee Walls	OF	17	23	1	0	1	1.4	1.000	-
Ken Walters	OF	56	73	4	2	0	1.4	.975	-
Ken Walters	1B	5	23	3	0	3	5.2	1.000	-
Ken Walters	3B	1	0	0	0	0	0.0	.000	-
George Williams	2B	15	23	36	2	9	4.1	.967	-
Jim Woods	3B	15	12	18	1	3	2.1	.968	-
TEAM TOTALS			4,150	1,803	146	478	3.3	.976	155

Data courtesy of Baseball-Almanac.com.

1961 Philadelphia Phillies Statmaster: Hitting

NAME	POS	GAMES	AVG	SLG	AB	H	2B	3B	HR	AB/HR	R	RBI	BB	SO	SB
Ruben Amaro	SS	135	.257	.349	381	98	14	9	1	381.0	34	32	53	59	1
Jack Baldschun	P	65	.000	.000	11	0	0	0	0	0.0	0	0	1	7	0
Paul Brown	P	5	.500	.500	2	1	0	0	0	0.0	0	0	0	0	0
John Buzhardt	P	41	.105	.140	57	6	2	0	0	0.0	2	1	3	29	0
Johnny Callison	OF	138	.266	.418	455	121	20	11	9	50.6	74	47	69	76	10
Jimmie Coker	C	11	.400	.560	25	10	1	0	1	25.0	3	4	7	4	1
Choo Choo Coleman	C	34	.128	.149	47	6	1	0	0	0.0	3	4	2	8	0
Wes Covington	OF	57	.303	.485	165	50	9	0	7	23.6	23	26	15	17	0
Tony Curry	OF	15	.194	.250	36	7	2	0	0	0.0	3	3	1	8	0
Clay Dalrymple	C	129	.220	.294	378	33	11	1	5	75.6	23	42	30	30	0
Bobby Del Greco	OF	41	.259	.357	112	29	5	0	2	56.0	14	11	12	17	0
Don Demeter	OF	106	.257	.432	382	98	18	4	20	19.1	54	68	19	74	2
Turk Farrell	P	5	.500	.500	2	1	0	0	0	0.0	1	0	0	1	0
Don Ferrarese	P	43	.171	.171	35	6	0	0	0	0.0	1	1	1	4	0
Tony Gonzalez	OF	126	.277	.437	426	118	16	8	12	35.5	58	58	49	66	15
Dallas Green	P	42	.152	.152	33	5	0	0	0	0.0	4	3	5	13	0
Pancho Herrera	1B	126	.258	.408	400	103	17	2	13	30.8	56	51	55	120	5
Darrell Johnson	C	21	.230	.246	61	14	1	0	0	0.0	4	3	3	8	0
Al Kenders	C	10	.174	.217	23	4	1	0	0	0.0	0	1	1	0	0
Joe Koppe	SS	6	.000	.000	3	0	0	0	0	0.0	1	0	0	0	0
Ken Lehman	P	42	.000	.000	6	0	0	0	0	0.0	1	0	0	1	0
Art Mahaffey	P	36	.127	.159	63	8	2	0	0	0.0	3	3	3	20	0

1961 Philadelphia Phillies Statmaster: Hitting (cont.)

NAME	POS	GAMES	AVG	SLG	AB	H	2B	3B	HR	AB/HR	R	RBI	BB	SO	SB
Bobby Malkmus	2B	121	.231	.327	342	79	8	2	7	48.9	39	31	20	43	1
Jack Meyer	P	1	.000	.000	0	0	0	0	0	0.0	0	0	0	0	0
Cal Neeman	C	19	.226	.258	31	7	1	0	0	0.0	0	2	4	8	1
Jim Owens	P	21	.074	.074	27	2	0	0	0	0.0	0	1	4	12	0
Robin Roberts	P	26	.091	.091	33	3	0	0	0	0.0	1	0	1	11	0
Bob Sadowski	3B	16	.130	.130	54	7	0	0	0	0.0	4	0	4	7	1
Chris Short	P	40	.162	.162	37	6	0	0	0	0.0	1	2	1	10	1
Bobby Gene Smith	OF	79	.253	.328	174	44	7	0	2	87.0	16	18	15	32	0
Charley Smith	3B	112	.248	.365	411	102	13	4	9	45.7	43	47	23	76	3
Frank Sullivan	P	49	.152	.152	33	5	0	0	0	0.0	2	2	5	10	0
Tony Taylor	2B	106	.250	.323	400	100	17	3	2	200.0	47	26	29	59	11
Elmer Valo	OF	50	.186	.302	43	8	2	0	1	43.0	4	8	8	6	0
Lee Walls	1B	91	.280	.425	261	73	6	4	8	32.6	32	30	19	48	2
Ken Walters	OF	86	.228	.328	180	41	8	2	2	90.0	23	14	5	25	2
George Williams	2B	17	.250	.250	36	9	0	0	0	0.0	4	1	4	4	0
Jim Woods	3B	23	.229	.417	48	11	3	0	2	24.0	6	9	4	15	0
TEAM TOTALS			.243	.357	5,213	1,265	185	50	103	50.6	584	549	475	928	56

Data courtesy of Baseball-Almanac.com.

1961 Philadelphia Phillies Statmaster: Pitcher

NAME	GAMES	W	L	W%	ERA	GS	CG	IP	HA	BB	SO	SHU
Jack Baldschun	65	5	3	.625	3.88	0	0	99.2	90	49	59	0
Paul Brown	5	0	1	.000	8.10	1	0	10.0	13	8	1	0
John Buzhardt	41	6	13	.250	4.49	27	6	202.1	200	65	92	1
Turk Farrell	5	2	1	.667	6.52	0	0	9.2	10	6	10	0
Don Ferrarese	42	5	12	.294	3.76	14	3	138.2	120	68	89	1
Dallas Green	42	2	4	.333	4.85	10	1	128.0	160	47	51	1
Ken Lehman	41	1	1	.500	4.26	2	0	63.1	61	25	27	0
Art Mahaffey	36	11	19	.367	4.10	32	12	219.1	205	70	158	3
Jack Meyer	1	0	0	.000	9.00	0	0	2.0	2	2	2	0
Jim Owens	20	5	10	.333	4.47	17	3	106.2	119	32	38	0
Robin Roberts	26	1	10	.091	5.85	18	2	117.0	154	23	54	0
Chris Short	39	6	12	.333	5.94	16	1	127.1	157	71	80	0
Frank Sullivan	49	3	16	.158	4.29	18	1	159.1	161	55	114	1
TEAM TOTALS		47	107	.305	4.61	155	29	1383.1	1,452	521	775	7

Data courtesy of Baseball-Almanac.com.

#9 | Tie: '50-'51-'52-'53-'54 Buccos

At Least They Were Consistent
The 1950–1954 Pittsburgh Pirates

> They finished last—on merit.
>
> —*Branch Rickey on the '52 Pirates,*
> *quoted from his AP obituary, December 1965*

Although they are one of the more consistently disappointing teams in to-day's major leagues, the Pittsburgh Pirates remain one of baseball's most storied franchises. With a Hall of Fame lineup that boasts such epic names as Honus Wagner, Pie Traynor, Hank Greenberg, Roberto Clemente, and Willie Stargell, it is hard to believe that they have become one of the least successful franchises in the modern game. At the end of the 2008 season, the team finished 27 out of 30 with a 67–95 record, which was not much of an improvement over their last place finish during the 2007 campaign. To date, the Pirates have not had a winning record since 1992.

Times have certainly changed, as the turn-of-the-twentieth-century Pirates were a National League juggernaut and dominated much of the early 1900s. Always a blue-collar team in a blue-collar town, Pittsburgh Pirates' Honus Wagner summed up the team's simple approach to success when he said, "There ain't much to being a ballplayer, if you're a ballplayer." The Pirates opened the century by winning three straight pennants (1901–1903). The 1902 team won 103 games and finished a mind-boggling 27 games ahead of second-place Brooklyn. Over these three seasons, Wagner hit an amazing .353, .330 and .355. It was an unforgettable period in Pittsburgh's sports legacy.

One era of baseball in the Steel City that many would rather forget is the 1950s "Buccos," more specifically, the 1950–1954 teams. Unfortunately, the immediate post–World War II years brought plenty of hope and heart-ache to the franchise. Despite acquiring a real superstar in Ralph Kiner, who led the National League in homers for seven seasons, the Pirates sank into quicksand. In 1952, they compiled one of the worst records in major league history, winning 42 games and losing 112 (.273) and finishing 54½ games out of first place. The 1950s stretch was nearly a half decade of disaster and represents one of the worst back-to-back-to-back-to-back performances in MLB history.

The Blame Game
The 1950 Pittsburgh Pirates (57–96)

Ralph Kiner, Elmer Riddle, Bing Crosby, and Wally Westlake (Carnegie Library of Pittsburgh)

The 1950 Pittsburgh Pirates played 153 games during the regular season, won 57, lost 96, and finished in eighth position. They played their home games at historic Forbes Field, where bleachers full of frustrated fans watched them end the season with a .373 winning percentage. The contradictory statistics they accumulated over the course of the season make this particular team interesting. The 1950 Pirates nearly led the league in some categories, while bringing up the rear in others. On paper, the Pirates of the "Nifty-Fifties" routinely defeated themselves.

For instance, the 1950 Bucs featured the stellar slugging of Ralph Kiner, who hit a whopping 47 round-trippers, but they also carried one of the worst pitching ensembles ever to step on a diamond. Ranked dead last in the entire National League, the Pirates' pitchers posted a miserable 4.33 ERA and not a single hurler who won more than one game finished the 1950 season with a winning record. Contrasting the ineptitude of the pitching staff, the Pirate fielders boasted a tremendous fielding percentage of .977, which was third best in the National League. In other words, they had no one to blame but themselves. And yet, this bottom-of-the-barrel staff had some hard-throwing big-name veterans:

- Cliff Chambers: 12–15, 4.30 ERA in 27 games
- Murry Dickson: 10–15, 3.80 ERA in 51 games
- Hank Borowy: 1–3, 6.39 ERA in 11 games
- Vern Law: 7–9, 4.92 ERA in 27 games
- Frank Barrett: 1–2, 4.15 ERA in 5 games
- Bill Macdonald: 8–10, 4.29 ERA in 32 games
- Vic Lombardi: 0–5, 6.60 ERA in 39 games
- Hal Gregg: 0–1, 13.50 ERA in 5 games
- Bob Chesnes: 3–3, 5.54 ERA in 9 games
- Harry Gumpert: 0–0, 5.40 ERA in 1 games
- Bill Werle: 8–16, 4.60 ERA in 48 games
- Forest "Woody" Main: 1–0, 4.87 ERA in 12 games
- Mel Queen: 5–14, 5.98 ERA in 12 games
- Windy McCall: 0–0, 9.45 ERA in 2 games
- Bill Pierro: 0–2, 10.55 ERA in 12 games
- Jim "Junior" Walsh: 1–1, 5.05 ERA in 38 games
- Frank Papish: 0–0, 27.00 ERA in 4 games
- Jack Phillips: 0–0, 7.20 ERA in 1 games
- Source: baseballhistorian.com

1950 Pirates Standings

NATIONAL LEAGUE	W	L	GB	PCT.
Philadelphia Phillies	91	63	-	.591
Brooklyn Dodgers	89	65	2	.578
New York Giants	86	68	5	.558
Boston Braves	83	71	8	.539
St. Louis Cardinals	78	75	12.5	.510
Cincinnati Reds	66	87	24.5	.431
Chicago Cubs	64	89	26.5	.418
Pittsburgh Pirates	57	96	33.5	.373

Data courtesy of Baseball-Almanac.com.

Art Imitates Life
The 1951 Pittsburgh Pirates (64–90)

Left Fielder and Future Broadcaster Ralph Kiner (Carnegie Library of Pittsburgh)

The 1951 Pirates franchise "slightly" improved from eighth place to seventh, scoring 689 runs, allowing 845 and raising the bar to a measly .416 winning percentage. Once again Kiner contributed at the plate, while the rest of the franchise struggled to keep afloat. Adding insult to injury was the fact that the team's perennial bottom dwelling inspired a Hollywood movie script.

Originally released in 1951, *Angels in the Outfield* told the story of a gritty but likeable manager with the ridiculous name of Guffy McGovern, who helms a last-place Pittsburgh team. Riding what appeared to be a never-ending losing streak, McGovern began hearing voices promising to help if he cleaned up his act. After a series of miraculous events transpired on the field, the team pulled itself out of the basement. However, a young orphan girl spilled the beans when she innocently told a reporter that she had witnessed angels helping out the Pirates, thus giving away McGovern's secret of success.

This unique black-and-white MGM film starred Paul Douglas and Janet Leigh and was directed by Clarence Brown. It was partially shot on location in Pittsburgh and contained extensive baseball action shots, most of which were filmed at Forbes Field. The filmmaker used footage of Kiner knocking balls out of the park for some scenes depicting home runs.

Unlike the modernized version that was released in 1994, the audience never saw the angels themselves, because a series of primitive prop-effects represented the heavenly beings' presence on screen. The dialogue in the film was also considerably different, as profanity was certainly not acceptable in 1950 films. The cuss words "spewed" by McGovern were dubbed with audio gibberish of scrambled recordings of his own voice.

Fortunately, the movie was released in October after the Pirates tanked another season, as the fan's reactions might have echoed the film's foul-mouthed skipper.

1951 Pirates Standings

NATIONAL LEAGUE	W	L	GB	PCT.
New York Giants	98	59	–	.624
Brooklyn Dodgers	97	60	1	.618
St. Louis Cardinals	81	73	15.5	.526
Boston Braves	76	78	20.5	.494
Philadelphia Phillies	73	81	23.5	.474
Cincinnati Reds	68	86	28.5	.442
Pittsburgh Pirates	64	90	32.5	.416
Chicago Cubs	62	92	34.5	.403

Data courtesy of Baseball-Almanac.com.

How Low Can You Go?
The 1952 Pittsburgh Pirates (42–112)

Pittsburgh's 1952 baseball club not only lowered the bar for performance, it dropped it on the ground, yelled, and then kicked dirt on it.

Despite low expectations in the local press, the 1952 team entered the season under the guise of promise. One of baseball's most celebrated figures, Branch Rickey, led it. The 70-year old general manager had already secured his place in history after single-handedly breaking major league baseball's color barrier by signing the first African-American ballplayer, Jackie Robinson. He later drafted the first Hispanic superstar, Roberto Clemente. Bill Meyer remained as manager, and both men struggled to field a team worthy of their investments.

Tensions in the front office remained high after the two-year contract of the team's star slugger, Ralph Kiner, expired before the 1952 season.[1] Kiner was the premier power hitter in baseball, but Rickey would not commit to resigning him, causing frustrations for both player and management. After a series of stalled negotiations, Kiner received permission to negotiate directly with the Pirates' owner. Surprisingly, John W. Galbreath agreed to a one-year, $90,000 contract, making Kiner the highest-paid player in the entire National League.

The wealthy outfielder remained at the top of his game and he extended his string of seasons leading the league in home runs to six in 1952. Unfortunately, his days in a Pirates uniform were still numbered. The slugger, who was selected to participate in the All-Star Game in six straight seasons (1948 to 1953) and whose career home run ratio is second only to Babe Ruth, ultimately was elected to the National Baseball Hall of Fame. Although the Pirates remained in the cellar for most of his tenure, Kiner still remains recognized as one of the game's greatest stars.

Even spring training was a disaster for the 1952 Buccos. According to the team's records, Gus Bell missed training time due to family-related car problems and illness and was sent back down to the minor leagues. Pitcher Bill Werle was suspended indefinitely and fined $500. (He was traded to the St. Louis Cardinals two weeks later.). Thirteen rookies, including four teenagers, made the Pirates' Opening Day roster.

Pittsburgh posted a surprising and respectable 2–2 record in the first four regular season games. Unfortunately, they then reeled off 16 losses in their next 17 outings and never again approached the .500 mark. The top three aces in the Pirate's bullpen won only one of their first nine games. Even Kiner's batting average plummeted from lack of support and sat at a mediocre .220 one month into the season. By mid-May, the club's ERA topped 5.0, and the team's 5–28 record for the month triggered immediate panic both in the stands and on the field.

Gus Bell was called up from the minors, but he was unable to ignite a spark in the Pirates' fledgling lineup. Kiner hit .241 with 13 home runs and

1952 Pittsburgh Pirates (Baseball Hall of Fame Library, Cooperstown, NY)

31 RBIs, but the Bucs still hit the midway point in the season with a 21–59 mark. Several of the Pirates' more reliable bats experienced epic slumps, including Jack Merson (0-for-35), Clyde McCullough (0-for-24), and Tony Bartiromo (0-for-29).

The second half of the season picked right up where the first half left off, as Pittsburgh went 2–11 in July. The team was mathematically eliminated from postseason competition with six weeks still left to play. By now, it appeared that everything the Pirates touched turned to dust. In August, the team called up a 20-year-old minor-league phenom named Ron Necciai, who had tossed a legendary 27-strikeout game. He surrendered five runs in his first inning in the major leagues. No one escaped the curse.

As the '52 season came to a close, Pittsburgh's record was a horrible 42–112. The Pirates' 23–54 performance (0.299 winning percentage) at home and 19–58–1 (0.247 winning percentage) away were the franchise's worst since the 1890 season, as well as the worst of any franchise since the 1935 Boston Braves. To date, the only nonexpansion team to finish lower was the 2003 Detroit Tigers.

Years later, Joe Garagiola shamelessly joked about the team Bucco fans would rather forget. In Joe Garagiola's *It's Anybody's Ball Game,* he said,

> My first baseman was George "Catfish" Metkovich from our 1952 Pittsburgh Pirates team, which lost 112 games. After a terrible series against the New York Giants, in which our center fielder made three throwing errors and let two balls get through his legs, manager Billy Meyer pleaded, "Can somebody think of something to help us win a game?" "I'd like to make a suggestion," Metkovich said. "On any ball hit to center field, let's just let it roll to see if it might go foul."

1952 Pirates Standings

NATIONAL LEAGUE	W	L	GB	PCT.
Brooklyn Dodgers	96	57	–	.627
New York Giants	92	62	4.5	.597
St. Louis Cardinals	88	66	8.5	.571
Philadelphia Phillies	87	67	9.5	.565
Chicago Cubs	77	77	19.5	.500
Cincinnati Reds	69	85	27.5	.448
Boston Braves	64	89	32	.418
Pittsburgh Pirates	42	112	54.5	.273

Data courtesy of Baseball-Almanac.com.

Rock Bottom
The 1953 Pittsburgh Pirates (50–104)

1953 Pittsburgh Pirates (Baseball Hall of Fame Library, Cooperstown, NY)

The 1953 Pirates had absolutely nowhere to go but up. After experiencing a record-setting train wreck that forever solidified their place in the annals of baseball's worst, Pittsburgh looked to the future.

However, that future would not include most of their key players, including several who were traded mid-season. In June Ralph Kiner, Joe Garagiola, Catfish Metkovich, and Howie Pollet were all traded to the Chicago Cubs. Gus Bell had already been shipped to the Cincinnati Reds prior to the season and Pete Castiglione was traded to the St. Louis Cardinals. It seemed that the management staff was eager to forget the last few years and start over. Unfortunately, things would not improve enough to move the team out of last place, as they limped in with a 50–104 record, only marginally better than the wretched 1952 team.

Despite their collective failure, one player on Pittsburgh's 1953 roster is worth mentioning: all-star pitcher Murry Dickson went from hero to zero in a Pirate uniform. Respected around the league for his inventive deliveries, Dickson was a former pennant-winning hurler who led the National League in defeats for three successive seasons (1952–1954).

Unfortunately, Dickson's tenure in Pittsburgh was filled with disappointment. In 1951, he won 20 games while losing 16 for the seventh-place

Pirates, which won only 64 contests for the entire season. He pitched 19 complete games that season, and followed with 21 more in 1952, when he won 14 and lost 21 for a last-place team that won only 42 games all year. (In retrospect, Dickson accounted for 31 percent of Pirate victories in 1951, and fully one-third of the team's wins in 1952.) He then dropped 19 decisions in 1953 and was traded to the Philadelphia Phillies.

1953 Pirates Standings

NATIONAL LEAGUE	W	L	GB	PCT.
Brooklyn Dodgers	105	49	–	.682
Milwaukee Braves	92	62	13	.597
Philadelphia Phillies	83	71	22	.539
St. Louis Cardinals	83	71	22	.439
New York Giants	70	84	35	.455
Cincinnati Reds	68	86	37	.442
Chicago Cubs	65	89	40	.422
Pittsburgh Pirates	50	104	55	.325

Data courtesy of Baseball-Almanac.com.

End of an Era
The 1954 Pittsburgh Pirates (53–101)

Perhaps the only positive highlight of Pittsburgh's 1954 season was the acquisition of second baseman Curt Roberts, the first black player to sign with the Pirates. Pittsburgh obtained Roberts from Denver of the Western League as part of a minor league working agreement before the 1954 season. It would be the only barrier broken that year. The prognosis for 1954 looked grim in Pittsburgh again, and the few fans who had remained had little hope in their team's ability to get out of the gutter.

A preseason article in the 1954 *Street and Smith's Yearbook* perfectly summed up the excruciating frustration that overshadowed the Pirates of this period:

> There's nothing but trouble ahead for the Pirates in '54. Last year, they peddled the longtime Forbes Field favorite, Ralph Kiner. Pressed for cash after a $325,000 deficit in 1953, the Pirates sent another star, Danny O'Connell, to the Milwaukee Braves for six players and financial balm estimated as high as $100,000. Though owned by wealthy people, including John Galbreath and Bing Crosby, the Pirates aren't throwing money around.

1954 Pittsburgh Pirates (Baseball Hall of Fame Library, Cooperstown, NY)

For O'Connell, Branch Rickey obtained three veterans and three rookies. The established players were pitcher Max Surkont, outfielder Sid Gordon, ticketed for third base, and Sam Jethroe, an outfielder Rickey originally sold to the Braves. The freshmen pitchers are Larry Lassalle, a southpaw who won 19 and lost 5 for Jacksonville; Fred Waters, 10–10 lefty at Lincoln, Neb.; and Curtis Raydon, also from Jacksonville. Rickey called it a long range deal. Fred Haney, his manager, wasn't quoted.

Another estimated $80,000 came rolling in when the tailenders dispatched 37-year-old Pitcher Murry Dickson to the Phillies, who also gave up an infielder and a pitcher in the transaction. With O'Connell and Dickson gone, the only remaining Pirate standout, unless 1954 proves otherwise, is Frank Thomas, powerful right-handed hitting outfielder who may be the club's new Ralph Kiner. Thomas, a rookie last year, belted 30 homers—seven more than Kiner accomplished in his first season.

Because the Pirates hit only 99 homers, Greenberg Gardens, which slashed the left field target by 30 feet, is coming down.

Most important new Pirate may be Gerald Lynch, 6–1, 180-pound outfielder drafted from Kansas City (minors) after he had led the Piedmont League at Norfolk in six batting categories, including 133 runs batted in and a .333 average. Among the veteran outfielders, in addition to Thomas, are Cal Abrams and Hal Rice. Preston Ward and Paul Smith will be pressed at first base by Dale Long, who hit 35 homers with Hollywood last year and was voted the Pacific Coast League's most valuable player.

Pitching help may come from George O'Donnell, 20–21 at Hollywood, and Nelson King, relief specialist from Denver, who had a 2.00 ERA while submitting a 15–3 record. Vern Law, 6–9 in 1951, comes back from military service apparently cured of a sore arm. If so, he could be a winner.

The Pirates lost 112 games in 1952 and were whipped 104 times last year, a sad commentary on a club that has an all-time league record of 4,432 victories against 3,841 defeats.

Source: Baseballhistorian.com

Unfortunately, the 1954 team did not disappoint their pessimistic critics, finishing 53–101 while refusing to let go of that last place slot. All in all, the 1950–1954 stretch for the Pittsburgh Pirates represents one of most futile periods for a single team in MLB history. In fact, the Pirates did not boast a winning season until 1958, Danny Murtaugh's first full season as their manager. Murtaugh is widely credited for inventing the concept of the closer by frequently playing pitcher Elroy Face late in close games.

Despite their atrocious showing throughout the early 1950s, the Pirates' brilliant general manager Branch Rickey established one of baseball's most successful farm and scouting systems. The seeds he planted later bloomed into several highly competitive teams that eventually became champions in the 1960s and late-1970s.

1954 Pirates Standings

NATIONAL LEAGUE	W	L	GB	PCT.
New York Giants	97	57	–	.630
Brooklyn Dodgers	92	62	5	.597
Milwaukee Braves	89	65	8	.578
Philadelphia Phillies	75	79	22	.487
Cincinnati Redlegs	74	80	23	.481
St. Louis Cardinals	72	82	25	.468
Chicago Cubs	64	90	33	.416
Pittsburgh Pirates	53	101	44	.344

Data courtesy of Baseball-Almanac.com.

#10 | The Worst Record of the Modern Era

The 1962 New York Mets (40–120)

Can't anybody here play this game?

—*Mets manager Casey Stengel, 1962*

For more than 70 years, New York City successfully hosted three major league baseball teams, the New York Yankees of the American League, and the New York Giants and Brooklyn Dodgers of the National League. The New York teams enjoyed a great deal of success, with each winning multiple pennants and World Series championships. There were even a couple of crosstown World Series, most notably when the Dodgers beat the Yankees in 1953.

In 1957, Giants majority owner Horace Stoneham, frustrated by the lack of support for the construction of a new stadium to replace ancient, decrepit Polo Grounds, decided to move his team to San Francisco. Only Joan Whitney Payson, one of the shareholders and directors of the Giants, voted no on the move to San Francisco. At the same time that Stoneham was negotiating the terms of his team's move to San Francisco, Dodgers owner Walter O'Malley decided to move his team to Los Angeles, meaning that for the first time in more than seven decades, New York found itself without a National League franchise. For five long, unhappy seasons, the Yankees were the only show in town.

Mrs. Payson, who was one of the wealthiest women in the world, was determined to bring National League baseball back to New York City as soon as possible. She joined forces with a prominent Wall Street lawyer named William A. Shea, who began by trying to find another team to move to New York. When those efforts failed, he decided to goad the National League owners to agree to expand the league. He enlisted the former general manager of the Dodgers, Branch Rickey, who brought instant credibility to the effort, and threatened to form a new major league, the Continental League.

1962 New York Mets (Baseball Hall of Fame Library, Cooperstown, NY)

With Mrs. Payson's money behind them, they took steps to organize their new league, including the introduction of legislation before Congress that would have limited the reserve clause and created free agency, a prospect that terrified the other National League owners.

The gambit succeeded. In 1960, afraid that the new league would get off the ground, the other owners of the National League caved and agreed to expand from 8 teams to 10 for the 1962 season. The two new teams would be the New York Metropolitans, who became known as the Mets, and the Houston Colt 45s (who were later renamed the Astros). The new team would play in the Polo Grounds for a couple of years until a new stadium could be built in Flushing, Queens. The Polo Grounds was literally falling apart. Also, the old stadium had odd dimensions. Because the baseball diamond sat in the middle of a rectangular football field, it was only 257 feet to left field and 279 feet to right, while the center field bleachers were 483 feet away. Only one player, Joe Adcock of the Braves, had managed to hit one out to center field in the long history of the ancient stadium.

George Weiss, who was the general manager during the dynasty years of the New York Yankees but was forced out when the owners of the team felt he was too old for the job, was hired to be the general manager of the new team. Weiss had to build an organization from the ground up. He began by hiring Casey Stengel, who won five consecutive World Series championships with the Yankees in the late 1940s and early 1950s, to manage the new team. The 73-year-old Stengel, known for his hilarious malapropisms, which were commonly called "Stengelese," was a living legend for winning 10 pennants in 12 years with the Yankees. For sure, Stengel faced a stern test. His coaches included Hall of Fame pitcher Red Ruffing, former Dodger Cookie Lavagetto and Solly Hemus, who managed the St. Louis Cardinals for part of the 1961 season.

Weiss decided to populate his roster with a combination of familiar New York heroes at the end of their careers and young, unproven players. An expansion draft would be held to fill out team rosters. "I want to thank all of those generous owners for giving us those great players that they did not want," declared Stengel. "Those lovely, generous owners."

Weiss drafted a catcher, Hobie Landrith, as the team's first draft pick. He acquired 35-year-old future Hall of Fame center fielder Richie Ashburn, a hero of the 1950 Philadelphia Phillies "Whiz Kids." Ashburn, who was known for his blazing speed and good defense as a young player, no longer had that speed. The vast tract of land that made up center field at the Polo Grounds would be a challenge for his creaky old legs. Weiss then traded draft pick Lee Walls for Dodger second baseman Charley Neal. He drafted 33-year-old outfielder Gus Bell, who was near the end of his productive career, shortstop Elio Chacon from the Cincinnati Reds, outfielder Joe Christopher from the Pirates, Felix Mantilla from the Braves, and Dodger hero Gil Hodges, who was at the end of his career.[1] He also drafted catcher Clarence "Choo Choo" Coleman from the Phillies. Coleman, who is featured later in this book, hit all of .128 for the 1961 Phillies and is probably the only player to be part of two of the worst teams in the history of Major League Baseball in two consecutive seasons.

Weiss also drafted 1957 rookie of the year first baseman Ed Bouchee from the Phillies. He took two promising young pitchers, Jay Hook (who had a degree in mechanical engineering from Northwestern University) from the Reds and Al Jackson from the Pirates. He took right-handed pitcher Roger Craig from the Dodgers, and a Cardinal pitcher named Bob Miller (later in the season, Weiss traded for another pitcher named Robert G. Miller, and the two roomed together on the road, meaning that all incoming phone calls for that room were directed to Bob Miller). He then

First Baseman Marv Throneberry
(AP Photo)

acquired left fielder/first baseman Frank Thomas, who had hit .281 and 27 homers for the 1961 Braves, for $128,000. At Stengel's request, Weiss acquired a promising, speedy young outfielder name Rod Kanehl, who quickly became a fan favorite in New York.

The 1962 Mets began the season with a roster filled with either has-beens like Gil Hodges or never-weres, such as Choo Choo Coleman. "I'll admit that our roster isn't exactly what we'd like it to be," admitted Weiss before the season. His strategy for filling the team's roster meant that the Mets were doomed to be awful for years until the farm system finally produced some talented young players.[2] Nobody expected this team to do much in its first season, least of all Casey Stengel. When asked by a reporter how he thought he'd do managing the team, Stengel replied, "I don't know. It ain't been managed yet." 1962 proved to be an incredibly long and unhappy season for the Mets.

They actually didn't do all that badly in the Grapefruit League season during spring training in Florida, posting a record of 13–15. Kanehl hit .400 during spring training and so did Don Zimmer. Roger Craig pitched 35 innings and posted a respectable ERA of 2.50. Many of the pundits actually picked the new Houston team to finish last in the National League, expecting the Mets to fight it out with the Phillies for ninth place. They were wrong.

The Mets arrived in St. Louis for their season opener on April 10, 1962. The team checked into its hotel. That night, most of the team—16 players— got stuck in an elevator at the team's hotel for 2½ hours, including opening night pitcher Roger Craig. "I knew it," sighed an exasperated Craig. "The first time in my life I'm going to open a season, I get stuck in an elevator. I'll probably be here for 24 hours." They were eventually rescued, but the incident set the tone for the entire season.

The Mets began their first regular season in St. Louis on April 11, 1962. Or, they were supposed to. The game was rained out. That was probably the best thing that happened to them the entire season. Instead, they played their inaugural game the next night and lost 11–4. The Cardinals scored their first run in the first inning when pitcher Roger Craig wound up, started his motion toward the plate, and dropped the ball with a runner on third. The home plate umpire called it a balk, and the runner scored. It was not an auspicious beginning. As Jimmy Breslin, the witty *New York Herald Tribune* columnist, put it, "The Mets' season was now officially shot."

They then returned home to New York, where the city held a ticker tape parade to welcome the new team, with Stengel leading the way. "They couldn't have picked a better manager to lead the parade down Broadway," remembered Rod Kanehl. "The fans loved him. You know, they didn't necessarily love him when he was a Yankee manager, but he was different when he was with the Mets. He was more patient. He knew that he didn't have the ball club, that we didn't have any pitching."

Eager fans desperate to see National League baseball once more packed the old Polo Grounds. Ashburn drove in the first run and was rewarded with a standing ovation. They lost 4–3, the second in what turned out to be a nine-game losing streak to begin the season. They lost by booting ground balls, by letting fly balls drop untouched, with base-running gaffes, and with really bad pitching. They often came up with new, creative ways to lose.

The Mets finally won a game in Pittsburgh on April 23, prompting Stengel to declare, "Ninety-nine more and we got the pennant." It was not to be. Instead, they reeled off losing streaks of 9, 11, 13, and 17 games. By Memorial Day, they were solidly entrenched in tenth place, a position they would not yield for the rest of the season, prompting Stengel to wonder aloud, "Can't anybody here play this game?" Desperate to find some way to win, Stengel used 49 different players over the course of the long season. "I don't know what's going on, but I know I've never seen it before," declared a frustrated Richie Ashburn.

Players came and went, but Weiss made a landmark move on May 9, acquiring first baseman Marv Throneberry from the Baltimore Orioles. Throneberry had a good stick, but he had bad hands. Nevertheless, the Mets faithful loved him, immediately dubbing him "Marvelous Marv," even though he was prone to strike out too much, hit into too many double plays, and was a defensive nightmare. He was 29, thickly built, and nearly bald. He chewed tobacco, had a thick Tennessee drawl, and by the end of the season, he was a living legend in New York. One day, Throneberry laced a line drive deep into the gap in the Polo Grounds. He put his head down and built up a head of steam, rounding first base, second base, and then chugged into third base, puffing and wheezing from the effort of legging out a triple. Ernie Banks, the Cubs' first baseman, looked at umpire Dusty Boggess and said, "Didn't touch the bag, you know, Dusty." When Boggess nodded, Banks called for the ball. He caught it, stepped on first base, and Boggess called Marvelous Marv out for missing the base. When Stengel came out to argue the call, Boggess said, "He didn't touch second, either." That ended the argument. "Things just sort of keep on happening to me," sighed Throneberry. That simple statement summed up the entire 1962 season for the Mets.

In April, Weiss obtained catcher Harry Chiti from the Cleveland Indians for a player to be named later. Chiti was a well-traveled 12-year veteran of the major leagues who hadn't seen a lot of playing time. He hit .195 in 15 games with the Mets. In June, the Indians came calling. They wanted their player to be named later, so Weiss had to act. He sent Chiti back to Cleveland, meaning that the catcher was traded for himself in just another absurd event in a season filled with absurd events.

The Mets won a total of 40 games that season, losing 120 along the way. They set the modern record for impotence, breaking the single season record for losses of 117 set by the 1916 Philadelphia Athletics, and finished 60½ games behind the pennant-winning San Francisco Giants. "Fellers, don't feel bad about this," declared Stengel, who was trying to make his team feel better about the dubious honors they racked up that year. "No one or two players could have done all this." They ended the long, frustrating season with a .333 winning percentage.

The Mets used seven different catchers that year, with Chris Cannizaro and Choo Choo Coleman leading the pack with 59 and 55 games, respectively. Ashburn led the team with a .306 average, clubbing a career-high seven homers. Ashburn promptly retired at the end of the season, accepting a job as a broadcaster with his old team, the Phillies, taking a pay cut to do so.[3] Gil Hodges, who had creaky knees, played in only 54 games, hitting .252 with nine homers. Third baseman Felix Mantilla had a solid season, hitting .275 with 11 homers and 59 RBIs. Left fielder Frank Thomas clouted 34 homers and drove in 94 runs in a respectable season. Former Yankee stalwart outfielder Gene Woodling, now 39 and in the twilight of his career, was acquired mid-season. Woodling hit .274 in 81 games with the Mets. Don Zimmer was lucky—he was traded only 14 games into his tenure with the team. Throneberry hit .244 with 16 homers and 49 RBIs. He also had 83 strikeouts in only 357 at bats, and he also made 17 errors in the field. The team's .240 batting average was 21 points below the National League average, and 38 points less than the pennant-winning Giants.

The team's defense was generally awful. The Mets committed a league-leading 210 errors and had only a .967 fielding percentage, the worst in the National League. They scored 617 runs, while giving up a staggering 948, meaning that they were outscored by 331 runs, or by an average of two runs per game.

The pitching was no better. The staff posted an awful 5.04 team ERA, half a run higher than the next worst pitching staff and more than a full run worse than the league average of 3.94. They gave up 1,577 hits, 577 walks, and 948 runs in 1,430 innings. Their pitching staff yielded 322 more runs than the fourth-place Pittsburgh Pirates did.

Roger Craig, the staff's best pitcher, went 10–24 with a 4.51 ERA.[4] Al Jackson went 8–20 with a 4.40 ERA. This was the first time since 1936 that a National League team boasted two 20-game losers.[5] The third starter, Jay Hook, nearly joined them in the 20-loss club, posting an 8–19 mark, with a 4.84 ERA. "He had good stuff," said catcher Norm Sherry of Hook, "but he seemed to make that bad pitch when he shouldn't. That always hurt him." Craig Anderson, who split the season between starting and the bull pen, posted an awful 3–17 record with a 5.35 ERA. Bob Miller, who had 21 starts, was 1–12, with a 4.89 ERA. Only reliever Craig MacKenzie had a winning record, posting a 5–4 mark.

"You look back on it," noted a Mets player that winter, "and you have to say 40 games is about all we could win. After all, we were playing against teams that had *all major leaguers* on them." For someone accustomed to winning, as Stengel was, 1962 had to have been a horrific experience. "Strangers are hard to manage," declared Stengel. "It was like spring training all year. But I expected to win more games. I was very much shocked."

Casey Stengel's Amazin' Mets, as he liked to call his team, set the modern gold standard for incompetence on a baseball diamond. It's likely to be a very, very long time before a team as bad as the 1962 Mets flashes across the baseball horizon again.

1962 New York Mets Stats: Fielding

NAME	POS	GAMES	PO	A	E	DP	TC/G	FLD%
Craig Anderson	P	50	8	36	2	3	0.9	.957
Richie Ashburn	OF	97	187	9	5	1	2.1	.975
Richie Ashburn	2B	?	5	4	1	1	5.0	.900
Gus Bell	RF	26	40	7	1	3	1.8	.979
Ed Bouchee	1B	19	137	23	4	16	8.6	.976
Chris Cannizzaro	C	56	218	34	7	3	4.6	.973
Chris Cannizzaro	RF	1	1	0	0	0	1.0	1.000
Elio Chacon	SS	110	204	332	22	64	5.1	.961
Elio Chacon	2B	2	2	1	0	0	1.5	1.000
Elio Chacon	3B	1	0	0	0	0	0.0	.000
Harry Chiti	C	14	62	4	2	1	4.9	.971
Joe Christopher	OF	94	133	5	4	4	1.5	.972
Galen Cisco	P	4	2	2	0	0	1.0	1.000

1962 New York Mets Stats: Fielding (cont.)

NAME	POS	GAMES	PO	A	E	DP	TC/G	FLD%
Choo Choo Coleman	C	44	187	22	1	2	4.8	.995
Cliff Cook	3B	16	14	21	5	2	2.5	.875
Cliff Cook	RF	10	11	0	1	0	1.2	.917
Roger Craig	P	42	23	54	4	4	1.9	.951
Ray Daviault	P	36	9	6	0	0	0.4	1.000
John DeMerit	OF	9	4	0	0	0	0.4	1.000
Sammy Drake	2B	10	21	21	1	6	4.3	.977
Sammy Drake	3B	6	3	5	1	0	1.5	.889
Larry Foss	P	5	2	1	0	0	0.6	1.000
Joe Ginsberg	C	2	9	2	0	1	5.5	1.000
Rick Herrscher	1B	10	75	8	0	9	8.3	1.000
Rick Herrscher	3B	6	3	7	2	1	2.0	.833
Rick Herrscher	OF	4	2	0	0	0	0.5	1.000
Rick Herrscher	SS	3	3	4	0	1	2.3	1.000
Jim Hickman	OF	124	265	7	8	0	2.3	.971
Dave Hillman	P	13	2	3	0	0	0.4	1.000
Gil Hodges	1B	47	315	32	5	23	7.5	.986
Jay Hook	P	37	22	31	3	2	1.5	.946
Willard Hunter	P	27	5	6	1	0	0.4	.917
Al Jackson	P	36	21	59	2	1	2.3	.976
Sherman Jones	P	8	3	5	0	0	1.0	1.000
Rod Kanehl	2B	62	183	187	22	53	6.3	.944
Rod Kanehl	3B	30	15	40	8	4	2.1	.873
Rod Kanehl	OF	20	21	1	1	0	1.2	.957
Rod Kanehl	1B	3	16	2	1	0	6.3	.947
Rod Kanehl	SS	2	0	0	0	0	0.0	.000
Ed Kranepool	1B	3	9	3	0	0	4.0	1.000
Clem Labine	P	3	0	2	0	0	0.7	1.000
Hobie Landrith	C	21	87	3	3	0	4.4	.968
Ken MacKenzie	P	42	3	16	2	3	0.5	.905
Felix Mantilla	3B	95	76	179	14	22	2.8	.948
Felix Mantilla	SS	25	28	48	4	10	3.2	.950
Felix Mantilla	2B	14	35	24	2	4	4.4	.967
Jim Marshall	1B	5	47	4	0	6	10.2	1.000
Jim Marshall	RF	1	0	0	0	0	0.0	.000
Bob Miller	P	33	14	32	2	3	1.5	.958
Bob Miller	P	17	2	3	0	1	0.3	1.000
Vinegar Bend Mizell	P	17	1	4	0	0	0.3	1.000

1962 New York Mets Stats: Fielding (cont.)

NAME	POS	GAMES	PO	A	E	DP	TC/G	FLD%
Herb Moford	P	7	2	1	0	0	0.4	1.000
Bob Moorhead	P	38	7	28	4	4	1.0	.897
Charlie Neal	2B	85	187	240	13	54	5.2	.970
Charlie Neal	SS	39	63	118	12	30	4.9	.938
Charlie Neal	3B	12	6	31	3	1	3.3	.925
Joe Pignatano	C	25	100	10	1	2	4.4	.991
Bobby Gene Smith	OF	6	12	0	0	0	2.0	1.000
Sammy Taylor	C	50	202	25	2	3	4.6	.991
Frank Thomas	LF	126	216	14	9	0	1.9	.962
Frank Thomas	1B	11	88	3	1	7	8.4	.989
Frank Thomas	3B	10	7	19	4	1	3.0	.867
Marv Throneberry	1B	97	785	77	17	87	9.1	.981
Gene Woodling	OF	48	68	0	1	0	1.4	.986
Don Zimmer	3B	14	12	37	2	3	3.6	.961
TEAM TOTALS			4,290	1,902	210	446	3.3	.967

Data courtesy of Baseball-Almanac.com.

1962 New York Mets Stats: Pitching

NAME	GAMES	W	L	W%	ERA	GS	CG	IP	HA	BB	SO	SHU
Craig Anderson	50	3	17	.150	5.35	14	2	131.1	150	63	62	0
Galen Cisco	4	1	1	.500	3.26	2	1	19.1	15	11	13	0
Roger Craig	42	10	24	.294	4.51	33	13	233.1	261	70	118	0
Ray Daviault	36	1	5	.167	6.22	3	0	81.0	92	48	51	0
Larry Foss	5	0	1	.000	4.63	1	0	11.2	17	7	3	0
Dave Hillman	13	0	0	.000	6.32	1	0	15.2	21	8	8	0
Jay Hook	37	8	19	.296	4.84	34	13	213.2	230	71	113	0
Willard Hunter	27	1	6	.143	5.57	6	1	63.0	67	34	40	0
Al Jackson	36	8	20	.286	4.40	33	12	231.1	244	78	118	4
Sherman Jones	8	0	4	.000	7.71	3	0	23.1	31	8	11	0
Clem Labine	3	0	0	.000	11.25	0	0	4.0	5	1	2	0
Ken MacKenzie	42	5	4	.556	4.95	1	0	80.0	87	34	51	0
Bob Miller	33	1	12	.077	4.89	21	1	143.2	146	62	91	0
Bob Miller	17	2	2	.500	7.08	0	0	20.1	24	8	8	0
Vinegar Bend Mizell	17	0	2	.000	7.34	2	0	38.0	48	25	15	0
Herb Moford	7	0	1	.000	7.20	0	0	15.0	21	1	5	0
Bob Moorhead	38	0	2	.000	4.53	7	0	105.1	118	42	63	0
TEAM TOTALS		40	120	.250	5.04	161	43	1430	1,577	571	772	4

Data courtesy of Baseball-Almanac.com.

1962 New York Mets Stats: Hitting

NAME	POS	GAMES	AVG	SLG	AB	H	2B	3B	HR	AB/HR	R	RBI	BB	SO	SB
Craig Anderson	P	50	.094	.094	32	3	0	0	0	0.0	2	0	1	12	0
Richie Ashburn	OF	135	.306	.393	389	119	7	3	7	55.6	60	28	81	39	12
Gus Bell	OF	30	.149	.198	101	15	2	0	1	101.0	8	6	10	7	0
Ed Bouchee	1B	50	.161	.287	87	14	2	0	3	29.0	7	10	18	17	0
Chris Cannizzaro	C	59	.241	.271	133	32	2	1	0	0.0	9	9	19	26	1
Elio Chacon	SS	118	.236	.296	368	87	10	3	2	184.0	49	27	76	64	12
Harry Chiti	C	15	.195	.220	41	8	1	0	0	0.0	2	0	1	8	0
Joe Christopher	OF	119	.244	.362	271	66	10	2	6	45.2	36	32	35	42	11
Galen Cisco	P	4	.000	.000	7	0	0	0	0	0.0	0	0	0	1	0
Choo Choo Coleman	C	55	.250	.441	152	38	7	2	6	25.3	24	17	11	24	2
Cliff Cook	3B	40	.232	.357	112	26	6	1	2	56.0	12	9	4	34	1
Roger Craig	P	42	.053	.053	76	4	0	0	0	0.0	1	2	4	33	0
Ray Daviault	P	36	.067	.067	15	1	0	0	0	0.0	0	0	1	8	0
John DeMerit	OF	14	.188	.375	16	3	0	0	1	16.0	3	1	2	4	0
Sammy Drake	2B	25	.192	.192	52	10	0	0	0	0.0	2	7	6	12	0
Larry Foss	P	5	.000	.000	1	0	0	0	0	0.0	0	0	0	0	0
Joe Ginsberg	C	2	.000	.000	5	0	0	0	0	0.0	0	0	0	1	0
Rick Herrscher	1B	35	.220	.340	50	11	3	0	1	50.0	5	6	5	11	0
Jim Hickman	OF	140	.245	.401	392	96	18	2	13	30.2	54	46	47	96	4
Dave Hillman	P	13	.000	.000	1	0	0	0	0	0.0	0	0	0	1	0
Gil Hodges	1B	54	.252	.472	127	32	1	0	9	14.1	15	17	15	27	0
Jay Hook	P	41	.203	.203	69	14	0	0	0	0.0	6	5	8	24	0
Willard Hunter	P	27	.231	.231	13	3	0	0	0	0.0	1	0	0	7	0
Al Jackson	P	44	.068	.096	73	5	2	0	0	0.0	5	2	2	27	0

1962 New York Mets Stats: Hitting (cont.)

NAME	POS	GAMES	AVG	SLG	AB	H	2B	3B	HR	AB/HR	R	RBI	BB	SO	SB
Sherman Jones	P	8	.429	.429	7	3	0	0	0	0.0	0	1	0	2	0
Rod Kanehl	2B	133	.248	.322	351	87	10	2	4	87.8	52	27	23	36	8
Ed Kranepool	1B	3	.167	.333	6	1	1	0	0	0.0	0	0	0	1	0
Clem Labine	P	3	.000	.000	0	0	0	0	0	0.0	0	0	0	0	0
Hobie Landrith	C	23	.289	.422	45	13	3	0	1	45.0	6	7	8	3	0
Ken MacKenzie	P	42	.083	.083	12	1	0	0	0	0.0	0	1	0	6	0
Felix Mantilla	3B	141	.275	.399	466	128	17	4	11	42.4	54	59	37	51	3
Jim Marshall	1B	17	.344	.656	32	11	1	0	3	10.7	6	4	3	6	0
Bob Miller	P	40	.122	.171	41	5	0	1	0	0.0	2	0	1	17	0
Bob Miller	P	17	.000	.000	1	0	0	0	0	0.0	0	0	0	0	0
Vinegar Bend Mizell	P	17	.250	.250	8	2	0	0	0	0.0	1	0	0	2	0
Herb Moford	P	7	.250	.250	4	1	0	0	0	0.0	0	0	0	1	0
Bob Moorhead	P	38	.045	.045	22	1	0	0	0	0.0	2	0	5	11	0
Charlie Neal	2B	136	.260	.388	508	132	14	9	11	46.2	59	58	56	90	2
Joe Pignatano	C	27	.232	.268	56	13	2	0	0	0.0	2	2	2	11	0
Bobby Gene Smith	OF	8	.136	.227	22	3	0	1	0	0.0	1	2	3	2	0
Sammy Taylor	C	68	.222	.329	158	35	4	2	3	52.7	12	20	23	17	0
Frank Thomas	OF	156	.266	.496	571	152	23	3	34	16.8	69	94	48	95	2
Marv Throneberry	1B	116	.244	.426	357	87	11	3	16	22.3	29	49	34	83	1
Gene Woodling	OF	81	.274	.405	190	52	8	1	5	38.0	18	24	24	22	0
Don Zimmer	3B	14	.077	.096	52	4	1	0	0	0.0	3	1	3	10	0
TEAM TOTALS			.240	.361	5,492	1,318	166	40	139	39.5	617	573	616	991	59

Data courtesy of Baseball-Almanac.com.

One Year of Wretchedness

The 1969 Seattle Pilots (64–98)

> The Pilots were a joke.
>
> —*Mike Marshall, original Seattle Pilot and*
> *1974 National League Cy Young Award winner*

Seattle was the home of successful minor league baseball franchises for more than 60 years. When major league baseball decided to expand before the 1969 season, Seattle seemed like an excellent choice for a new major league expansion team. However, the new team faced significant challenges. The new team would have to begin its tenure in tiny, ancient Sick's Stadium, which was not up to major league standards. It seated only 11,000, and it was in such bad shape that attendance fell for the final three seasons that the California Angels' AAA team played there, 1966 through 1968. One of the team's pitchers, Jim Bouton, left a detailed description of the old ballpark, calling it a "graveyard for pitchers, home-run heaven of the major leagues. The clubhouse is small and crowded and there's no rug, just rubber runners on the cement floor and the lockers are small and close together." Others remembered the uncomfortable folding metal chairs in the clubhouse, instead of the comfortable surroundings they were accustomed to in other major league ballparks.

The place left a lot to be desired as a major league baseball stadium. "It was like a nice high school field or average college stadium," said outfielder Jim Gosger. "I played in AAA places that were much nicer." Another player said, "It needed a lot of improvement." The new team would have to play in the decrepit little bandbox until a new stadium could be built to take its place.

The new team also had incompetent ownership. Dewey Soriano played for the Seattle Rainiers of the Pacific Coast League (PCL) as a young man, and was the president of the PCL in 1966. He and his brothers, Max and Milton, formed Pacific Northwest Sports for the purpose of obtaining a

1969 Seattle Pilots (Baseball Hall of Fame Library, Cooperstown, NY)

major league expansion team for Seattle. The Sorianos recruited William Daley, the former owner of the Cleveland Indians, for their ownership group to prove to the other major league owners that they had an experienced baseball man among their ranks. Daley owned 47 percent, while the Soriano brothers controlled 34 percent of the stock in the corporation.

In 1967, the American League voted to expand from 10 teams to 12, largely to resolve a huge dispute that arose when Charles O. Finley moved the A's from Kansas City to Oakland. Kansas City would get one of the new teams to replace the departed A's. The National League also expanded, with new teams in San Diego and Montreal. Where would the other new American League team land? The bid of the Sorianos won, but not without major strings attached. For Seattle to get a major league team, the seating capacity of Sick's Stadium would have to be expanded to 30,000 prior to Opening Day of the 1969 season and the voters of Seattle would have to approve a $40 million bond package for the construction of a new domed stadium. Construction had to begin no later than December 31, 1970. If construction had not commenced by then, the other owners retained the right to move the team.

With that, the Sorianos began building an organization for their new team. They hired Marvin Milkes as the new team's general manager. Milkes had worked in the California Angels organization, but he had never served as a general manager. He quickly proved that he was not up to the task. The new team began its life with incompetent ownership and incompetent management.

After bragging that they would land a lucrative contract and holding out for outrageous sums of money, the Sorianos found themselves without a television contract, meaning that no local television station covered the hometown team during its inaugural season. It also meant that the team missed out on a critical source of revenue. It was not an auspicious beginning for the new franchise, which was already undercapitalized. The lack of a television contract all but insured that the Sorianos would not be able to support their new team financially.

A contest was held to name the new team. The name Pilots won the contest, ironically finishing ahead of the name Mariners. The name supposedly linked the Seattle area's intimate involvement in the nautical and aviation industries.

Having named the team, the Sorianos now had to work on developing the brand. Management developed several uniform schemes. The first uniforms were quite plain: white for home, gray for away, with the word PILOTS spelled out on the chest, with a blue cap featuring a yellow "S." However, this simple scheme did not last long. Another, more flamboyant scheme was developed. The uniform was styled after an airline captain's uniform, with a garish logo and gold leaves and gold braids, in the military style known derisively as "scrambled eggs," were

added to the caps. "I thought they were going give us a boat with that cap," recalled pitcher Gary Bell. "I didn't particularly like all of that stuff on the bill." The whole getup was hideous, and they were probably the most unusual uniforms ever worn by major leaguers. "We look like goddamn clowns," grumbled relief pitcher Jim Bouton at the beginning of the season. Looking

Left Fielder / Designated Hitter
Tommy Davis (Seattle Pilots)

back at the uniforms years later, many of the players expressed fondness for the unusual uniforms, and many said that they liked the hats.

Just after the 1968 World Series, the Sorianos hired St. Louis Cardinal third base coach Joe Schultz as the first manager of the Pilots. Schultz had a nondescript 10-year career in the major leagues, and spent more than 20 years as a coach. The Cardinals had just won back-to-back World Series appearances in 1967 and 1968. "He was a character and a good baseball guy," remembered one pitcher. "He kept us loose." Schultz encouraged his team to go out and win one and then head back to the locker room to pound a few beers. His players loved him for it. The baseball lifer appeared to be a good choice to serve as a manager, but Schultz proved himself to be inept in his one year as a major league manager.

Schultz brought Ron Plaza with him from the Cardinals to serve as first base coach. He was the only coach that Schultz got to pick himself because Milkes refused to permit Schultz to choose his own coaching staff as a matter of team policy. Milkes chose the rest of the coaching staff. Sal Maglie, the ace of the New York Giants of the 1950s, was chosen as pitching coach, and Frank Crosetti, who had played with Babe Ruth with the New York Yankees, was brought in to teach and coach third base. Eddie O'Brien, the athletic director at Seattle University, was made bull pen coach as a favor to enable him to qualify for five years in the major leagues so he could collect a pension. This was a nice gesture, but it was hardly a reason to make a man a major league coach when he had never before been a coach.[1]

With a manager in place, it was now time to add players. Jim Bouton, who had won 21 games with the New York Yankees in 1963 and 18 during the regular season and 2 more in the 1964 World Series, was purchased from the Yankees for $20,000. Bouton had injured his arm in 1965 and was no longer a fireballer. Instead, he learned to throw the knuckleball, and spent a couple of years toiling in the minor leagues while mastering the difficult flutterball. Milkes got the Yankees to agree to pay $8,000 of Bouton's $20,000 salary for 1969. Milkes also purchased slick-fielding first baseman Mike Hegan from the Yankees.

Most of the rest of the roster was filled out through the expansion draft. All major league teams were required to leave several players unprotected, so that the four new expansion teams could select them. These players were usually either has-beens or never-weres, meaning that there was little chance of the expansion teams finishing anywhere but last. The 1969 expansion draft was no exception. Since both leagues added teams, the new Kansas City Royals and Seattle Pilots drafted only from American

League teams and the new San Diego Padres and Montreal Expos drafted from only National League teams.

Milkes chose the only power hitter available, first baseman Don Mincher, a former all-star. He selected former Cincinnati Reds all-star infielder Tommy Harper, and Tommy Davis, who won two batting titles with the Los Angeles Dodgers in 1962 and 1963. However, Davis suffered a severe ankle injury in 1965, and never recovered fully from it, making him expendable by 1969. Milkes selected Ray Oyler, a fine fielding but weak-hitting shortstop from the Detroit Tigers, who won the World Series in 1968. Third baseman Rich Rollins, who was an all-star with the Minnesota Twins, but was in the twilight of his career, was also selected. A knee injury shortened his season and ended his playing career the next season.

Beside Bouton, the pitching choices included Gary Bell, a former three-time all-star who was nearing the end of his career, Steve Barber, a former 20-game winner with the Baltimore Orioles, and Jack Aker, a relief specialist. As Barber later put it, "The club was supposed to be built around me and Gary Bell. It just so happened that Bell was at the end of his career, and I couldn't pitch most of the year." With the two veteran hurlers who were supposed to be the mainstays of the pitching staff so ineffective, failure became inevitable.

In addition, Milkes purchased the contract of young Mike Marshall from the Tigers; Marshall was a highly touted prospect who had won 15 games at AAA Toledo in 1968. After leaving the Pilots' organization, Marshall became one of the best relief pitchers in the history of major league baseball, winning the 1974 National League Cy Young Award while a member of the pennant-winning Los Angeles Dodgers. Milkes also selected a handsome, fiery outfield prospect named Lou Piniella.

As management tried to build a team, the City of Seattle tried to ready old Sick's Stadium to host major league baseball. However, they could not do so until after the end of the 1968 PCL season, meaning that all work had to be completed in about six months. When bids for the expansion of the stadium came in much higher than expected, the seating capacity was reduced from 28,500 seats to 25,000 seats, a reduction approved reluctantly by the other American League owners. After squabbling and labor disputes, construction did not begin until January 1, 1969. Work was not completed until after the season was already underway. "When you walk in on opening day and you see that big crane there and they are still putting the stadium seats together, you kinda wonder what's going to go on here," recalled Gosger. The fates seemed to be aligned against the new team before the first pitch was thrown at spring training.

Unfortunately, the beginning of spring training was delayed in 1969. Major league baseball had only recently unionized, and the union chose to hold its first players' strike that winter if no new contract was in place by the time spring started. The strike only lasted 10 days, but it hurt the four expansion teams, which were trying to build something from the ground up. The Pilots won their first exhibition game, with first baseman Greg Goossen serving as the "designated pinch hitter" for the pitcher in an experiment being tried that would hopefully add more offense to games by keeping weak-hitting hurlers from coming to the plate.[2] "Are they trying to tell me something about my glove?" wondered Goossen. Schultz foolishly and boldly predicted that the Pilots would finish third in their division after that first exhibition game.

The team scored a lot of runs during the Cactus League season, but it quickly became obvious that the pitching staff left a great deal to be desired. Barber began suffering from arm trouble that plagued him the entire season. Bouton's knuckler was inconsistent. Nevertheless, the Pilots finished the Grapefruit League season with a respectable 12–16 record.

Milkes began making moves. He traded infielder Chico Salmon to the Baltimore Orioles for pitcher Gene Brabender. He sent Piniella to the Kansas City Royals for outfielder Steve Whitaker and pitcher John Gelnar. Schultz did not like Piniella and had no confidence in his ability, so Milkes unloaded him. Piniella won the 1969 American League Rookie of the Year award and had a successful 18-year major league career, finishing with a .291 career batting average. After retiring as a player, he became a manager, winning a World Series championship with the Yankees, and several division championships with the Seattle Mariners, in a great twist of irony.

Forty-two-year-old pitcher Bill Henry made the team coming out of training camp, but retired on April 3. "What am I doing keeping younger guys from a chance to earn a living?" asked Henry. "I'm 42 years old. I've had 13 years in the big leagues. I don't really belong here." And with that, another roster spot opened up.

The Pilots broke camp and headed north. "The most significant event in Seattle baseball history takes place tonight at Anaheim Stadium," declared the *Seattle Post Intelligencer* on April 8, 1969. "Seattle begins its first major league season, the climax, for fans in the area, of years of waiting." And so it was.

Hegan hit the team's first home run in the top of the first inning, staking the Pilots to a 4–0 lead. They hung on to beat the California Angels, 4–3, with Marty Pattin posting the franchise's first victory. They lost the second game, splitting the series with the Angels, and then headed north to Seattle for the team's first home game.

The team arrived on April 10 and was treated to a parade through downtown Seattle. However, in a sign of things to come, a crowd of only 500 awaited their arrival. While the parade went on, workers continued trying to get Sick's Stadium ready. Only 6,000 new seats had been installed, increasing its capacity to 17,000, and the new scoreboards were installed a couple of hours before the first home game began. The new right-field bleachers were not installed until May. There were gaping holes in the left-field fence, and the decrepit little bandbox was nowhere near ready to host major league baseball. However, the game would not wait for the stadium to be completed, and play began with the team's home opener on April 11, 1969.

With Commissioner Bowie Kuhn, American League President Joe Cronin, and former Rainiers players in attendance and in front of a sellout crowd of 17,850, the home season for the Seattle Pilots began. After homers by Rich Rollins and Don Mincher and his own two-run double, Gary Bell won the home opener, 7–0, pitching a complete game shutout against the Chicago White Sox. They won their next game against the White Sox and were 3–1.

The Pilots went 7–11 in April, and were 8–17 by May 7. Pattin and Marshall both pitched well, but the team scored few runs in their support. Things then turned around for the Pilots, who got good pitching and timely hitting, winning seven of nine games, and drawing good attendance to old Sick's Stadium. After a superb performance during the month of May by right-handed pitcher Diego Segui, the Pilots unexpectedly reached .500. As long as the veteran players remained healthy, the team at least had a chance to be respectable. However, the older players soon began to break down, and so did the fortunes of the Pilots.

The new team got no respect. In June, when the Pilots flew to New York for a game against the Yankees, sportswriter Vic Ziegel of the *New York Post* wrote, "Today Mel Stottlemyre goes after his seventh victory, and Gene Brabender goes after . . . whatever the Gene Brabenders of the world go after." The infuriated Brabender, who stood 6-foot-6 inches and weighed 245 pounds, cut an intimidating site. "He looks like if you got a hit off him," said catcher Jim Pagliaroni of Brabender, "he'd crush your spleen." The big pitcher wanted to find Ziegel and inflict bodily harm on him. Instead, Brabender pitched a superb game and beat the Yankees and Stottlemyre 2–1, making the scribe eat his words. The Pilots went 14–15 in June and were in third place, at 34–39, on June 30. Perhaps Schultz's prognostication about where his team would finish was correct.

Milkes continued shuffling players in and out. Between trades and sending players back and forth to the team's AAA affiliate in Vancouver, the Pilots set a major league record by using 53 different players over the course of the season, including 36-year-old rookie outfielder Billy Williams, who spent 17 seasons in the minor leagues before finally getting a major league at bat. At times, it felt like the clubhouse door was actually a revolving door as players came and went.

Unfortunately, the wheels came off in July. The Pilots went 9–20 in July, but still managed to hang on to third place. Pitcher John Gelnar lost two games in one day, taking the loss when a game suspended in the 17th inning resumed on July 20, and then he also lost the regular game. The skid continued throughout August, and attendance plummeted. Less than 10,000 attended games on average, which did not bode well for the future of the franchise. With no television contract to entice people to come to games, the team floundered financially, and it was obvious that the team would lose money for the season. By August, the Sorianos owed the City of Seattle so much rent money that the team was nearly locked out of Sick's Stadium. They lost 15 out of 16 games during the second half of August as the skid spiraled out of control. To his great consternation, Tommy Davis, who was the team's leader and who liked Seattle, was traded to the Astros for outfielder Sandy Valdespino and highly touted outfield prospect Danny Walton, leaving the team leaderless. "After they traded Tommy Davis I thought our club lost enthusiasm," said catcher Gerry McNertney. By August 31, the Pilots had a 49–81 record and were in sole possession of last place.

There was one bright spot as the season wound down. On September 8, Milkes promoted highly regarded right-handed pitcher Miguel Fuentes from Vancouver, and the rookie responded by twirling a seven-hit complete game in his major league debut. Young Fuentes appeared in eight games, and pitched effectively. It looked like the young hurler would have a bright future in the major leagues. Unfortunately, he was shot and killed in a bar fight in his native Puerto Rico during the off-season and never got to show how good he might have been. His short tenure with the Pilots was undoubtedly the most tragic of any player's.

Thankfully, the season ended on October 2, with the Pilots firmly in possession of last place. They finished at 64–98, narrowly avoiding 100 losses; by contrast, the National League Padres and Expos both posted records of 52–110. Although Dewey Soriano had predicted that more than 1,000,000 would attend Pilots' games, only 677,944 showed up. The Sorianos later claimed that they lost $1 million for the 1969 season and that they had only $100,000 in available funds to begin the 1970 season.

Some of the Pilots had decent seasons. First baseman Don Mincher, who represented the team at the All-Star game and got a hit off Bob Gibson, a future Hall of Famer and the National League's best pitcher, hit .246 with 25 homers and 78 RBIs. Tommy Harper led the majors with 73 stolen bases. Mike Hegan hit .292. Young outfielders Wayne Comer and Steve Hovley both performed well after being called up from Vancouver, and Goossen blasted 10 homers and hit .309. However, the poor performance of most of the Pilots' hitters dragged the team batting average down to a meager .234.

The team's pitching staff demonstrated the same lack of consistency. Gene Brabender proved to be the team's only reliable starting pitcher. Diego Segui had an outstanding season, posting a remarkable 12–6 record with a 3.35 ERA and 12 saves. Reliever Bob Locker posted a 2.18 ERA with six saves, while John O'Donoghue had a respectable 2.96 ERA and six saves, meaning that the bull pen was the only reliable portion of the pitching staff. Some of the young hurlers, such as John Gelnar, Skip Lockwood, and Dick Baney, all demonstrated promise. At the same time, veterans who had been expected to contribute to the starting rotation failed miserably. Gary Bell was traded to the White Sox for Locker in May, Steve Barber spent most of the season on the disabled list, and Jim Bouton was traded to the Houston Astros for hurler Dooley Womack in August after posting inconsistent numbers throughout the season with a management that did not trust his knuckleball.[3] The team finished the season with an unacceptable 4.35 ERA.

After the end of the season, Milkes fired the entire coaching staff, and followed by terminating Schultz in November. The firing of Schultz surprised most of the players, who really liked him and his managing style. He chose Dave Bristol, former manager of the Cincinnati Reds, to replace Schultz. Schultz never managed in the major leagues again. However, redoing the coaching staff was the least of Marvin Milkes' problems. The bigger issue was whether there would even be a team for him to run.

By the end of the 1969 season, the Sorianos were in dire financial straits. The team's atrocious attendance, combined with the lack of television revenue, meant that they were in deep trouble. Mix in the fact that little progress had been made on building a new stadium to replace Sick's Stadium, and the future did not look bright at all for major league baseball in Seattle. A local businessperson agreed to purchase the team until he learned just how much debt was involved. When the new ownership group was unable to raise sufficient funds to complete the transaction, the team was sold to a group from Milwaukee led by car dealer Bud Selig for $13.5 million. Although the team was already in spring training, it was sold, meaning that the Pilots had only a single season in Seattle. To the shock of most of the players, the team relocated to Milwaukee and got a new name: the Brewers. "I think everybody wanted to get out of there," recalled pitcher John Donaldson when asked about the move to Milwaukee years later.

Ironically, the 1970 Brewers only won one more game than the 1969 Pilots, but nearly 1,000,000 fans flocked to Milwaukee's County Stadium to see them play. Selig and his new ownership group proved that Milwaukee could successfully maintain a major league baseball franchise, and the Brewers continue to play there to this day, although they joined the National League in a realignment of teams and divisions in 1997. The Brewers have only been in postseason play three times in 40 years, including one losing World Series appearance in 1982, meaning that moving the team did not guarantee success.

In 1977, major league baseball returned to Seattle in the form of another expansion team called the Mariners. This time, however, the team had a real stadium to play in, in the form of the Kingdome, the domed stadium anticipated by the American League owners in 1967. The loss of the Pilots permitted the city administrators to learn some valuable lessons, and to prepare properly for the advent of a new expansion team, unlike the chaos of 1969. The Mariners have enjoyed great success in their 34 years, winning several division titles under fiery manager Lou Piniella.

Thus ended the sad, strange saga of the 1969 Seattle Pilots, who set the modern gold standard for miserable failures in the single season of their existence.

1969 Seattle Pilots Schedule

GAME	DATE / BOX SCORE	OPPONENT	SCORE	DECISION	RECORD
1	04–08–1969	at California Angels	4–3	W	1–0
2	04–09–1969	at California Angels	3–7	L	1–1
3	04–11–1969	vs Chicago White Sox	7–0	W	2–1
4	04–12–1969	vs Chicago White Sox	5–1	W	3–1
5	04–13–1969	vs Chicago White Sox	7–12	L	3–2
6	04–14–1969	vs Kansas City Royals	1–2	L	3–3
7	04–16–1969	vs Minnesota Twins	4–6	L	3–4
8	04–19–1969	at Chicago White Sox	5–1	W	4–4
9-I	04–20–1969	at Chicago White Sox	2–3	L	4–5
10-II	04–20–1969	at Chicago White Sox	3–13	L	4–6
11	04–21–1969	at Kansas City Royals	4–1	W	5–6
12	04–22–1969	at Kansas City Royals	1–2	L	5–7
13	04–23–1969	at Kansas City Royals	3–4	L	5–8
14	04–25–1969	vs Oakland Athletics	2–14	L	5–9
15	04–26–1969	vs Oakland Athletics	6–3	W	6–9
16	04–27–1969	vs Oakland Athletics	5–13	L	6–10
17	04–29–1969	vs California Angels	1–0	W	7–10
18	04–30–1969	at Minnesota Twins	4–6	L	7–11
19	05–01–1969	at Minnesota Twins	1–4	L	7–12
20	05–02–1969	at Oakland Athletics	7–8	L	7–13
21	05–03–1969	at Oakland Athletics	2–3	L	7–14
22-I	05–04–1969	at Oakland Athletics	6–4	W	8–14
23-II	05–04–1969	at Oakland Athletics	7–11	L	8–15
24	05–06–1969	vs Boston Red Sox	2–12	L	8–16
25	05–07–1969	vs Boston Red Sox	4–5	L	8–17
26	05–09–1969	vs Washington Senators	2–0	W	9–17
27	05–10–1969	vs Washington Senators	16–13	W	10–17
28	05–11–1969	vs Washington Senators	6–5	W	11–17
29	05–12–1969	vs New York Yankees	8–4	W	12–17
30	05–13–1969	vs New York Yankees	5–3	W	13–17
31	05–14–1969	vs New York Yankees	4–5	L	13–18
32	05–16–1969	at Boston Red Sox	10–9	W	14–18
33	05–17–1969	at Boston Red Sox	1–6	L	14–19
34	05–18–1969	at Boston Red Sox	9–6	W	15–19
35	05–20–1969	at Washington Senators	5–6	L	15–20
36	05–21–1969	at Washington Senators	6–2	W	16–20
37	05–22–1969	at Washington Senators	7–6	W	17–20
38	05–23–1969	at Cleveland Indians	1–7	L	17–21

1969 Seattle Pilots Schedule (cont.)

GAME	DATE / BOX SCORE	OPPONENT	SCORE	DECISION	RECORD
39	05–24–1969	at Cleveland Indians	8–2	W	18–21
40	05–25–1969	at Cleveland Indians	3–2	W	19–21
41	05–27–1969	vs Baltimore Orioles	8–1	W	20–21
42	05–28–1969	vs Baltimore Orioles	5–9	L	20–22
43	05–30–1969	vs Detroit Tigers	5–8	L	20–23
44	05–31–1969	vs Detroit Tigers	2–3	L	20–24
45	06–01–1969	vs Detroit Tigers	8–7	W	21–24
46	06–02–1969	vs Cleveland Indians	8–2	W	22–24
47	06–03–1969	vs Cleveland Indians	1–3	L	22–25
48	06–04–1969	vs Cleveland Indians	4–10	L	22–26
49	06–06–1969	at Baltimore Orioles	1–5	L	22–27
50	06–07–1969	at Baltimore Orioles	0–10	L	22–28
51	06–08–1969	at Baltimore Orioles	7–5	W	23–28
52	06–09–1969	at Detroit Tigers	3–2	W	24–28
53	06–10–1969	at Detroit Tigers	0–5	L	24–29
54	06–11–1969	at Detroit Tigers	3–4	L	24–30
55	06–13–1969	at New York Yankees	2–1	W	25–30
56	06–14–1969	at New York Yankees	5–4	W	26–30
57	06–15–1969	at New York Yankees	0–4	L	26–31
58	06–16–1969	at Chicago White Sox	3–8	L	26–32
59-I	06–18–1969	at Chicago White Sox	3–7	L	26–33
60-II	06–18–1969	at Chicago White Sox	6–5	W	27–33
61	06–19–1969	at Chicago White Sox	10–13	L	27–34
62-I	06–20–1969	vs Kansas City Royals	5–3	W	28–34
63-II	06–20–1969	vs Kansas City Royals	2–6	L	28–35
64	06–21–1969	vs Kansas City Royals	1–0	W	29–35
65	06–22–1969	vs Kansas City Royals	5–1	W	30–35
66-I	06–24–1969	vs Chicago White Sox	4–6	L	30–36
67-II	06–24–1969	vs Chicago White Sox	6–7	L	30–37
68	06–25–1969	vs Chicago White Sox	3–1	W	31–37
69	06–26–1969	vs Chicago White Sox	3–2	W	32–37
70-I	06–27–1969	at California Angels	3–5	L	32–38
71-II	06–27–1969	at California Angels	5–2	W	33–38
72	06–28–1969	at California Angels	3–0	W	34–38
73	06–29–1969	at California Angels	2–8	L	34–39
74	07–01–1969	at Oakland Athletics	7–1	W	35–39
75	07–02–1969	at Oakland Athletics	0–5	L	35–40
76	07–03–1969	at Oakland Athletics	4–6	L	35–41
77-I	07–04–1969	at Kansas City Royals	2–13	L	35–42

1969 Seattle Pilots Schedule (cont.)

GAME	DATE / BOX SCORE	OPPONENT	SCORE	DECISION	RECORD
78-II	07–04–1969	at Kansas City Royals	2–3	L	35–43
79	07–05–1969	at Kansas City Royals	4–6	L	35–44
80	07–06–1969	at Kansas City Royals	9–3	W	36–44
81	07–07–1969	vs California Angels	1–5	L	36–45
82	07 08–1969	vs California Angels	3–1	W	37–45
83-I	07–09–1969	vs California Angels	8–0	W	38–45
84-II	07–09–1969	vs California Angels	0–5	L	38–46
85	07–11–1969	at Minnesota Twins	3–9	L	38–47
86	07–12–1969	at Minnesota Twins	1–11	L	38–48
87-I	07–13–1969	at Minnesota Twins	2–5	L	38–49
88-II	07–13–1969	at Minnesota Twins	4–5	L	38–50
89	07–15–1969	vs Oakland Athletics	2–6	L	38–51
90	07–16–1969	vs Oakland Athletics	1–6	L	38–52
91	07–17–1969	vs Oakland Athletics	2–8	L	38–53
92-I	07–18–1969	vs Minnesota Twins	2–1	W	39–53
93-II	07–18–1969	vs Minnesota Twins	3–2	W	40–53
94	07–19–1969	vs Minnesota Twins	7–11	L	40–54
95	07–20–1969	vs Minnesota Twins	0–4	L	40–55
96	07–24–1969	vs Boston Red Sox	8–6	W	41–55
97	07–25–1969	vs Boston Red Sox	6–7	L	41–56
98	07–26–1969	vs Boston Red Sox	8–5	W	42–56
99	07–27–1969	vs Boston Red Sox	3–5	L	42–57
100	07–29–1969	vs Washington Senators	2–4	L	42–58
101	07–30–1969	vs Washington Senators	4–3	W	43–58
102	07–31–1969	vs Washington Senators	6–7	L	43–59
103	08–01–1969	vs New York Yankees	2–4	L	43–60
104	08–02–1969	vs New York Yankees	4–5	L	43–61
105	08 03 1969	vs New York Yankees	3–5	L	43–62
106	08–05–1969	at Boston Red Sox	9–2	W	44–62
107	08–06–1969	at Boston Red Sox	6–5	W	45–62
108	08–07–1969	at Boston Red Sox	4–5	L	45–63
109	08–08–1969	at Washington Senators	3–10	L	45–64
110	08–09–1969	at Washington Senators	8–6	W	46–64
111	08–10–1969	at Washington Senators	5–7	L	46–65
112	08–11–1969	at Cleveland Indians	8–2	W	47–65
113	08–12–1969	at Cleveland Indians	5–6	L	47–66
114	08–13–1969	at Cleveland Indians	5–3	W	48–66
115	08–15–1969	vs Baltimore Orioles	1–2	L	48–67
116	08–16–1969	vs Baltimore Orioles	3–15	L	48–68

1969 Seattle Pilots Schedule (cont.)

GAME	DATE / BOX SCORE	OPPONENT	SCORE	DECISION	RECORD
117	08–17–1969	vs Baltimore Orioles	1–4	L	48–69
118	08–18–1969	vs Baltimore Orioles	3–12	L	48–70
119	08–19–1969	vs Detroit Tigers	3–5	L	48–71
120	08–20–1969	vs Detroit Tigers	3–4	L	48–72
121	08–21–1969	vs Detroit Tigers	6–7	L	48–73
122	08–22–1969	vs Cleveland Indians	8–9	L	48–74
123	08–23–1969	vs Cleveland Indians	3–7	L	48–75
124	08–24–1969	vs Cleveland Indians	5–6	L	48–76
125	08–26–1969	at Baltimore Orioles	2–1	W	49–76
126	08–27–1969	at Baltimore Orioles	2–7	L	49–77
127	08–28–1969	at Baltimore Orioles	3–4	L	49–78
128	08–29–1969	at Detroit Tigers	1–6	L	49–79
129	08–30–1969	at Detroit Tigers	3–4	L	49–80
130	08–31–1969	at Detroit Tigers	2–7	L	49–81
131-I	09–01–1969	at New York Yankees	1–6	L	49–82
132-II	09–01–1969	at New York Yankees	5–1	W	50–82
133	09–02–1969	at New York Yankees	4–5	L	50–83
134	09–04–1969	vs Kansas City Royals	3–5	L	50–84
135	09–05–1969	vs Kansas City Royals	5–4	W	51–84
136	09–06–1969	vs Kansas City Royals	2–6	L	51–85
137	09–07–1969	vs Kansas City Royals	7–6	W	52–85
138-I	09–08–1969	vs Chicago White Sox	2–1	W	53–85
139-II	09–08–1969	vs Chicago White Sox	5–1	W	54–85
140	09–10–1969	at Oakland Athletics	9–4	W	55–85
141	09–11–1969	at Oakland Athletics	3–6	L	55–86
142-I	09–12–1969	vs California Angels	4–1	W	56–86
143-II	09–12–1969	vs California Angels	1–1	T	56–86–1
144-I	09–13–1969	vs California Angels	6–4	W	57–86–1
145-II	09–13–1969	vs California Angels	2–4	L	57–87–1
146	09–14–1969	vs California Angels	2–4	L	57–88–1
147	09–15–1969	at Kansas City Royals	3–2	W	58–88–1
148	09–16–1969	at Kansas City Royals	1–2	L	58–89–1
149-I	09–17–1969	at Chicago White Sox	4–6	L	58–90–1
150-II	09–17–1969	at Chicago White Sox	1–2	L	58–91–1
151	09–19–1969	at Minnesota Twins	1–2	L	58–92–1
152	09–20–1969	at Minnesota Twins	2–3	L	58–93–1
153	09–21–1969	at Minnesota Twins	4–3	W	59–93–1
154	09–22–1969	at California Angels	5–4	W	60–93–1
155	09–23–1969	at California Angels	4–5	L	60–94–1

1969 Seattle Pilots Schedule (cont.)

GAME	DATE / BOX SCORE	OPPONENT	SCORE	DECISION	RECORD
156	09–24–1969	at California Angels	1–3	L	60–95–1
157	09–25–1969	vs Minnesota Twins	5–1	W	61–95–1
158	09–26–1969	vs Minnesota Twins	4–3	W	62–95–1
159-I	09–28–1969	vs Minnesota Twins	2–5	L	62–96–1
160-II	09–28–1969	vs Minnesota Twins	4–1	W	63–96–1
161	09–30–1969	vs Oakland Athletics	4–8	L	63–97–1
162	10–01–1969	vs Oakland Athletics	4–3	W	64–97–1
163	10–02–1969	vs Oakland Athletics	1–3	L	64–98–1

Data courtesy of Baseball-Almanac.com.

#12 | In Need of Forgiveness

The 1973 San Diego Padres (60–102)

The San Diego Padres came into the National League in 1969 as part of the same expansion that brought about the short-lived Seattle Pilots. They took their name from a Pacific Coast League (PCL) team that began playing in San Diego in 1936 and won the PCL championship in 1937 behind 18-year-old outfielder Ted Williams. With constant sunshine, warm weather, and a rich history in the Pacific Coast League, San Diego was a natural choice for a major league expansion team when the National League decided to expand in 1969. The team's original owner was C. Arnholt Smith, a prominent San Diego businessperson and former owner of the PCL Padres. Smith was involved in banking, tuna fishing, hotels, real estate, and an airline.

The new team got a new stadium to play in. Built in 1967 to house both baseball and football, cavernous Jack Murphy Stadium was not friendly to hitters: the center-field wall was 420 feet from home plate, and the left- and right-field power alleys were 375 feet away. It also had walls 17 feet tall, meaning that one had to really hit a blast to clear those walls. However, the stadium was new and gleaming, and it helped to attract fans to see their very bad new baseball team play.[1]

Buzzie Bavasi, the longtime general manager of the Brooklyn and Los Angeles Dodgers, was hired to be the team's first president and general manager, meaning that a veteran and knowledgeable baseball man would be in charge of the team's day-to-day operations in the team's new stadium. In spite of these pluses, the team really struggled. The Padres finished last in each of their first six seasons in the National League West, losing 100 games or more four times. There were few bright spots for the new franchise, which had little talent to work with.

1970 San Diego Padres (Baseball Hall of Fame Library, Cooperstown, NY)

The one real bright spot during the team's first years was first baseman Nate Colbert, taken from the Houston Astros organization during the expansion draft. Colbert was a big man who was a reliable slugger. He had his best day in the major leagues on August 1, 1972, when he cracked 5 homers and drove in 13 runs in a doubleheader. He tied the record for homers in a doubleheader and shattered Stan Musial's record of 11 runs batted in. The Padres swept the Braves 9–0 and 11–7 that day. Colbert slugged 38 homers and drove in 111 runs in 1972, logging 67 extra base hits. He finished a remarkable eighth in the National League most valuable player balloting in 1972, finishing second to Cincinnati Reds Hall of Famer Johnny Bench in homers, and set a record that still stands for driving in the highest percentage of his team's runs over the course of a season. He was the Padres' representative to the National League All-Star team for the years 1971–1973 and still holds the franchise record for career home runs.

Preston Gomez managed the Padres from 1969 to the beginning of the 1972 season, losing 110 games in 1969, 99 in 1970, 100 in 1971, and another 7 in 11 games in 1972. Gomez was fired. Third-base coach Don Zimmer, a baseball lifer who survived the 1962 New York Mets, became the team's new manager. Zimmer posted a 54–88 record for the rest of the season, lending

Nate Colbert gets congratulations from the
Padres' batboy (AP Photo/CEK)

some hope that the Padres might finally be improving. Zimmer did the best he could. "I always had an answer for whatever move I made. Maybe it wasn't the answer they wanted to hear," declared Zimmer, "but I always had a reason for what I did." However, that optimism was not warranted. Zimmer lasted only one full season as manager of the Padres, 1973.

Other than Colbert, the Padres' opening day lineup had little talent to offer. The season opened hopefully enough, with the Padres winning their first two games against the Los Angeles Dodgers. They promptly reeled off five straight losses and never came close to being above .500 again for the rest of the season. They had a six-game losing streak and then lost 10 in a row in June. They followed that with an eight-game losing streak in July. When it was all said and done, the Padres finished 60–102, and were shut out 19 times. They finished 39 games out first place, and 16½ games behind the fifth-place Atlanta Braves. The Padres were undisputedly the worst team in the National League that year. Zimmer was fired as manager after the end of the season.

Only 611,826 fans clicked the turnstiles at Jack Murphy Stadium for the entire 1973 season, for an average attendance of 7,553 per game. The lack of attendance, combined with the team's ongoing lack of success, meant that Arnholt Smith had major financial difficulties. Unless something changed soon, Smith would run out of money and would have to sell the team.

The Padres' season ended strangely. The National League East had only one team finish above .500—the New York Mets—who won the division with a pathetic 82–79 record. However, as the season wound down, the Mets dueled with the Pittsburgh Pirates for the division crown. A mid-season game between the Padres and the Pirates was rained out and would only be made up if it became necessary to do so. Although the Padres believed that their season ended on September 29, it didn't. Instead, they had to play the makeup game with the Pirates, which was played in Pittsburgh.

The Padres won the game and eliminated the Pirates, ending the most bizarre season that the National League has ever seen.

The Padres actually fielded a ball club that was occasionally capable of scoring some runs. They had a team batting average of .241 with 112 homers and 516 RBIs, including several players who put up respectable numbers at the plate.

Colbert had another good year, although his power production dropped off significantly from his 1972 career highs due to a bad back. In spite of the physical problems, Colbert still hit .270 with 22 homers and 80 RBIs. However, he also had 146 strikeouts in 529 at bats, or one every 3.7 at bats. Outfielder Clarence "Cito" Gaston hit .250 with 16 homers and 57 RBIs. Third baseman Dave Roberts hit .286 with 21 homers and 64 RBIs in 127 games even though he was a defensive liability. Rookie outfielder Johnny Grubb had an excellent season. Grubb hit a respectable .311 with 8 homers and 37 RBIs in 113 games as the team's lead-off hitter. Bespectacled catcher Fred Kendall had a career year, hitting .282 with 10 homers and 39 RBIs in 145 games.

The team's pitching staff left a great deal to be desired. Dr. Steve Arlin, who was also a practicing dentist in the off-season, was the staff ace. Arlin went 11–14 with an ERA of 5.10 and nearly no-hit the Phillies in July for what would have been the franchise's first no-hitter. Righty Bill Greif went 10–17, but had a respectable ERA of 3.21. Righty Clay Kirby posted a dismal record of 8–18 with an ERA of 4.79. The bullpen featured the likes of Vicente Romo, who had a record of 2–3 with a 3.70 ERA and 7 saves. Workhorse lefty Rich Troedson, a rookie, went 7–9 with an ERA of 4.25 with one save in 152.1 innings. The team had an ERA of 4.16.

Two rookies made their major league debuts during the course of the 1973 season. Randy Jones, a 23-year-old southpaw pitcher, made his big league debut on June 16, 1973. Jones appeared in 20 games in 1973, going 7–6 with a respectable ERA of 3.16. Two years later, in 1975, Jones went 20–12 with a 2.24 ERA and won the Cy Young Award in 1976, posting an outstanding 22–14 record with a 2.74 ERA. However, Jones pitched 600 innings those two years, which took a major toll on his arm. Jones was never the same again after 1976 and was out of baseball with a career losing record by 1982. However, for two years, he was one of the finest pitchers in the game, the first really effective pitcher to emerge from the Padres' farm system, and the first Padre to develop a following of his own.

Three days after Jones made his debut on June 16, the Padres promoted a 21-year-old outfielder from St. Paul, Minnesota, named Dave Winfield.

Winfield stood 6-foot 6-inches tall and weighed 220 pounds. He was an awesome physical specimen and an outstanding all-around athlete. Winfield starred at two sports—basketball and baseball—at the University of Minnesota. He was the most valuable player of the College World Series in 1973, as a pitcher. Upon graduating, he was drafted by the Padres, the Atlanta Hawks of the National Basketball Association, the Utah Stars of the American Basketball Association, and, even though he had never played football in college, by the Minnesota Vikings of the National Football League. He was the first man ever drafted in three different sports. Winfield chose baseball, and was in the major leagues by June of his first professional season.

He singled in his first major league at bat. He appeared in 56 games in 1973, hitting a solid .277 with 3 homers and 12 RBIs in 141 at bats. Winfield played the outfield, where his rifle of an arm could be used to its best advantage. Thus began a Hall of Fame career in which Dave Winfield played 22 years, amassed 3,110 hits, 475 homers, 1,833 RBIs, and a career batting average of .283. He spent eight of those years with the Padres, and when he was inducted into the Baseball Hall of Fame in 2001, he went in as a Padre. The Padres, in turn, retired his uniform number 31. Winfield was the first great player to emerge from the Padres' farm system, and he provided a portent of better days to come.

Two other members of the 1973 Padres had significant achievements. Thirty-two-year-old catcher Pat Corrales, who appeared in 29 games for the Padres in his final season in the major leagues, retired and became a coach. In 1978, he became the manager of the Texas Rangers, and in 1983, he led the Philadelphia Phillies to the National League pennant, but lost to Baltimore in the World Series. Outfielder Cito Gaston retired at the end of the 1978 season and also became a coach. Partway through the 1989 season, Gaston was named manager of the Toronto Blue Jays, and he successfully led that team to two consecutive World Series championships in 1992 and 1993. Two players of mediocre talent, who proved to be excellent major league managers, came from the same terrible Padres teams of the early 1970s.

The Padres did not break the .500 mark for a season until they won the National League West in 1984, and their lack of success nearly cost the city its team. After the 1973 season, the Padres were on the verge of being sold to grocery magnate Joseph Danzansky, who intended to relocate the team to Washington, DC, which had lost its American League team to Texas after the 1971 season. New uniforms were designed, and Topps issued its 1974 baseball cards with "Washington National League" on about half of the Padres' players' cards. A San Diego judge ruled that he could not stop the team from moving, but determined that the city could recover damages since 15 years remained on the lease for Jack Murphy Stadium. Not knowing what a jury might find as damages for a 15-year lease for a major league baseball team, Smith changed his mind and elected to sell the team to Ray Kroc, the co-founder of the McDonald's restaurant chain. Kroc was determined the keep the team in San Diego, and it remains there to this day.

Since the dark days of the early 1970s, the Padres have won the National League West five times, in 1984, 1996, 1998, 2005, and 2006. They won the National League pennant twice, in 1984 and 1998, losing in the World Series both times. However, the prospect of simply going .500 was still a long way off in 1973. The Padres remained mired in their misery until they finally finished above .500 once in 1978. They did not break the magical .500 mark again until 1985, 15 years after the team was founded.

1973 San Diego Padres Stats: Fielding

NAME	POS	GAMES	PO	A	E	DP	TC/G	FLD%
Dwain Anderson	SS	39	42	81	9	15	3.4	.932
Dwain Anderson	3B	6	0	12	2	0	2.3	.857
Steve Arlin	P	34	11	21	0	4	0.9	1.000
Mike Caldwell	P	55	12	29	2	1	0.8	.953
Dave Campbell	2B	27	68	73	3	18	5.3	.979
Dave Campbell	1B	3	10	0	0	0	3.3	1.000
Dave Campbell	3B	2	1	3	1	1	2.5	.800
Nate Colbert	1B	144	1,300	98	11	124	9.8	.992
Mike Corkins	P	47	8	8	4	0	0.4	.800
Pat Corrales	C	28	130	6	2	1	4.9	.986
Bob Davis	C	5	32	0	2	0	6.8	.941
Cito Gaston	OF	119	198	16	12	4	1.9	.947
Bill Greif	P	36	11	24	1	0	1.0	.972
Johnny Grubb	OF	102	229	11	3	1	2.4	.988
Johnny Grubb	3B	2	0	0	0	0	0.0	.000
Enzo Hernandez	SS	67	106	190	7	42	4.5	.977
Dave Hilton	3B	47	40	88	4	11	2.8	.970
Dave Hilton	2B	23	39	53	2	8	4.1	.979
Randy Jones	P	20	3	24	1	0	1.4	.964
Fred Kendall	C	138	749	64	13	7	6.0	.984
Clay Kirby	P	34	9	19	3	1	0.9	.903

1973 San Diego Padres Stats: Fielding (cont.)

NAME	POS	GAMES	PO	A	E	DP	TC/G	FLD%
Leron Lee	OF	84	154	7	5	0	2.0	.970
Gene Locklear	LF	37	77	2	4	0	2.2	.952
Dave Marshall	RF	8	14	0	0	0	1.8	1.000
Don Mason	2B	1	1	2	1	1	4.0	.750
Bob Miller	P	18	0	2	0	0	0.1	1.000
Jerry Morales	OF	100	214	5	2	1	2.2	.991
Rich Morales	2B	79	176	239	5	45	5.3	.988
Rich Morales	SS	10	15	24	0	4	3.9	1.000
Ivan Murrell	OF	37	69	2	3	0	2.0	.959
Ivan Murrell	1B	24	180	14	2	14	8.2	.990
Fred Norman	P	12	4	14	0	0	1.5	1.000
Dave Roberts	3B	111	77	245	20	25	3.1	.942
Dave Roberts	2B	12	15	31	4	6	4.2	.920
Vicente Romo	P	49	5	15	2	1	0.4	.909
Gary Ross	P	58	8	10	0	2	0.3	1.000
Frank Snook	P	18	2	7	0	0	0.5	1.000
Derrel Thomas	SS	74	115	227	32	39	5.1	.914
Derrel Thomas	2B	47	96	97	5	27	4.2	.975
Rich Troedson	P	50	5	34	0	0	0.8	1.000
Dave Winfield	OF	36	64	1	3	0	1.9	.956
Dave Winfield	1B	1	1	0	0	0	1.0	1.000
TEAM TOTALS		—	4,290	1,798	170	403	3.4	.973

Data courtesy of Baseball-Almanac.com.

1973 San Diego Padres Stats: Hitting

NAME	POS	GAMES	AVG	SLG	AB	H	2B	3B	HR	AB/HR	R	RBI	BB	SO	SB
Dwain Anderson	SS	53	.121	.121	107	13	0	0	0	0.0	11	3	14	29	2
Steve Arlin	P	34	.167	.183	60	10	1	0	0	0.0	2	5	4	21	0
Mike Caldwell	P	56	.143	.143	35	5	0	0	0	0.0	2	0	1	12	0
Dave Campbell	2B	33	.224	.255	98	22	3	0	0	0.0	2	8	7	15	1
Nate Colbert	1B	145	.270	.450	529	143	25	2	22	24.0	73	80	54	146	9
Mike Corkins	P	48	.212	.515	33	7	1	0	3	11.0	6	5	2	14	0
Pat Corrales	C	29	.208	.264	72	15	2	1	0	0.0	7	3	6	10	0
Bob Davis	C	5	.091	.091	11	1	0	0	0	0.0	1	0	0	5	0
Cito Gaston	OF	133	.250	.405	476	119	18	4	16	29.8	51	57	20	88	0
Bill Greif	P	36	.098	.098	61	6	0	0	0	0.0	3	1	4	28	0
Johnny Grubb	OF	113	.311	.445	389	121	22	3	8	48.6	52	37	37	50	9
Enzo Hernandez	SS	70	.223	.239	247	55	2	1	0	0.0	26	9	17	14	15
Dave Hilton	3B	70	.197	.299	234	46	9	0	5	46.8	21	16	19	35	2
Randy Jones	P	20	.167	.188	48	8	1	0	0	0.0	2	2	1	22	0
Fred Kendall	C	145	.282	.396	507	143	22	3	10	50.7	39	59	30	35	3
Clay Kirby	P	35	.093	.111	54	5	1	0	0	0.0	1	1	1	21	0
Leron Lee	OF	118	.237	.297	333	79	7	2	3	111.0	36	30	33	61	4
Gene Locklear	OF	67	.240	.351	154	37	6	1	3	51.3	20	25	21	22	9
Dave Marshall	OF	39	.286	.338	49	14	5	0	0	0.0	4	4	8	9	0
Don Mason	2B	8	.000	.000	8	0	0	0	0	0.0	0	0	0	2	0
Bob Miller	P	18	.000	.000	2	0	0	0	0	0.0	0	0	0	1	0
Jerry Morales	OF	122	.281	.420	388	109	23	2	9	43.1	47	34	27	55	6

1973 San Diego Padres Stats: Hitting (cont.)

NAME	POS	GAMES	AVG	SLG	AB	H	2B	3B	HR	AB/HR	R	RBI	BB	SO	SB
Rich Morales	2B	90	.164	.197	244	40	6	1	0	0.0	9	16	27	36	0
Ivan Murrell	OF	93	.229	.429	210	48	13	1	9	23.3	23	21	2	52	2
Fred Norman	P	12	.136	.136	22	3	0	0	0	0.0	1	0	1	5	0
Dave Roberts	3B	127	.286	.472	479	137	20	3	21	22.8	56	64	17	83	11
Vicente Romo	P	49	.125	.125	16	2	0	0	0	0.0	2	1	1	2	0
Gary Ross	P	58	.000	.000	4	0	0	0	0	0.0	0	0	0	2	0
Frank Snook	P	18	.000	.000	2	0	0	0	0	0.0	0	0	0	2	0
Derrel Thomas	SS	113	.238	.260	404	96	7	1	0	0.0	41	22	34	52	15
Rich Troedson	P	50	.175	.175	40	7	0	0	0	0.0	1	1	1	18	0
Dave Winfield	OF	56	.277	.383	141	39	4	1	3	47.0	9	12	12	19	0
TEAM TOTALS			.244	.351	5,457	1,330	198	26	112	48.7	548	516	401	966	88

Data courtesy of Baseball-Almanac.com.

1973 San Diego Padres Stats: Pitching

NAME	GAMES	W	L	W%	ERA	GS	CG	IP	HA	BB	SO	SHU
Steve Arlin	34	11	14	.440	5.10	27	7	180.0	156	72	98	3
Mike Caldwell	55	5	14	.263	3.74	13	3	149.0	146	53	86	1
Mike Corkins	47	5	8	.385	4.50	11	2	122.0	130	61	82	0
Bill Greif	36	10	17	.370	3.21	31	9	199.1	181	62	120	3
Randy Jones	20	7	6	.538	3.16	19	6	139.2	129	37	77	1
Clay Kirby	34	8	18	.308	4.79	31	4	191.2	214	66	129	2
Bob Miller	18	0	0	.000	4.11	0	0	30.2	29	12	15	0
Fred Norman	12	1	7	.125	4.26	11	1	74.0	72	29	49	0
Vicente Romo	49	2	3	.400	3.70	1	0	87.2	85	46	51	0
Gary Ross	58	4	4	.500	5.42	0	0	76.1	93	33	44	0
Frank Snook	18	0	2	.000	3.62	0	0	27.1	19	18	13	0
Rich Troedson	50	7	9	.438	4.25	18	2	152.1	167	59	81	0
TEAM TOTALS		60	102	.370	4.16	162	34	1430	1,461	548	845	10

Data courtesy of Baseball-Almanac.com.

#13 | Fundamentally Flawed
The 1988 Baltimore Orioles (54–107)

> Master the Fundamentals: All good ballplayers
> start with the basics, and stick with them to keep
> their standard of performance high.
>> —*Cal Ripken Sr. in* The Ripken Way

The St. Louis Browns team was one of the original franchises of the American League. However, it was the second St. Louis team to have the name "Browns." The original Browns eventually became known as the St. Louis Cardinals and played in the National League (the 1898 Browns are profiled in this book). The Milwaukee Brewers relocated to St. Louis for the 1902 season and were renamed the Browns, joining the American League as one of its charter franchises.

The Browns had a long history of frustration and of losing. From 1902 through 1922, they had only four winning seasons, and won only one American League pennant, in 1944 (losing in the World Series to their crosstown rivals, the Cardinals, 4 games to 2). The team had only 12 winning seasons out of the 52 that they played in St. Louis. With able-bodied talent badly depleted by World War II, the 1945 edition of the Browns featured an outfielder named Pete Gray, who had only one arm.

In 1951, the colorful and controversial Bill Veeck purchased the team. He thought up wild promotions that people either loved or hated, including signing a 3-foot 7-inch, 65-pound midget named Eddie Gaedel to a major league contract. Gaedel, wearing the peculiar number ⅛, went to the plate as a pinch hitter and walked on four pitches. The president of the American League voided Gaedel's contract the next day.

Believing St. Louis was too small to host two major league teams, Veeck launched an all-out campaign to try to drive the Cardinals out of town. The campaign nearly succeeded. Instead, the team was sold to the Busch family of Anheuser-Busch brewing fame, and the Cardinals now had the

1988 Baltimore Orioles (Baseball Hall of Fame Library, Cooperstown, NY)

financial wherewithal to withstand the onslaught. Veeck tried to move the Browns back to Milwaukee, but the other American League owners, who despised Veeck, blocked the move. Instead, the team was sold to a group of investors and moved to Baltimore, Maryland, in the fall 1954.

The new owners changed the team name to the Orioles, and they did all they could to try to disassociate themselves from the losing tradition of St. Louis. With new ownership in place, the team's fortunes gradually changed. By 1966, a young Orioles team loaded with talent defeated the Los Angeles Dodgers in the World Series, beginning a 17-year run of dominating the American League's Eastern Division. They lost to the Miracle Mets in the 1969 World Series, and then defeated the Cincinnati Reds in the 1970 World Series. Featuring four 20-game winners, the 1971 Orioles won the Eastern Division handily, but lost to the Pittsburgh Pirates in the World Series. They won the American League East in 1973 and 1974, and then lost to the Pirates again in the 1979 World Series. They won another World Series championship in 1983, ending a long run of dominance. Over a period of 21 years, the Orioles posted a record of 1,873–1,470, finishing 403 games over .500 for the era. Their organization was the envy of baseball, and was generally considered the finest organization in the game during this period.

By 1988, five years removed from their last World Series championship, things had changed dramatically for the Orioles. The team's farm system, long the envy of baseball, had been depleted. Earl Weaver, who led them to so many wins, retired in 1982. Joe Altobelli, who won the 1983 World Series, was fired during the 1985 season. Weaver briefly returned to manage the team, but lasted only the partial 1985 season and the 1986 season before retiring again. Cal Ripken Sr. who spent more than 35 years in the Orioles' system as player, coach, and manager, took the helm in 1987. The team went 67–95 and finished sixth in the American League East.

Ripken had one real distinction: He was the first major league manager to manage two of his sons at the same time. Younger son Billy played second base and older son Cal Jr. played shortstop. The 1988 edition of the Orioles featured two first-ballot Hall of Famers in Cal Jr. and first baseman Eddie Murray. Ripken and Murray, who were both in the prime of their careers in 1988, each retired with more than 3,000 career hits and combined for nearly 950 homers between them. A big right-handed pitcher with an overpowering fastball named Curt Schilling also made his major league debut that year.

Fans didn't know what to expect. The Orioles lost 42 of their final 56 games to end the 1987 season. Management spent the off-season retooling the roster such that only 11 players from the 1987 season opener were on the 1988 season opening roster. The team was one of the older teams in baseball, and it was, by far, the slowest team in the majors. The O's lost their Opening Day game to the Milwaukee Brewers 12–0 before a Memorial Stadium record crowd of 52,395 fans. "You can't judge us by one game," declared pitcher Mike Boddicker. He was wrong. It was about to get a lot worse.

The Orioles reeled off 21 consecutive losses to begin the season. "We lost in every way," said second baseman Billy Ripken. "We scored runs and gave up more, and then sometimes when we didn't score, we gave up just a little, but it was enough." Manager Ripken was fired six games into the losing streak and was replaced by Orioles Hall of Famer Frank Robinson. Before the streak ended, President Ronald Reagan expressed his sympathy for the team's plight, and priests and psychologists offered their assistance. The streak looked like this:

1988 Baltimore Orioles Losing Streak

GAME	DATE	OPPONENT	SCORE	DECISION	RECORD
1	04-04-1988	vs Milwaukee Brewers	0-12	L	0-1
2	04-06-1988	vs Milwaukee Brewers	1-3	L	0-2
3	04-08-1988	at Cleveland Indians	0-3	L	0-3
4	04-09-1988	at Cleveland Indians	1-12	L	0-4
5	04-10-1988	at Cleveland Indians	3-6	L	0-5
6	04-11-1988	at Cleveland Indians	2-7	L	0-6
7	04-12-1988	vs Kansas City Royals	1-6	L	0-7
8	04-13-1988	vs Kansas City Royals	3-9	L	0-8
9	04-14-1988	vs Kansas City Royals	3-4	L	0-9
10	04-15-1988	vs Cleveland Indians	2-3	L	0-10
11	04-16-1988	vs Cleveland Indians	0-1	L	0-11
12	04-17-1988	vs Cleveland Indians	1-4	L	0-12
13	04-19-1988	at Milwaukee Brewers	5-9	L	0-13
14	04-20-1988	at Milwaukee Brewers	6-8	L	0-14
15	04-21-1988	at Milwaukee Brewers	1-7	L	0-15
16	04-22-1988	at Kansas City Royals	1-13	L	0-16
17	04-23-1988	at Kansas City Royals	3-4	L	0-17
18	04-24-1988	at Kansas City Royals	1-3	L	0-18
19	04-26-1988	at Minnesota Twins	2-4	L	0-19
20	04-27-1988	at Minnesota Twins	6-7	L	0-20
21	04-28-1988	at Minnesota Twins	2-4	L	0-21

Data courtesy of Baseball-Almanac.com.

The players kept hoping it would get better. After the fifth loss, reliever Tom Niedenfuer said, "Every team in the majors is going to lose five games in a row at some point. Ours are just coming at the beginning." After game seven, the team had been outscored 49-8 for the season to date. On April 19, they lost to the Brewers again in an epic show of ineptitude, 9-5, featuring four errors, two passed balls, two missed signs, a base-running blunder, a misjudged fly ball, and a blown lead. The loss tied the 1904 Washington Senators and the 1920 Detroit Tigers for most losses at the beginning of the season, a record that they shattered a day later. The next day, a sign appeared on the outfield wall: 0-162. THAT'S WHY WE CALL THEM THE O'S. When the Brewers completed their series sweep on April 21, the Orioles broke their 34-year-old franchise mark for most consecutive losses with 15. When Bret Saberhagen beat them 3-1 in Kansas City on April 24, the team boasted an anemic .198 batting average for the season. The next day, President Reagan called to encourage them and asked what he could do to help. Manager Frank Robinson responded by asking the Gipper if he could play first base. However, it was not enough. The Orioles still lost their 19th straight game on April 26.

"You can laugh about it now, but at the time, going through it, that was miserable," recalled reliever Mark Thurmond. "Absolute torture. I remember waking up and thinking 'Hey, we're already out of it.' That was pretty depressing. We were not a very good team. That was obvious. There were some players who could play and put up some good numbers at other places, but anything that could go wrong did. Add that to the fact that we weren't very good to begin with, and you have a streak."

When "the Birds" lost again on April 27, they tied the 1906 Boston Red Sox and the 1916 and 1943 Philadelphia Athletics for the American League's longest losing streaks. "It's like World Series pressure," said shortstop Ripken, who knew what he was talking about. "That's the only way to describe it. That's the way it is." Another Oriole showed remarkable candor and honesty when asked about the epic losing streak. "We got a bunch of old guys who are over the hill, or going over it, and a bunch of young guys who just can't play baseball," he said. "We're trying. We just don't have any talent."

General Manager Roland Hemond had led the 1983 Chicago White Sox to a division championship; ironically, the Sox lost to the Orioles in the American League Championship Series. Hemond had brought an extra suit to the ballpark on the night that the Sox clinched the division. The suit was drenched in champagne and was later put on display in a glass case at Comiskey Park. After the 20th consecutive loss, White Sox owner Eddie Einhorn sent the suit to Hemond, still sticky with champagne, to wear. When it arrived, Hemond quickly put it on. Although Hemond hoped it would work to break the streak, he was disappointed.

The O's shattered the record for futility the next night, as the streak culminated with an American League record 21 straight losses, prompting legendary baseball columnist Tom Boswell to write, "This could be the day. Please, let this be the day. It is written on every Orioles face on every pitch. They have the World Series look. Drawn, worried, faces so seriously, studiously intent that the idea of a smile or a word of idle infield chatter is unthinkable. You need binoculars to see that truth in the Baltimore Orioles' faces, but it is there, plain as 21 losses in a row."

They finally won for the first time that year on April 29, during their 22nd game of the season, defeating the Milwaukee Brewers 9–0, featuring homers by Cal Ripken Jr. and Murray and with Hemond still wearing the champagne-soaked suit. "It didn't smell too good, but it worked," recalled Hemond. "After the last out, a friend sitting behind me said, 'What about it, Roland?' He poured beer all over me."

Although their epic streak was finally over, the Orioles had set one major league record—for most consecutive losses to open the season—and one American League record—for most consecutive losses—along the way. By the time they finally won their first game of the season, the O's were already pretty much out of the pennant race, and April hadn't ended yet.

On top of everything else that went wrong that season, team owner Edward Bennett Williams died on August 21 after a long battle with cancer, and longtime trainer Ralph Salvon also died during the season. With all that the Orioles players had to deal with on the field, the off-field distractions only made things worse.

On May 2, 1988, the Orioles released their popular longtime left-handed starter Scott McGregor, who had spent his entire career in Baltimore. In a 13-year career, McGregor went 138–108, including a 20-win season in 1980. By 1988, his array of junk was no longer getting major league hitters out, and it was clear that he was done. After receiving the news, McGregor went back into the clubhouse to pack his bags. Catcher Terry Kennedy summed it all up nicely when he said, "You lucky SOB: you don't have to play here anymore."

The Orioles ended the season at 54–107, finishing 34½ games behind the division-winning Boston Red Sox and 23½ games behind the sixth-place Cleveland Indians. They lost 16 of their last 19 games. They had only 20 road wins for the season. Their last home game ended with yet another loss. After losing their last home game to the Yankees, 5–1, the players removed their jerseys and raffled them off to fans as part of a promotion, providing a fitting ending to a strange season in which the Orioles lost their first nine home games. Despite a league-high seven lost home dates due to weather, the Birds still drew more than 1.6 million fans.

Murray hit .284 with 28 homers and 84 RBIs in a subpar season. Cal Ripken Jr. hit .264 with 23 homers and 81 RBIs. Outfielder Fred Lynn, nearing the end of a fine career, was only a shadow of the player who had electrified the American League during the 1970s. He hit only .252 with 18 homers and a meager 37 RBIs. Outfielder Joe Orsulak hit a respectable .288 with 8 homers and 27 RBIs. Second baseman Billy Ripken hit an anemic .207 with only 2 homers and 34 RBIs. The Orioles had a miserable team batting average of .238, with 137 homers and only 517 RBIs in the worst season of their franchise history. Their .238 mark was the lowest team batting average in the major leagues in six years.

The pitching wasn't much better. Mike Boddicker, who was a mainstay of the 1983 world championship team, posted a 6–12 mark with a respectable 3.86 ERA, and he was the best of a bad pitching staff. Righty Jose Bautista went 6–15 with a 4.30 ERA. Southpaw Jeff Ballard went 8–13 with a 4.40 ERA. Righty Jay Tibbs went 4–15 with an ugly 5.39 ERA. Veteran righty Mike Morgan went 1–6 with a 5.43 ERA. Twenty-one-year-old right-hander Curt Schilling made his major league debut on September 7, 1988. He went 0–3 in four appearances, giving up 22 hits in 14.2 innings and posting an atrocious ERA of 9.82, which was not an auspicious beginning to what became a superb major league career.[1] A total of 23 pitchers toiled unsuccessfully for the Orioles that year, combining for a team ERA of 4.55 and surrendering 1,506 hits in 1,416 innings pitched.

The Orioles also played atrocious defense that year. For a franchise whose history featured superb defense and speed, the 1988 edition's lack of defense was embarrassing. The 1988 Orioles had a team fielding percentage of only .978, the franchise's worst fielding percentage since 1959. This team never had a chance.

Team manager Frank Robinson left the following valediction for his 1988 Orioles: "I'll tell you what about that team. It wasn't that they didn't try. They just didn't have the talent," he said. "It wasn't there. Sometimes we didn't play good baseball, like in the [Seattle] Kingdome when we had three or four guys come over for a ball, and it dropped, and we lost 5–4. But we didn't get blown out but about one or two times in that streak. We just didn't have the talent to win. We tried."

There wasn't much else to say about one of the worst teams in the history of major league baseball. However, the team cleaned house over the winter, including trading away Eddie Murray, who had grown disgruntled in Baltimore. These moves opened up roster slots for talented young players to step up from the minor leagues. The 1989 Orioles went 87–75, and finished in second place in the American League East. Their improvement was the fourth best in the history of major league baseball to date. However, the remarkable turnaround did little to ease the sting of their epic 21-game losing streak to open the 1988 season.

1988 Baltimore Orioles Statmaster: Fielding

NAME	POS	GAMES	PO	A	E	DP	TC/G	FLD%
Don Aase	P	35	2	3	0	1	0.1	1.000
Brady Anderson	CF	49	156	1	3	0	3.3	.981
Jeff Ballard	P	25	9	13	0	3	0.9	1.000
Jose Bautista	P	33	27	11	1	3	1.2	.974
Mike Boddicker	P	21	12	15	2	0	1.4	.931
Butch Davis	OF	10	16	1	0	1	1.7	1.000
Butch Davis	DH	1	0	0	0	0	-	-
Gordon Dillard	P	2	0	1	0	0	0.5	1.000
Jim Dwyer	DH	17	0	0	0	0	-	-
Jim Dwyer	OF	2	3	0	0	0	1.5	1.000
Ken Gerhart	OF	93	192	3	5	1	2.2	.975
Ken Gerhart	DH	3	0	0	0	0	-	-
Rene Gonzales	3B	80	45	153	7	19	2.6	.966
Rene Gonzales	2B	14	17	29	1	6	3.4	.979
Rene Gonzales	SS	2	1	3	0	1	2.0	1.000
Rene Gonzales	RF	1	1	0	0	0	1.0	1.000
Rene Gonzales	1B	1	2	0	0	0	2.0	1.000
John Habyan	P	7	5	1	0	0	0.9	1.000
Pete Harnisch	P	2	2	2	0	0	2.0	1.000
Keith Hughes	RF	31	59	4	2	2	2.1	.969
Keith Hughes	DH	1	0	0	0	0	-	-
Terry Kennedy	C	79	332	23	2	3	4.5	.994
Tito Landrum	OF	12	15	0	0	0	1.3	1.000
Tito Landrum	DH	1	0	0	0	0	-	-
Fred Lynn	OF	83	216	1	2	0	2.6	.991
Fred Lynn	DH	2	0	0	0	0	-	-
Scott McGregor	P	4	1	5	0	0	1.5	1.000
Bob Milacki	P	3	4	3	0	1	2.3	1.000
Mike Morgan	P	22	9	9	0	1	0.8	1.000
Eddie Murray	1B	103	867	106	11	101	9.6	.989
Eddie Murray	DH	58	0	0	0	0	-	-
Carl Nichols	C	13	66	12	1	2	6.1	.987
Carl Nichols	RF	3	5	1	0	0	2.0	1.000
Tom Niedenfuer	P	52	3	5	1	1	0.2	.889
Dickie Noles	P	2	0	0	0	0	0.0	.000
Gregg Olson	P	10	1	2	0	0	0.3	1.000
Joe Orsulak	OF	117	228	6	5	2	2.0	.979
Oswaldo Peraza	P	19	8	11	3	1	1.2	.864

1988 Baltimore Orioles Statmaster: Fielding (cont.)

NAME	POS	GAMES	PO	A	E	DP	TC/G	FLD%
Billy Ripken	2B	149	309	440	12	110	5.1	.984
Billy Ripken	3B	2	1	0	0	0	0.5	1.000
Billy Ripken	DH	1	0	0	0	0	-	-
Cal Ripken, Jr.	SS	161	284	480	21	119	4.9	.973
Wade Rowdon	3B	8	5	13	1	1	2.4	.947
Wade Rowdon	LF	5	2	1	0	0	0.6	1.000
Wade Rowdon	DH	5	0	0	0	0	-	-
Bill Scherrer	P	4	0	0	0	0	0.0	.000
Curt Schilling	P	4	0	0	1	0	0.3	.000
Dave Schmidt	P	41	18	20	1	2	1.0	.974
Rick Schu	3B	72	56	108	11	7	2.4	.937
Rick Schu	DH	9	0	0	0	0	-	-
Rick Schu	1B	4	38	2	0	1	10.0	1.000
Larry Sheets	OF	76	139	9	4	0	2.0	.974
Larry Sheets	DH	50	0	0	0	0	-	-
Larry Sheets	1B	3	20	3	0	3	7.7	1.000
Doug Sisk	P	52	9	16	3	1	0.5	.893
Pete Stanicek	LF	65	128	4	2	2	2.1	.985
Pete Stanicek	2B	16	21	20	2	5	2.7	.953
Pete Stanicek	DH	1	0	0	0	0	-	-
Jeff Stone	OF	21	23	3	1	1	1.3	.963
Jeff Stone	DH	1	0	0	0	0	-	-
Mickey Tettleton	C	80	361	31	3	1	4.9	.992
Mark Thurmond	P	43	3	8	1	0	0.3	.917
Jay Tibbs	P	30	17	18	0	0	1.2	1.000
Jim Traber	1B	57	459	58	5	51	9.2	.990
Jim Traber	DH	30	0	0	0	0	-	-
Jim Traber	OF	11	22	1	1	0	2.2	.958
Mark Williamson	P	37	9	14	1	0	0.6	.958
Craig Worthington	3B	26	20	53	3	4	2.9	.961
TEAM TOTALS			4,248	1,726	119	457	2.9	.980

Data courtesy of Baseball-Almanac.com.

1988 Baltimore Orioles Statmaster: Hitting

NAME	POS	GAMES	AVG	SLG	AB	H	2B	3B	HR	AB/HR	R	RBI	BB	SO	SB
Don Aase	P	35	.000	.000	0	0	0	0	0	0.0	0	0	0	0	0
Brady Anderson	OF	53	.198	.271	177	35	8	1	1	177.0	17	9	8	40	6
Jeff Ballard	P	25	.000	.000	0	0	0	0	0	0.0	0	0	0	0	0
Jose Bautista	P	33	.000	.000	0	0	0	0	0	0.0	0	0	0	0	0
Mike Boddicker	P	21	.000	.000	0	0	0	0	0	0.0	0	0	0	0	0
Butch Davis	OF	13	.240	.280	25	6	1	0	0	0.0	2	0	0	8	1
Gordon Dillard	P	2	.000	.000	0	0	0	0	0	0.0	0	0	0	0	0
Jim Dwyer	DH	35	.226	.226	53	12	0	0	0	0.0	3	3	12	11	0
Ken Gerhart	OF	103	.195	.344	262	51	10	1	9	29.1	27	23	21	57	7
Rene Gonzales	3B	92	.215	.266	237	51	6	0	2	118.5	13	15	13	32	2
John Habyan	P	7	.000	.000	0	0	0	0	0	0.0	0	0	0	0	0
Pete Harnisch	P	2	.000	.000	0	0	0	0	0	0.0	0	0	0	0	0
Keith Hughes	OF	41	.194	.324	108	21	4	2	2	54.0	10	14	16	27	1
Terry Kennedy	C	85	.226	.298	265	60	10	0	3	38.3	20	16	15	53	0
Tito Landrum	OF	13	.125	.208	24	3	0	1	0	0.0	2	2	4	6	0
Fred Lynn	OF	87	.252	.482	301	76	13	1	18	16.7	37	37	28	66	2
Scott McGregor	P	4	.000	.000	0	0	0	0	0	0.0	0	0	0	0	0
Bob Milacki	P	3	.000	.000	0	0	0	0	0	0.0	0	0	0	0	0
Mike Morgan	P	22	.000	.000	0	0	0	0	0	0.0	0	0	0	0	0
Eddie Murray	1B	161	.284	.474	603	171	27	2	28	21.5	75	84	75	78	5
Carl Nichols	C	18	.191	.213	47	9	1	0	0	0.0	2	1	3	10	0
Tom Niedenfuer	P	52	.000	.000	0	0	0	0	0	0.0	0	0	0	0	0

1988 Baltimore Orioles Statmaster: Hitting (cont.)

NAME	POS	GAMES	AVG	SLG	AB	H	2B	3B	HR	AB/HR	R	RBI	BB	SO	SB
Dickie Noles	P	2	.000	.000	0	0	0	0	0	0.0	0	0	0	0	0
Gregg Olson	P	10	.000	.000	0	0	0	0	0	0.0	0	0	0	0	0
Joe Orsulak	OF	125	.288	.422	379	109	21	3	8	47.4	48	27	23	30	9
Oswaldo Peraza	P	19	.000	.000	0	0	0	0	0	0.0	0	0	0	0	0
Billy Ripken	2B	150	.207	.258	512	106	18	1	2	256.0	52	34	33	63	8
Cal Ripken, Jr.	SS	161	.264	.431	575	152	25	1	23	25.0	87	81	102	69	2
Wade Rowdon	3B	20	.100	.100	30	3	0	0	0	0.0	1	0	0	6	1
Bill Scherrer	P	4	.000	.000	0	0	0	0	0	0.0	0	0	0	0	0
Curt Schilling	P	4	.000	.000	0	0	0	0	0	0.0	0	0	0	0	0
Dave Schmidt	P	41	.000	.000	0	0	0	0	0	0.0	0	0	0	0	0
Rick Schu	3B	89	.256	.363	270	69	9	4	4	67.5	22	20	21	49	6
Larry Sheets	OF	136	.230	.343	452	104	19	1	10	45.2	38	47	42	72	1
Doug Sisk	P	52	.000	.000	0	0	0	0	0	0.0	0	0	0	0	0
Pete Stanicek	OF	83	.230	.310	261	60	7	1	4	65.3	29	17	28	45	12
Jeff Stone	OF	26	.164	.180	61	10	1	0	0	0.0	4	1	4	11	4
Mickey Tettleton	C	86	.261	.424	283	74	11	1	11	25.7	31	37	28	70	0
Mark Thurmond	P	43	.000	.000	0	0	0	0	0	0.0	0	0	0	0	0
Jay Tibbs	P	30	.000	.000	0	0	0	0	0	0.0	0	0	0	0	0
Jim Traber	1B	103	.222	.324	352	78	6	0	10	35.2	25	45	19	42	1
Mark Williamson	P	37	.000	.000	0	0	0	0	0	0.0	0	0	0	0	0
Craig Worthington	3B	26	.185	.284	81	15	2	0	2	40.5	5	4	9	24	1
TEAM TOTALS			.238	.359	5,358	1,275	199	20	137	39.1	550	517	504	869	69

Data courtesy of Baseball-Almanac.com.

1988 Baltimore Orioles Statmaster: Pitching

NAME	GAMES	W	L	W%	ERA	GS	CG	IP	HA	BB	SO	SHU
Don Aase	35	0	0	.000	4.05	0	0	46.2	40	37	28	0
Jeff Ballard	25	8	12	.400	4.40	25	6	153.1	167	42	41	1
Jose Bautista	33	6	15	.286	4.30	25	3	171.2	171	45	76	0
Mike Boddicker	21	6	12	.333	3.86	21	4	147.0	149	51	100	0
Gordon Dillard	2	0	0	.000	6.00	1	0	3.0	3	4	2	0
John Habyan	7	1	0	1.000	4.30	0	0	14.2	22	4	4	0
Pete Harnisch	2	0	2	.000	5.54	2	0	13.0	13	9	10	0
Scott McGregor	4	0	3	.000	8.83	4	0	17.1	27	7	10	0
Bob Milacki	3	2	0	1.000	0.72	3	1	25.0	9	9	18	1
Mike Morgan	22	1	6	.143	5.43	10	2	71.1	70	23	29	0
Tom Niedenfuer	52	3	4	.429	3.51	0	0	59.0	59	19	40	0
Dickie Noles	2	0	2	.000	24.30	2	0	3.1	11	0	1	0
Gregg Olson	10	1	1	.500	3.27	0	0	11.0	10	10	9	0
Oswaldo Peraza	19	5	7	.417	5.55	15	1	86.0	98	37	61	0
Bill Scherrer	4	0	1	.000	13.50	0	0	4.0	8	3	3	0
Curt Schilling	4	0	3	.000	9.82	4	0	14.2	22	10	4	0
Dave Schmidt	41	8	5	.615	3.40	9	0	129.2	129	38	67	0
Doug Sisk	52	3	3	.500	3.72	0	0	94.1	109	45	26	0
Mark Thurmond	43	1	8	.111	4.58	6	0	74.2	80	27	29	0
Jay Tibbs	30	4	15	.211	5.39	24	1	158.2	184	63	82	0
Mark Williamson	37	5	8	.385	4.90	10	2	117.2	125	40	69	0
TEAM TOTALS		54	107	.335	4.55	161	20	1416.0	1,506	523	709	2

Data courtesy of Baseball-Almanac.com.

#14 | A Complete Massacre
The 1991 Cleveland Indians (57–105)

> Remember, fans, Tuesday is Die Hard Night. Free
> admission for anyone who was actually alive the last
> time the Indians won the pennant.
> —*Harry Doyle (Bob Uecker) in the film Major League*

The Cleveland Indians were one of American League's eight charter franchises. The team was founded in 1901, but actually began play in 1900 as the Lake Shores, while the American League was officially a minor league. Then called the Cleveland Blues, the team played in League Park until moving permanently to Cleveland Municipal Stadium in 1946. The team's name was changed to the Indians in 1914. The Indians had some success during the first 50 years of their existence. They won the 1920 World Series, and then beat the Boston Red Sox in a one-game playoff to take the 1948 American League pennant with a team that featured African-American stars and future Hall of Famers Larry Doby and Leroy "Satchel" Paige. They then won the World Series, beating the Boston Braves in six games. The 1954 edition of "the Tribe" set a major league record with 111 wins and only 43 losses but then lost to the New York Giants in the World Series. Although nobody knew it then, 41 years would pass before the Indians returned to the Fall Classic.

In 1960, however, General Manager Frank "Trader" Lane made a trade that cursed the Indians, much as trading Babe Ruth cursed the Boston Red Sox. Rocky Colavito, a slugging right fielder and fan favorite, was traded to the Detroit Tigers for banjo-hitting outfielder Harvey Kuenn. Thus, the Indians traded the defending American League home-run king for the 1959 American League batting average leader. Kuenn hit .359 that year. After the trade, Colavito hit 30 or more homers four times and made three All-Star teams. Kuenn, on the other hand, played only one season for the Tribe before being traded for aging pitcher Johnny Antonelli and unproven outfielder Willie Kirkland. Thus was born the Curse of Rocky Colavito, which continues to haunt the Indians to this day.

Left Fielder and Crowd Combatant Albert Belle (AP Photo/Mark Duncan)

The Indians went through a long dry spell. The 1970s, in particular, were a decade of misery for Tribe fans. The Indians finished last from 1969 through 1975, including the infamous 1974 Dime a Beer Night that led to an on-field riot and a game forfeited by the Tribe. No American League team lost more games in the 1970s than did the Cleveland Indians. They escaped the cellar and finished as high as fourth in their division before sinking back to the depths in 1982. By 1985, the Tribe was deeply immersed in last place, losing 102 games and finishing 39½ games out of first place. In 1990, the team finished 77–85, but still finished fourth in the American League East Division.

The team was desperate to regain its past glory, and was not afraid to make trades to try to do so. General Manager Hank Peters began in 1989 by trading popular first baseman/outfielder Joe Carter to the San Diego Padres for two unproven players, catcher Sandy Alomar Jr. and third baseman Carlos Baerga in an unpopular move with the fans. Alomar was named 1989 Rookie of the Year, and also won three Gold Glove awards. Baerga quickly became one of the best players in the American League, making three All-Star teams in a row. The fans soon changed their tune, but two good players do not a successful team make.

In addition, the farm system was beginning to produce some good young players. Jim Thome, a hulking first baseman with a lot of power (Thome is one of only 8 members of the 600 home run club), made his major league debut in 1991, and Albert Belle, a brawny, moody, but talented outfielder, cracked the regular lineup that year. Prospects were beginning to brighten significantly for the Tribe for the 1991 season.

During the off-season, Peters acquired speedy leadoff hitter/center fielder Alex Cole from the St. Louis Cardinals. Cole hit .300 and stole 40 bases in just 63 games for the Cardinals. To exploit Cole's range in the outfield and speed afoot, Peters had the outfield fence moved back at Cleveland's immense, crumbling Municipal Stadium, and raised the center field portion to look something like Fenway Park's Green Monster, prompting left-handed relief pitcher Jesse Orosco to call it the "Blue Ant." Cole hit an infield chopper in a spring training game, stumbled out of the batter's box, fell, and separated his shoulder. He was never the same again. Although he hit .295 for the Indians in 1991, he stole only 27 bases in 122 games. It was not an auspicious beginning for a team that was the subject of great expectations. The outfield wall was returned to its original configuration for the 1992 season, and Cole was traded. The great experiment lasted a single season.

When the regular season began, the team didn't get off to the sort of start that the front office desired. Manager John McNamara, a baseball lifer who led the 1986 Boston Red Sox to a heartbreaking World Series defeat, was fired about halfway through the season, and Mike Hargrove took over. Hargrove was a former Indians standout player who won the 1974 American League Rookie of the Year Award with the Texas Rangers, and who accumulated a batting average of .290 and 1,614 hits in his major league career. Hargrove, who was known as the "Human Rain Delay" for his long, deliberate, and exasperating routine at the plate, was popular with the Indians' fans. "Grover," as Hargrove was also known, went 32–53 for the balance of the season.

The 1991 Tribe finished 57–105, dead last in the American League East, 34 games behind the World Champion Toronto Blue Jays. As the season dragged on, tempers grew short. In September, after a glut of makeup doubleheaders, Hargrove quipped, "I never knew anybody who said they liked doubleheaders except Ernie Banks, and I think he was lying." The year of 1991 was a long and unhappy season for Cleveland fans and players alike.

Other than Albert Belle and Carlos Baerga, the Tribe packed little punch. Belle was mercurial, to say the least. He was a surly, angry young man with vast talent who was also a recovering alcoholic. He hit .282 with 28 homers, 31 doubles, and 95 RBIs in just 123 games, demonstrating the sort of natural ability that led to a 50-homer season just four years later. However, he was thin-skinned and had a hair trigger on his foul temper. One day during the long summer of 1991, a fan heckled him badly about his alcohol abuse and stint in rehabilitation. Belle lost his temper, turned, and winged a baseball at the man. "He threw a line drive that hit the guy in the chest," noted an Indians beat writer. "This was in the days before ESPN, so there was no replay of it. 'Did I just see what I thought I just saw?' We'd heard about his problems in the minor leagues and college, but this was the first tangible evidence this guy was going to be a problem for this team." Belle's surliness eventually drove him out of Cleveland, but not before he accomplished great feats that helped change the fortunes of the Tribe.

Baerga established himself as a legitimate star, hitting a solid .288, with 11 homers and 69 RBIs. The next year, 1992, Baerga broke out, hitting .312 with 20 homers and 105 RBIs, making the American League All-Star team. He had three more dominant seasons before being traded to the New York Mets in 1996.

Sandy Alomar Jr., the popular and talented catcher, was hindered by injuries and only played in 51 games, hitting an anemic .217 with no homers and only 7 RBIs. Shortstop Felix Fermin hit .262 and played solid defense, but he was little threat at the plate. Veteran designated hitter and outfielder Chris James, who was almost at the end of his career, had a bad season in 1991, hitting only .238 with 5 homers and 41 RBIs. Although he didn't retire until 1995, 1991 was James' last season as a regular. Second baseman Jerry Browne hit only .228 with 1 homer and 29 RBIs. The Tribe had a great deal of trouble finding regular outfielders, third basemen, and catchers. A number of different players rotated through these important positions, but none played with any sort of regularity, perhaps because none showed any reliability. As a consequence, the Indians used 28 different position players throughout the season, but nothing helped. The team hit .254, but had only 79 homers and 546 RBIs.

The pitching staff didn't fare much better, although two competent starters that became important cogs in the successful years that followed anchored the staff. Workhorse righty Charles Nagy had his first full year in the majors in 1991. He went 10–15 with a 4.13 ERA in 211.1 innings. Southpaw Greg Swindell, who won 18 games for the Tribe in 1988, went 9–16 with a respectable ERA of 3.48 in 238 innings pitched. Righty Eric King went 6–11 with a 4.60 ERA. Knuckleballer Tom Candiotti went 7–6 with a good ERA of 2.24. Hard-luck Rod Nichols went 2–11 but had a decent ERA of 3.54.

The bullpen featured a couple of good hurlers. Reliable lefty Jesse Orosco went 2–0 with a 3.74 ERA in 47 appearances. Doug Jones, who was one of the best and most reliable closers in baseball, had an uncharacteristic, atrocious year in 1991. He went 4–8 with a bloated 5.54 ERA and only seven saves; in 1992, Jones had 36 saves and a sparkling ERA of 1.85. The nucleus of a solid and reliable pitching staff was there. However, in 1991, the prospects of success remained a chimera. In 1991, they had a team ERA of 4.24 and gave up 1,551 hits in 1,441.1 innings pitched.

Better days lay ahead for the Tribe. In 1992, Hargrove led them out of the basement, finishing fourth. During the strike-shortened 1994 season, the Indians went 66–47 and finished second in the American League Central Division. They won their division for the next five straight seasons, 1995–1999, and went to the World Series twice. They lost to the Atlanta Braves in the 1995 Series and to the upstart Florida Marlins in 1999, relying on the nucleus of everyday players and pitchers that suffered through the miserable 1991 season.

The Indians had played in dank, cavernous Municipal Stadium for years. The old ballpark was crumbling, and it was a terrible place to watch a game, with obstructed view seats throughout the entire lower deck. The Indians badly needed a new stadium, and had needed one for years. Fortunately, in 1990, voters passed levies to fund the construction of new baseball and football stadiums for Cleveland, and work on the new ballpark would begin in January 1992. A bright, beautiful new stadium would be ready in 1994, so a better place to play was also just around the corner.

However, the Curse of Rocky Colavito, which doomed the Tribe to so many last place finishes over the last 50 years, remains in place. They still have not won another World Series, and they continue to toil to escape the Curse. In 1991, the Curse buried the Indians in the basement, where they remained for the entire long, miserable season.

1991 Cleveland Indians Statmaster: Fielding

NAME	POS	GAMES	PO	A	E	DP	TC/G	FLD%
Mike Aldrete	1B	47	313	22	2	31	7.2	.994
Mike Aldrete	LF	16	21	1	0	0	1.4	1.000
Mike Aldrete	DH	7	0	0	0	0	-	-
Beau Allred	OF	42	105	1	3	0	2.6	.972
Beau Allred	DH	1	0	0	0	0	-	-
Sandy Alomar, Jr.	C	46	280	19	4	4	6.6	.987
Sandy Alomar, Jr.	DH	4	0	0	0	0	-	-
Carlos Baerga	3B	89	54	183	14	14	2.8	.944
Carlos Baerga	2B	75	163	238	12	59	5.5	.971
Carlos Baerga	SS	2	0	0	1	0	0.5	.000
Eric Bell	P	10	2	1	0	0	0.3	1.000
Albert Belle	OF	89	170	8	9	1	2.1	.952
Albert Belle	DH	32	0	0	0	0		-
Willie Blair	P	11	2	5	0	1	0.6	1.000
Denis Boucher	P	5	0	5	1	1	1.2	.833
Jerry Browne	2B	47	80	109	7	17	4.2	.964
Jerry Browne	LF	17	26	0	1	0	1.6	.963
Jerry Browne	3B	15	7	32	6	4	3.0	.867
Jerry Browne	DH	7	0	0	0	0	-	-
Tom Candiotti	P	15	9	10	0	0	1.3	1.000
Alex Cole	OF	107	256	6	8	1	2.5	.970
Alex Cole	DH	6	0	0	0	0	-	-
Bruce Egloff	P	6	2	1	0	0	0.5	1.000
Jose Escobar	SS	5	5	5	0	0	2.0	1.000
Jose Escobar	2B	4	10	8	0	4	4.5	1.000
Jose Escobar	3B	1	0	0	0	0	0.0	.000
Felix Fermin	SS	129	214	372	12	74	4.6	.980
Jose Gonzalez	OF	32	52	1	1	0	1.7	.981
Mauro Gozzo	P	2	0	0	0	0	0.0	.000
Glenallen Hill	OF	33	89	0	2	0	2.8	.978
Glenallen Hill	DH	1	0	0	0	0	-	-
Shawn Hillegas	P	51	7	8	0	1	0.3	1.000
Mike Huff	OF	48	96	3	1	1	2.1	.990
Mike Huff	2B	2	1	3	0	0	2.0	1.000
Brook Jacoby	1B	55	379	32	5	27	7.6	.988
Brook Jacoby	3B	15	11	29	0	3	2.7	1.000
Chris James	DH	60	0	0	0	0	-	-

1991 Cleveland Indians Statmaster: Fielding (cont.)

NAME	POS	GAMES	PO	A	E	DP	TC/G	FLD%
Chris James	OF	39	78	2	0	1	2.1	1.000
Chris James	1B	15	95	8	0	7	6.9	1.000
Reggie Jefferson	1B	26	252	24	2	28	10.7	.993
Doug Jones	P	36	7	10	0	1	0.5	1.000
Eric King	P	25	9	14	2	2	1.0	.920
Wayne Kirby	OF	21	40	1	0	0	2.0	1.000
Garland Kiser	P	7	0	0	0	0	0.0	.000
Tom Kramer	P	4	1	0	0	0	0.3	1.000
Mark Lewis	2B	50	87	140	8	29	4.7	.966
Mark Lewis	SS	36	42	91	1	18	3.7	.993
Luis Lopez	C	12	34	2	0	0	3.0	1.000
Luis Lopez	1B	10	75	7	2	7	8.4	.976
Luis Lopez	DH	6	0	0	0	0	-	-
Luis Lopez	3B	1	0	0	0	0	0.0	.000
Luis Lopez	LF	1	0	0	0	0	0.0	.000
Ever Magallanes	SS	2	0	1	0	0	0.5	1.000
Jeff Manto	3B	32	21	58	6	12	2.7	.929
Jeff Manto	1B	14	75	3	2	5	5.7	.975
Jeff Manto	C	5	13	2	0	0	3.0	1.000
Jeff Manto	LF	1	0	0	0	0	0.0	.000
Carlos Martinez	DH	41	0	0	0	0	-	-
Carlos Martinez	1B	31	229	12	8	30	8.0	.968
Luis Medina	DH	5	0	0	0	0	-	-
Jeff Mutis	P	3	1	1	0	0	0.7	1.000
Charles Nagy	P	33	17	20	2	4	1.2	.949
Rod Nichols	P	31	10	14	1	1	0.8	.960
Steve Olin	P	48	3	8	0	2	0.2	1.000
Jesse Orosco	P	47	3	3	0	0	0.1	1.000
Dave Otto	P	18	1	16	1	0	1.0	.944
Tony Perezchica	SS	6	2	4	0	1	1.0	1.000
Tony Perezchica	3B	3	0	1	0	0	0.3	1.000
Tony Perezchica	2B	2	1	6	0	0	3.5	1.000
Tony Perezchica	DH	1	0	0	0	0	-	-
Rudy Seanez	P	5	0	0	0	0	0.0	.000
Jeff Shaw	P	29	4	11	2	2	0.6	.882
Joel Skinner	C	99	504	38	5	4	5.5	.991
Greg Swindell	P	33	7	30	1	2	1.2	.974
Eddie Taubensee	C	25	89	6	2	1	3.9	.979

1991 Cleveland Indians Statmaster: Fielding (cont.)

NAME	POS	GAMES	PO	A	E	DP	TC/G	FLD%
Jim Thome	3B	27	12	60	8	6	3.0	.900
Efrain Valdez	P	7	0	1	0	0	0.1	1.000
Sergio Valdez	P	6	0	0	0	0	0.0	.000
Mike Walker	P	5	1	1	0	0	0.4	1.000
Turner Ward	OF	38	65	1	0	0	1.7	1.000
Mitch Webster	OF	10	24	0	0	0	2.4	1.000
Mark Whiten	OF	67	166	11	7	2	2.7	.962
Mark Whiten	DH	3	0	0	0	0	-	-
Mike York	P	14	2	3	0	0	0.4	1.000
TEAM TOTALS			4,324	1,712	149	408	2.9	.976

Data courtesy of Baseball-Almanac.com.

1991 Cleveland Indians Statmaster: Hitting

NAME	POS	GAMES	AVG	SLG	AB	H	2B	3B	HR	AB/HR	R	RBI	BB	SO	SB	OBP	SB%	CS
Mike Aldrete	1B	85	.262	.322	183	48	6	1	1	183.0	22	19	36	37	1	.380	.333	2
Beau Allred	OF	48	.232	.328	125	29	3	0	3	41.7	17	12	25	35	2	.359	.500	2
Sandy Alomar, Jr.	C	51	.217	.266	184	40	9	0	0	0.0	10	7	8	24	0	.264	.000	4
Carlos Baerga	3B	158	.288	.398	593	171	28	2	11	53.9	80	69	48	74	3	.346	.600	2
Eric Bell	P	10	.000	.000	0	0	0	0	0	0.0	0	0	0	0	0	.000	.000	0
Albert Belle	OF	123	.282	.540	461	130	31	2	28	16.5	60	95	25	99	3	.323	.750	1
Willie Blair	P	11	.000	.000	0	0	0	0	0	0.0	0	0	0	0	0	.000	.000	0
Denis Boucher	P	5	.000	.000	0	0	0	0	0	0.0	0	0	0	0	0	.000	.000	0
Jerry Browne	2B	107	.228	.269	290	66	5	2	1	290.0	28	29	27	29	2	.292	.333	4
Tom Candiotti	P	15	.000	.000	0	0	0	0	0	0.0	0	0	0	0	0	.000	.000	0
Alex Cole	OF	122	.295	.354	387	114	17	3	0	0.0	58	21	58	47	27	.386	.614	17
Bruce Egloff	P	6	.000	.000	0	0	0	0	0	0.0	0	0	0	0	0	.000	.000	0
Jose Escobar	SS	10	.200	.200	15	3	0	0	0	0.0	0	1	1	4	0	.250	.000	0
Felix Fermin	SS	129	.262	.302	424	111	13	2	0	0.0	30	31	26	27	5	.307	.556	4
Jose Gonzalez	OF	33	.159	.261	69	11	2	1	1	69.0	10	4	11	27	8	.284	1.000	0
Mauro Gozzo	P	2	.000	.000	0	0	0	0	0	0.0	0	0	0	0	0	.000	.000	0
Glenallen Hill	OF	37	.262	.410	122	32	3	0	5	24.4	15	14	16	30	4	.345	.667	2
Shawn Hillegas	P	51	.000	.000	0	0	0	0	0	0.0	0	0	0	0	0	.000	.000	0
Mike Huff	OF	51	.240	.336	146	35	6	1	2	73.0	28	10	25	30	11	.364	.846	2
Brook Jacoby	1B	66	.234	.333	231	54	9	1	4	57.8	14	24	16	32	0	.289	.000	1
Chris James	DH	115	.238	.318	437	104	16	2	5	87.4	31	41	18	61	3	.273	.429	4
Reggie Jefferson	1B	26	.198	.287	101	20	3	0	2	50.5	10	12	3	22	0	.219	.000	0

1991 Cleveland Indians Statmaster: Hitting (cont.)

NAME	POS	GAMES	AVG	SLG	AB	H	2B	3B	HR	AB/HR	R	RBI	BB	SO	SB	OB?	SB%	CS
Doug Jones	P	36	.000	.000	0	0	0	0	0	0.0	0	0	0	0	0	.000	.000	0
Eric King	P	25	.000	.000	0	0	0	0	0	0.0	0	0	0	0	0	.000	.000	0
Wayne Kirby	OF	21	.209	.256	43	9	2	0	0	0.0	4	5	2	6	1	.239	.333	2
Garland Kiser	P	7	.000	.000	0	0	0	0	0	0.0	0	0	0	0	0	.000	.000	0
Tom Kramer	P	4	.000	.000	0	0	0	0	0	0.0	0	0	0	0	0	.000	.000	0
Mark Lewis	2B	84	.264	.318	314	83	15	1	0	0.0	29	30	15	45	2	.293	.500	2
Luis Lopez	C	35	.220	.293	82	18	4	1	0	0.0	7	7	4	7	0	.261	.000	0
Ever Magallanes	SS	3	.000	.000	2	0	0	0	0	0.0	0	0	1	1	0	.333	.000	0
Jeff Manto	3B	47	.211	.313	128	27	7	0	2	64.0	15	13	14	22	2	.306	1.000	0
Carlos Martinez	DH	72	.284	.397	257	73	14	0	5	51.4	22	30	10	43	3	.310	.600	2
Luis Medina	DH	5	.063	.063	16	1	0	0	0	0.0	0	0	1	7	0	.118	.000	0
Jeff Mutis	P	3	.000	.000	0	0	0	0	0	0.0	0	0	0	0	0	.000	.000	0
Charles Nagy	P	33	.000	.000	0	0	0	0	0	0.0	0	0	0	0	0	.000	.000	0
Rod Nichols	P	31	.000	.000	0	0	0	0	0	0.0	0	0	0	0	0	.000	.000	0
Steve Olin	P	48	.000	.000	0	0	0	0	0	0.0	0	0	0	0	0	.000	.000	0
Jesse Orosco	P	47	.000	.000	0	0	0	0	0	0.0	0	0	0	0	0	.000	.000	0
Dave Otto	P	18	.000	.000	0	0	0	0	0	0.0	0	0	0	0	0	.000	.000	0
Tony Perezchica	SS	17	.364	.455	22	8	2	0	0	0.0	4	0	3	5	0	.440	.000	0
Rudy Seanez	P	5	.000	.000	0	0	0	0	0	0.0	0	0	0	0	0	.000	.000	0
Jeff Shaw	P	29	.000	.000	0	0	0	0	0	0.0	0	0	0	0	0	.000	.000	0
Joel Skinner	C	99	.243	.303	284	69	14	0	1	284.0	23	24	14	67	0	.279	.000	2
Greg Swindell	P	33	.000	.000	0	0	0	0	0	0.0	0	0	0	0	0	.000	.000	0

1991 Cleveland Indians Statmaster: Hitting (cont.)

NAME	POS	GAMES	AVG	SLG	AB	H	2B	3B	HR	AB/HR	R	RBI	BB	SO	SB	OBP	SB%	CS
Eddie Taubensee	C	26	.242	.303	66	16	2	1	0	0.0	5	8	5	16	0	.288	.000	0
Jim Thome	3B	27	.255	.367	98	25	4	2	1	98.0	7	9	5	16	1	.298	.500	1
Efrain Valdez	P	7	.000	.000	0	0	0	0	0	0.0	0	0	0	0	0	.000	.000	0
Sergio Valdez	P	6	.000	.000	0	0	0	0	0	0.0	0	0	0	0	0	.000	.000	0
Mike Walker	P	5	.000	.000	0	0	0	0	0	0.0	0	0	0	0	0	.000	.000	0
Turner Ward	OF	40	.230	.300	100	23	7	0	0	0.0	11	5	10	16	0	.300	.000	0
Mitch Webster	OF	13	.125	.125	32	4	0	0	0	0.0	2	0	3	9	2	.200	.500	2
Mark Whiten	OF	70	.256	.422	258	66	14	4	7	36.9	34	26	19	50	4	.310	.667	2
Mike York	P	14	.000	.000	0	0	0	0	0	0.0	0	0	0	0	0	.000	.000	0
TEAM TOTALS			.254	.350	5,470	1,390	236	26	79	69.2	576	546	449	888	84	.313	.592	58

Data courtesy of Baseball-Almanac.com.

1991 Cleveland Indians Statmaster: Pitching

NAME	GAMES	W	L	W%	ERA	GS	CG	IP	HA	BB	SO	SHU	SV	HRA
Eric Bell	10	4	0	1.000	0.50	0	0	18.0	5	5	7	0	0	0
Willie Blair	11	2	3	.400	6.75	5	0	36.0	58	10	13	0	0	7
Denis Boucher	5	1	4	.200	8.34	5	0	22.2	35	8	13	0	0	6
Tom Candiotti	15	7	6	.538	2.24	15	3	108.1	88	28	86	0	0	6
Bruce Egloff	6	0	0	.000	4.76	0	0	5.2	8	4	8	0	0	0
Mauro Gozzo	2	0	0	.000	19.28	2	0	4.2	9	7	3	0	0	0
Shawn Hillegas	51	3	4	.429	4.34	3	0	83.0	67	46	66	0	7	7
Doug Jones	36	4	8	.333	5.54	4	0	63.1	87	17	48	0	7	7
Eric King	25	6	11	.353	4.60	24	2	150.2	166	44	59	1	0	7
Garland Kiser	7	0	0	.000	9.64	0	0	4.2	7	4	3	0	0	0
Tom Kramer	4	0	0	.000	17.36	0	0	4.2	10	6	4	0	0	1
Jeff Mutis	3	0	3	.000	11.68	3	0	12.1	23	7	6	0	0	1
Charles Nagy	33	10	15	.400	4.13	33	6	211.1	228	66	109	1	0	15
Rod Nichols	31	2	11	.154	3.54	16	3	137.1	145	30	76	1	1	6
Steve Olin	48	3	6	.333	3.36	0	0	56.1	61	23	38	0	17	2
Jesse Orosco	47	2	0	1.000	3.74	0	0	45.2	52	15	36	0	0	4
Dave Otto	18	2	8	.200	4.23	14	1	100.0	108	27	47	0	0	7
Rudy Seanez	5	0	0	.000	16.20	0	0	5.0	10	7	7	0	0	2
Jeff Shaw	29	0	5	.000	3.36	1	0	72.1	72	27	31	0	1	6
Greg Swindell	33	9	16	.360	3.48	33	7	238.0	241	31	169	0	0	21
Efrain Valdez	7	0	0	.000	1.50	0	0	6.0	5	3	1	0	0	0
Sergio Valdez	6	1	0	1.000	5.51	0	0	16.1	15	5	11	0	0	3
Mike Walker	5	0	1	.000	2.08	0	0	4.1	6	2	2	0	0	0
Mike York	14	1	4	.200	6.75	4	0	34.2	45	19	19	0	0	2
TEAM TOTALS		57	105	.352	4.24	162	22	1441.1	1,551	441	862	3	33	110

Data courtesy of Baseball-Almanac.com.

#15 | Scaredy Cats
The 2003 Detroit Tigers (43–119)

> High or low in the standings, the Detroit Tigers have always been a fighting baseball club, snarling and scrapping to the finish.
>
> —*Fred Lieb in* The Detroit Tigers *(1946)*

The Detroit Tigers are one of the American League's charter members, and one of only four original members still playing in the same city where the team began.[1] Originally called the Wolverines, the Tigers began play in the American League in 1901. Some of the greatest players to ever take the field were Tigers, including Ty Cobb, Hank Greenberg, Charlie Gehringer, and Al Kaline. The Tigers won American League pennants in 1907, 1908, and 1909, losing in the World Series each time. After a decade of mediocrity in the 1920s, they finally broke through in 1935. After losing the 1934 World Series to the St. Louis Cardinals' "Gas House Gang," the Tigers got revenge the next year, defeating the Chicago Cubs 4–2 for their first world championship.

With the timely return of slugger Hank Greenberg from military duty in 1945 and superb pitching by Virgil "Fire" Trucks, "Prince Hal" Newhouser, and Dizzy Trout, the Tigers stormed to another championship that fall, once again defeating the Cubs. However, the team fell into mediocrity again after that championship. Despite winning 101 games in 1961, a fine Tigers team still finished second behind the New York Yankees, one of the few times that a team won more than 100 games and did not make the postseason. In 1968, riding pitcher Denny McLain's 31–4 season, the Tigers ran away with the American League pennant and then defeated a fine St. Louis Cardinals team in the World Series. After winning the American League Eastern Division in 1972, the Tigers began another slow decline that lasted the balance of the 1970s.

In 1979, future Hall of Famer George "Sparky" Anderson, who managed the great Cincinnati Reds "Big Red Machine" teams of the 1970s, was hired

Jeremy Bonderman hands the ball over to manager Jim Leyland (AP Photo/Ed Zurga)

to manage the team, and he built another world champion. Riding the bats of shortstop Alan Trammell, catcher Lance Parrish, and MVP outfielder Kirk Gibson, the 1984 Tigers blew through the regular season, the American League playoffs, and defeated the San Diego Padres in the World Series. They lost in the American League Championship Series in 1987 before yet another decline set in. From 1994 to 2005, the Tigers did not have a winning record. By 2002, the Tigers were ready for a complete overhaul.

There really was no good reason for the downfall of the venerable franchise, other than that it had a history of this sort of thing. The team moved into gleaming new Comerica Park in 2000, attracting sellout crowds, and seemingly moving in the right direction. Instead, they spiraled out of control in a series of moves beginning with the signing of free agent outfield disaster Juan Gonzalez, bad amateur drafts, and poor management at the top that seemed uncommitted to spending the money necessary to build a competitive team.

In 2001, team owner Mike Ilitch hired Dave Dombrowski, former general manager of the world champion 1997 Florida Marlins, as team president. Dombrowski was brought in to break the inertia that had settled in since 1984, and to get the team back on the winning track. When the 2002 team started the season 0–6, Dombrowski fired unpopular General Manager Randy Smith (who had given expensive long-term contracts to sign players who proved unproductive, such as outfielder Juan Gonzalez) and popular manager Phil Garner, and assumed the general manager duties himself. Bench coach Luis Pujols was named interim manager, and after leading the team to a 55–106 record, Pujols was let go. In the interim, Dombrowski cleaned house, unloading many of the team's veterans for young talent. "Sometimes you have to take a step backward to regroup and go forward," he declared.

Determined to blow it all up and start over, Dombrowski brought back the trio of players who had led the team to the 1984 world championship to run the team on the field. Trammell was named manager and Parrish and Gibson were hired as coaches. They faced a stern task. Nobody expected the 2003 edition of the Tigers to be good, but nobody expected what happened, either. Nobody could have predicted the epic meltdown that the Tigers suffered that year.

Trammell did not have much talent to work with. Other than longtime Tiger outfielder Bobby Higginson, who hit 30 homers in 2000, and 29-year-old designated hitter Dmitri Young, there wasn't much else other than a trio of young pitchers who faced their baptism of fire in 2003. The truth was that the trio probably should have spent the season in the minor leagues, but the Tigers did not have the luxury of giving them another year of experience before tossing them into the breach. Those three young hurlers had a wretched season, leading the majors in losses: Mike Maroth (9–21), Jeremy Bonderman (6–19), and Nate Cornejo (6–17). Maroth had the most losses in a season since Jim Bonham of the Cubs and Randy Jones of the Cubs both lost 22 in 1974.

The Tigers reeled off nine straight losses to open the season, and were outscored 54–14 during that ugly losing streak. By the end of April, the Tigers were 3–21, and it was obvious that they were going to dwell in the cellar for the entire season. And it just got worse from there. By mid-June, Maroth was 1–11 and Bonderman was 2–10, and the Tigers' management gave serious consideration to holding them out of the pitching staff in the hope of avoiding any serious, long-term psychological injuries to the young hurlers. By the end of July, the Tigers were already 50 games under .500 as losing streak blended into losing streak. The Tigers suffered through losing streaks of 11 games, 10 games, 9 games, and two different 8-gamers. Longtime broadcaster Ernie Harwell, a member of the baseball Hall of Fame, summed the 2003 season up nicely: "Even when it rains, it's almost a celebration."

When it was all over, the team posted a mark of 43–119, the worst since Casey Stengel's 1962 Mets. They lost their 100th game on August 30. As the team's fortunes sank, attendance plummeted, in spite of the gleaming new ballpark. "You tell people you've got tickets, and they laugh at you," said one fan. "We can't even give them away on eBay." They were outscored by a stunning 928–591 over the course of the long season. Maroth's grandmother died on the day that he lost number 20. Trammell's mother died during the season's final weeks. The misery just kept coming.

The Tigers lost their 117th game of the season on September 21, 2003. "We're just about out of gas," admitted Trammell. "I think it's just the losing, the day in and day out . . . it's probably a little too much for us to overcome." They still had seven games left, meaning that they only had to lose four out of those last seven games to shatter the record for futility set by Stengel's Mets 41 years earlier. "Obviously it's a big deal because it's a record," said third-year catcher Brandon Inge. "No one wants to be looked at as the worst team ever." Young, one of the few veterans on the team, chimed in. "It's on everybody's mind, man," he admitted. "It's a number we're going to have to live with if we reach it." Remarkably, the Tigers rallied and won five of the last seven games, leaving them one loss short of the record set by the Mets.

The next-to-last game was against the Minnesota Twins, who jumped out to an 8–0 lead. The Tigers rallied to win the game 9–8, scoring the winning run on a wild pitch on a strikeout in the bottom of the ninth inning. The Tigers then beat the Twins again the next day 9–4, behind six strong innings by Maroth. After the final game, Dmitri Young made an odd but prophetic statement. "A few years down the road, I can look back and say this was the beginning of a dynasty," he declared. "This was the beginning of a rebuilding process. We started from scratch with flour, eggs and sugar."

Dombrowski was more realistic. "Nobody likes to lose and we were losing every day," he said. "But the way we finished told you that there was still fight in the team. We could've folded, but battled back and won. It was exciting to win those last two games."

Young had a good season, and had good reason to look forward to in 2004. He led the team by hitting .297, with 29 homers and 85 RBIs. Higginson, who was plagued with hamstring problems all season, had a subpar year. He hit only .235 with 14 homers and only 52 RBIs. Outfielder Craig Monroe hit .240 with 23 homers and 70 RBIs. The third outfielder, Alex Sanchez, hit a respectable .289, but with only 1 homer and 29 RBIs. First baseman Carlos Pena hit .248 with 18 homers and 50 RBIs. Third baseman Shane Halter hit a mere .217 with 12 homers and only 30 RBIs. Catcher Brandon Inge hit an anemic .203 while slick-fielding shortstop Ramon Santiago hit only .225. As a team, the Tigers hit .240, with 153 homers and 553 RBIs.

The team's pitching staff was atrocious. Maroth went 9–21 with an ERA of 5.73. Bonderman went 6–19 with an ERA of 5.56. Cornejo went 6–17 with an ERA of 4.67. Adam Bernero went 1–12 with an ugly ERA of 6.08. Gary Knotts was 3–8, with an ERA of 6.04. The bullpen had one bright light. Jamie Walker was 5–3, with three saves and an ERA of 3.32 in 78 games. The rest went downhill from there. The staff, which used 20 different pitchers that long summer, had a bad team ERA of 5.32, and gave up a staggering 1,616 hits in 1438.2 innings pitched.

Dombrowski realized that the debacle was not Trammell's fault and said that Trammell had done a fine job with the team in spite of it all. He gave Trammell a second chance the next year, and the Tigers rewarded him by improving to 72–90. When they stagnated at 71–91 in 2005, Dombrowski fired Trammell and replaced him with fiery Jim Leyland. Leyland, who had won the 1997 World Series under Dombrowski, carried off a miracle in 2006. With the nucleus of free agent catcher Ivan Rodriguez, pitchers Nate Robertson, Fernando Rodney and Jason Bonderman (who went 14–8 with a 4.08 ERA that year), the Tigers finished second in their division with a record of 95–67, but secured a wild card slot in the playoffs. They won the divisional playoff and then won the American League Championship Series for an unlikely World Series appearance just three years after going 43–119. Although the Tigers did not win the 2006 Fall Classic, their presence there was a testimony to Dombrowski's vision. However, that vision seemed terribly unlikely during that long, miserable summer of 2003.

The Tigers faced a long, uphill battle just to reach mediocrity after their run at baseball immortality in 2003. That they accomplished their goal and made it back to the World Series just three years later proved that good things can happen to teams with a vision and with the fortitude to stick it out long enough for that vision to take shape.

2003 Detroit Tigers Statmaster: Fielding

NAME	POS	GAMES	PO	A	E	DP	TC/G	FLD%
Matt Anderson	P	23	1	2	1	0	0.2	.750
Steve Avery	P	19	4	3	0	1	0.4	1.000
Adam Bernero	P	18	6	14	0	1	1.1	1.000
Hiram Bocachica	CF	5	9	1	0	0	2.0	1.000
Hiram Bocachica	LF	1	2	0	0	0	2.0	1.000
Jeremy Bonderman	P	33	14	25	1	2	1.2	.975
Nate Cornejo	P	32	15	34	2	4	1.6	.961
Eric Eckenstahler	P	20	0	0	1	0	0.1	.000
Franklyn German	P	45	1	5	0	1	0.1	1.000
Shane Halter	3B	50	36	98	2	12	2.7	.985
Shane Halter	SS	27	33	62	5	14	3.7	.950
Shane Halter	2B	24	40	74	0	12	4.8	1.000
Shane Halter	1B	12	84	4	2	13	7.5	.978
Shane Halter	PH	10	-	-	-	-	-	-
Shane Halter	DH	4	0	0	0	0	-	-
Shane Halter	LF	2	0	0	0	0	0.0	.000
Shane Halter	PR	2	-	-	-	-	-	-
Bobby Higginson	RF	117	248	4	5	0	2.2	.981
Bobby Higginson	DH	8	0	0	0	0	-	-
Bobby Higginson	PH	6	-	-	-	-	-	-
Bobby Higginson	CF	1	1	0	0	0	1.0	1.000
A.J. Hinch	C	27	110	6	2	0	4.4	.983
A.J. Hinch	PH	1	-	-	-	-	-	-
Omar Infante	SS	63	117	211	13	53	5.4	.962
Omar Infante	3B	4	1	8	1	1	2.5	.900
Omar Infante	2B	2	3	3	0	2	3.0	1.000
Omar Infante	PR	2	-	-	-	-	-	-
Brandon Inge	C	104	500	67	2	11	5.5	.996
Brandon Inge	PR	2	-	-	-	-	-	-
Gene Kingsale	CF	23	52	0	1	0	2.3	.981
Gene Kingsale	LF	8	14	0	0	0	1.8	1.000
Gene Kingsale	PH	4	-	-	-	-	-	-
Gene Kingsale	DH	4	0	0	0	0	-	-
Gene Kingsale	PR	3	-	-	-	-	-	-
Danny Klassen	3B	13	15	24	0	3	3.0	1.000
Danny Klassen	2B	4	12	16	1	4	7.3	.966
Danny Klassen	PH	4	-	-	-	-	-	-

2003 Detroit Tigers Statmaster: Fielding (cont.)

NAME	POS	GAMES	PO	A	E	DP	TC/G	FLD%
Danny Klassen	SS	3	5	8	2	0	5.0	.867
Danny Klassen	PR	1	-	-	-	-	-	-
Gary Knotts	P	20	8	15	0	1	1.2	1.000
Wilfredo Ledezma	P	34	4	7	0	0	0.3	1.000
Shane Loux	P	11	3	5	0	0	0.7	1.000
Mike Maroth	P	33	9	42	2	2	1.6	.962
Chris Mears	P	29	3	5	0	2	0.3	1.000
Craig Monroe	LF	75	148	6	4	1	2.1	.975
Craig Monroe	RF	38	72	2	3	0	2.0	.961
Craig Monroe	PH	18	-	-	-	-	-	-
Craig Monroe	DH	12	0	0	0	0	-	-
Craig Monroe	CF	2	1	0	0	0	0.5	1.000
Craig Monroe	PR	1	-	-	-	-	-	-
Warren Morris	2B	89	182	271	6	83	5.2	.987
Warren Morris	PH	11	-	-	-	-	-	-
Warren Morris	PR	1	-	-	-	-	-	-
Eric Munson	3B	91	68	150	19	13	2.6	.920
Eric Munson	PH	8	-	-	-	-	-	-
Eric Munson	DH	2	0	0	0	0	-	-
Dean Palmer	DH	22	0	0	0	0	-	-
Dean Palmer	PH	2	-	-	-	-	-	-
Dean Palmer	3B	1	0	4	0	0	4.0	1.000
Dean Palmer	1B	1	9	1	0	0	10.0	1.000
Craig Paquette	1B	5	42	1	0	4	8.6	1.000
Craig Paquette	LF	3	8	0	0	0	2.7	1.000
Craig Paquette	PH	3	-	-	-	-	-	-
Craig Paquette	RF	2	2	0	0	0	1.0	1.000
Danny Patterson	P	19	3	3	1	0	0.4	.857
Carlos Pena	1B	128	1,135	91	13	130	9.7	.990
Carlos Pena	PH	3	-	-	-	-	-	-
Carlos Pena	DH	1	0	0	0	0	-	-
Ben Petrick	LF	18	34	0	1	0	1.9	.971
Ben Petrick	CF	14	26	2	1	1	2.1	.966
Ben Petrick	C	6	25	0	0	0	4.2	1.000
Ben Petrick	RF	3	1	0	0	0	0.3	1.000
Ben Petrick	1B	2	3	0	0	0	1.5	1.000
Nate Robertson	P	8	2	6	0	0	1.0	1.000
Fernando Rodney	P	27	0	3	0	0	0.1	1.000

2003 Detroit Tigers Statmaster: Fielding (cont.)

NAME	POS	GAMES	PO	A	E	DP	TC/G	FLD%
Matt Roney	P	45	7	11	2	0	0.4	.900
Cody Ross	RF	6	15	0	2	0	2.8	.882
Alex Sanchez	CF	99	278	1	6	0	2.9	.979
Alex Sanchez	PH	5	-	-	-	-	-	-
Alex Sanchez	PR	2	-	-	-	-	-	-
Ramon Santiago	SS	85	141	248	10	68	4.7	.975
Ramon Santiago	2B	53	105	153	10	45	5.1	.963
Ramon Santiago	PH	4	-	-	-	-	-	-
Brian Schmack	P	11	1	1	0	0	0.2	1.000
Steve Sparks	P	42	6	12	1	5	0.5	.947
Chris Spurling	P	66	1	7	0	0	0.1	1.000
Andres Torres	CF	36	80	1	1	0	2.3	.988
Andres Torres	RF	16	20	3	0	1	1.4	1.000
Andres Torres	PH	7	-	-	-	-	-	-
Andres Torres	PR	4	-	-	-	-	-	-
Andres Torres	DH	3	0	0	0	0	-	-
Andres Torres	LF	1	2	0	0	0	2.0	1.000
Matt Walbeck	C	55	172	16	4	1	3.5	.979
Matt Walbeck	PH	5	-	-	-	-	-	-
Matt Walbeck	PR	2	-	-	-	-	-	-
Jamie Walker	P	78	4	11	1	1	0.2	.938
Kevin Witt	DH	36	0	0	0	0	-	-
Kevin Witt	1B	27	214	20	0	31	8.7	1.000
Kevin Witt	PH	20	-	-	-	-	-	-
Kevin Witt	LF	13	20	0	0	0	1.5	1.000
Kevin Witt	3B	5	1	4	0	0	1.0	1.000
Dmitri Young	DH	75	0	0	0	0	-	-
Dmitri Young	LF	61	125	5	2	2	2.2	.985
Dmitri Young	3B	16	8	37	8	5	3.3	.849
Dmitri Young	PH	7	-	-	-	-	-	-
Dmitri Young	1B	1	5	0	0	0	5.0	1.000
Ernie Young	DH	4	0	0	0	0	-	-
Ernie Young	PH	1	-	-	-	-	-	-
TEAM TOTALS			4,316	1,813	138	530	2.6	.978

Data courtesy of Baseball-Almanac.com.

2003 Detroit Tigers Statmaster: Hitting

NAME	POS	GAMES	AVG	SLG	AB	H	2B	3B	HR	AB/HR	R	RBI	BB	SO	SB
Matt Anderson	P	23	.000	.000	0	0	0	0	0	0.0	0	0	0	0	0
Steve Avery	P	19	1.000	1.000	1	1	0	0	0	0.0	1	0	0	0	0
Adam Bernero	P	18	.000	.000	4	0	0	0	0	0.0	0	0	0	1	0
Hiram Bocachica	OF	6	.045	.091	22	1	1	0	0	0.0	1	0	0	7	0
Jeremy Bonderman	P	33	.000	.000	2	0	0	0	0	0.0	0	0	0	2	0
Nate Cornejo	P	32	.000	.000	4	0	0	0	0	0.0	0	0	0	4	0
Eric Eckenstahler	P	20	.000	.000	0	0	0	0	0	0.0	0	0	0	0	0
Franklyn German	P	45	.000	.000	0	0	0	0	0	0.0	0	0	0	0	0
Shane Halter	3B	114	.217	.342	360	78	5	2	12	30.0	33	30	27	77	2
Bobby Higginson	OF	130	.235	.369	469	110	13	4	14	33.5	61	52	59	73	8
A.J. Hinch	C	27	.203	.392	74	15	3	1	3	24.7	7	11	3	18	0
Omar Infante	SS	69	.222	.258	221	49	6	1	0	0.0	24	8	18	37	6
Brandon Inge	C	104	.203	.339	330	67	15	3	8	41.3	32	30	24	79	4
Gene Kingsale	OF	39	.208	.275	120	25	3	1	1	120.0	11	8	10	17	1
Danny Klassen	3B	22	.247	.356	73	18	3	1	1	73.0	9	7	4	26	0
Gary Knotts	P	20	.000	.000	1	0	0	0	0	0.0	0	0	0	0	0
Wilfredo Ledezma	P	34	.000	.000	0	0	0	0	0	0.0	0	0	0	0	0
Shane Loux	P	11	.000	.000	0	0	0	0	0	0.0	0	0	0	0	0
Mike Maroth	P	33	.500	.500	2	1	0	0	0	0.0	0	0	1	0	0
Chris Mears	P	29	.000	.000	0	0	0	0	0	0.0	0	0	0	0	0
Craig Monroe	OF	128	.240	.449	425	102	18	1	23	18.5	51	70	27	89	4
Warren Morris	2B	97	.272	.373	346	94	13	2	6	57.7	37	37	23	42	4
Eric Munson	3B	99	.240	.441	313	75	9	0	18	17.4	28	50	35	61	3

2003 Detroit Tigers Statmaster: Hitting (cont.)

NAME	POS	GAMES	AVG	SLG	AB	H	2B	3B	HR	AB/HR	R	RBI	BB	SO	SB
Dean Palmer	DH	26	.140	.163	86	12	2	0	0	0.0	3	6	9	28	0
Craig Paquette	1B	11	.152	.152	33	5	0	0	0	0.0	2	0	0	5	0
Danny Patterson	P	19	.000	.000	0	0	0	0	0	0.0	0	0	0	0	0
Carlos Pena	1B	131	.248	.440	452	112	21	6	18	25.1	51	50	53	123	4
Ben Petrick	OF	43	.225	.375	120	27	6	0	4	30.0	18	12	8	30	0
Nate Robertson	P	8	.000	.000	0	0	0	0	0	0.0	0	0	0	0	0
Fernando Rodney	P	27	.000	.000	0	0	0	0	0	0.0	0	0	0	0	0
Matt Roney	P	45	.500	.500	2	1	0	0	0	0.0	0	0	0	1	0
Cody Ross	OF	6	.211	.421	19	4	1	0	1	19.0	1	5	1	3	0
Alex Sanchez	OF	101	.289	.355	394	114	13	5	1	394.0	43	22	18	46	44
Ramon Santiago	SS	141	.225	.284	444	100	18	1	2	222.0	41	29	33	66	10
Brian Schmack	P	11	.000	.000	0	0	0	0	0	0.0	0	0	0	0	0
Steve Sparks	P	42	.000	.000	0	0	0	0	0	0.0	0	0	0	0	0
Chris Spurling	P	66	.000	.000	0	0	0	0	0	0.0	0	0	0	0	0
Andres Torres	OF	55	.220	.298	168	37	4	3	1	168.0	23	9	10	35	5
Matt Walbeck	C	55	.174	.239	138	24	4	1	1	138.0	11	6	3	26	0
Jamie Walker	P	78	.000	.000	0	0	0	0	0	0.0	0	0	0	0	0
Kevin Witt	DH	93	.263	.407	270	71	9	0	10	27.0	25	26	15	68	1
Dmitri Young	DH	155	.297	.537	562	167	34	7	29	19.4	78	85	58	130	2
Ernie Young	DH	5	.182	.182	11	2	0	0	0	0.0	0	0	0	5	0
TEAM TOTALS			.240	.375	5,466	1,312	201	39	153	35.7	591	553	439	1,099	98

Data courtesy of Baseball-Almanac.com.

2003 Detroit Tigers Statmaster: Pitching

NAME	GAMES	W	L	W%	ERA	GS	CG	IP	HA	BB	SO	SHU
Matt Anderson	23	0	1	.000	5.40	0	0	23.1	25	9	13	0
Steve Avery	19	2	0	1.000	5.63	0	0	16.0	19	7	6	0
Adam Bernero	18	1	12	.077	6.08	17	0	100.2	104	41	54	0
Jeremy Bonderman	33	6	19	.240	5.56	28	0	162.0	193	58	108	0
Nate Cornejo	32	6	17	.261	4.67	32	2	194.2	236	58	46	0
Eric Eckenstahler	20	0	0	.000	2.87	0	0	15.2	9	15	12	0
Franklyn German	45	2	4	.333	6.04	0	0	44.2	47	45	41	0
Gary Knotts	20	3	8	.273	6.04	18	0	95.1	111	47	51	0
Wilfredo Ledezma	34	3	7	.300	5.79	8	0	84.0	99	35	49	0
Shane Loux	11	1	1	.500	7.12	4	0	30.1	37	12	8	0
Mike Maroth	33	9	21	.300	5.73	33	1	193.1	231	50	87	0
Chris Mears	29	1	3	.250	5.44	3	0	41.1	50	11	21	0
Danny Patterson	19	0	0	.000	4.08	0	0	17.2	15	4	19	0
Nate Robertson	8	1	2	.333	5.44	8	0	44.2	55	23	33	0
Fernando Rodney	27	1	3	.250	6.07	0	0	29.2	35	17	33	0
Matt Roney	45	1	9	.100	5.45	11	0	100.2	102	48	47	0
Brian Schmack	11	1	0	1.000	3.46	0	0	13.0	14	4	4	0
Steve Sparks	42	0	6	.000	4.72	0	0	89.2	95	34	49	0
Chris Spurling	66	1	3	.250	4.68	0	0	77.0	78	22	38	0
Jamie Walker	78	4	3	.571	3.32	0	0	65.0	61	17	45	0
TEAM TOTALS		43	119	.265	5.32	162	3	1438.2	1,616	557	764	0

Data courtesy of Baseball-Almanac.com.

Hall of Shame

#1 | Worst Season
From Heroes to Zeroes
The 1884 Wilmington Quicksteps

> Simmons pulled his team from the field and disbanded
> them due to lack of fan interest, on September 21, 1884.
> There wasn't one fan in the stands.
> —*Baseball Reference (Union Association)*

All sports teams can have a bad season. This book is full of them. However, one team in particular may have had the worst season ever in the history of professional baseball. These lovable losers were the 1884 Wilmington Quicksteps, who went a miserable 2–16 and are most likely the reason that Delaware still does not have a major-league franchise today. Theirs is truly a bittersweet tale of burning bright to burning out.

The Quicksteps franchise was originally part of the Inter-State Baseball Association of Professional Baseball Clubs, which was founded in 1883. The following year, the league was reorganized into the amateur Eastern League and Wilmington's team looked to be a strong contender early on. In fact, the Quicksteps had built such a reputation that major league ball clubs began challenging them to exhibition games. Living up to their hype, Wilmington defeated both the Washington Nationals and the Baltimore Monumentals.

During their regular season in the Eastern League, the Quicksteps played like champions and won the league's title with an impressive 50–12 record. Unfortunately, baseball's popularity had not caught on yet and the attendance at the home games lacked. Additionally, the teams' domination in the Eastern League may have given the Wilmington players a false sense of pride. After all, they earned their accolades while playing minor-league teams of very low caliber. They soon received a dose of "pro-ality."

Late in the 1884 season, the Union Association's founder, Henry Lucas, who also owned the St. Louis Maroons, convinced Quicksteps skipper Joe Simmons to join with the financially struggling Philadelphia Keystones and move over to his league. Both teams jumped at the opportunity due to their dreadful ticket sales and the lack of what they considered to be "worthy"

Right-Handed Pitcher and Outfielder Daniel Casey (Library of Congress)

competition. Ironically, Simmons had played in the major league National Association for three seasons and even played and managed during his final year with the Keokuk Westerns , who went 1–13. Perhaps this was a sign of things to come.

Still riding the momentum of its amateur championship, Wilmington's team won its major-league opener 4–3, once again defeating the Washington Nationals. Unfortunately, this victory marked the apex of its season, as the team plummeted dramatically in the standings. As the "Q'steps," as the team was sometimes called, lost game after game, the team's more valuable players began to revolt. Many believed that their contracts did not legally bind them after the team migrated from one league into another without their consent. Their frustration was understandable, as they went from minor-league heroes to major-league zeroes.

The team's captain, shortstop Oyster Burns, eventually left for Baltimore and a $900 a month paycheck. Teammate Dennis Casey followed and played in the Monumentals' outfield for a salary of $700 per month. Both players had been making a measly $150 per month in Wilmington. Other players also left for a pay raise, including catcher Tony Cusick, who became a Keystone for $375 per month. The remaining only marquee player was Ed Nolan, who pitched Wilmington to its only other win (again over Washington).

By the time of their second "W," the Quicksteps' season was absolutely meaningless, as St. Louis' team had already locked up the pennant. With a dwindling box office and virtually nonexistent fan base, the future looked grim for Wilmington. An equally disgruntled Simmons debated canceling the team's remaining games and prepared to disband the franchise altogether.

On September 21, 1884, the Quicksteps showed up for a game against the Kansas City Cowboys to an empty Union Street Park. Adding to their embarrassing no-show was the inability of Wilmington to pay the minimum

$60 fee required for visiting teams. Prior to the first pitch, the players were pulled off the field and the team was officially dissolved. The Milwaukee Grays immediately filled their spot in the Union Association.[1]

In the end, the 1884 Quicksteps finished dead last with a .111 winning percentage, and tallied the worst seasonal record ever recognized by major league baseball. It was also the first time that a baseball team folded after failing to complete even a single campaign. Their 1884 comparative stats told the tale:

Monthly Splits:

MONTH (GAMES)	WON	LOST	WIN %
August (10)	1	9	0.100
September (8)	1	7	0.125

Team versus Team Splits:

OPPONENT (GAMES)	WON	LOST	WIN %
Baltimore Monumentals (1)	0	1	0.000
Boston Unions (5)	0	5	0.000
Cincinnati Outlaw Reds (3)	1	2	0.333
St. Louis Maroons (4)	0	4	0.000
Washington Nationals (5)	1	4	0.200

Score-Related Splits:

TYPE (GAMES)	WON	LOST	WIN %
Shutouts (4)	1	3	0.250
1-Run Games (4)	2	2	0.500
Blowouts (9)	0	9	0.000

Several of Wilmington's players went on to successful careers in the major leagues, including the mutinous team captain Oyster Burns, who jumped ship for the Baltimore franchise. He finished the season with a respectable .290 batting average with 6 home runs and 23 runs-batted-in. In 1888, Burns signed with the Brooklyn Bridegrooms for a whopping $4,000 and began to earn his pay. In 1889, he tallied a meager 5 round-trippers, but had 100 RBIs and a .304 batting average. Two seasons later, Burns hit a career-high 13 homers and had 128 RBIs. Over the next three years he tallied 83, 96, and 107 RBIs. In 1890, the veteran catcher hit an impressive .354 and finished his career with the New York Giants.

Over the years, several new teams were established in Wilmington, including the 1885 Blue Hens, who carried on the town's tradition by going 5–28 before being sold to Atlantic-City; the 1889 Hens, who finished 4–16; the 1890 Peach Growers, who managed a 29–66 mark; and the 1896 Peaches, who were rotten and posted a 58–79 record. None of them, however, approached the lowlights of the original Quicksteps, whose appalling performance in 1884 has never been equaled.

1884 Wilmington Quicksteps Schedule

GAME	DATE	OPPONENT	SCORE	DECISION	RECORD
1	08–18–1884	at Washington Nationals	4–3	W	1–0
2	08–19–1884	at Washington Nationals	2–4	L	1–1
3	08–21–1884	at Washington Nationals	1–12	L	1–2
4	08–22–1884	at Washington Nationals	0–14	L	1–3
5	08–23–1884	at Washington Nationals	4–10	L	1–4
6-I	08–25–1884	at Boston Unions	0–0	L F	1–5
7-II	08–25–1884	at Boston Unions	0–6	L	1–6
8	08–27–1884	at Boston Unions	1–7	L	1–7
9	08–28–1884	at Boston Unions	4–5	L	1–8
10	08–30–1884	at Boston Unions	0–3	L	1–9
11	09–02–1884	vs Cincinnati Outlaw Reds	3–2	W	2–9
12	09–03–1884	vs Cincinnati Outlaw Reds	3–7	L	2–10
13	09–05–1884	vs Cincinnati Outlaw Reds	1–6	L	2–11
14	09–06–1884	vs St. Louis Maroons	2–4	L	2–12
15	09–08–1884	vs St. Louis Maroons	3–9	L	2–13
16	09–09–1884	vs St. Louis Maroons	3–11	L	2–14
17	09–10–1884	vs St. Louis Maroons	1–7	L	2–15
18	09–12–1884	at Baltimore Monumentals	3–4	L	2–16

Data courtesy of Baseball-Almanac.com.

#2 | Worst Investment
Money for Nothing
The $100-Plus Million 2008 Seattle Mariners

> But can this 100-loss season be repeated? Right now,
> I'm actually wondering how they're going to avoid
> that happening. This team is a train wreck, through
> and through.
>
> —*Geoff Baker of the* Seattle Times

An old saying goes, "Money can't buy everything, but it sure as hell helps." Virtually every professional sports team of the modern era has become a huge moneymaking corporation, and the owners and athletes are now multimillionaires. Big names with bigger contracts are the norm, and only the inflated egos of today's so-called "marquee" players match these inflated salaries.

Over the last decade, financially superior teams like the New York Yankees and Boston Red Sox have drawn fire for their notorious spending habits, which has unfairly enabled them to sign a majority of the available free agent all-stars. Major league baseball has attempted to temper these economic advantages through revenue sharing, but there are still teams whose entire infield-combined salaries do not equal that of a richer team's star player.

That said, money doesn't always guarantee winning, and there have been many record-setting contracts executed that ultimately resulted in a bust. This may be an acceptable attrition rate when it happens to an individual player, but what happens when a whole team fails to earn its paycheck? The answer is a devastating twofold disaster on and off the ball field. Perhaps no team has better embodied the sin of frivolous overspending than the "poor" 2008 Seattle Mariners.

After completing its first winning season in four years, Seattle's club repositioned itself as a major contender in the American League's West Division. As expected, the "M's" bolstered its advantage by signing several acquisitions in the off-season. Each of these moves met with intense scrutiny. Historically, the Mariners had a terrible track record with the exchange

Seattle Mariners starting pitcher Erik Bedard (AP Photo/Marcio Jose Sanchez)

of player personnel. General Manager Bill Bavasi, who took over the spot in 2003, had been the point person on multiple Seattle transactions that failed to deliver results. However, in the 2008 season, he set a new high for signing lows.

Bavasi's resume included the premature trading of players such as Asdrubal Cabrera, Shin-Soo Choo, Carlos Guillen, Rafael Soriano, and Matt Thornton. He also signed several mediocre free agents such as Miguel Batista, Richie Sexson, Scott Spiezio, Carlos Silva, and Jarrod Washburn to lengthy, expensive contracts. Perhaps the worst transaction following the 2007 campaign was his exchange of five players, including the promising Adam Jones and Chris Tillman, for pitcher Erik Bedard. Ironically Bedard made just 15 starts before requiring shoulder surgery, which revealed that he did not have a simple labrum tear as expected.

Still, the future looked bright on Opening Day 2008 when the newly revamped, $118-million Mariners took the field. Many commentators in the sports press projected Seattle to go far, maybe even to the postseason, and the fans in the stands planned for the playoffs, too.

One hopeful reporter boldly predicted, "Expect the M's to make that final leap from 2nd string to real contention this year. The Angels acquired Jon Garland, who this particular analyst thinks is badly overrated and Torii Hunter (similarly overrated), lost their only good defensive infielder (Orlando Cabrera) and may have lost Kelvim Escobar for a significant chunk of the 2008 season with an undisclosed shoulder ailment. I believe this year, the Mariners will make the playoffs, though it's far from guaranteed."

The Mariners opened the season with a 5–2 victory over the Texas Rangers (they won their first and last games), perhaps creating a false sense of hope in all in attendance. Unfortunately, much like their weather, dark skies were just ahead for both Seattle's team and their fans.

Within a few weeks of collapse after collapse, it became apparent that something was dreadfully wrong. In late May, local writer Matt Eddy stated, "The 2008 Mariners are a study in dysfunction. They don't hit, they don't pitch and they don't catch the ball, a formula that has produced the worst run differential in the American League."

Along the way, they set a litany of unwanted records for a franchise with a monumental payroll. Their longest winning streak of the entire 2008 season was a measly four games, but their longest losing string was a whopping 12. By September, they stood at 57–87, and on September 23, they became the first club to spend $100 million in payroll and lose 100 games by falling to the Anaheim Angels 5–4 for a season mark of 58–100. The Mariners shamefully finished the season with a 61–101 record (.377), finishing last in the American League and second worst in all of major league baseball. They slipped 27 games from the previous season and chalked up the franchise's worst overall performance in 25 years.

Seattle's sports reporters in particular vocalized their disgust and disappointment with the team in the papers and online. Joseph Franco of the *Bleacher Report* recalled, "I experienced one of the Mariners' few wins at Safeco Field against the Rays, but, even though they won, the stadium seemed empty, and fans were disgruntled. 'Fire Armstrong!' yells (referring to team President Chuck Armstrong) broke the crowd's silence."

Matthew Carruth of the *Hardball Times* posted, "Yes, they faced some bad luck. The number and extent of the injuries they encountered were unfortunate and would have hurt any team. They also dealt with unlucky hitters in the form of line drives not going for hits as often as would be expected. Those unlucky breaks would have turned any good team into an average one, but combined with a lack of planning reminiscent of FEMA-circa Katrina, it created a crater so large as to finally swallow the front office."

The backlash against the front office during this marathon of mediocrity was equally severe. General Manager (GM) Bill Bavasi was fired in June when the team stood at 24–45. Skipper John McLaren followed him into the unemployment line three days later. Associate GM Lee Pelekoudas and bench coach Jim Riggleman stepped into the vacancies on an interim basis. First baseman Richie Sexson and designated hitter Jose Vidro were released due to their lack of performance on the field.

In October, the team signed new general manager Jack Zduriencik, a popular scouting director for Milwaukee's team, who was named as Baseball America's "2007 Executive of the Year." Zduriencik earned his reputation by executing a brilliant rebuilding plan that turned the Brewers from a perennial also-ran to a playoff contender. He immediately hired former Oakland Athletics bench coach Don Wakamatsu as his manager, named former Brewers staff member Tom McNamara as his scouting director, and promoted Mariners coordinator of instruction Pedro Grifol to farm director.

Zduriencik also tempered the team's spending in 2009, and the team spent less on the draft ($2.5 million) than any other major league baseball club. Only time will tell whether his radical approach will "pay off" in the long run.

2008 Seattle Mariners Roster

#	PITCHERS	HEIGHT	WEIGHT	THROWS	BATS	DATE OF BIRTH
58	Cha Seung Baek	6–04	190	Right	Right	1980–05–29
43, 42, 43	Miguel Batista	6–00	160	Right	Right	1971–02–19
45	Erik Bedard	6–01	186	Left	Left	1979–03–05
48	Roy Corcoran	5–10	170	Right	Right	1980–05–11
41	R.A. Dickey	6–03	205	Right	Right	1974–10–29
31	Ryan Feierabend	6–03	190	Left	Left	1985–08–22
54	Sean Green	6–06	230	Right	Right	1979–04–20
34	Felix Hernandez	6–03	170	Right	Right	1986–04–08
36	Cesar Jimenez	5–11	180	Left	Left	1984–11–12
57	Mark Lowe	6–03	190	Right	Left	1983–06–07
26	Randy Messenger	6–06	245	Right	Right	1981–08–13
35	Brandon Morrow	6–03	190	Right	Right	1984–07–26
59	Eric O'Flaherty	6–02	195	Left	Left	1985–02–02
20	J.J. Putz	6–05	220	Right	Right	1977–02–22
53, 42, 53	Arthur Rhodes	6–02	206	Left	Left	1969–10–24
18	Ryan Rowland-Smith	6–03	205	Left	Left	1983–01–26
52	Carlos Silva	6–04	225	Right	Right	1979–04–23
60	Justin Thomas	6–03	225	Left	Left	1984–01–18

2008 Seattle Mariners Roster (cont.)

#	PITCHERS	HEIGHT	WEIGHT	THROWS	BATS	DATE OF BIRTH
56	Jarrod Washburn	6–01	187	Left	Left	1974–08–13
40	Jared Wells	6–04	200	Right	Right	1981–10–31
49	Jake Woods	6 01	190	Left	Left	1981–09–03
#	CATCHERS	HEIGHT	WEIGHT	THROWS	BATS	DATE OF BIRTH
15	Jamie Burke	6–00	195	Right	Right	1971–09–24
9	Jeff Clement	6–01	215	Right	Left	1983–08–21
2	Kenji Johjima	6–00	200	Right	Right	1976–06–08
32	Rob Johnson	6–01	200	Right	Right	1983–07–22
#	INFIELDERS	HEIGHT	WEIGHT	THROWS	BATS	DATE OF BIRTH
29, 42, 29	Adrian Beltre	5–11	170	Right	Right	1978–04–07
5	Yuniesky Betancourt	5–10	190	Right	Right	1982–01–31
13	Miguel Cairo	6–00	160	Right	Right	1974–05–04
23	Tug Hulett	5–10	185	Right	Left	1983–02–28
39	Bryan LaHair	6–05	220	Right	Left	1982–11–05
4, 42, 4	Jose Lopez	6–02	170	Right	Right	1983–11–24
10	Greg Norton	6–01	190	Right	Both	1972–07–06
44	Richie Sexson	6–06	205	Right	Right	1974–12–29
27	Matt Tuiasosopo	6–02	223	Right	Right	1986–05–10
61	Luis Valbuena	5–10	200	Right	Left	1985–11–30
3	Jose Vidro	5–11	175	Right	Both	1974–08–27
#	OUTFIELDERS	HEIGHT	WEIGHT	THROWS	BATS	DATE OF BIRTH
50	Wladimir Balentien	6–02	190	Right	Right	1984–07–02
16	Willie Bloomquist	5–11	180	Right	Right	1977–11–27
28	Raul Ibanez	6–02	210	Right	Left	1972–06–02
25	Charlton Jimerson	6 03	210	Right	Right	1979–09–22
12	Mike Morse	6–04	220	Right	Right	1982–03–22
8	Jeremy Reed	6–00	185	Left	Left	1981–06–15
51	Ichiro Suzuki	5–09	160	Right	Left	1973–10–22
6	Brad Wilkerson	6–00	200	Left	Left	1977–06–01

Data courtesy of Baseball-Almanac.com.

#3 | Worst Collapse
Rotten to the (Big Apple) Core
The 2007 New York Mets

> Mets fans generally tend to assume the worst, so these days their depression is superimposed on their baseline dysphoria.
>
> —*Dr. Alan Manevitz,*
> *a psychiatrist who regularly attends Mets games*
> (New York Daily News, *2007)*

The resurrected New York Mets entered the 2007 baseball season defending their first Eastern Divisional Championship since 1988. The newly appointed and tremendously popular Willie Randolph left the crosstown rival Yankees staff and managed the franchise to an impressive 97–65 season. They had used the reinvigorating marketing slogan of "The Team—The Time—The Mets" and remained a preseason favorite among local sports prognosticators. Unfortunately their Cinderella follow-up season ended horrifically after the Mets perpetrated one of the biggest team breakdowns in memory.

The 2007 opener revealed a team that was still riding high on the mo-

mentum of the 2006 campaign. The Mets swept the St. Louis Cardinals and immediately jumped into first place in the National League East. An unlikely hero named John Maine, New York's underappreciated hurler, remained undefeated for the entire month of April and was named the National League's "Pitcher of the Month." And franchise slugger David Wright contributed to the cause by carrying over a hitting streak that began in 2006 and extended to a franchise-record

Mets fan voicing his disappointment
(AP Photo/Kathy Kihonicek)

26 games. It appeared, at least early on, that no one could stop this ferocious New York Mets juggernaut offensively or defensively.

May at Shea Stadium looked even better than April as pitching replacement Jorge Sosa came to the mound strong and posted a 4–1 record for the month. His 8–1 victory moved the team into sole possession of first place, where the Mets remained untouched until the final week of the season. Sosa's teammate Wright also maintained his slugging percentage and boasted 8 home runs and 22 RBIs during May. The Mets dominated their competition through the month, and finished May with an impressive 19–9 mark. They had a 4½-game lead going into June, and it looked like they would have a return engagement in the postseason. But it was not to be. Summer was not kind to the New Yorkers.

After losing six straight games in June, the Mets became the first team in major league history to play six consecutive series against six different playoff teams (Tigers, Dodgers, Yankees, Twins, Athletics, and Cardinals) from the prior season. This challenge proved too difficult, as the Mets lost 9 out of 12 contests. They then broke out of their slump by winning five out of the last six games.

Skipper Willie Randolph was fired in June and bench coach Jerry Manuel, a former "American League Manager of the Year" for the Chicago White Sox, took the reins for the rest of the year. It was a frustrating end for the 53-year-old Randolph, who was set to be a National League coach during the upcoming All-Star Game at Yankee Stadium. As the first black manager in all of New York's baseball history, Randolph's early dismissal resulted in cries of racism.

New York limped into the All-Star break with a decent 48–39 record. They held a slim two-game lead over the Atlanta Braves, but their inconsistent play had opened the door for opponents to play catch-up.

In August, the Mets traveled to historic Wrigley Field and won two out of three from the Central Division first-place Cubs. They then defeated the National League West first-place Diamondbacks a week later, propelling them into the second week of September 21 games over .500 and a record of 83–62. Martínez returned from an injury just in time for the playoff deadline, and a renewed sense of purpose swept through the clubhouse. By September 17, the Mets held first place in the National League East with an 83–66 record and a 2½-game lead over the charging Phillies. Still, they remained plagued by several disappointing losses that quickly narrowed the gap. New York lost four in a row, including a three-game sweep by Philadelphia.

The Mets' pitching staff, improved by some free-agent ace signings, accomplished several impressive individual records throughout the 2007 campaign.[1] Future Hall of Famers Pedro Martínez and Tom Glavine each reached milestones. Martínez notched his 3,000th strikeout and Glavine earned his 300th win. Meeting the playoff roster deadline of September 1, the Mets front office filled several holes in the lineup by picking up Luis Castillo and Jeff Conine.

Despite these moves, things continued to go badly for the Mets down the stretch. Poor pitching and random contributions at the plate devastated the team in close contests. Defeats at the hands of bad teams only added insult to injury. Instead of schooling bad teams like they had in the spring months, New York lost five out of six games with the fourth-place Washington Nationals. They also lost on September 28, falling into second place for the first time in four months. The Mets pulled themselves back into a tie with Philadelphia, but even their best players were slipping fast.

On the next-to-the-last day in September, the Mets faced the Florida Marlins, with hopes of shoring up the National League East or at least forcing a one-game playoff. Unfortunately, Tom Glavine shockingly surrendered seven runs in the first inning, as the Mets fell 8–1. The Phillies took advantage of the epic collapse by the Mets and capped a miraculous victory over the spoiler Nationals to literally steal the National League East title from their rivals. Not even the "Miracle Mets" could have saved them.

As the City of Brotherly Love erupted in jubilee, Mets fans erupted in agony after riding the highest peaks and darkest depths during the 2007 season. Some sports columnists called it one of the worst collapses in sports history. Ironically, many experts compared New York's collapse to that of the 1964 Phillies, who surrendered a 6½-game lead in the last 12 games.[2] In the end, the 2007 Mets completed the season with a disappointing record of 88 wins and 74 losses. They placed second in the National League East, and third in the Wild Card standings. They have not been back to the playoffs since.

The Mets' beat reporters immediately began criticizing the team's fall from grace and statistically declared their breakdown as *the* worst in modern memory. In a scathing piece titled "The Mets Are the Biggest Chokers of Them All," *Associated Content* reporter Zac Wassink proclaimed, "The 2007 Mets finished just one game behind the Phillies in the NL East. That means that all the Mets had to do was win two more games during their home stand at the end of the season in order to win the NL East. Instead, the Mets lost to the Nationals (73–89), the Cardinals (78–84) and the Marlins

(71–91) in six out of the last seven games of the season. I want to reiterate that all of those games were played at Shea."

He added,

At the end of August the Mets played a four-game series at Philadelphia. At that point New York still had the division well in hand. A split of the series would have done major damage to the psyche of the Phillies, not to mention threatening the chance that they would come back and take the NL East. Instead, the Mets got swept on the road in a series that included Billy Wagner blowing the final game, after the Mets made a comeback of their own by scoring five runs in the top of the eighth. In the middle of September the two teams faced off again, this time at Shea Stadium. The Mets had just finished taking two out of three from the Atlanta Braves, thus completely burying the Braves in the NL East. Instead of doing the same to the Phillies the Mets were swept again, blowing leads in the first two games of the series. How big are those two games now? Those two games are the difference between the Mets playing baseball in October and sitting on the couch watching those ridiculous Dane Cook "Actober" commercials.

Perhaps the New York Met's storied history as the "comeback kids" made their 2007 collapse all the more unpalatable. After debuting in 1962 as one of the worst teams ever in professional baseball, the "Amazin' Mets" climbed to the top in 1969 and were reincarnated four years later as the team that "Ya' Gotta Believe."

God only knows what kinds of nicknames the disappointed fans in blue and orange bestowed upon their team following the 2007 debacle, but you can probably bet they were not suitable for a kid's T-shirt.

2007 New York Mets Schedule

GAME	DATE/BOX SCORE	OPPONENT	SCORE	DECISION	RECORD
1	04–01–2007	at St. Louis Cardinals	6–1	W	1–0
2	04–03–2007	at St. Louis Cardinals	4–1	W	2–0
3	04–04–2007	at St. Louis Cardinals	10–0	W	3–0
4	04–06–2007	at Atlanta Braves	11–1	W	4–0
5	04–07–2007	at Atlanta Braves	3–5	L	4–1
6	04–08–2007	at Atlanta Braves	2–3	L	4–2
7	04–09–2007	vs Philadelphia Phillies	11–5	W	5–2
8	04–11–2007	vs Philadelphia Phillies	2–5	L	5–3
9	04–12–2007	vs Philadelphia Phillies	5–3	W	6–3
10	04–13–2007	vs Washington Nationals	3–2	W	7–3
11	04–14–2007	vs Washington Nationals	2–6	L	7–4
12	04–17–2007	at Philadelphia Phillies	8–1	W	8–4
13	04–18–2007	at Florida Marlins	9–2	W	9–4
14	04–19–2007	at Florida Marlins	11–3	W	10–4
15	04–20–2007	vs Atlanta Braves	3–7	L	10–5
16	04–21–2007	vs Atlanta Braves	7–2	W	11–5
17	04–22–2007	vs Atlanta Braves	6–9	L	11–6
18	04–23–2007	vs Colorado Rockies	6–1	W	12–6
19	04–24–2007	vs Colorado Rockies	2–1	W	13–6
20	04–25–2007	vs Colorado Rockies	5–11	L	13–7
21	04–27–2007	at Washington Nationals	3–4	L	13–8
22	04–28–2007	at Washington Nationals	6–2	W	14–8
23	04–29–2007	at Washington Nationals	1–0	W	15–8
24	04–30–2007	vs Florida Marlins	6–9	L	15–9
25	05–01–2007	vs Florida Marlins	2–5	L	15–10
26	05–02–2007	vs Florida Marlins	6–3	W	16–10
27	05–03–2007	at Arizona Diamondbacks	9–4	W	17–10
28	05–04–2007	at Arizona Diamondbacks	5–3	W	18–10
29	05–05–2007	at Arizona Diamondbacks	6–2	W	19–10
30	05–06–2007	at Arizona Diamondbacks	1–3	L	19–11
31	05–07–2007	at San Francisco Giants	4–9	L	19–12
32	05–08–2007	at San Francisco Giants	4–1	W	20–12
33	05–09–2007	at San Francisco Giants	5–3	W	21–12
34	05–11–2007	vs Milwaukee Brewers	5–4	W	22–12
35	05–12–2007	vs Milwaukee Brewers	3–12	L	22–13
36	05–13–2007	vs Milwaukee Brewers	9–1	W	23–13
37	05–14–2007	vs Chicago Cubs	5–4	W	24–13
38	05–15–2007	vs Chicago Cubs	1–10	L	24–14

2007 New York Mets Schedule (cont.)

GAME	DATE/BOX SCORE	OPPONENT	SCORE	DECISION	RECORD
39	05–16–2007	vs Chicago Cubs	8–1	W	25–14
40	05–17–2007	vs Chicago Cubs	6–5	W	26–14
41	05–18–2007	vs New York Yankees	3–2	W	27–14
42	05–19–2007	vs New York Yankees	10–7	W	28–14
43	05–20–2007	vs New York Yankees	2–6	L	28–15
44	05–22–2007	at Atlanta Braves	1–8	L	28–16
45	05–23–2007	at Atlanta Braves	3–0	W	29–16
46	05–24–2007	at Atlanta Braves	1–2	L	29–17
47	05–25–2007	at Florida Marlins	6–2	W	30–17
48	05–26–2007	at Florida Marlins	7–2	W	31–17
49	05–27–2007	at Florida Marlins	6–4	W	32–17
50	05–29–2007	vs San Francisco Giants	5–4	W	33–17
51	05–30–2007	vs San Francisco Giants	0–3	L	33–18
52	05–31–2007	vs San Francisco Giants	4–2	W	34–18
53	06–01–2007	vs Arizona Diamondbacks	1–5	L	34–19
54	06–02–2007	vs Arizona Diamondbacks	7–1	W	35–19
55	06–03–2007	vs Arizona Diamondbacks	1–4	L	35–20
56	06–05–2007	vs Philadelphia Phillies	2–4	L	35–21
57	06–06–2007	vs Philadelphia Phillies	2–4	L	35–22
58	06–07–2007	vs Philadelphia Phillies	3–6	L	35–23
59	06–08–2007	at Detroit Tigers	3–0	W	36–23
60	06–09–2007	at Detroit Tigers	7–8	L	36–24
61	06–10–2007	at Detroit Tigers	7–15	L	36–25
62	06–11–2007	at Los Angeles Dodgers	3–5	L	36–26
63	06–12–2007	at Los Angeles Dodgers	1–4	L	36–27
64	06–13–2007	at Los Angeles Dodgers	1–9	L	36–28
65	06–15–2007	at New York Yankees	2–0	W	37–28
66	06–16–2007	at New York Yankees	8–11	L	37–29
67	06–17–2007	at New York Yankees	2–8	L	37–30
68	06–18–2007	vs Minnesota Twins	8–1	W	38–30
69	06–19–2007	vs Minnesota Twins	0–9	L	38–31
70	06–20–2007	vs Minnesota Twins	2–6	L	38–32
71	06–22–2007	vs Oakland Athletics	9–1	W	39–32
72	06–23–2007	vs Oakland Athletics	1–0	W	40–32
73	06–24–2007	vs Oakland Athletics	10–2	W	41–32
74	06–25–2007	vs St. Louis Cardinals	2–1	W	42–32
75	06–26–2007	vs St. Louis Cardinals	3–5	L	42–33
76	06–27–2007	vs St. Louis Cardinals	2–0	W	43–33

2007 New York Mets Schedule (cont.)

GAME	DATE/BOX SCORE	OPPONENT	SCORE	DECISION	RECORD
77-I	06–29–2007	at Philadelphia Phillies	6–5	W	44–33
78-II	06–29–2007	at Philadelphia Phillies	5–2	W	45–33
79	06–30–2007	at Philadelphia Phillies	8–3	W	46–33
80	07–01–2007	at Philadelphia Phillies	3–5	L	46–34
81	07–02–2007	at Colorado Rockies	2–6	L	46–35
82	07–03–2007	at Colorado Rockies	3–11	L	46–36
83	07–04–2007	at Colorado Rockies	7–17	L	46–37
84	07–05–2007	at Houston Astros	6–2	W	47–37
85	07–06–2007	at Houston Astros	0–4	L	47–38
86	07–07–2007	at Houston Astros	5–3	W	48–38
87	07–08–2007	at Houston Astros	3–8	L	48–39
88	07–12–2007	vs Cincinnati Reds	3–2	W	49–39
89	07–13–2007	vs Cincinnati Reds	4–8	L	49–40
90	07–14–2007	vs Cincinnati Reds	2–1	W	50–40
91	07–15–2007	vs Cincinnati Reds	5–2	W	51–40
92	07–16–2007	at San Diego Padres	1–5	L	51–41
93	07–17–2007	at San Diego Padres	7–0	W	52–41
94	07–18–2007	at San Diego Padres	4–5	L	52–42
95	07–19–2007	at Los Angeles Dodgers	13–9	W	53–42
96	07–20–2007	at Los Angeles Dodgers	4–1	W	54–42
97	07–21–2007	at Los Angeles Dodgers	6–8	L	54–43
98	07–22–2007	at Los Angeles Dodgers	5–4	W	55–43
99	07–24–2007	vs Pittsburgh Pirates	8–4	W	56–43
100	07–25–2007	vs Pittsburgh Pirates	6–3	W	57–43
101	07–26–2007	vs Pittsburgh Pirates	4–8	L	57–44
102	07–27–2007	vs Washington Nationals	2–6	L	57–45
103-I	07–28–2007	vs Washington Nationals	3–1	W	58–45
104-II	07–28–2007	vs Washington Nationals	5–6	L	58–46
105	07–29–2007	vs Washington Nationals	5–0	W	59–46
106	07–31–2007	at Milwaukee Brewers	2–4	L	59–47
107	08–01–2007	at Milwaukee Brewers	8–5	W	60–47
108	08–02–2007	at Milwaukee Brewers	12–4	W	61–47
109	08–03–2007	at Chicago Cubs	6–2	W	62–47
110	08–04–2007	at Chicago Cubs	2–6	L	62–48
111	08–05–2007	at Chicago Cubs	8–3	W	63–48
112	08–07–2007	vs Atlanta Braves	3–7	L	63–49
113	08–08–2007	vs Atlanta Braves	4–3	W	64–49
114	08–09–2007	vs Atlanta Braves	6–7	L	64–50
115	08–10–2007	vs Florida Marlins	3–4	L	64–51

2007 New York Mets Schedule (cont.)

GAME	DATE/BOX SCORE	OPPONENT	SCORE	DECISION	RECORD
116	08–11–2007	vs Florida Marlins	5–7	L	64–52
117	08–12–2007	vs Florida Marlins	10–4	W	65–52
118	08–14–2007	at Pittsburgh Pirates	5–4	W	66–52
119	08–15–2007	at Pittsburgh Pirates	10–8	W	67–52
120	08–16–2007	at Pittsburgh Pirates	7–10	L	67–53
121	08–17–2007	at Washington Nationals	6–2	W	68–53
122	08–18–2007	at Washington Nationals	7–4	W	69–53
123	08–19–2007	at Washington Nationals	8–2	W	70–53
124	08–21–2007	vs San Diego Padres	7–6	W	71–53
125	08–22–2007	vs San Diego Padres	5–7	L	71–54
126	08–23–2007	vs San Diego Padres	8–9	L	71–55
127	08–24–2007	vs Los Angeles Dodgers	5–2	W	72–55
128	08–25–2007	vs Los Angeles Dodgers	4–3	W	73–55
129	08–26–2007	vs Los Angeles Dodgers	2–6	L	73–56
130	08–27–2007	at Philadelphia Phillies	2–9	L	73–57
131	08–28–2007	at Philadelphia Phillies	2–4	L	73–58
132	08–29–2007	at Philadelphia Phillies	2–3	L	73–59
133	08–30–2007	at Philadelphia Phillies	10–11	L	73–60
134	08–31–2007	at Atlanta Braves	7–1	W	74–60
135	09–01–2007	at Atlanta Braves	5–1	W	75–60
136	09–02–2007	at Atlanta Braves	3–2	W	76–60
137	09–03–2007	at Cincinnati Reds	10–4	W	77–60
138	09–04–2007	at Cincinnati Reds	11–7	W	78–60
139	09–05–2007	at Cincinnati Reds	0–7	L	78–61
140	09–07–2007	vs Houston Astros	11–3	W	79–61
141	09–08–2007	vs Houston Astros	3–1	W	80–61
142	09–09–2007	vs Houston Astros	4–1	W	81–61
143	09–10–2007	vs Atlanta Braves	3–2	W	82–61
144	09–11–2007	vs Atlanta Braves	5–13	L	82–62
145	09–12–2007	vs Atlanta Braves	4–3	W	83–62
146	09–14–2007	vs Philadelphia Phillies	2–3	L	83–63
147	09–15–2007	vs Philadelphia Phillies	3–5	L	83–64
148	09–16–2007	vs Philadelphia Phillies	6–10	L	83–65
149	09–17–2007	at Washington Nationals	4–12	L	83–66
150	09–18–2007	at Washington Nationals	8–9	L	83–67
151	09–19–2007	at Washington Nationals	8–4	W	84–67
152	09–20–2007	at Florida Marlins	7–8	L	84–68
153	09–21–2007	at Florida Marlins	9–6	W	85–68
154	09–22–2007	at Florida Marlins	7–2	W	86–68

2007 New York Mets Schedule (cont.)

GAME	DATE/BOX SCORE	OPPONENT	SCORE	DECISION	RECORD
155	09–23–2007	at Florida Marlins	7–6	W	87–68
156	09–24–2007	vs Washington Nationals	4–13	L	87–69
157	09–25–2007	vs Washington Nationals	9–10	L	87–70
158	09–26–2007	vs Washington Nationals	6–9	L	87–71
159	09–27–2007	vs St. Louis Cardinals	0–3	L	87–72
160	09–28–2007	vs Florida Marlins	4–7	L	87–73
161	09–29–2007	vs Florida Marlins	13–0	W	88–73
162	09–30–2007	vs Florida Marlins	1–8	L	88–74

Data courtesy of Baseball-Almanac.com.

#4 | Worst Pitching Staff
Scoring 10 Runs a Game But Still Losing
The 1930 Philadelphia Phillies

The Philadelphia Phillies called tiny Baker Bowl home during the 1930s. The little stadium featured tin-covered outfield fences, meaning that baseballs rebounded off them with a loud "boom."[1] The tiny bandbox featured a right-field fence that loomed only 272 feet away from home plate, meaning that it was a hitter's paradise. And the 1930 Phillies could hit. They took advantage of new baseballs that featured a hitter-friendly resilient core and flatter seams. Featuring future Hall of Fame left-fielder Chuck Klein, the 1930 Phils posted a team batting average of .315. Every regular position player on the team hit at least .282 that year.

Klein had a monster year. He hit .386, with 250 base hits, including 59 doubles and 40 homers. He scored 158 runs and drove in a staggering 170.[2] Right-fielder Lefty O'Doul, a failed pitcher who had been converted to the outfield, nearly matched him. O'Doul hit .383, with 202 hits, 37 doubles, and 22 homers. He scored 122 runs and drove in 97. Third baseman Pinky Whitney hit .342 with 207 hits and 117 RBIs. The team scored 944 runs and just pounded the ball all over their friendly little ballpark. This Phillies team set franchise records for hits, singles, doubles, total bases, runs, and runs batted in, all of which still stand, nearly 80 years later.

With that kind of offense, one would think that the Phils would have won the National League.

PHILADELPHIA BALL PARK OF NATIONAL LEAGUE, PHILADELPHIA, PA.

Philadelphia's beloved ballpark: The Baker Bowl (Library of Congress)

Wrong. This team posted a 52–102 record and finished dead last. Why? Because opposing teams hit a staggering .350 against what has to be the worst pitching staff in the history of major league baseball. The team's ERA was an incredible 6.71. The Phillies also made matters much worse by leading the National League with 239 errors, 23 more than the next worse fielding team. The atrocious pitching and awful fielding combined for a total of 1,199 runs being scored against the Phillies that year, a record for wretchedness that stands to this day. The Phightin' Phils regularly scored 10 runs per game and still lost.

"Fidgety Phil" Collins was the only member of the pitching staff to have a decent season, posting a 16–11 record and an ERA of 4.78. The right-hander was the only Phillies hurler with an ERA less than 5.0. Supporting him was righty Claude Willoughby, who went 4–17 with a ghastly ERA of 7.59. Willoughby gave up a staggering 241 hits in only 153 innings. Southpaw Les Sweetland posted a 7–15 record with an ERA of 7.71. He surrendered 271 hits in 160 innings. Right-hander Ray Benge went 11–15 with a 5.70 ERA. Righty starter Hap Collard was 6–12 and 6.80, and right-handed relief pitcher Hal Elliott was 6–11 with a 7.67 ERA, meaning that he gave up least one run in every appearance that season.

Even Grover Cleveland "Pete" Alexander, one of the greatest pitchers to ever toe the rubber, put up terrible numbers in his final major league season. Alexander, who went 31–10 with a 1.22 ERA for the National League champion 1915 Phillies, was now 43 years old and clearly at the end of the line of a glorious career that featured a record of 373–208 and a guaranteed spot in the Hall of Fame. In 9 appearances in 1930, Alexander went 0–3, with an astronomical 9.14 ERA. The old righty gave up an unfathomable 40 hits in just 22⅓ innings. He wisely retired after 19 years in the major leagues before further tainting his otherwise magnificent career.

It's difficult to imagine a pitching staff much worse than the one employed by the 1930 Philadelphia Phillies. Indeed, the 1930 Phillies staff richly deserves the hard-earned title of worst pitching staff in the history of major league baseball, establishing a record for wretchedness that will probably never be eclipsed.

1930 Philadelphia Phillies Statmaster: Pitching

NAME	GAMES	W	L	W%	ERA	GS	CG	IP	HA	BB	SO	SHU
Grover Alexander	9	0	3	.000	9.14	3	0	21.2	40	6	6	0
Ray Benge	38	11	15	.423	5.70	29	14	225.2	305	81	70	0
Hap Collard	30	6	12	.333	6.80	15	4	127.0	188	39	25	0
Phil Collins	47	16	11	.593	4.78	25	17	239.0	287	86	87	1
Hal Elliott	48	6	11	.353	7.67	11	2	117.1	191	58	37	0
Snipe Hansen	22	0	7	.000	6.72	9	1	84.1	123	38	25	0
Lou Koupal	13	0	4	.000	8.59	4	1	36.2	52	17	11	0
John Milligan	9	1	2	.333	3.18	2	1	28.1	26	21	7	0
Chet Nichols	16	1	2	.333	6.79	5	1	59.2	76	16	15	0
Buz Phillips	14	0	0	.000	8.04	1	0	43.2	68	18	9	0
Harry Smythe	25	0	3	.000	7.79	3	0	49.2	84	31	9	0
By Speece	11	0	0	.000	13.27	0	0	19.2	41	4	9	0
Les Sweetland	34	7	15	.318	7.71	25	8	167.0	271	60	36	1
Claude Willoughby	41	4	17	.190	7.59	24	5	153.0	241	68	38	1
TEAM TOTALS		52	102	.338	6.71	156	54	1372.2	1,993	543	384	3

Data courtesy of Baseball-Almanac.com.

#5 | Worst Scandal
Cheaters Never Win
The 1919 "Black Sox" Scandal

> Regardless of the verdict of juries, no player that
> throws a ball game, no player that entertains propos-
> als or promises to throw a game, no player that sits
> in a conference with a bunch of crooked players and
> gamblers where the ways and means of throwing
> games are discussed, and does not promptly tell his
> club about it, will ever play professional baseball.
> —*Commissioner Kenesaw Mountain Landis*

Even a casual baseball fan can tell you a little something about the Black Sox scandal of 1919. The very fiber that held the game together was challenged when the news broke a year after the series that a fix was on from the first inning of the first game of the 1919 World Series. Eight members of the participating White Sox, including pitchers Eddie Cicotte and Claude (Lefty) Williams, outfielders Joe Jackson and Happy Felsch, first baseman Chick Gandil, shortstop Swede Risberg, third baseman Buck Weaver, and reserve infielder Fred McMullin were all charged with conspiring to fix the outcome of the Fall Classic against the Cincinnati Reds. Cynics realized that something was fishy before the series even started when the pregame betting odds reversed shortly before the first game. Chicago's White Sox were originally slated as heavy favorites, but later became underdogs to the Cincinnati Reds. Despite the rumors, most fans and members of the press accepted the games to be fairly and honestly played, but all that changed in 1920 when suspicions turned into confessions.

The first game of the 1919 scandal featured an outstanding and "authentic" performance by the Reds' pitcher Dutch Ruether. In addition to going the distance in a six hitter, he went three for three with two triples and three runs batted in. Greasy Neale, who led his team in hitting at .351, also performed well at the plate in tandem with teammate Jake Daubert. The White Sox put on quite a show themselves, losing 9–1 in questionable fashion. Nothing changed the following day as Cincinnati's Slim Sallee faired the same, tossing a 4–2 Game 2 victory that was scaled by a Larry

1919 Chicago "Black Sox" (Baseball Hall of Fame Library, Cooperstown, NY)

Kopf two-run triple in the fourth. Dickey Kerr, an up-and-coming White Sox rookie, drew the start for Game 3. Apparently untouched by the scandal, the tough left-hander refused to roll over and threw a three-hit 3–0 winner to put Chicago back in the race (whether they wanted to be or not).

The inspired Reds, unaware that a fix was on, pitched back-to-back shutouts in Games 4 and 5 on the arms of Jimmy Ring (2–0) and Hod Eller (5–0), who sat down six consecutive batters. But wait! It wasn't over yet . . . In any other year, the series would have ended there, but 1919 was different. Due to the intense postwar interest, the commissioner of baseball decided to extend this Fall Classic to a best-of-nine affair.

To curb further suspicion, the Black Sox made a reasonable effort and rebounded in the following two games with 5–4 and 4–1 victories. Cincinnati "dominated" the final outing "with a little help" from their crooked rivals in a 10–5 stomp that started with four runs in the first inning. The Reds unexpectedly won their first World Championship in their first Fall Classic appearance. Unfortunately, the victory turned bittersweet after the scandal blew up a year later. The Black Sox camouflaged their deception by being selective in their misdeeds. Joe Jackson batted a series-leading

.375 but acknowledged that he had let up in key situations. Buck Weaver also performed well at the plate by hitting .324. Chick Gandil had game-deciding hits in two outings and Eddie Cicotte tossed a one-run game to avoid elimination.

After a lengthy investigation in 1920, the members of Chicago's tainted team were surprisingly acquitted the following year despite their own confessions (which were recanted later). All of the players involved were banned from baseball because of their undeniable link to gamblers. The league offices constantly denied accusations from the press that professional baseball itself was in on the take and made every effort to assure the fans that the 1919 scandal was an isolated incident. "Regardless of the verdict of juries," commissioner Kenesaw Mountain Landis said in a statement, "no player that throws a ball game, no player that entertains proposals or promises to throw a game, no player that sits in a conference with a bunch of crooked players and gamblers where the ways and means of throwing games are discussed, and does not promptly tell his club about it, will ever again play professional baseball."

Although fan favorite "Shoeless Joe" Jackson maintained his innocence until his death in 1951, he had, in fact, previously confessed to the act on September 28, 1920. On being called as a witness before a Cook County grand jury investigating the scandal, he submitted to an interview.

The transcripts of that session were recorded in a signed confession, and then swiftly disappeared because, it is believed, of a cynical deal cut between the White Sox owner, Charles A. Comiskey, and the gambler Arnold Rothstein. The lack of hard evidence helped Jackson and his teammates escape criminal convictions.

Three years later, when Jackson sued Comiskey and baseball to be reinstated—Commissioner Landis had banned him despite the court's

Outfielder "Shoeless" Joe Jackson
(Library of Congress)

decision—the confession mysteriously resurfaced, and Jackson lost the suit. Jackson's testimony is damning, conflicting, and compelling all at the same time, and some have argued for decades that the confession was coerced. Following are excerpts:

> Q. (By assistant state's attorney Hartley L. Replogle): Did anybody pay you any money to help throw that Series in favor of Cincinnati?
>
> A. They did.
>
> Q. How much did they pay you?
>
> A. They promised me $20,000 and paid me 5.
>
> Q. (Did Mrs. Jackson) know that you got $5,000 for helping throw these games?
>
> A. She did . . . yes.
>
> Q. What did she say about it?
>
> A. She said she thought it was an awful thing to do.
>
> Q. That was after the fourth game?
>
> A. I believe it was, yes.
> (Jackson said that Lefty Williams, the Chicago pitcher, was the intermediary between him and the gamblers.)
>
> Q. When did he promise the $20,000?
>
> A. It was to be paid after each game.
> (But Jackson got only $5,000, thrown onto his hotel bed by Williams after the fourth game. Jackson was asked what he said to Williams.)
>
> A. I asked him what the hell had come off here.
>
> Q. What did he say?
>
> A. He said (Chick) Gandil (the Chicago first baseman, and player ringleader) said we all got a screw . . . that we got double-crossed. I don't think Gandil was crossed as much as he crossed us.
>
> Q. At the end of the first game you didn't get any money, did you?
>
> A. No, I did not, no, sir.
>
> Q. What did you do then?
>
> A. I asked Gandil what is the trouble? He says, "Everything is all right." He had it.
>
> Q. Then you went ahead and threw the second game, thinking you would get it then, is that right?
>
> A. We went ahead and threw the second game.
> After the third game I says, "Somebody is getting a nice little jazz, everybody is crossed." He said, "Well, Abe Attel and Bill Burns had crossed him." Attel and Burns were gamblers in the conspiracy.
> (Then Jackson was asked about the fourth game of the Series.)

Q. Did you see any fake plays?

A. Only the wildness of (Eddie) Cicotte (Chicago pitcher).

Q. Did you make any intentional errors yourself that day?

A. No sir, not during the whole series.

Q. Did you bat to win?

A. Yes.

Q. And run the bases to win?

A. Yes, sir.

Q. And field the balls at the outfield to win?

A. I did. . . . I tried to win all the games.

Q. Weren't you very much peeved that you only got $5,000 and you expected to get 20?

A. No, I was ashamed of myself.

Q. Where did you put the $5,000 (that Williams gave him)?

A. I put it in my pocket.

Q. What did Mrs. Jackson say about it?

A. She felt awful bad about it, cried about it a while.

Q. Had you ever played crooked baseball before this?

A. No, sir, I never had.

Q. You think now Williams may have crossed you, too?

A. Well, dealing with crooks, you know, you get crooked every way. This is my first experience and last.

The sting of these revelations was far-reaching and personally felt by both the fans and the media. Nevertheless, some refused to believe the accusations or the verdict of the criminal court. For example, Francis C. Richter, editor for the *Reach Baseball Guide,* wrote the following in 1920:

Any man who knows anything at all about base ball and base ball players knows absolutely that both the game and its exemplars are absolutely honest so far as its public presentation is concerned, and any man who insinuates that the 1919 World's Series was not honorably played by every participant therein not only does not know what he is talking about, but is a menace to the game quite as much as the gamblers would be if they had the ghost of a chance to get in their nefarious work.

In 2009, ESPN Senior Writer Rob Neyer voiced his own sentiments about the scandal that still stains the legacies of the participants 89 years after their betrayal, writing:

Joe Jackson agreed to throw the World Series, and he received $5,000 for doing so. The evidence that he actually did throw the Series is slightly less than conclusive, but in a way that's irrelevant. He certainly knew what was going on, and he probably helped. And that's all we need to know. Shoeless Joe's not a god, nor even a ghost. He was a man who happened to play baseball exceptionally well. Frankly, he doesn't deserve all this adulation, and if he were still with us he probably wouldn't understand it. As David Fleitz writes in his fine book, *Shoeless: The Life and Times of Joe Jackson:*

> Joseph Jackson died in 1951 but lives on as Shoeless Joe, more a myth than a man, a ghostly figure walking out of a cornfield wanting nothing more than to play the game he loved. The real Joe Jackson, the South Carolina mill hand and small-town businessman, would smile and shake his head at the legend that surrounds Shoeless Joe today. Strangers leaving flowers at his grave, paying tens of thousands of dollars for his autograph, writing emotional letters to the commissioner of baseball. For what, really? Joe Jackson played baseball, that's all. Played the game, made some money, got into a little scrape up north, and came back home to South Carolina. That's all.
>
> Hey, I'm as sentimental as the next guy. I cry when I watch *The Natural,* and I think Iowa really is something like heaven. But Joe Jackson and his cohorts committed a truly evil crime, compromising the integrity of their profession and violating the trust of their fans.

To this day, participants in the Black Sox conspiracy have been denied entry into the Baseball Hall of Fame, and the controversy surrounding the 1919 Fall Classic still resonates. Shelves full of books and a number of major motion pictures and documentaries have been produced over the years all claiming to have the "real" story.

In the late 1990s, a movement to reinstate Joe Jackson sprung up. In 1998, the South Carolina General Assembly passed a resolution requesting that Jackson be reinstated as a member in good standing in professional baseball, thereby qualifying him for induction into Cooperstown. In 1999, U.S. Sen. Strom Thurmond, R-S.C., petitioned MLB Commissioner Bud Selig to reinstate Shoeless Joe. These efforts failed, and Jackson and the other Black Sox scalawags remain ostracized from the game they besmirched.

Perhaps Connie Mack had it right when he said: "Jackson's fall from grace is one of the real tragedies of baseball. I always thought he was more sinned against than sinning."

1919 World Series: Composite Statistics

CINCINNATI REDS: COMPOSITE HITTING STATISTICS													
NAME	POS	G	AB	H	2B	3B	HR	R	RBI	AVG	BB	SO	SB
Jake Daubert	1b	8	29	7	0	1	0	4	1	.241	1	2	1
Pat Duncan	of	8	26	7	2	0	0	3	8	.269	2	2	0
Hod Eller	p	2	7	2	1	0	0	2	0	.286	0	2	0
Ray Fisher	p	2	2	1	0	0	0	0	0	.500	0	0	0
Heinie Groh	3b	8	29	5	2	0	0	6	2	.172	6	4	0
Larry Kopf	ss	8	27	6	0	2	0	3	2	.222	3	2	0
Dolf Luque	p	2	1	0	0	0	0	0	0	.000	0	1	0
Sherry Magee	ph	2	2	1	0	0	0	0	0	.500	0	0	0
Greasy Neale	of	8	28	10	1	1	0	3	4	.357	2	5	1
Bill Rariden	c	5	19	4	0	0	0	0	2	.211	0	0	1
Morrie Rath	2b	8	31	7	1	0	0	5	2	.226	4	1	2
Jimmy Ring	p	2	5	0	0	0	0	0	0	.000	0	2	0
Edd Roush	of	8	28	6	2	1	0	6	7	.214	3	0	2
Dutch Ruether	p-2	3	6	4	1	2	0	2	4	.667	1	0	0
Slim Sallee	p	2	4	0	0	0	0	0	0	.000	0	0	0
Jimmy Smith	pr	1	0	0	0	0	0	0	0	.000	0	0	0
Ivey Wingo	c	3	7	4	0	0	0	1	1	.571	3	1	0
TOTALS			251	64	10	7	0	35	33	.255	25	22	7

CHICAGO WHITE SOX: COMPOSITE HITTING STATISTICS													
NAME	POS	G	AB	H	2B	3B	HR	R	RBI	AVG	BB	SO	SB
Eddie Cicotte	p	3	8	0	0	0	0	0	0	.000	0	3	0
Eddie Collins	2b	8	31	7	1	0	0	2	1	.226	1	2	1
Shano Collins	of	4	16	4	1	0	0	2	0	.250	0	0	0
Happy Felsch	of	8	26	5	1	0	0	2	3	.192	1	4	0
Chick Gandil	1b	8	30	7	0	1	0	1	5	.233	1	3	1
Joe Jackson	of	8	32	12	3	0	1	5	6	.375	1	2	0
Bill James	p	1	2	0	0	0	0	0	0	.000	0	1	0
Dickie Kerr	p	2	6	1	0	0	0	0	0	.167	0	0	0
Nemo Leibold	of	5	18	1	0	0	0	0	0	.056	2	3	1
Grover Lowdermilk	p	1	0	0	0	0	0	0	0	.000	0	0	0
Byrd Lynn	c	1	1	0	0	0	0	0	0	.000	0	0	0
Erskine Mayer	p	1	0	0	0	0	0	0	0	.000	0	0	0
Fred McMullin	ph	2	2	1	0	0	0	0	0	.500	0	0	0
Eddie Murphy	ph	3	2	0	0	0	0	0	0	.000	0	1	0
Swede Risberg	ss	8	25	2	0	1	0	3	0	.080	5	3	1
Ray Schalk	c	8	23	7	0	0	0	1	2	.304	4	2	1
Buck Weaver	3b	8	34	11	4	1	0	4	0	.324	0	2	0
Roy Wilkinson	p	2	2	0	0	0	0	0	0	.000	0	1	0
Lefty Williams	p	3	5	1	0	0	0	0	0	.200	0	3	0
TOTALS			263	59	10	3	1	20	17	.224	15	30	5

Data courtesy of Baseball-Almanac.com.

1919 World Series: Composite Statistics (cont.)

CINCINNATI REDS: COMPOSITE PITCHING STATISTICS

NAME	W	L	G	GS	CG	S	SH	IP	ERA	H	SO	ER	BB
Hod Eller	2	0	2	2	2	0	1	18.0	2.00	13	15	4	2
Ray Fisher	0	1	2	1	0	0	0	7.2	2.35	7	2	2	2
Dolf Luque	0	0	2	0	0	0	0	5.0	0.00	1	6	0	0
Jimmy Ring	1	1	2	1	1	0	1	14.0	0.64	7	4	1	6
Dutch Ruether	1	0	2	2	1	0	0	14.0	2.57	12	1	4	4
Slim Sallee	1	1	2	2	1	0	0	13.1	1.35	19	2	2	1
TOTALS	5	3	12	8	5	0	2	72.0	1.63	59	30	13	15

CHICAGO WHITE SOX: COMPOSITE PITCHING STATISTICS

NAME	W	L	G	GS	CG	S	SH	IP	ERA	H	SO	ER	BB
Eddie Cicotte	1	2	3	3	2	0	0	21.2	2.91	19	7	7	5
Bill James	0	0	1	0	0	0	0	4.2	5.79	8	2	3	3
Dickie Kerr	2	0	2	2	2	0	1	19.0	1.42	14	6	3	3
Grover Lowdermilk	0	0	1	0	0	0	0	1.0	9.00	2	0	1	1
Erskine Mayer	0	0	1	0	0	0	0	1.0	0.00	0	0	0	1
Roy Wilkinson	0	0	2	0	0	0	0	7.1	1.23	9	3	1	4
Lefty Williams	0	3	3	3	1	0	0	16.1	6.61	12	4	12	8
TOTALS	3	5	13	8	5	0	1	71.0	3.42	64	22	27	25

Data courtesy of Baseball-Almanac.com.

#6 | Worst Call
*61 in '61
Maris Gets the Asterisk

> Ah, bullshit. It was you Rodge. You did it, you son of a
> bitch. Nobody can ever take that away from you.
> — *Mickey Mantle (Thomas Jane) to Roger Maris*
> *(Barry Pepper) in the Billy Crystal film *61*

When modern baseball fans look back at all the classic record-breaking moments that they have witnessed in their lifetime, one number probably stands out in their minds—the number 62. Why? Because most of them could never forget the excitement and pageantry of watching Mark McGwire and Sammy Sosa set new standards in 1998 by both breaking the all-time single season home run record, the most revered record in all of sports.

For the first time in a long time, America's passion for the game resembled the glory days, when it truly was our nation's pastime and the players were larger-than-life heroes. And although their legacy has come under scrutiny due to the steroids scandal that has stained the entire era, both McGwire and Sosa received credit for giving major league baseball a much-needed shot in the arm (no pun intended).

Despite the fact that another suspicious slugger named Barry Bonds has since set the new magic number at 73, their race seemed more romantic and brought a lot of overdue attention to the man whose record they were chasing, Roger Maris. It also seemed more fitting that they were both competing to break the record, just as Maris and his teammate Mickey Mantle had in 1961. Both contests were between two friends pushing each other to be better on and off the field—neither allowing their competitiveness to get in the way of their friendship or allowing their friendship to get in the way of their competitiveness.

The press dubbed them the "M&M Boys," and their story provides an incredible example of the impact sports can have when two teammates who are as opposite as can be come together to create something special together. To understand this, one has to look at both men individually to really understand what they accomplished together.

Right-Fielder and "Bronx Bombardier" Roger Maris (Library of Congress)

Roger Maris was a great ballplayer who never got the respect he deserved.[1] Unfortunately, the press never really considered him "hero" material, but when examining his life on and off the field, you realize that he was the ideal hero. He was a good husband, father, and athlete who was more concerned with the success of his team than with his own individual stats, an attitude seldom seen in today's game.

No record ever hung around a player's neck like an albatross than did Roger Maris' 61 homers in 1961. As late as the 1980 All-Star Game, he fumed, "They acted as though I was doing something wrong, poisoning the record books or something. Do you know what I have to show for 61 home runs? Nothing. Exactly nothing." In surpassing Babe Ruth's supposedly unsurpassable record, Maris faced the hostility of the baseball public on several fronts.

First, although he had been the 1960 American League Most Valuable Player (MVP), he was a .269 hitter, still an unknown quantity unworthy of dethroning America's greatest sports hero. That he played the game with a ferocious intensity and that he was a brilliant right fielder and an exceptional base runner, well, that was irrelevant.

Second, for most of the season Maris wasn't the only batter chasing the ghost of the Babe. His teammate Mickey Mantle, the successor to Ruth, to Lou Gehrig, and to Joe DiMaggio, was the people's choice. Mantle hit the 500-foot home runs that thrilled fans. Mantle garnered support as the season-long duel headed toward September.

Maris? He was merely efficient, a left-handed hitter who had just the right swing to take advantage of the friendly short porch in Yankee Stadium's right field. He rarely hit a homer farther than 400 feet, and he had almost no charisma. That 1961 season was the first year of expansion, and the first year of the expanded 162-game season. With the addition of two teams to the American League, many hitters had their greatest seasons, such as Detroit's Norm Cash, who somehow hit .361, corked bat and all. Expansion also meant an expanded schedule. Ruth set his record in 1927 in a 154-game season, and many believed that the only way to legitimately break his record was to do so in 154 games, not 162.

So, for many people, Maris' feat would be tainted if he needed more than 154 games to break Ruth's record. Commissioner Ford Frick even announced that if Maris took more than 154 games to break the record, it would go into the record books as a separate accomplishment from Ruth's, with an asterisk. "As a ballplayer, I would be delighted to do it again," Maris remarked. "As an individual, I doubt if I could possibly go through it again. They even asked for my autograph at mass." As always, Maris was being honest. He once said about playing baseball for a living, "It's a business. If I could make more money down in the zinc mines, I'd be mining zinc." Could anyone have been more unlike the Babe?

In his first game in Yankee pinstripes, Maris singled, doubled, and smacked two home runs. His 1960 MVP numbers included a league-leading 112 RBIs and 39 home runs, only one behind league-leader Mantle, although he missed 18 games with injuries. In 1961, Maris stayed healthy and played 161 games, a career high. As he and Mantle made their charge at Ruth's home run record, the Yankees even considered switching Maris, who batted third, and Mantle, who batted fourth, to give Mantle a better shot at the record.

If the switch had been made, Maris almost certainly would not have broken the record. Consider this: Maris did not receive one intentional walk in 1961. After all, who would walk Maris to get to Mantle? The pressure to beat Ruth became so intense for Maris that clumps of his hair fell out. "I never wanted all this hoopla," Maris said. "All I wanted is to be a good ballplayer, hit 25 or 30 homers, drive in around a hundred runs, hit

.280, and help my club win pennants. I just wanted to be one of the guys, an average player having a good season."

Mantle suffered a hip injury in the middle of September that forced him out of the lineup and out of the race. Even with Mantle out of the lineup, Maris kept it up and went into the 154th game of the season in Baltimore with 58 homers. He gave it his best shot that night. He hit number 59 and then hit a long foul on his second-to-last at bat. Alas, in his last at bat, against tough knuckleballer Hoyt Wilhelm, he hit a checked-swing grounder. "Maybe I'm not a great man, but I damn well want to break the record," he said. He finally did it on the last day of the season against the Red Sox's Tracy Stallard. Fittingly, the long fly only traveled about 340 feet into Yankee Stadium's short right-field porch. Maris garnered back-to-back MVP honors after driving in a league leading 142 runs.

As expected, major league baseball (MLB) Commissioner (and the Babe's ghostwriter) Ford C. Frick ruled that because Maris had played a 162-game schedule (as opposed to Ruth's 154), his record would be listed officially with a qualifying asterisk, an edict that stood until 1991. Although Maris never experienced the same outrageous success with the bat, his consistency as a power hitter continued, and he clubbed 275 home runs during his 12-year career.

Maris remained bitter about the experience for the rest of his life. Speaking at the 1980 All-Star Game, he said of the 1961 season, "They acted as though I was doing something wrong, poisoning the record books or something. Do you know what I have to show for 61 home runs? Nothing. Exactly nothing." Later, Maris even surmised that it might have been better all along had he not broken the record or even threatened it at all.

Mickey Mantle, like Maris, was also an exceptional athlete from the Midwest, but with a press-friendly personality and movie-star good looks that made him a fan favorite both on and off the field. The "Mick" fit the Yankee persona perfectly, and his contributions to the pinstripes were on par with the long line of Yankee legends that came before him. Mickey represented what America is all about: a young kid from the Midwest, going to the big city, living the American dream and becoming a sports legend. A courageous player, he achieved greatness despite an arrested case of osteomyelitis, numerous injuries, and frequent surgeries.

The powerful Yankee switch-hitter belted 536 homers (many of the tape-measure variety), won the American League home run and slugging titles four times, collected 2,415 hits, and batted .300 or more 10 times. The three-time MVP was named to 20 All-Star teams. He holds numerous World Series records, including most home runs (18).

They were opposites, yes, but they were also equals. Both summed up their careers perfectly. Mickey said, "It was all I lived for, to play baseball." and Roger was quoted as saying, "All I wanted was to be a good ballplayer."

Maris has not been elected to the National Baseball Hall of Fame, but his teammate Mantle was elected unanimously in his first year of eligibility. Many historians credit Ford Frick's decision to "footnote" Maris' epic achievement as preventing him from being put on the ballot. Others simply state that Maris did not have the cumulative statistics to warrant such an honor. Ironically, the decision to add the asterisk has also stained the commissioner's legacy.

The first MLB leader not to have a political background, Ford Frick was a multitalented journalist with experience in teaching, ghost writing, and advertising. After graduating from DePauw University, Frick took a position as an English teacher at Colorado High School and also freelanced as a beat writer for the *Colorado Springs Gazette*. Two years later, he left teaching to become the supervisor of training in the rehabilitation division of the War Department for four states (Colorado, Utah, New Mexico, and Wyoming). Although the position was important, Frick could not ignore his "writer's bug," and briefly worked for the *Rocky Mountain News* in Denver before returning to Colorado Springs to open his own advertising agency and write a weekly editorial column for the *Colorado Springs Telegraph*.

An enthusiastic baseball fan, Frick landed his dream job in 1922 after joining the sports staff of the *New York American*. The following year, he moved on to the *Evening Journal,* where he covered the New York Yankees and eventually became a ghostwriter for Babe Ruth. Things got even better when he finally left the typewriter behind in favor of the microphone to become a sportscaster with station WOR. A rising figure in the sports media, Frick was named the first director of the National League Service Bureau and was put in charge of all publicity for major league baseball. He excelled at the position and was later elected as the president of the National League, succeeding John A. Heydler.

His first act as president was a passionate proposal for the establishment of a National Baseball Museum to honor the greatest players ever to take the field. This, of course, led to the founding of the Hall of Fame. He was also instrumental in saving several franchises from bankruptcy, including the Brooklyn Dodgers, Philadelphia Phillies, Boston Braves, Cincinnati Reds, and the Pittsburgh Pirates. Immensely popular among the owners, he remained president of the National League until 16 of the owners elected him commissioner in September 1951.

Frick was responsible for many changes in the reconstruction, expansion, and transition of baseball during his tenure as commissioner. Some of the major changes included the growth from 8 to 10 teams in each league, the establishment of multiple national television contracts, a league draft and college scholarship system, and the introduction of baseball on the international level in countries such as Japan, Central America, Holland, Italy, and Africa.

Not unlike the major league baseball founders, Frick was criticized on several occasions for policies that did not agree with the public's view. The verdict surrounding Roger Maris' single-season home-run record remained at the top of that list. That decision stood for the next 30 years and remained as a black eye on Frick's otherwise stellar career. Frick was inducted into the Hall of Fame that he helped to establish in 1970. He also became the namesake of the Ford C. Frick Award, which is given to outstanding Hall of Fame broadcasters.

In 1991, then MLB Commissioner Fay Vincent officially removed the asterisk from the record. Unfortunately, Roger Maris passed away in 1985 and never received full credit for his unparalleled athletic accomplishment.

61 Home Runs by Roger Maris

HR	GAME	DATE/BOX	PITCHER	TEAM	THROWS	WHERE	INNING
1	11	04–26–1961	Paul Foytack	Detroit	Right	Away	5th
2	17	05–03–1961	Pedro Ramos	Minnesota	Right	Away	7th
3	20	05–06–1961	Eli Grba	Los Angeles	Right	Away	5th
4	29	05–17–1961	Pete Burnside	Washington	Left	Home	8th
5	30	05–19–1961	Jim Perry	Cleveland	Right	Away	1st
6	31	05–20–1961	Gary Bell	Cleveland	Right	Away	3rd
7	32	05–21–1961	Chuck Estrada	Baltimore	Right	Home	1st
8	35	05–24–1961	Gene Conley	Boston	Right	Home	4th
9	38	05–28–1961	Cal McLish	Chicago	Right	Home	2nd
10	40	05–30–1961	Gene Conley	Boston	Right	Away	3rd
11	40	05–30–1961	Mike Fornieles	Boston	Right	Away	8th
12	41	05–31–1961	Billy Muffett	Boston	Right	Away	3rd
13	43	06–02–1961	Cal McLish	Chicago	Right	Away	3rd
14	44	06–03–1961	Bob Shaw	Chicago	Right	Away	8th
15	45	06–04–1961	Russ Kemmerer	Chicago	Right	Away	3rd
16	48	06–06–1961	Ed Palmquist	Minnesota	Right	Home	6th
17	49	06–07–1961	Pedro Ramos	Minnesota	Right	Home	3rd
18	52	06–09–1961	Ray Herbert	Kansas City	Right	Home	7th
19	55	06–11–1961	Eli Grba	Los Angeles	Right	Home	3rd

61 Home Runs by Roger Maris (cont.)

HR	GAME	DATE/BOX	PITCHER	TEAM	THROWS	WHERE	INNING
20	55	06–11–1961	Johnny James	Los Angeles	Right	Home	7th
21	57	06–13–1961	Jim Perry	Cleveland	Right	Away	6th
22	58	06–14–1961	Gary Bell	Cleveland	Right	Away	4th
23	61	06–17–1961	Don Mossi	Detroit	Left	Away	4th
24	62	06–18–1961	Jerry Casale	Detroit	Right	Away	8th
25	63	06–19–1961	Jim Archer	Kansas City	Left	Away	9th
26	64	06–20–1961	Joe Nuxhall	Kansas City	Left	Away	1st
27	66	06–22–1961	Norm Bass	Kansas City	Right	Away	2nd
28	74	07–01–1961	Dave Sisler	Washington	Right	Home	9th
29	75	07–02–1961	Pete Burnside	Washington	Left	Home	3rd
30	75	07–02–1961	Johnny Klippstein	Washington	Right	Home	7th
31	77	07–04–1961	Frank Lary	Detroit	Right	Home	8th
32	78	07–05–1961	Frank Funk	Cleveland	Right	Home	7th
33	82	07–09–1961	Bill Monbouquette	Boston	Right	Home	7th
34	84	07–13–1961	Early Wynn	Chicago	Right	Away	1st
35	86	07–15–1961	Ray Herbert	Chicago	Right	Away	3rd
36	92	07–21–1961	Bill Monbouquette	Boston	Right	Away	1st
37	95	07–25–1961	Frank Baumann	Chicago	Left	Home	4th
38	95	07–25–1961	Don Larsen	Chicago	Right	Home	8th
39	96	07–25–1961	Russ Kemmerer	Chicago	Right	Home	4th
40	96	07–25–1961	Warren Hacker	Chicago	Right	Home	6th
41	106	08–04–1961	Camilo Pascual	Minnesota	Right	Home	1st
42	114	08–11–1961	Pete Burnside	Washington	Left	Away	5th
43	115	08–12–1961	Dick Donovan	Washington	Right	Away	4th
44	116	08–13–1961	Bennie Daniels	Washington	Right	Away	4th
45	117	08–13–1961	Marty Kutyna	Washington	Right	Away	1st
46	118	08–15–1961	Juan Pizarro	Chicago	Left	Home	4th
47	119	08–16–1961	Billy Pierce	Chicago	Left	Home	1st
48	119	08–16–1961	Billy Pierce	Chicago	Left	Home	3rd
49	124	08–20–1961	Jim Perry	Cleveland	Right	Away	3rd
50	125	08–22–1961	Ken McBride	Los Angeles	Right	Away	6th
51	129	08–26–1961	Jerry Walker	Kansas City	Right	Away	6th
52	135	09–02–1961	Frank Lary	Detroit	Right	Home	6th
53	135	09–02–1961	Hank Aguirre	Detroit	Left	Home	8th
54	140	09–06–1961	Tom Cheney	Washington	Right	Home	4th
55	141	09–07–1961	Dick Stigman	Cleveland	Left	Home	3rd
56	143	09–09–1961	Mudcat Grant	Cleveland	Right	Home	7th

61 Home Runs by Roger Maris (cont.)

HR	GAME	DATE/BOX	PITCHER	TEAM	THROWS	WHERE	INNING
57	151	09–16–1961	Frank Lary	Detroit	Right	Away	3rd
58	152	09–17–1961	Terry Fox	Detroit	Right	Away	12th
59	155	09–20–1961	Milt Pappas	Baltimore	Right	Away	3rd
60	159	09–26–1961	Jack Fisher	Baltimore	Right	Home	3rd
61	163	10–01–1961	Tracy Stallard	Boston	Right	Home	4th

Data courtesy of Baseball-Almanac.com.

#7 | Worst Team Year-In and Year-Out

Abandon Ship
The Pittsburgh Pirates and 19-Plus Straight Losing Seasons (and Counting)

> No one wants to lose this many games. It sucks. The
> bottom line is, it sucks. I hate to cuss, but nobody
> likes it, nobody wants it.
>
> *—Pirates manager John Russell*
> *(whose 2010 club reached 82 losses quicker than*
> *any other team in the 18-year span)*

The 2009 Pittsburgh Pirates set the new gold standard for futility over the long haul. By losing more than 82 games, the Pirates made 2009 their 17th straight losing season, shattering the old record, held by the 1933–1948 Philadelphia Phillies, although the Phils had 30 losing seasons in 31 years between 1918 and 1948. The Buccos ended the season with a mark of 62–99, and finished 28½ games out of first place in their division. "We can't worry about it. It is what it is," Pirates manager John Russell said of the streak. "Unfortunately, we're not happy with where we are in terms of wins and losses, and we've got a lot of work to do. But we believe in what we're doing. We've developed some very good young players, and we're looking forward to continuing to build. Unfortunately, we can't do anything about the 17 years."

"Setting a major league mark for losing hurts and it hits particularly hard for us because everyone in this organization is extraordinarily proud to be a part of a franchise that has such a long and rich history of winning," team president Frank Coonelly said. Nevertheless, his team lost 11 out of 12 to achieve their 82nd loss of the season on September 8, 2009. The record-setting loss mathematically eliminated the Pirates from the pennant race. It was quite a fall from grace for a franchise that won five World Series from 1909 to 1979 and sent 13 players to the Hall of Fame.

It took the Pirates 317 different players to accomplish such a dubious honor, including the following landmarks:

(We Should Be GMs.)

- The Pirates' cumulative record as of the end of the 2009 season was 1,158–1,501, for a .436 winning percentage. The 1997 edition went 79–83, which was the closest the team has come to reaching .500 since the streak began in 1993. The 2001 team went 62–100.
- Over the course of the streak, the Bucs have finished last 10 times and next to last 3 times. Their highest place finish was 1997, when they went 79–83. They have spent only 79 days in first place—an average of only 11 days per year—over the course of the streak, with 32 of those days occurring in the aberrant year of 1997.
- The latest date in any year that the Pirates topped .500 was August 26, 1997, when they were 67–66. Since 2000, the latest date was May 29, 2004. The 2009 edition was 12–11 on May 2 and then never topped .500 again. Other than the 1997 team, no Pirate team has been in first place any later than April 25. In this decade alone, the latest date was May 29, 2004.
- The Pirates can claim *the* professional sports record for most consecutive losing seasons. The Vancouver Canucks of the NHL had 15 straight losing seasons, 1976–1991, while the NBA's Kansas City/Sacramento

Kings of 1983–1998 also had a 15-year losing streak. From 1983 to 1996, the Tampa Bay Buccaneers of the NFL had a 14-year losing streak.

Over the course of the season, the Pirates' management unloaded most of the team's limited talent in return for prospects. "We know these moves are going to be incredibly unpopular," Neal Huntington, the team's general manager, said. "But this is how we're going to rebuild this franchise. We're trying to create a winner. We have no interest in getting to .500 once and then losing for five years."

The 2010 edition of the Pirates was even worse. The 2010 team posted a 57–105 record, which was the worst record in the major leagues. They ended up a distant 34 games out of first place in the National League Central Division, only further adding to their legacy of suffering. The end of the 2010 season marked their 18th straight losing season, adding to their record run of futility. In 2011, they prolonged their suffering into the next decade by posting a 72–90 record.

For the sake of their fans, let's hope that Huntington was correct in his assessment. Although the Buccos have a *long* way to go to match the 31-year-long run of futility set by the Phillies, they now own the longest losing season streak in the history of professional sports in North America, and their fans deserve better.

19 Seasons of Futility in the Steel City

YEAR	RECORD	MANAGER	FINISH
2011	72–90	Clint Hurdle	4/6
2010	57–105	John Russell	6/6
2009	62–99	John Russell	6/6
2008	67–95	John Russell	6/6
2007	68–94	Jim Tracy	6/6
2006	67–95	Jim Tracy	5/6
2005	67–95	Lloyd McClendon and Pete Mackinin	6/6
2004	72–89	Lloyd McClendon	5/6
2003	75–87	Lloyd McClendon	4/6
2002	72–89	Lloyd McClendon	4/6
2001	62–100	Lloyd McClendon	6/6
2000	69–93	Gene Lamont	5/6
1999	78–83	Gene Lamont	3/6
1998	69–93	Gene Lamont	6/6
1997	79–83	Gene Lamont	2/5
1996	73–89	Jim Leyland	5/5
1995	58–86	Jim Leyland	5/5
1994	53–61	Jim Leyland	3/5
1993	75–87	Jim Leyland	5/7
1992	96–66	Jim Leyland	1/6

Source: Pittsburgh Post-Gazette

#8 | Top 10 Worst Plays

A baseball game is simply a nervous breakdown
divided into nine innings.
> —*Earl Wilson, starting pitcher for the*
> *Red Sox, Tigers, and Padres*

Shocking, shameful, surprising, and even *silly* are just some of the words that fittingly describe the following recollections. In his book, *Baseball's Biggest Bloopers,* Dan Gutman wrote:

Some ballplayers are remembered for their home runs and great plays—but imagine being famous for blowing the game! People are still talking about Fred Snodgrass, who dropped a fly ball in 1912; Bill Buckner, first baseman for the Boston Red Sox, who should never have gotten out of bed on October 25, 1986; and poor Fred Merkle, who in his first game in the majors made the most famous mistake in baseball history.

Of course, every baseball fan has his or her favorite memories they'd rather forget. Here are our personal selections for the worst moments ever to take place on or off the ball field. There are 10 "winners" (in no particular order):

Bill Buckner's Blooper

> I really had to forgive, not the fans of Boston, per se,
> but I would have to say in my heart I had to forgive the
> media for what they put me and my family through.
> —*Bill Buckner (after throwing out the first pitch*
> *at an April 2008 Red Sox game)*

Perhaps the most recalled fielding error in the history of major league baseball (an Internet Google search for "buckner's error" brings up 46,000 hits), this goof remains the biggest blemish ever to hang over the memory a ballplayer's career. Unfortunately, it also shadows what would otherwise be a respectable legacy. Bill Buckner was a journeyman player who amassed a resume over a 20-year period that included such notable achievements as a National League batting title for hitting .324 in 1980, an All-Star selection in 1981, and 2,700 career hits accumulated while playing for the Los Angeles Dodgers, Chicago Cubs, Boston Red Sox, California Angels, and Kansas City Royals. He was also noted for his base-running skills and twice finished in the top 10 for stolen bases. Buckner twice led the league in doubles and became a key member of the Boston Red Sox American League pennant winner in 1986. That team rose to the top of the American League and went up against the surprising New York Mets for the World Championship. On October 25, Boston led the best-of-seven World

First Baseman Bill Buckner Vacates the Field (Library of Congress)

Series, three games to two, and had a two-run lead with two outs in the bottom of the 10th inning. The Red Sox were about to clinch their first World Series championship since 1918, and were finally about to escape the Curse of the Bambino.

The National League's best came back to tie the game after Calvin Schiraldi surrendered three straight singles. Adding insult to injury, Bob Stanley came on in relief and threw a wild pitch. Mookie Wilson followed at the plate and fouled off several offerings before hitting what appeared to be an easy grounder straight to Bill Buckner at first base. As Red Sox fans watched in horror, the ball casually rolled under the awkwardly positioned fielder's glove, through Buckner's legs and into the grass of the outfield. Base runner Ray Knight took advantage of the blooper and sprinted home for the winning score. This forced a Game 7, which the Mets won to clinch their second World Series title.

For Buckner, the error unfairly redefined his entire legacy in the game of baseball. The Boston media treated Buckner particularly unkindly, and it took years before he could forgive them for sullying his memory at Fenway Park. He retired in 1990 and moved his family to Boise, Idaho, where he invested in real estate. Over the years, the event became ingrained in American pop-culture by being referred to in poems, songs, and movies. The baseball that escaped Buckner's grasp was later auctioned for $93,000.

Ironically, Buckner also played a supporting role in another baseball milestone. As a left-fielder for the Los Angeles Dodgers, he climbed the fence in an attempt to catch Hank Aaron's 715th home run on April 8, 1974. He missed that one, too.

Pete Rose Ruins Ray Fosse

> I don't remember Pete Rose's 4,192nd hit that broke Ty Cobb's longstanding record . . . but I will never forget the image of Rose running over Ray Fosse in the 1970 All-Star Game.
>
> —*Brett Neal, on ESPN's*
> *"Baseball's Other Great Moments."*

Baseball is seldom considered a full-contact sport because the competition does not require the brutal violence of, say, a football or hockey game. Still, there are moments in the course of a contest that can become physically heated. Unfortunately, these rare instances often result in player injuries that can be career ending, or even life threatening. One such tragedy occurred during the 1970 All-Star Game, where Pete Rose, aka "Charlie Hustle," committed what is generally considered to be one of the biggest hits ever laid on a ballplayer.

The American League (AL) entered the 1970 Midsummer Classic determined to break the embarrassing eight-game losing streak that plagued

Pete Rose and Ray Fosse Collide at Home (AP Photo)

it throughout the previous decade. AL manager Earl Weaver anticipated strong pitching being the Junior Circuit's best chance against the National League's power hitters. It appeared to be working, as most of the game was a pitcher's duel. Finally, the streak appeared to be a bad memory as the American League took a 4–1 lead going into the bottom of the ninth.

Then it happened . . . The Nationals hooked into Catfish Hunter, who gave up a leadoff home run to Dick Dietz. Singles by the next three batters followed, and a Roberto Clemente sacrifice sent the game into extra innings. In the bottom of the 12th, Pete Rose singled, and then went to second on another single by Billy Grabarkewitz. Jim Hickman lined a single to center. Kansas City Royals' outfielder Amos Otis charged the ball and fired a rocket to the plate for a play on Rose. Catcher Ray Fosse tried mightily to block the plate, but Rose was determined to score, and it was no contest. He bowled over Fosse, who was dazed by the collision, and scored the winning run. The impact not only resulted in a 5–4 victory, it also permanently rearranged Fosse's left shoulder, prematurely ending his budding career.

Tragically, Fosse was having the best season of his life, and had amassed 16 home runs at the All-Star break in 1970, as well as a 23-game hitting streak during the first half of the season. Adding to the heartache was the fact that it was only his second year in the major leagues. The impact of Rose's cross-body block left Fosse with a fractured bone in his shoulder, but X-rays taken at a Cincinnati hospital did not reveal the damage. Fosse kept playing, but he could never lift his arm, and his numbers dropped dramatically. To this day, he suffers from painful arthritis in that shoulder. Although Rose denies ever intentionally trying to level Fosse, he clearly had no intention of sliding as he neared the plate.

Revenge came later, in a way, after Rose was sentenced to jail for tax evasion. He served a portion of that sentence at a prison in Marion, Illinois, which just happened to be Ray Fosse's hometown. Apparently, the two never visited while Pete was incarcerated there.

Fred Merkle's Boner

> Considered by John McGraw, manager of the Giants, as a
> shrewd and aggressive player, Merkle also packed a wal-
> lop at the plate in the days of the "dead" ball.
> —New York Times *Obituary (March 3, 1956)*

Fred Merkle's contribution to the annals of baseball history reads less like a sports story and more like a comedic script. Why? Well, the term *bone-head* can be directly credited to the young Ohioan. Entering the game as a 19 year old and the youngest player in the entire National League, Merkle played infield for 16 seasons with the New York Giants, Brooklyn Robins, and Chicago Cubs of the National League. After playing in the International League from 1921 to 1925, he appeared in eight games with the New York Yankees before retiring in 1926. Despite his impressive list of employers, one incident that occurred in his rookie season has forever stained the memory of Fred Merkle.

The error took place during a 1908 game between the New York Giants and the Chicago Cubs. That day, he committed a tragic base-running boo-boo that quickly became known as "Merkle's Boner," and forever christened him with the moniker "Bonehead." In the bottom of the ninth-inning, the young first baseman came to bat with two down and a tie score of 1–1. Merkle's teammate "Moose" McCormick was on first base and advanced to third when Merkle came through with a clutch single. Al Birdwell followed suit, driving McCormick home for the apparent win. The spectators, under the impression that the game was over, ran onto the field to celebrate. Merkle, also thinking the game was concluded, fled the field and casually entered the Giants' clubhouse without ever touching second base.

Infielder and "Not-so-Giant" Fred Merkle (Library of Congress)

Johnny Evers, who was covering second, recognized the rookie's mistake, immediately retrieved the ball and stepped on the bag. He then appealed to umpire Hank O'Day, who called Merkle out on a force play, nullifying both McCormick's run and the win. The Giants and the Cubs ended the season tied for first place and held a rematch at the Polo Grounds on October 8. Unfortunately for Merkle, the Cubs won the makeup contest, 4–2, and walked off the field with the National League pennant. Giants skipper John McGraw was furious at the league office for robbing him of a victory, but he never blamed Merkle for his mistake.

Ironically, Chicago won the 1908 World Series, but has not repeated the feat since (as the publication date of this book).

George Brett's Pine Tar Incident

> The Royals and the Yankees hated each other. To this
> day, whenever I see Lou Piniella or one of those Yankees,
> we talk about how we hated those guys.
> —*George Brett, Baseball-Almanac.com*

One of baseball's greatest meltdowns occurred when the New York Yankees took on the Kansas City Royals in 1983's "Great Pine Tar Incident." As Yankee ace Goose Gossage attempted to protect a 4–3 advantage, George Brett smacked a two-run homer, putting his team in the lead. Until home plate umpire Tim McClelland called him out for having more than 18 inches of pine tar from the end of his bat, that is. Minor use of pine tar was acceptable because the sticky substance aided baseball players to improve their grip at the plate. According to Rule #1.10(c) of the Official Rules of Major League Baseball, batters may apply pine tar only from the handle of the bat extending up for 18 inches. However, Brett's bat appeared to have been coated with the sticky substance much further up the barrel.

As the all-star third baseman crossed the plate, New York manager Billy Martin approached the umpire and requested that Brett's bat be examined. Earlier in the season, Martin and other members of his team had noticed the large amount of pine tar used by the Royals slugger. With Brett watching from the dugout, McClelland and the rest of the umpiring crew inspected the bat by measuring it against the width of home plate (which is 17 inches). They determined that the amount of pine tar on the bat's handle clearly exceeded that allowed by MLB regulations. McClelland then pointed at Brett in the dugout and signaled that he was out. The call nullified the homerun and also ended the game. An enraged George Brett immediately rushed onto the field and had to be physically restrained by Kansas City manager Dick Howser and his teammates. One commentator later stated that he became the first player in baseball history to "hit a game-*losing* home run."

The Royals skipper immediately protested McClelland's verdict, which was reversed by American League President Lee MacPhail several weeks later. MacPhail ruled that the game should resume with two out in the top of the ninth inning with the Royals up 5–4, and that Brett was to be ejected for his outburst. On August 18 (an off day for both teams), the game resumed from the point of Brett's home run,

George Brett Reacts to his Disallowed Homer (Library of Congress)

and his team clinched the 5–4 win in front of a crowd of only 1,200 without the future Hall of Famer in the lineup.

Years later, the infamous "tar bat" joined its owner in the Baseball Hall of Fame, where it has been on display since 1987.

Cap Anson's Racist Reluctance

> I often think of going to some other city to play. A Chicago crowd is the worst in the world. I've stood their taunts and hisses for fifteen years, and it's beginning to weary me. I've come to the conclusion that it can't be deviltry on their part. If it was they would let up once in awhile. It's nothing more than a lack of brains.
>
> —*Cap Anson in the Chicago Daily News*

According to his player biography, "Adrian Constantine Anson known by the nicknames 'Cap' (for 'Captain') and 'Pop,' was a professional baseball player in the National Association and major league baseball. He played a record 27 consecutive seasons, and was regarded as one of the greatest players of his era and one of the first superstars of the game." What this introduction conveniently omitted is the fact that Cap Anson was also guilty of actively instigating rampant racism while helping to establish segregation in professional baseball that lasted for decades. On several occasions,

Anson refused to take the field when the opposing roster included black players. Although this practice of believing in white supremacy was not uncommon in that day, many allege that Anson intentionally used his popularity in Chicago while playing for the White Stockings to widen the divide between whites and blacks both on the field and off.

His racial intolerance came to the forefront on August 10, 1883, when Anson refused to play an exhi-

Ball-Playing Bigot Cap Anson (Library of Congress)

bition game against the Toledo Blue Stockings because their catcher, Moses Fleetwood Walker, was African American. On July 14, 1887, when Anson's team played an exhibition game against the Newark Little Giants, an African-American player named George Stovey was listed in the papers as the starting pitcher. Anson objected so vehemently to the press that the Giants benched their black ace, fearing a backlash from the fans. Anson repeated this racist reaction in September of 1888, when he saw that Walker was once again listed on a lineup card at an exhibition game at Syracuse. He pressured his opponents to find a white replacement, and they complied.

In a related decision, the International League owners voted 6 to 4 to exclude African-American players from future contracts. Many point to Anson's actions as triggering this lamentable decision. Professional baseball did not willingly admit another black player until 1946, when Jackie Robinson broke baseball's "color barrier" by signing with the Brooklyn Dodgers' minor league team in Montreal.

Anson carried his racist attitudes off the field as well, as evidenced by his description of Clarence Duval, Chicago's black team mascot. In his autobiography, *A Ball Player's Career,* Anson wrote, "Clarence was a little darkey that I had met some time before while in Philadelphia, a singer and dancer of no mean ability, and a little coon whose skill in handling the baton would have put to the blush many a bandmaster of national reputation. . . . Outside of his dancing and his power of mimicry he was, however, a 'no account n—r,' and more than once did I wish that he had been left behind."

Despite his controversial past, Cap Anson was judged on his athletic abilities and was elected to the national Baseball Hall of Fame in 1939. To this day, some opinionated fans believe that Anson should be banned from the Hall of Fame because of his racist legacy.

Player's Strikes ('72, '81, '94)

> Baseball is too much of a sport to be a business and too
> much of a business to be a sport.
>
> *—Phillip Wrigley, 1956*

Eighty-six games were cancelled due to the first general players' strike, which was eventually resolved on April 13, 1972. Concessions came after both the owners and players agreed on a $500,000 increase in pension fund payments. In an effort to prevent paying the players for the work

Major League Baseball Commissioner Bud
Selig (AP Photo/Paul Conners)

stoppage, the league decided not to make up the missed contests. As a result, some teams only played 153 games that year. Unfortunately, the 1972 walkout was merely a portent of things to come.

On May 29, 1981, the executive board of the Players' Association voted unanimously to strike again due to the unresolved issue of free agent compensation. The deadline was extended briefly, however, after the National Labor Relations Board heard the Players' Association's unfair labor complaint. At 12:30 A.M. on June 12, union chief Marvin Miller announced the players' strike, beginning the longest labor action in American sports history to date. By the time the season finally resumed on August 10, 706 games (38 percent of the major league schedule) had been canceled. As a result of the two-month strike, major league owners elected to split the 1981 season into two halves, with the first-place teams from each half in each division meeting in a best-of-five divisional playoff series. As a result, the Oakland A's, New York Yankees, Philadelphia Phillies, and Los Angeles Dodgers were guaranteed playoff spots as first-half divisional champions.

In 1994, the Major League Players Association rejected an owners' salary cap proposal that asked players to split all revenues 50–50. In addition, the owners proposed that salary arbitration be eliminated, in return for which free agency for players could be reached after four years in the majors instead of six. As negotiations heated up, the owners decided to withhold $7.8 million that they were obligated to pay into the players' pension and benefit plans. The final straw fell after the Senate Judiciary Committee failed to approve antitrust legislation that left the players with little choice but to strike.

On September 14, the remainder of the baseball season was canceled 34 days into the players' strike. As a result, the World Series was also called off for the first time since 1904. Three months later, the owners unilaterally implemented a salary cap when negotiations remained at a standstill. The strike continued into the 1995 season, when players' union chief Donald

Fehr declared all 835 unsigned major league players to be free agents in response to unilateral contract changes made by the owners. Five bills aimed
at ending the baseball strike were introduced into Congress and President
Bill Clinton ordered both players and owners to resume bargaining and
reach an agreement by February 6. The deadline passed with no compromises, and baseball's executive counsel approved the use of replacement
players for spring training and regular season games.

Finally, on April 25, the 234-day-long strike finally ended, although replacement umpires called the opening games. The regular officials continued to be locked out until May 3. In September, a three-judge panel
in New York voted unanimously to uphold the injunction that ended the
strike. Although the owners appealed the decision, the panel determined
that the Players Relations Committee had illegally attempted to eliminate
free agency and salary arbitration.

Babe Slugs Umpire Brick Owens

> It wasn't a love tap. I really socked him—right in the jaw.
> — *Babe Ruth*

Babe Ruth is responsible for many of the greatest moments in the history of
professional baseball. Unfortunately, he is also guilty of committing some
of the worst. One event, in particular, took place during the 1917 season
when the then hot-tempered Red Sox pitcher walked off the mound and
punched the home plate umpire in the face. In a year that had already seen
the United States dragged into an ongoing world war, Ruth's reaction still
seemed extreme. After all, baseball had yet to become the wartime escape
for the masses. In the end, 10 million combatants were killed and more
than 20 million were wounded.

Fortunately in this particular engagement, the only one wounded was
Clarence "Brick" Owens, the umpire. Brick was one of the game's most respected officials and his career spanned three decades. (He worked in the
National League in 1908 and 1912–1913, and in the American League from
1916 through 1937. He later officiated in the World Series in 1918, 1922,
1925, 1928, and 1934, serving as crew chief for the last two series. He also
worked the All-Star Game in 1934.)

In 1917, during a game against the Washington Senators, Babe Ruth
walked the first batter that he faced. He immediately challenged Umpire

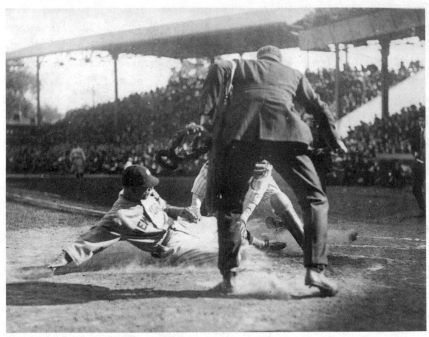

Umpire Making a Call Against the Yankees (Library of Congress)

Owen's call of a fourth ball and was ejected for arguing with an official. Not deterred, Ruth became so incensed that he approached the batter's box and slugged Owens in the face. Ruth was restrained and dragged from the field as Brick Owens lived up to his nickname and returned to his duties at the plate. Ernie Shore replaced Ruth and not only picked the walked runner off first base, he then retired the next 26 batters he faced. Ironically, MLB record books officially regard this game as a combined "no-hitter" by Ruth and Shore, even though it appears that the only hit to occur at the plate during a Washington turn was Ruth's slugging of Owens.

Disco Demolition Night Debacle

> Disco Demolition Night was the beginning of the end.
> —*The Bee Gees*

On July 12, 1979, WLUP-FM's "Disco Demolition Night" at Chicago's Comiskey Park went terribly wrong, as close to 90,000 fans turned up to receive discounted tickets for a doubleheader and eventually rioted on the field.

The promotional event was initiated by local disc jockey Steve Dahl, who was fired after his former station WDAI went to a 24–7 disco format. Dahl, along with his new radio partner, Garry Meier, declared war on the format and even created the anti-disco-dancing organization called the "Insane Coho Lips Anti-Disco Army." The DJs also recorded a parody of the popular Rod Stewart hit "Do Ya' Think I'm Sexy?" that was appropriately titled "Do You Think I'm Disco?" Bill and Mike Veeck of the White Sox organization worked closely with the sales staff at WLUP to devise a catchy promotion in which attendees would exchange their unwanted disco records for cheap tickets (98 cents, representing the station's number on the dial, 97.9). The albums would then be placed into a large bin or crate set in the middle of the outfield and exploded.

Unfortunately, things did not go as planned. The additional attendance unexpectedly ballooned from the anticipated 5,000 to almost 70,000 before the game began. Impatient fans began climbing the fences and walls, as the off-ramps to the stadium from the Dan Ryan Expressway had to be closed. After the crate was stuffed to capacity with records, the gate staff stopped collecting them. As the first game progressed, fans began throwing the vinyl albums like Frisbees, injuring bystanders. According to one account of the event in the *Chicago Tribune,* "After the first game, Dahl, dressed in army fatigues and helmet, along with Lorelei Shark, WLUP's first 'Rock Girl' and bodyguards, went out to center field. The large box containing the collected

Chicago's White Sox Park on Disco Demolition Night (AP Photo/Fred Jewell)

records was rigged with a bomb. When it exploded, the bomb tore a hole in the outfield grass surface and thousands of fans immediately rushed the field." Chicago police in riot gear rushed in to help clear the field of more than 20,000 unruly spectators. Miraculously, only 6 people were injured and 39 were arrested for disorderly conduct.

After a delay of 1 hour and 16 minutes, the umpires determined that the ball field was unplayable and called the second game between the White Sox and visiting Detroit Tigers. The following day, American League President Lee MacPhail awarded the Tigers a 9–0 forfeit win after the embarrassing catastrophe made the front page of every newspaper in Chicago. In the *Chicago Sun-Times,* one headline read "The Horror at Comiskey," while another called it "The most dangerous promotion in the history of sports."

Top 10 Songs of 1979 (8 were disco):

1	My Sharona, The Knack
2	Bad Girls, Donna Summer
3	Le Freak, Chic
4	Do Ya' Think I'm Sexy, Rod Stewart
5	Reunited, Peaches and Herb
6	I Will Survive, Gloria Gaynor
7	Hot Stuff, Donna Summer
8	Y.M.C.A., Village People
9	Ring My Bell, Anita Ward
10	Sad Eyes, Robert John

Mickey Owen's Passed Ball

> I would've been completely forgotten if I hadn't missed that pitch.
>
> —*Mickey Owen*

More than any other sport, baseball is a game in which *everything* is tallied and measured. Statistics are just as important as any other historical aspect of the game, and box scores and scorecards remain as timeless testaments to the countless moments of triumph and tragedy that make up its legacy. One stat in particular stands out more than any other due to its shameful connotation: the "error." It is the single recorded moment in sports where everyone knows exactly when and where a player made a

Mickey Owen's Day of Infamy (Library of Congress)

mistake. Lou Brock said, "You can't be afraid to make errors! You can't be afraid to be naked before the crowd, because no one can ever master the game of baseball, or conquer it. You can only challenge it."

That said, sometimes an error can be so damning that it condenses an entire career into a single unfortunate play. Brooklyn Dodgers catcher Mickey Owen experienced this in spades. Owen played in the major leagues for 13 seasons and was an outstanding positional player with a strong and accurate arm. Unfortunately, much like Fred Merkle and Bill Buckner, his legacy was forever cast in stone following a disastrous play that overshadowed an otherwise all-star career. The former catcher's worst achievement dominated his July 15, 2005, obituary in the *New York Times,* which stated·

On the afternoon of Oct. 5, 1941, the Yankees were trailing the Dodgers, 4–3, at Ebbets Field in Game 4 of the World Series and were down to their final out with Brooklyn about to tie the Series at two games apiece. Tommy Henrich, the Yankees' star outfielder, was at the plate facing the ace reliever Hugh Casey, with nobody on base and a full count. Casey threw a pitch that broke sharply, and Henrich swung and missed. The home plate umpire, Larry Goetz, signaled a strikeout and the game was seemingly over. But the pitch hit the heel of Owen's glove and skipped away for a passed ball. As Owen chased the ball near the Dodgers' dugout, Henrich raced to first base. Joe DiMaggio followed with a single to left, then Charlie Keller hit a ball high off the right-field screen, scoring Henrich and DiMaggio and giving the Yankees a 5–4 lead. After Bill Dickey walked, Joe Gordon doubled to make the score 7–4. The Dodgers went down quickly in the ninth, and the Yankees had a lead of three games to one. They captured the World Series the next day, inspiring the enduring headline in the *Brooklyn Eagle,* "Wait Till Next Year."

A dejected Owens feared that he would be forever loathed by the Dodger faithful, but his anxieties were quickly put to rest. In an interview given on the 25th anniversary of the gaffe, he told the *Saturday Evening Post* that he had received more than 4,000 wires and letters of support in the wake of the mistake, which he claimed gave him the strength to continue on.

Owen later played for both the Chicago Cubs and the Boston Red Sox before retiring and founding the Mickey Owen Baseball School in Miller, Missouri. Passed ball drills were no doubt part of the curriculum for catchers.

Brooklyn Dodgers Go West

> I am a young girl of 16 and enjoy baseball to great
> extents. If the Dodgers move to Los Angeles I will no
> longer enjoy the right given to me by my creator. Please
> keep them here. Baseball keeps a lot of us teenagers off
> the streets and prevents juvenile delinquency.
> —*Gloria Cerrato to New York City*
> *Mayor Robert Wagner, 1957*

Perhaps no event in the history of baseball resulted in more resentment than the relocation of the Brooklyn Dodgers to the West Coast in 1957. Team owner Walter O'Malley was a shrewd businessperson who had been trying to expand his operations in New York for several years. Although his team's beloved Ebbets Field had become a landmark in the city's borough, it was more than 40 years old and was beginning to show its age. Limited to a maximum capacity of only 32,000 seats, Ebbets could not compete financially with the likes of Yankee Stadium, which doubled its capacity. Ticket sales had also dropped in recent years, as the Dodgers couldn't even fill the seats during a pennant race. The team drew only 13,423 fans per

Diehard Dodgers Fans (Library of Congress)

game in 1955, down from the 23,474 they'd averaged in 1947. This, along with the inability to purchase land suitable for a new ballpark, disappointed O'Malley and he began to explore potential locations for his franchise.

As the 1957 season progressed, a rumor began circulating that the team might be leaving town. Many loyal Dodgers fans could not imagine that "Dem Bums" would ever abandon them and chose to ignore the gossip. Behind the scenes, officials from the city of Los Angeles offered O'Malley what the city of New York would not: prime real estate for the construction of a new field. Although the city of Los Angeles' original proposal had been written for the Washington Senators, it was also a perfect fit for the Dodgers.

In October of that year, O'Malley announced that after 68 seasons in the Big Apple, his team would be moving to Los Angeles. Desperate for major league baseball, West Coast fans welcomed the relocated franchise with open arms. The team played in the Los Angeles Memorial Coliseum for the first several years while the new stadium was built in Chavez Ravine. During the first season in Dodger Stadium (1962), the team averaged 34,014 fans per game (more than the total capacity of Ebbets Field).

Seeing the potential of an untapped market for financial gain, New York Giants owner Horace Stoneham followed suit and moved his team to San Francisco, leaving the New York Yankees as the only baseball team left in New York City. Six months later, on April 18, 1958, the newly transplanted

Dodgers played their first game in Los Angeles, defeating the neighboring Giants 6–5 before 78,672 fans at the Coliseum, which was built for football and had odd dimensions for baseball.

Few fans in Los Angeles or New York were aware of the architectural vision that O'Malley had fostered as far back as the 1940s. According to records, one design featured a translucent dome (17 years before the Houston Astrodome opened). Other proposed innovations included closed circuit television sets in stadium restaurants; a club level with terraced areas for tables; a cascading fountain in center field with multicolor spotlights triggered after a home run; and trams to transport fans from the parking lots to their seating levels.

For Brooklyn fans left behind, these ballpark innovations mattered little, as the relocation of their heroes was a far too painful reality. Many stated that they would never forgive the team or its owner, and their bitterness has lasted for generations. Even today, "true-blue" Dodger fans refuse to acknowledge the Los Angeles version of their beloved franchise. In their eyes, the team died the day it fled to California.

#9 | Worst Players

How does one define *the* worst player in all of professional baseball history? Is it a poorly scouted rookie who never pans out, or a grizzled veteran whose best days were far behind him?

Could it be a poor trade acquisition, or maybe an injured player who never quite healed? In today's modern game there are far too many factors that could affect a player's fall from grace, and there is a list a mile long of ball players who were supposed to make it big in the majors but never came close to fulfilling expectations.

Therefore, we have simply selected four especially bad players from days gone by who never had a good season, ever. The irony is that these "famous failures" inevitably would have been all but forgotten if they were actually any good:

Worst Batter
Bill Bergen

Birth Name:	William Aloysius Bergen
Nickname:	Bill
Born On:	06–13–1878
Born In:	North Brookfield, Massachusetts
Died On:	12–19–1943
Died In:	Worcester, Massachusetts
Cemetery:	St. John Cemetery, Worcester, Massachusetts
College:	None attended
Batted:	Right
Threw:	Right
Height:	6–0
Weight:	184
First Game:	05–06–1901 (Age 22)
Last Game:	09–20–1911
Draft:	Not applicable

William Aloysius Bergen was an athletic anomaly whose talents on the baseball field were so contradictory as to be almost unbelievable at times. A capable defenseman behind the plate, Bergen unfortunately became the complete opposite when standing next to it. In fact, at times it seemed that the batter's box was a virtual "Black Hole" of sorts that sucked away all of this catcher's offensive abilities to play professional ball. And although the subjective title for the "all-time worst hitter" can be debated ad nauseum among statisticians, there is absolutely no doubt that William Bergen ("the batter") belongs at or near the top of that list.

A typical season at the plate for Bergen would see him play in anywhere from 80 to 100 games, posting a batting average ranging from the .130s to the .180s, approximately 15 RBIs and, of course, absolutely no home runs.

Born in North Brookfield, Massachusetts, in June 1878, Bill Bergen showed promise as a talented fielder at an early age. Despite his one-dimensional skill set, he somehow lasted 11 seasons in the major leagues with the Cincinnati Reds and Brooklyn Dodgers. In spite of a long career, Bergen's defensive claim to fame has been severely tarnished by his complete ineptitude on the offensive side of the diamond. In 1906, a Pittsburgh sportswriter took Bergen to task for his lack of focus on the game. Perhaps this was a sign of things to

Bill Bergen (Baseball Hall of Fame Library, Cooperstown, NY)

come. "Bergen is a fine catcher, and would be finer still but for his desire to live well," wrote the sportswriter. "Out this way we have rumors that now and then Bergen is late reporting for duty, all because he met some friends who will invite him to have a bite to eat, etc. Not caring about being churlish, he accepts, and will look on life as a round of pleasure. Time will come when the Brooklyn man will get down to solid base playing and forget good things in the pleasure line." Or maybe not.

Bergen had 3,028 at bats in his career, compiling an abysmal batting average in the .170s, marking the all-time record worst for players who compiled more than 2,500 at bats. His career on-base percentage (OBP) is .194, and he is the only player with at least 500 at bats with an OBP less than .200. In his busiest season (112 games in 1909), Bergen posted a miserable .139 batting average (BA), with just 48 hits in 346 at bats and only 3 extra-base hits (for a pathetic .156 slugging average [SA]). Both his BA and SA stand as all-time lows for any player with more than 300 at bats in a season. That same year, Bergen set another unwanted record for futility by going 46 at bats in a row without a base hit, the longest streak ever by a position player.

Shamefully, from 1904 on, Dodger pitchers as a group outhit Bergen, .169 to .162. By 1911, his average sank to a career-low .132 with just 10 RBIs in 227 at bats. Few others have ever compared to such miserable offensive stats. The *Bill James Historical Baseball Abstract* currently lists Bill Bergen in their all-time Lowest Batting Average category twice: in 1909 at .139 and lifetime at .175.

That said, this National Leaguer's contributions to the game as a catcher stand in stark contrast to those made at the plate. Bergen currently holds the number nine slot on the all-time list for assists by a catcher with 1,444, an especially notable accomplishment for a player who was never a full-time participant. Bergen also received the accolade of "Best Catcher" from the *Sporting News* in 1908, and in 1909, he set an MLB record with a magnificent .989 fielding percentage. On August 23, 1909, he set a major league record by gunning down six St. Louis Cardinal base stealers in a single game, a record that still stands today. Historian Charles Faber called Bergen the third-best defensive catcher ever in his book *Baseball Ratings,* while *Total Baseball* currently ranks him as the fifth-best defensive catcher of all time.

Our criticisms, however, deal strictly with Bergen's performances with a bat and not the ones with his glove, the ones in which he was caught swinging, or at least trying to. Ironically, the Dodgers team that Bergen played for boasted a losing record every year that he was on the team, bottoming out with a 48–104 record in 1905. Eventually, Bergen's lack of offense became too disappointing to overlook, and he was demoted to the minor leagues, where he continued to play ball until 1914. He then coached and managed before retiring in 1920. In retrospect, it is truly amazing that someone who was such a gifted fielder could be such a poor hitter.

On a side note, Bergen's brother was Marty Bergen, who played for the Boston Beaneaters and became infamous for murdering his family and then committing suicide. Bill Bergen was recorded in the press as saying that "The ghosts got to him and never let him go."

Bill Bergen Hitting Stats

YR	TEAM	G	AB	R	H	2B	3B	HR	GS	RBI	BB	IBB	SO	SH	SF	HBP	GIDP	AVG	OBP	SLG
1901	Reds	87	308	15	55	6	4	1	0	17	8	-	-	10	-	0	-	.179	.199	.234
1902	Reds	89	322	19	58	8	3	0	0	36	14	-	-	6	-	0	-	.180	.214	.224
1903	Reds	58	207	21	47	4	2	0	0	19	7	-	-	4	-	0	-	.227	.252	.266
1904	Superbas	96	329	17	60	4	2	0	0	12	9	-	-	9	-	0	-	.182	.204	.207
1905	Superbas	79	247	12	47	3	2	0	0	22	7	-	-	11	-	0	-	.190	.213	.219
1906	Superbas	103	353	9	56	3	3	0	0	19	7	-	-	12	-	0	-	.159	.175	.184
1907	Superbas	51	138	2	22	3	0	0	0	14	1	-	-	4	-	0	-	.159	.165	.181
1908	Superbas	99	302	8	53	8	2	1	0	15	5	-	-	13	-	0	-	.175	.189	.215
1909	Superbas	112	346	16	48	1	1	1	0	15	10	-	-	16	-	0	-	.139	.163	.156
1910	Superbas	89	249	11	40	2	1	0	0	14	6	-	39	18	-	0	-	.161	.180	.177
1911	Dodgers	84	227	8	30	3	1	0	0	10	14	-	42	9	-	0	-	.132	.183	.154
YR	TEAM	G	AB	R	H	2B	3B	HR	GS	RBI	BB	IBB	SO	SH	SF	HBP	GIDP	AVG	OBP	SLG
CAREER 11 YEARS		947	3,028	138	516	45	21	2	0	193	88	-	81	112	-	0	-	.170	.194	.201

Data courtesy of Baseball-Almanac.com.

Worst Pitcher
Jim Hughey

Birth Name:	James Ulysses Hughey
Nickname:	Coldwater Jim
Born On:	03–08–1869
Born In:	Wakeshma, Michigan
Died On:	03–29–1945
Died In:	Coldwater, Michigan
Cemetery:	Lester Cemetery, Coldwater, Michigan
College:	None Attended
Batted:	Unknown
Threw:	Right
Height:	6–0
Weight:	Unknown
First Game:	09–29–1891 (Age 22)
Last Game:	09–30–1900
Draft:	Not Applicable

More than a century after he first climbed atop the pitchers mound, James Ulysses Hughey is still unequivocally remembered as major league baseball's "anti-ace." He was a righty for the Milwaukee Brewers (1891), Chicago Colts (1893), Pittsburgh Pirates (1896–1897), St. Louis Browns/St. Louis Cardinals (1898 and 1900), and Cleveland Spiders (1899).

As the last pitcher to lose 30 outings in a single season, Hughey's cumulative stats don't lie. In 1899, he led the National League in losses. Over seven seasons, he boasted a 29–80 win-loss record, 145 games (113 started), 100 complete games, 28 games finished, 1 save, 1,007 innings pitched, 1,271 hits allowed, 748 runs allowed, 545 earned runs allowed, 21 home runs allowed, 317 walks allowed, 250 strikeouts, 46 hit batsmen, 37 wild pitches, and a 4.87 lifetime ERA. Yes, that's almost a 5.0 earned run average!

In retrospect, Jim Hughey's historically lackluster performance is even more startling in light of the successful seasons that the promising pitcher assembled at the highest levels of the minor leagues before being called up to the majors. According to a bio penned by SABR historian Craig Lammers, "Hughey started his professional career in the Indiana State League. The '*Coldwater Courier*' reported, 'Baseball experts say Hughey is making a great record in the Indiana League. He has an upshot that no other pitcher has got onto and one that puzzles all the batters.'"

Although statistics for that first season are not available, Hughey played

Jim Hughey and Family (Library of Congress)

well enough to be signed by Fond du Lac of the Wisconsin State League for the 1891 campaign. According to the *Daily Reporter,* the young pitcher earned the moniker of "Smiling Jim" early on. One account in the paper stated that, "When the hopes of the visitors would be raised by two men on bases, Hughey would smile sarcastically and strike out the batters." Later he would earn the nickname "Coldwater Jim," which stuck.

In August 1891, Cincinnati's fledging baseball franchise disbanded and was replaced by Milwaukee's minor league team, which opted to retain some of its own players and others inherited from Cincinnati. Milwaukee also purchased the contracts of promising minor leaguers, including Jim Hughey. Although he only started a single game while wearing the Wisconsin uniform, it was a winning effort. The American Association folded in December, leaving the Baltimore Orioles, St. Louis Browns, Louisville Colonels, and Washington Senators to be absorbed into the National League the following season. Milwaukee was not as fortunate.

The following year Hughey moved on to Kansas City of the Western League. By now, he was known for his curve ball and led the league with 111 strikeouts in 21 games before that league also folded in July. He then finished the season with Macon Central Cities of the Southern League. He began 1893 with Macon Central and pitched competently enough to earn a trial with Cap Anson's struggling Chicago Colts. In 1894, the Western League was revived and Hughey returned to Toledo with the White Stockings. Surprisingly, he compiled a 26–11 record with 99 strikeouts in 334 innings. He carried this momentum into the 1894 effort, winning 22 of 37 decisions and upping his strikeout total to 150 in 318 innings. The future finally looked bright for the journeyman right-hander.

These back-to-back performances in 1893 and 1894 caught the attention of Connie Mack, who was then managing the Pittsburgh Pirates. Much to the pitcher's dismay, the Pirates purchased Hughey's contract. Perhaps Hughey's patience was wearing thin, because he had no problems voicing his displeasure with moving to the Steel City. In 1896, he declared, "I'm not stuck on pitching ball in the Big League. When I was in the Western League I received as much salary and had an easier time of it. The newspapers do not roast the players in the Western League (the *Blade* excluded); though in the big league the men are subjected to severe roasts if they lose two or three games, especially the pitchers. Of course the pitcher is invariably blamed when his team loses."

After years of bouncing from town to town and team to team, dealing with injuries and unwanted trades, league collapses, consolidations, and other matters not under his control, a disgruntled Hughey fell into a downward spiral that ultimately ruined his legacy. Although he still had the occasional good outing, Hughey's overall performance was never consistently right again. In 1899, he finished the season with a dismal 4–30 record and an atrocious 5.41 era. No MLB pitcher has ever matched it.

In 1902, a desperate Hughey joined the Toledo Mud Hens, which was part of the newly re-formed American Association. On returning to Ohio, the aging hurler admitted that he had avoided conditioning during the off-season, hoping to avoid the chronic arm problems he'd suffered during the previous campaign. Unfortunately, that decision plagued him for the rest of the season. Early in the year, he was routinely self-defeated by inconsistency, wildness, and a total loss of control in the latter part of games. Further complicating matters was his being on a bad team that fell into last place early in the season and never escaped. This collapse marked the beginning of the end for "Coldwater Jim."

Hughey's physical decline eventually matched his mental deterioration. Sportswriters lambasted him in the papers, saying that he was "getting too fat." Later in the season they declared:

As fat and saucy as ever, Jeems Hughey wandered out onto the diamond yesterday afternoon at Armory Park with the avowed intention of making the downtrodden [Minneapolis] Millers look like a lot of selling platers. The Michigan marvel miscalculated somewhere. His benders were not the mysteries they were once. The misfits from St. Anthony's Falls took a kink or two out of them in the very first inning, and from that time on Jeems began to lose flesh. By the time the game was half over the fat boy had lost so much of his corpulency that his clothes did not fit. Along toward the finish, his uniform was hanging on him in folds. Jeems had the same old grunt but somehow or other he couldn't fool 'em.

With a forgettable 8–21 record, Hughey was finally released at his own request. Despite his best efforts, he never pulled out of the slump that became his baseball legacy. Despite a promising start, his overall career record ended up as one of the worst in the history of professional baseball. Still, it has been written that Jim Hughey remained proud of his career and enjoyed talking about the game. Ironically, older residents of the Coldwater, Michigan, area remember two crossed baseball bats and the name "Home Run Farm" painted onto the small barn at the pitcher's place. This may seem a strange choice of imagery for a baseball pitcher, but it somehow made perfect sense for old "Smiling Jim."

Worst Catcher
John Humphries

Birth Name:	John Henry Humphries
Nickname:	None
Born On:	11–12–1861
Born In:	North Gower, Ontario, Canada
Died On:	11–29–1933
Died In:	Salinas, California
Cemetery:	Cremated
College:	Cornell University
Batted:	Left
Threw:	Left
Height:	6–00
Weight:	185
First Game:	07–07–1883 (Age 21)
Last Game:	08–01–1884
Draft:	Not Applicable

Perhaps the worst of the worst, John Humphries' major league career only lasted two ghastly seasons. A cursory examination of his cumulative statistics demonstrates why. A Canadian who was born in North Gower, Ontario, Humphries was selected over other candidates due to his dubious achievements behind the plate. As a rare left-handed catcher with the New York Gothams in 1883, he tallied a whopping 20 errors in 23 games. And his contributions with the bat weren't far behind. With a .112 batting average, a .120 on-base-percentage, a .121 slugging-percentage (in 107 at bats) and

Jim Hughey Pitching Stats

YEAR	TEAM	G	GS	GF	W	L	PCT	ERA	CG	SHO	SV	IP	BFP	H	ER	R	HR	BB	IBB	SO	WP	HBP	BK	HLD
1891	Brewers	2	1	1	1	0	1.000	3.00	1	0	0	15.0	0	18	5	6	0	3	-	9	0	0	0	-
1893	Colts	2	2	0	0	1	.000	11.00	1	0	0	9.0	0	14	11	16	0	3	-	4	0	0	0	-
1896	Pirates	25	14	9	6	8	.429	4.99	11	0	0	155.0	0	171	86	108	3	67	-	48	4	0	0	-
1897	Pirates	25	17	7	6	10	.375	5.06	13	0	1	149.1	0	193	84	115	3	45	-	38	7	7	0	-
1898	Browns	35	33	-	7	24	.226	3.93	31	0	0	283.2	0	325	124	-	2	71	-	74	-	-	-	-
1899	Spiders	36	34	2	4	30	.118	5.41	32	0	0	283.0	0	403	170	244	9	88	-	54	10	22	0	-
1900	Cardinals	20	12	7	5	7	.417	5.19	11	0	0	112.2	0	147	65	90	4	40	-	23	5	6	0	-
CAREER		G	GS	GF	W	L	PCT	ERA	CG	SHO	SV	IP	BFP	H	ER	R	HR	BB	IBB	SO	WP	HBP	BK	HLD
7 YEARS		145	113	26	29	80	.266	4.87	100	0	1	1,007.2	0	1,271	545	579	21	317	-	250	26	35	0	-

John Humphries: Fielding Stats

TEAM	POS	G	GS	OUTS	TC	TC/G	CH	PO	A	E	DP	PB	CASB	CACS	FLD%	RF	ZR
1883 Gothams	C	20	-	-	124	6.2	101	71	30	23	3	31	-	-	.815	0.00	-
1883 Gothams	OF	12	-	-	17	1.4	14	13	1	3	0	n/a	n/a	n/a	.824	0.00	-
1884 Nationals	1B	4	-	-	36	9.0	34	33	1	2	0	n/a	n/a	n/a	.944	0.00	-
1884 Nationals	C	35	-	-	281	8.0	250	198	52	31	6	44	-	-	.890	0.00	-
1884 Nationals	OF	12	-	-	36	3.0	25	25	0	11	0	n/a	n/a	n/a	.694	0.00	-
1884 Gothams	C	20	-	-	193	9.7	173	138	35	20	2	21	-	-	.896	0.00	-
CAREER	POS	G	GS	OUTS	TC	TC/G	CH	PO	A	E	DP	PB	CASB	CACS	FLD%	. RF	ZR
C TOTALS		75	0	0	598	8.0	524	407	117	74	11	96	N/A	N/A	.876	0.00	-
OF TOTALS		24	0	0	53	2.2	39	38	1	14	0	N/A	N/A	N/A	.736	0.00	-
1B TOTALS		4	0	0	36	9.0	34	33	1	2	0	N/A	N/A	N/A	.944	0.00	-
2 YEARS		103	-	-	687	6.7	597	478	119	90	11	96	N/A	N/A	.869	0.00	-

Data courtesy of Baseball-Almanac.com.

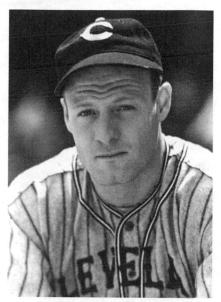

John Humphries (Baseball Hall of Fame Library, Cooperstown, NY)

a 6-for-64 start in the 1894 season, he had nowhere to go but up. Or so one would think.

Unfortunately, yet understandably, Humphries' days in the Big Apple were numbered and he was dropped by the Gothams and picked up by the Washington Nationals of the American Association. Like their new catcher, the Nats faired poorly, finishing with a 12–51 record and a collective team batting average of .200. Humphries picked right up where he left off and made 74 errors in just 75 games. The result was an unimaginably atrocious fielding percentage of .876. Adding insult to injury, he was moved out from behind the plate and then committed 19 errors in 24 games as a right fielder. By the end of the 1884 season, he had tallied 90 errors in his 103 games played (for an average of 0.9 per game) and 1.7 errors committed for every hit.

Being the first major "Ivy" league player to come from Cornell University, John Humphries set the bar extremely low for his fellow classmates. However, his deplorable play on the diamond did not keep him from being elected to the "Big Red's" Hall of Fame. And as disturbing as Humphries' play was, he is an important member in the lineage of ballplayers from the "Great White North."

Beginning with his predecessor Bill Phillips, who played with the Cleveland Blues in 1879, more than 200 Canadian-born players have played in the major leagues, including Eric Bedard, Eric Gagne, and Larry Walker. In 1887, Canadian Tip O'Neil won the Triple Crown with the St. Louis Browns, hitting .435, with 14 home runs, and 106 RBIs. Born in Chatham, Ontario, Ferguson Jenkins, the only Canadian-born Hall of Famer, won 284 games and had 49 shutouts from 1965 to 1983 with the Philadelphia Phillies, Chicago Cubs, Texas Rangers, and Boston Red Sox. Today, baseball is particularly popular in British Colombia, home of current major leaguers Justin Morneau, Rich Harden, and Jason Bay.

Today, there is little reference to John Humphries, the ball player. Within two years of his tenure with them, the New York Gothams became known as the Giants. They won four pennants in the 1880s, but by the turn of the new century they were floundering. The "original" Washington Nationals disbanded, only to reappear in 2005 when America's "National Pastime" returned to the nation's capital for the first time in 33 years, after major league baseball approved the relocation of the Montreal Expos to Washington, DC. Ironically, the announcement came one day before the anniversary of the final game of Washington's second team, the Senators, in 1971.

Worst Fielder
Tony Suck (Yes. That's his real name.)

Birth Name:	Charles Anthony Suck
Nickname:	Tony
Born On:	06–11–1858
Born In:	Chicago, Illinois
Died On:	01–29–1895
Died In:	Chicago, Illinois
Cemetery:	Oak Woods Cemetery, Chicago, Illinois
College:	None Attended
Batted:	Unknown
Threw:	Unknown
Height:	5–09
Weight:	164
First Game:	08–09–1883 (Age 25)
Last Game:	10–15–1884
Draft:	Not Applicable

Few players in major league baseball have been named as appropriately as Tony Suck, and one can only wonder if his parents somehow knew that their son would grow up to become one of the most inept infielders in the history of the game. His career statistics are staggeringly bad, and according to Jay Jaffe's detailed analysis in *The Man Who Lived Up to His Name*, he may very well be the most ineffective athlete ever to don a baseball cap.

According to Jaffe's findings, "In a career that lasted only 58 games over two seasons (1883 and 1884), Suck hit a whopping .151 (31-for-205). And a punchless .151 it was, too; only two of those hits were doubles, and none of them homers. His career slugging percentage was .161, with his on-base percentage of .205." Suck also committed more than 30 errors in 32 games at catcher (.894 PCT), 16 errors in 15 games at shortstop (.754 PCT), and 5 errors in 13 games in the outfield (.783 PCT), with 10 of those games in centerfield.

Buffalo Bisons (Library of Congress)

In 1883, Suck debuted with the Buffalo Bisons of the National League, although he only started in two outings. During that short time, he went 0–7 at the plate and committed three errors in his only game as a catcher. It was a less-than-stellar start to a major league career that only went downhill from there. After being cut by the Bisons, Suck returned as a member of the fledgling Union Association, which fell into financial ruin and disbanded before the year's end. Modern baseball experts, most notably Bill James, have argued that the Union Association (UA) was not even of a major league caliber and could not have possibly competed with the Nationals and Americans. James also believes that the Pacific Coast League and Negro National League had more deserving talent than the UA. Therefore, it somehow seems fitting that Suck played there.

His short-lived time in the Union Association was spent with the 34–39 Chicago Browns, who then folded and were replaced by the Pittsburgh Stogies, who also followed suit and were soon replaced by the St. Paul Saints of the Northwest League. It seems that every team that the .149-hitting, 46-in-53 game-error-making Suck '"touched" met its doom. Somehow, and in spite of it all, he retained his major league status and completed the season, starting three games for the one of the league's more promising franchises, the Baltimore Monumentals. The "Mons" finished with a 58–47 record, but that had little to do with Suck's acquisition. In fact, he went 3-for-10 while committing four errors in three games as catcher. Not surprisingly, he was cut at the end of the season and never played in the majors again.

With a track record as deplorable as Tony Suck's, sports statisticians have debated whether he was mathematically the worst baseball player of all time. Using a complicated series of algorithms and a searchable database, Jay Jaffe identified all of the players in baseball history with more than 200 plate appearances and a batting average below .180 (who were not pitchers). He then selected 50 players who fit the criteria and sorted them by On Base Percentage Plus Slugging Percentage (OPS+), which expresses a player's OPS relative to a park-adjusted league average. A 40 OPS+ means that a player falls about 30 percent below average in both On Base Percentage (OBP) and Slugging Percentage (SLG). OPS represents a player's on-base percentage plus slugging and the league's on-base plus slugging percentage. OBP equals a player's on-base percentage and the league's on-base percentage. We told you it was complicated!

After crunching the data, Jaffe concluded that Suck's OPS+ was a 25, which actually put him at number 13 on the list. His career numbers are as follows:

Games = 98
At Bats = 364
Hits = 52
Doubles = 0
Triples = 0
Homers = 0
Runs = 34
Base-On Balls = 19
Strikeouts = 41
Batting Average = .143
On-Base % = .188
Slugging % = .151

Still, there are few MLB players (if any) that "stunk it up" on both sides of the plate as consistently as Tony Suck did. Despite his failures at the major league level, Suck was considered to be a nice guy and remained a highly regarded individual in Chicago's minor league baseball community. He continued to play both semi-pro and amateur ball up until his premature death of pneumonia at the young age of 36.

Tony Suck Composite Stats

TONY SUCK HITTING STATS

YR	TEAM	G	AB	R	H	2B	3B	HR	GS	RBI	BB	IBB	SO	SH	SF	HBP	GIDP	AVG	OBP	SLG
1883	Bisons	2	7	1	0	0	0	0	0	0	1	-	-	-	-	0	-	.000	.125	.000
1884	Browns	43	153	15	22	2	0	0	0	0	12	-	-	-	-	0	-	.144	.206	.157
1884	Stogies	10	35	3	6	0	0	0	0	0	1	-	-	-	-	0	-	.171	.194	.171
1884	Monumentals	3	10	2	3	0	0	0	0	0	0	-	-	-	-	0	-	.300	.300	.300
CAREER		G	AB	R	H	2B	3B	HR	GS	RBI	BB	IBB	SO	SH	SF	HBP	GIDP	AVG	OBP	SLG
	2 YEARS	58	205	21	31	2	0	0	0	0	14	-	-	-	-	0	-	.151	.205	.161

TONY SUCK FIELDING STATS

	TEAM	POS	G	GS	OUTS	TC	TC/G	CH	PO	A	E	DP	PB	CASB	CACS	FLD%	RF	ZR
1883	Bisons	C	1	-	-	7	7.0	4	4	0	3	0	4	-	-	.571	0.00	-
1883	Bisons	LF	1	-	-	0	0.0	0	0	0	0	0	n/a	n/a	n/a	.000	0.00	-
1884	Browns	3B	1	-	-	0	0.0	0	0	0	0	0	n/a	n/a	n/a	.000	0.00	-
1884	Browns	C	28	-	-	260	9.3	235	136	49	25	3	15	-	-	.904	0.00	-
1884	Browns	OF	12	-	-	23	1.9	18	15	3	5	0	n/a	n/a	n/a	.783	0.00	-
1884	Browns	SS	15	-	-	65	4.3	49	16	33	16	1	n/a	n/a	n/a	.754	0.00	-
1884	Monumentals	C	3	-	-	34	11.3	30	25	5	4	0	4	-	-	.882	0.00	-
CAREER		POS	G	GS	OUTS	TC	TC/G	CH	PO	A	E	DP	PB	CASB	CACS	FLD%	RF	ZR
	C TOTALS		32	0	0	301	9.4	269	215	54	32	3	23	N/A	N/A	.894	0.00	-
	SS TOTALS		15	0	0	65	4.3	49	16	33	16	1	N/A	N/A	N/A	.754	0.00	-
	OF TOTALS		12	0	0	23	1.9	18	15	3	5	0	N/A	N/A	N/A	.783	0.00	-
	3B TOTALS		1	0	0	0	0.0	0	0	0	0	0	N/A	N/A	N/A	.000	0.00	-
	LF TOTALS		1	0	0	0	0.0	0	0	0	0	0	N/A	N/A	N/A	.000	0.00	-
	2 YEARS		61	-	-	389	6.4	336	246	90	53	4	23	N/A	N/A	.864	0.00	-

Data courtesy of Baseball-Almanac.com.

Grand "Champion"
Clarence "Choo Choo" Coleman

Birth Name:	Clarence Coleman
Nickname:	Choo Choo
Born On:	08–25–1937
Born In:	Orlando, Florida
Died On:	n/a
College:	None Attended
Batted:	Left
Threw:	Right
Height:	5–09
Weight:	165
First Game:	04–16–1961 (Age 23)
Last Game:	04–23–1966
Draft:	Not Applicable

The 1961 Philadelphia Phillies made the list of the worst teams in major league history, immortalized for their epic 23-game losing streak. The next year, the New York Mets, playing their inaugural season, set the gold standard for horrible baseball teams by losing 120 games. Two men provide a common link. Outfielder Bobby Gene Smith played for the 1961 Phillies and appeared in eight games for the 1962 Mets before being traded to Chicago Cubs. However, the true common link—the *You Stink!* Grand Champion— was catcher Clarence "Choo Choo" Coleman.

In 1961, Coleman, a 23-year-old native of Orlando, Florida, stood 5-feet 9-inches and weighed 165 pounds, and batted lefty. "He [Coleman] is quick on the base paths," observed legendary baseball writer Roger Angell in his 1982 book *Late Innings,* "but this is an attribute that is about as essential for catchers as neat handwriting." He was no defensive wizard, either. "Nobody could try any harder than this guy," recalled pitcher Clem Labine. "He was a boxer—someone who doesn't catch the ball most of the time, but he'd keep it in front of him." Angell was more colorful in his description, saying that Coleman "caught as though he were fighting a swarm of bees."

The little catcher was a man of few words. "He'd carry on a conversation with you," recalled a Met teammate, "but to keep it going, you had to do most of the talking." Ralph Kiner, the Hall of Fame outfielder and long-time Met broadcaster once interviewed Coleman after a game. "What's your wife's name, and what's she like?" inquired Kiner. "Her name is Mrs. Coleman, and she likes me," responded Choo Choo. The interview ended

Clarence "Choo Choo" Coleman (Baseball Hall of Fame Library, Cooperstown, NY)

shortly thereafter. He was also incapable of remembering the names of his teammates, and they razzed him mercilessly for it. Coleman good-naturedly shrugged it off.

Choo Choo was a hard-core pull hitter. "Choo Choo used to hit foul balls to right field," remembered a minor league teammate, "not just foul balls, but very foul balls. He didn't want to change the way he hit, because then he couldn't hit his foul balls. He was using his shoulders to swing the bat. It was such a bizarre way to hit. I don't know how anyone could even entertain it."

Coleman made his major league debut in Philadelphia in 1961. He appeared in 34 games, and had 47 at bats. He had only 6 hits in those 47 at bats, meaning that his batting average with the Phillies was a dismal .128. The Mets selected him in the expansion draft. He did not make the team out of spring training and was assigned to the Mets' AAA team in Buffalo. He was hitting only .195 at Syracuse when he was called up. He caught Casey Stengel's eye. A few days later, the Old Perfessor told a sportswriter, "Do you know who my player of the year is? My player of the year is Choo Choo Coleman and I have him for only two days. He runs very good."

Stengel's infatuation did not last. Choo Choo appeared in 55 games for the 1962 Mets, hitting .250 in 152 at bats. The left-handed pull hitter took advantage of the short porch in right field of the Polo Grounds, slugging six homers. He played in 106 games for the 1963 edition of the Mets, hitting only .178 with 3 homers in 247 at bats. He also committed 15 errors and had 11 passed balls in 1963, demonstrating that he was no Gold Glover behind the plate. He appeared in six more games for the Mets in 1966, and then disappeared from the major leagues. His career batting average was an atrocious .197 in 462 at bats.

Choo Choo Coleman deserves immortality as the *You Stink!* Grand Champion, having played for two of the very worst teams in the history of major league baseball, and playing badly at that. Here's to you, Choo Choo. Baseball history is much richer for your contributions.

Choo Choo Coleman Composite Stats

CHOO CHOO COLEMAN HITTING STATS

YR	TEAM	G	AB	R	H	2B	3B	HR	GS	RBI	BB	IBB	SO	SH	SF	HBP	GIDP	AVG	OBP	SLG
1961	Phillies	34	47	3	6	1	0	0	0	4	2	0	8	0	0	1	1	.128	.180	.149
1962	Mets	55	152	24	38	7	2	6	0	17	11	2	24	1	1	1	1	.250	.303	.441
1963	Mets	106	247	22	44	0	0	3	0	9	24	3	49	1	0	5	4	.178	.264	.215
1966	Mets	6	16	2	3	0	0	0	0	0	0	0	4	0	0	0	0	.188	.188	.188
CAREER		G	AB	R	H	2B	3B	HR	GS	RBI	BB	IBB	SO	SH	SF	HBP	GIDP	AVG	OBP	SLG
4 YEARS		201	462	51	91	8	2	9	0	30	37	5	85	2	1	7	6	.197	.266	.281

CHOO CHOO COLEMAN FIELDING STATS

YR	TEAM	POS	G	GS	OUTS	TC	TC/G	CH	PO	A	E	DP	PB	CASB	CACS	FLD%	RF	ZR
1961	Phillies	C	14	-	-	43	3.1	42	38	4	1	1	1	-	-	.977	0.00	-
1962	Mets	C	44	-	-	210	4.8	209	187	22	1	2	5	-	-	.995	0.00	-
1963	Mets	C	91	-	-	487	5.4	472	418	54	15	9	11	-	-	.969	0.00	-
1963	Mets	LF	1	-	-	0	0.0	0	0	0	0	0	n/a	n/a	n/a	.000	0.00	-
1966	Mets	C	5	-	-	27	5.4	26	24	2	1	0	0	-	-	.963	0.00	-
CAREER		POS	G	GS	OUTS	TC	TC/G	CH	PO	A	E	DP	PB	CASB	CACS	FLD%	RF	ZR
C TOTALS			154	0	0	767	5.0	749	667	82	18	12	17	N/A	N/A	.977	0.00	-
LF TOTALS			1	0	0	0	0.0	0	0	0	0	0	N/A	N/A	N/A	.000	0.00	-
4 YEARS			155	-	-	767	4.9	749	667	82	18	12	17	N/A	N/A	.977	0.00	-

Data courtesy of Baseball-Almanac.com.

Red Sox Owner Bob Quinn (Library of Congress)

Worst Owners
The Not-So-Mighty Quinns

The Quinn family spans four generations of baseball management. No other family has spent as many years in baseball management. And no other family has experienced as much baseball misery as the Quinns.

The patriarch was James Aloysius Robert "Bob" Quinn. Born in Columbus, Ohio, in 1870, Bob Quinn was a minor league catcher. When his playing days ended, he became general manager of a series of teams, including the Columbus Senators of the American Association and the St. Louis Browns of the American League. In 1923, he led a group that purchased the Boston Red Sox, presiding over some of the worst teams in the history of the American League. After selling the Red Sox to Tom Yawkey in 1933, he became president and general manager of the crosstown Boston Braves at the end of the 1935 season, the worst in Braves' history. He retired in 1945 without ever having won a pennant. Bob Quinn died in 1954.

His son, John J. Quinn, followed his father into the baseball business. He served as general manager of the Boston and Milwaukee Braves from 1945 to 1958, winning three pennants and one World Series championship in 1957. And then he tainted his fine record, spending 13 years as general manager of the Philadelphia Phillies, from 1959 until his forced retirement in June 1972. Quinn was the general manager (GM) of the Phillies during one of the worst periods in the long history of a franchise that has suffered more losses than any other. His record as GM of the Phillies was an awful 963–1116 record during his 12 full seasons, for a wining percentage of .463.

John Quinn's son Bob served as general manager of the Yankees, Reds, and Giants, and his other son Jack spent many years in the front office of the Cleveland Indians and also served as general manager of the St. Louis Blues hockey team.

Although the Quinns' dedication to the game of baseball is commendable, and their contributions many, it's hard to imagine two general managers who oversaw as many losing seasons and as much abject misery than did father and son Bob and John Quinn, who are the *You Stink!* Grand Champions for front office executives.

Disappointment
on the Diamond

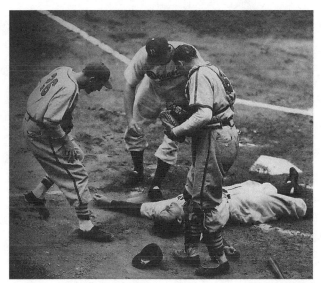

Cardinals Pitcher Bob Bowman Beans Brooklyn's Joe Medwick
(Library of Congress)

★ | A Timeline of Terribleness

Most fans with even a casual interest in the game of baseball could probably evoke one or two "highlight reel" performances recalling the greatest moments in major league baseball history. Some may cite Babe Ruth calling his shot during Game 3 of the 1932 World Series, while others might select Willie Mays' magnificent over-the-shoulder catch that saved two runs in Game 1 of the 1954 Fall Classic. Another might remember Bobby Thomson's "shot heard round the world" that nabbed the pennant for the 1951 Giants, or Reggie "Mr. October" Jackson's three homerun night in Game 6 of the 1977 Series. That said, it might be more difficult for one to identify the worst performances or moments in the game. Why? Because in most cases the fans are still trying to forget them! The following timeline chronicles some of the worst moments in professional baseball history.

A timeline format as it is written in sequential order from 1877 to 2011:

1877

The National League experienced its first scandal when the *Louisville Courier* newspaper reported a fix involving their Louisville Grays. After compiling a 27–12 record, the Grays lost eight in a row while Boston won 13 out of 15 to snatch the pennant. Despite a thorough investigation and several suspensions, sufficient proof that a crime was committed did not exist.

1880

In October 1880, the National League outlawed Sunday baseball and also banned the sale of beer at all games. Cincinnati refused to comply and was expelled from the league by National League President William Hulbert.

1882

The Chicago White Stockings set a major league record by scoring a 35–4 win over the Cleveland Blues. Outfielder-turned-pitcher Dave Rowe surrendered 29 hits (including 10 doubles and 7 walks) in his only appearance on the mound.

1883

The American Association champion Philadelphia Athletics lost their first eight postseason exhibition games, resulting in the cancellation of a "World Series" against the National League pennant-winning Boston Beaneaters.

1884

Decades before Jackie Robinson "officially" broke baseball's color barrier, Moses Fleetwood Walker played 46 major league games for the American Association's Toledo Blue Stockings. Despite hitting .263 in 1884, Walker tallied 37 errors, which led to his early release.

1889

On June 22, 1889, the Louisville Colonels of the American Association set an unwanted major league record by registering their 26th consecutive loss.

The short-lived Players League folded in December, returning all of the players to their original teams. The Pittsburgh franchise deviated from the agreement and signed second baseman Louis Bierbauer, who originally belonged to the Philadelphia Phillies. After being accused in the papers of being "Pirates," the team adopted the nickname and refused to return Bierbauer to its cross-state rivals.

1895

Before a game with the visiting Cleveland Spiders, the entire Chicago Colts team was arrested for "inciting, aiding and abetting the forming of a noisy crowd on a Sunday." Reverend W. W. Clark and the "Sunday Observance League" had protested the concept of baseball on Sunday and instigated the police action. After owner Jim Hart posted bail, 10,000 fans remained to watch the "wanted men" beat the visitors 13–4.

1898

On April 16, 1898, approximately 100 people (out of a crowd of 4,000) were injured after a fire (caused by a lit cigar) broke out in the grandstands of Sportsman's Park in St. Louis during a game between the Browns and visiting Chicago Orphans. Within half an hour, the entire bleachers and left-field stands were completely destroyed.

1901

On April 28, 1901, Cleveland Indians rookie pitcher Charles Baker surrendered an American League record 23 singles in a 13–1 loss to the Chicago White Stockings.

With two outs in the ninth, Milwaukee Brewers pitcher Bill Reidy set a major league record by surrendering 10 consecutive hits in a 13–2 loss to the Boston Somersets on June 2, 1901.

At the December 1901 league meeting, the Milwaukee Brewers franchise was officially dropped from the American League and was replaced by the St. Louis Browns.

1902

In July 1902, the Baltimore Orioles forfeited a game to St. Louis and their team to the league. With only five players available for the lineup, the

American League's front office borrowed backup players from several other teams and maintained the franchise for the remainder of the season. The team then folded.

1903

On May 6, 1903, the Chicago White Stockings committed 12 errors and the Detroit Tigers answered with six of their own. The combined "18-E debacle" set a modern major league record for the most errors (by two teams) in a single game.

Boston Brave Wiley Pratt became the only twentieth-century pitcher to lose two complete games in one day. Pratt allowed 14 hits, while striking out 12, en route to 1–0 and 5–3 Pittsburgh Pirates victories.

The inaugural World Series was a resounding success and represented the first step in healing the bruised egos of both the veteran National and fledgling American Leagues. Pittsburgh and Boston went head-to-head for eight games, proving that great baseball between the two leagues was possible and that a merger would benefit the growth of the sport. Unfortunately, and in spite of the concept's popularity, some owners still disagreed with the idea of interleague play, and in 1904, the World Series was prematurely cancelled.

1904

Boston Americans (Red Sox) shortstop Bill O'Neill set an unwanted major league record when he became the only twentieth-century player to record six errors during a 13-inning 5–3 loss to the St. Louis Browns.

After pitching a record-setting season with 41 wins and 454 innings in 55 games, New York Highlanders (Yankees) ace Jack Chesbro "crashed and burned" after losing control of a spitball that sailed over his catcher's head and allowed the American League pennant-losing run to score from third.

Frank Chance of the Chicago Cubs set a painful major league mark after being hit by pitches four times in one day during a May 30, 1904, doubleheader against the Cincinnati Reds. In the first game, "The Peerless Leader" actually lost consciousness after being tagged in the head by Jack Harper.

John T. Brush, president of the National League champion New York Giants, refused to play the returning American League champion Boston Americans. He was quoted as stating that he refused to compete with a "representative of the inferior American League." Surprisingly, Brush regretted the decision and later that year proposed to continue with the series as originally conceived. His about-face spawned the "Brush Rules," a set of guidelines relating to the on-field play and off-field finances of the World Series, which exist to this day.

1905

In 1905, the National League Board of Directors acquitted St. Louis Cardinal right-hander Jack Taylor of charges of throwing games. Despite the verdict, Taylor was still fined $300 for using poor judgment and practicing bad conduct.

1906

In August 1906, the Boston Americans set an unwanted major league record by suffering four straight shutout losses (0–3 on August 2; 0–4 on August 3; 0–1 on August 4; and 0–4 on August 6).

Prior to the 1906 season, National League umpire Hank O'Day unsuccessfully proposed that the batter's box be outlined with white rubber strips (rather than chalk) to prevent batters from erasing them with their spikes.

1907

Popular Boston Americans outfielder/manager Chick Stahl committed suicide in West Baden Springs, Indiana, while traveling with the team. A note left behind stated, "Boys, I just couldn't help it. You drove me to it."

A riot broke out during a July 8, 1907, Chicago Cubs–Brooklyn Dodgers game after Cubs manager Frank Chance, who was being pelted with empty bottles, threw one back into the crowd and clocked a young boy. After losing 5–0, the angry New York crowd rushed from the stands, forcing Chance to escape Washington Park in an armored car with a police escort.

1908

The 1908 Washington Senators set an unwanted American League record after being shut out 29 times.

In 1908, and despite overwhelming evidence to the contrary (after a two-year investigation by the Mills Committee), National League President A. G. Mills mistakenly declared that Abner Doubleday had, indeed, invented the sport of baseball at Cooperstown, New York, in 1839. Ninety-nine years later, a special committee from the Baseball Hall of Fame inducted Alexander Cartwright for originating baseball's original concepts and sportswriter Henry Chadwick for the invention of the box score.

1909

The National League deprived umpires of the ability to levy fines and declared that all relief pitchers must retire at least one batter before being relieved.

On July 3, 1909, the St. Louis Cardinals tied an unwanted major league mark by committing 17 errors during a doubleheader loss to the Cincinnati Reds, (10–2 and 13–7).

1910

On April 22, 1910, the Braves and Phillies combined for a major league record fewest at bats by two teams in nine innings: 48 (25 for Boston, 23 for Philadelphia). The record was tied the following season, but remained unbeaten until 1964.

1911

On September 28, 1911, several hundred fans witnessed one of the worst contests in American League history, as the New York Yankees and St. Louis Browns combined to accumulate 29 hits, 20 walks, 12 errors, and 15 stolen bases en route to an 18–12 (NY) final.

On May 22, 1911, Boston Braves pitcher Cliff Curtis set a major league record by recording his 23rd consecutive loss (beginning on June 13, 1910) in a 3–1 defeat by the St, Louis Cardinals.

1912

The St. Louis Cardinals set a major league record on April 16, 1912, by embarrassing the Chicago Cubs in a 20–5 massacre at Robison Field, a mark that stood until 1922.

1913

The Boston Red Sox set a major league record for frustration on July 3 by totaling 15 hits off the Washington Senators' Walter Johnson during a 1–0 shutout.

In December, the *Sporting News* reported that 15 men (none well known) had died from various baseball-inflicted injuries during the 1913 season, according to a list compiled by J. R. Vickery of Chicago.

1914

Cleveland Indians shortstop Ray Chapman stumbled his way into an unwanted record on June 20, 1914, by committing four errors in the fifth inning during a 7–1 loss to the New York Yankees at League Park II.

During the second game of an August 1914 doubleheader in Washington, Detroit Tigers pitcher Hooks Dauss combined with four Senators aces to hit a record seven batters for a major league mark that remained unmatched until the 1971 season.

Fans witnessed the debut of the short-lived Federal League after John T. Powers of Chicago convinced a group of entrepreneurs that the growing popularity of baseball could support a third major league. Eight teams began the league's inaugural season, with clubs based in Brooklyn, Chicago, St. Louis, and Pittsburgh as well as Baltimore, Kansas City, Buffalo, and Indianapolis, which had been the home for AAA teams. All eight cities constructed brand new ballparks, including the Chicago Whales, who played in what would eventually be known as Wrigley Field.

1915

On December 1, 1915, organized baseball agreed to a formal "peace treaty" with the Federal League, ending a two-year political war. The Federals agreed to disband after the American and National Leagues both agreed to pay an enormous sum of $600,000 for distribution to team owners, to absorb two franchises (one into the American League and one into the National League), and to recognize all former players as eligible picks at a Federal-controlled auction.

In 1915, the American League officially banned the "emery ball," a pitch introduced by Russ Ford in 1910. While a semi-pro pitcher, Ford had accidentally discovered that a scuffed baseball could be made to break sharply. He began doctoring the ball intentionally, using emery paper to scuff it up, and disguised his pitches as spitballs, which, at the time, were legal.

1916

On April 11, 1916, the World Champion Boston Red Sox suffered an embarrassing 1–0 loss during an exhibition game against young men from Boston College.

On May 9, 1916, the Philadelphia Athletics and Detroit Tigers combined to set a major league record with 30 walks during a 16–2, "Motor City" win. A's pitchers issued 19 free passes (and went on to finish the season with 715). Detroit added 11 more the following day for a two-game major league record of 29 walks.

1917

In April 1917, the Cincinnati Reds purchased Olympic icon Jim Thorpe from the Giants, but eventually sent him back to New York in August. Thorpe never experienced the same success on a baseball diamond that he had in the Olympics and retired after an undistinguished six-season career.

Organized baseball officially terminated relations with the players' union in 1917, leaving the players without representation. Players Fraternity President Dave Fultz called off a strike in which the players were attempting to eliminate a 10-day clause, whereby teams refused to pay any injured player after 10 days.

America's entry into World War I, combined with an unusually wet spring, led to the postponement of 48 National League games in the first month of the 1917 season. As a result, half of all major league clubs showed losses for the year, and 8 of 20 minor league teams folded before the end of the season. On a side note, the American League petitioned the United States Army to assign drill sergeants to each team for daily pregame drills.

1918

Cincinnati Reds manager Christy Mathewson suspended first baseman Hal "Prince Hal" Chase indefinitely on August 9, 1918, after suspecting him of taking bribes to fix games. Chase was eventually reinstated and returned to play for the New York Giants in 1919.

1919

The National League voted to ban the use of "spitballs" by all new pitchers. The ban was formally worked out by the Rules Committee the following February, and was expanded to include the use of all foreign substances (saliva, resin, talcum powder, paraffin) as well as any other alterations (shine or emery) to balls by pitchers.

The 1919 World Series ignited the infamous "Black Sox" scandal after eight members of the participating White Sox, including pitchers Eddie Cicotte and Claude (Lefty) Williams, outfielders Joe Jackson and Happy Felsch, first baseman Chick Gandil, shortstop Swede Risberg, third baseman Buck Weaver, and reserve infielder Fred McMullin were all charged with conspiring to fix the outcome of the Fall Classic against the Cincinnati Reds. To this day, the participants in the conspiracy have been denied entry into the Baseball Hall of Fame.

1920

On January 5, 1920, the New York Yankees officially announced the purchase of Babe Ruth from the Boston Red Sox. The disgruntled pitcher had been unable to reach a contract agreement and was sold to Colonel Jacob Ruppert's Yankees for $100,000 (plus a loan collateralized by Fenway Park). It took 87 years for Boston to win another World Series title. Generations of Red Sox fans blamed it on the "Curse of the Bambino."

The Detroit Tigers lost their first 13 games, tying the major league mark for consecutive losses at the start of a season set by the 1904 Washington Senators.

Tragedy struck the Cleveland Indians organization when a Carl Mays pitch beaned 29-year-old shortstop Ray Chapman. Chapman died the following day from a fractured skull.

Several hours before the start of Game 4 of the 1920 Fall Classic, Brooklyn Robins standout Rube Marquard (a Cleveland native), was arrested after attempting to sell a World Series ticket to an undercover police officer for $350. Marquard was found guilty and ordered to pay a fine and court costs totaling $3.80. Adding insult to injury, his hometown opponents won the game 5–1.

The Joint Rules Committee voted to ban the use of all foreign substances (saliva, resin, talcum powder, paraffin) as well as any other alterations (shine or emery) to balls by pitchers. As a result, the American League opted to allow two pitchers from each club the option to use a spitball for one more season. The Nationals set no limitations as long as all "practicing" pitchers were identified, and any other pitcher who was caught cheating would be suspended for a minimum of 10 days.

1921

On August 2, 1921, a Chicago jury rendered a verdict of "not guilty" in the criminal trial of the infamous "Black Sox," who had been accused of throwing the 1919 World Series in favor of the Cincinnati Reds. Ignoring the verdict, Commissioner Judge Kenesaw Mountain Landis banned all eight defendants from major league baseball for life. "Regardless of the verdict of juries," the commissioner said in a statement, "no player that throws a ball game, no player that entertains proposals or promises to throw a game, no player that sits in a conference with a bunch of crooked players and gamblers where the ways and means of throwing games are discussed, and does not promptly tell his club about it, will ever again play professional baseball."

1922

On July 13, 1922, 68 fans, representing the smallest crowd in Fenway Park's long and illustrious history, turned out to watch the visiting St. Louis Browns shut out Alex Ferguson and the Boston Red Sox 2–0.

On August 25, 1922, the Chicago Cubs edged the Philadelphia Phillies, 26–23, in one of the worst combined pitching performances in baseball history. The game featured 51 hits, 23 walks, and 10 errors with the Phillies stranding 16 men on base and the Cubs leaving 9.

1923

On September 16, 1923, a riot broke out in Chicago after umpire Charlie Moran made an "out" call at second base on Sparky Adams. Commissioner Judge Kenesaw Mountain Landis was in attendance and shook his cane at the angry mob as Moran and the other officials were pelted by hundreds of empty bottles. After holding up play for more than 15 minutes, the game resumed with the visiting New York Giants winning 10–6.

1926

During a September 3, 1926, outing against the Boston Braves, the New York Giants set a National League record by recording an astounding 12 runs in the fifth inning. The mid-game rally devastated the Braves, who were unable to recover en route to an embarrassing 17–3 disaster.

On May 8, 1926, a fire partially destroyed the bleachers along the left field line at Fenway Park. Surprisingly, Red Sox management opted not to replace the seats.

1927

During a May 14, 1927, game between the Philadelphia Phillies and St. Louis Cardinals, a section of 10 rows of the right-field stands at Philadelphia's Baker Bowl collapsed, spilling hundreds of fans onto spectators below. There were many injuries, but the only one death caused by the crowd's ensuing stampede and not the collapsing bleachers.

The New York Yankees' grand finale for their epic 1927 season, the World Series, was the quickest ever played, and lasted only 74 hours and 15 minutes. The Yankees became the first American League team to sweep a World Series in only the second sweep in World Series history (the other being the "Miracle Braves" over the Athletics in 1914). The Yankees trailed a total of only two innings during the entire series, outscoring the Pirates 23–10. Only once did Pittsburgh score more than one run in an inning (during Game 4). Fans of the badly beaten "Buccos" spared no words in voicing their disappointment and lambasted them in the press.

1928

Washington Senators pitcher Milt Gaston set another unusual American League record by scattering 14 hits en route to a 9–0 shutout over the Cleveland Indians on July 10, 1928.

Following a 1928 Labor Day doubleheader rainout, the Boston Braves played a record nine consecutive doubleheaders between September 4 and the 15: with the Brooklyn Dodgers on the 4th and 5th, then Philadelphia Phillies on the 7th and 8th, followed by the New York Giants on the 10th, 11th, 13th, and 14th, and finally with the Chicago Cubs on the 15th. Starting with Philadelphia, the Braves also set an unwanted record by dropping five consecutive games, including all four against the Giants.

On December 11, 1928, National League President John Heydler first proposed the concept of a designated hitter (also known as the *tenth regular*). Heydler contended that the fans were tired of seeing weak hitting pitchers come up to bat and that the incorporation of a designated hitter would improve the quality of play and speed up the game.

1929

On May 1, 1929, the first-place Philadelphia Athletics scored a whopping eight runs off Boston Red Sox pitcher Milt Gaston on the way to an embarrassing 24–6 massacre at Fenway Park. The 24 runs matched a franchise record previously set in the "Ty Cobb protest game" in 1912, and the 29 hits set another franchise mark.

1930

On May 9, 1930, the New York Yankees' and Detroit Tigers' outfields combined for a meager two putouts, setting an American League record that has never been equaled. The National League record for outfielder idleness was previously set at one putout when the Pittsburgh Pirates took on the "Brooklyn Superbas" in August 1910.

1931

On July 7, 1930, the St. Louis Browns and Chicago White Sox met for a 12-inning marathon in which not a single strikeout was recorded. The 10–8 decision still remains the longest game in major league history not to record a single "K."

On April 2, a 17-year-old female named Jackie Mitchell, of the Double A "Chattanooga Lookouts," took the mound against the mighty New York Yankees in a spring training exhibition. The first two batters she faced from "Murderers Row" were Babe Ruth and Lou Gehrig. After seven pitches Mitchell fanned the "Sultan of Swat" and the "Iron Horse," back-to-back. Within a month, women were officially banned from professional baseball.

1932

After holding several hearings following the 1932 season, Baseball Commissioner Judge Kenesaw Mountain Landis cleared Rogers Hornsby of charges of fraudulently "borrowing" money from several Chicago Cubs players. The investigation was initiated after Windy City newspapers reported that Hornsby had obtained money from players to bet on horse races or to share in joint ventures.

1933

On March 11, 1933, a substantial earthquake rocked the Los Angeles area, interrupting an exhibition game between the Chicago Cubs and New York Giants. As fans exited the grandstands amid panic, players from both teams huddled in the center of the diamond until the tremors stopped.

1934

On August 4, Reggie Grabowski of the 1934 Philadelphia Phillies set an unwanted National League record by surrendering 11 hits (and runs) in the ninth inning against the New York Giants in a humiliating 21–4 loss.

Baseball Commissioner Judge Kenesaw Mountain Landis, who was granted absolute power in 1920 after the Black Sox scandal had tainted the game, denied participant Shoeless Joe Jackson's appeal for reinstatement in January of 1934.

Due to declining attendance, both the 1934 St. Louis Cardinals and St. Louis Browns discontinued radio broadcasts from Sportsman's Park in an effort to promote ticket sales. All games had been aired since 1926, but only on weekdays for the last two years.

1935

In November 1935, the National League temporarily assumed control of the bankrupt Boston Braves after several attempts to sell the club failed. Finishing the season with 115 losses, (a record that remained until the 1962 expansion New York Mets lost 120), the foundering franchise barely managed a winning percentage of .248, which remains the worst in the twentieth century.

1936

On April 26, 1936, Philadelphia Phillies catcher Earl Grace set an unwanted major league record by allowing Brooklyn Dodgers shortstop Ben Geraghty to get on base twice as a result of two separate catcher interference calls (tipped bat).

After purchasing the foundering Boston Braves in 1936, the team owners asked a local newspaper person to choose a new nickname for the franchise based on suggestions made by the fans. After hundreds of entries, the moniker Boston "Bees" was selected. Unfortunately, it never caught on and was changed back to the Braves after the 1940 season.

1937

On May 3, 1937, the New York Giants tied an unusual major league record by playing an entire nine-inning game against the Boston Bees without engaging their outfielders in a single play. The Bees outfield managed only three putouts themselves, winning 3–1.

In January 1937, Cincinnati fell victim to its worst flooding disaster ever, as rising water overwhelmed the lower city limits and Crosley Field. At its peak, river water covered the infield diamond and lower grandstands with as much as 21 feet of water. Taking advantage of a photographic opportunity, Reds pitchers Gene Schott and Lee Grissom rowed a boat out from the center field wall for a once-in-a-lifetime image that appeared in newspapers across the country.

1938

On May 5, 1938, Philadelphia Phillies pitcher Hal Kelleher set two unwanted major league records by surrendering 12 runs to 16 Chicago Cub batters in the eighth inning of a 21–2 massacre. Joe Marty led the attack with four hits for four runs and four runs batted in.

On June 18, a jilted Babe Ruth signed on as a Brooklyn Dodgers coach for the remainder of the season. Desperately seeking a management position, the "Sultan of Swat" agreed to participate in many exploitive "noncoaching-related" publicity stunts, including appearing in uniform before games for batting demonstrations.

1939

On May 2, 1939, New York Yankee Lou Gehrig, also known as the "Iron Horse," voluntarily benched himself "for the good of the team." Gehrig's consecutive-game streak thus ended at 2,130. After being diagnosed with amyotrophic lateral sclerosis (later renamed Lou Gehrig's Disease), the ailing first baseman was forced to retire with a .143 batting average and only a single run batted in.

In November 1939, an "off-season" experiment known as the "National Professional Indoor Baseball League" debuted to poor reviews. Headed by President Tris Speaker, the league boasted 10 clubs, including one in each major league city except Washington. Unfortunately, the novel concept of playing baseball indoors during the winter months failed at the ticket gates miserably, and the league was disbanded within a month.

1940

On May 7, 1940, the Brooklyn Dodgers fell 18 2 as the St. Louis Cardinals totaled 49 total bases on 20 hits; 13 knocks went for extra-bases, and 7 were home runs. The rally set a National League record for most extra bases for long hits with 29.

Brooklyn Dodgers' reliever Carl Doyle dropped the ball (and the game) after giving up 16 hits and 14 runs (in just four innings), as the Cincinnati Reds tallied 27 hits and a 23–2 victory. To make matters worse, Doyle also hit four Cincinnati batters with pitches to tie a National League record, initiating a bitter rivalry between the teams that lasted for decades. Four days later, Doyle was dealt to the St. Louis Cardinals.

Walter Johnson, who had won 416 games for the Washington Senators, lost the 1940 election as the Republican candidate for the U.S. House of Representatives from Maryland. Although Johnson's political career ended before it began, his career on the field never seemed to end. He compiled statistics that included the following: 16 straight wins (1912), a string of 56 scoreless innings and a 36–7 (1.09) mark in 1913, 5 wins, 3 of them shut-outs, in 9 days (1908), 66 triumphs over Detroit, the most for any American League pitcher against any one team, 200 victories in 8 seasons and 300 victories in 14 seasons.

1941

Joe DiMaggio's 56 game hitting streak finally ended on July 17, 1941, thanks to solid pitching by Cleveland Indians pitchers Al Smith and Jim Bagby. Despite stopping the "Yankee Clipper," the Tribe was unable to stop the rest of the Yankees and lost 6–5 in front of 60,000 fans.

On August 19, 1941, Frankie Frisch, manager of the Pittsburgh Pirates, was ejected from the second game of a doubleheader after appearing on the field waving an umbrella to protest the playing conditions at Brooklyn's Ebbets Field. American artist Norman Rockwell later transformed the humorous argument into a famous oil painting titled *Bottom of the Sixth*.

In response to the notorious "bean ball wars" of the 1940 season, the Brooklyn Dodgers inserted protective liners into their caps as a safety precaution. The rising aggressions between pitchers and batters had resulted in the serious injury and hospitalization of Joe Medwick, Billy Jurges, and others. Although the thin liners were hardly noticeable, many players around the league criticized them as a distraction.

1942

On August 14, the New York Yankees infield combined to turn seven double plays (a major league record) during an 11–2 massacre of the Philadelphia Athletics. All-star catcher Bill Dickey gunned down two runners following third strikes, and Phil Rizzuto, Johnny Murphy, and Red Rolfe combined on five others. The Yankees finished the season with 190 double plays, just falling short of their previous record of 194 that was set in 1941.

On the same day his wife gave birth to a son, Chicago Cubs shortstop Lennie Merullo set a major league record by committing four separate errors in the second inning of a 1942 nightcap against the Boston Braves. Despite the new father's poor play, the Cubs won 12–8 after losing the first game, 10–6.

On March 18, 1942, two black players, Jackie Robinson and Nate Moreland, requested walk-on tryouts with the Chicago White Sox during a spring training session in Pasadena. Manager Jimmie Dykes reluctantly allowed them to work out with the ball club, but dismissed both without an offer.

In 1942, the *Sporting News* published a controversial editorial calling for continued segregation on the ball field and in the stands. The unfortunate column stated that members of each race "prefer to draw their talents from their own ranks and both groups know their crowd psychology and do not care to run the risk of damaging their own game." Fortunately, segregation in major league baseball ended in 1947.

1943

On August 24, the miserable Philadelphia Athletics recorded their 20th loss in a row, tying the American League mark for consecutive defeats. Luckily, they avoided breaking the record by scoring eight runs on the home Chicago White Sox in the bottom half of the doublehcader.

In 1943, major league baseball approved a new "official" ball that was comprised of reclaimed cork and balata, which were two suitable materials that were not needed in the war effort. Officials insisted that the ball would have the resiliency of the old version, but players later complained of an inability to drive the "overripe grapefruits" and pointed out the lack of home runs as a result.

1944

Despite running a close race for first place in the American League, the St. Louis Browns recorded the worst AL attendance on September 29, 1944, when an embarrassing total of only 6,172 fans witnessed their sweep of a doubleheader against the New York Yankees. The following day, attendance doubled to 12,982 as Dennis Galehouse pitched the entire game, winning 2–0 for his ninth victory of the year. Two days later, the Browns were tied with the Detroit Tigers and boasted their first sellout in more than 20 years, as 37,815 packed Sportsman's Park to watch their "forgotten" team clinch the pennant on the final day of the season.

One of baseball's worst franchises, the 1944 Philadelphia Phillies attempted to induce public support by announcing a fan-based contest to rename the team. Mrs. Elizabeth Crooks, who was given a $100 war bond and a season ticket, submitted the winning entry of "Blue Jays." Her entry, which later ended up on another team's uniform, was chosen over a number of monikers ranging from the Daisies to the Stinkers. The new name was used as the unofficial team title for 1944–1945 season, but was abandoned in 1946, though the team was still occasionally referred to in newspaper accounts as the "Blue Jays" through 1949.

1945

Major league owners canceled the 1945 All-Star Game due to wartime travel restrictions. Eight simultaneous games were scheduled in place of the Midsummer Classic, pitting the National and American Leagues against one another in interleague play.

1946

The 1946 American League All-Stars embarrassed the National League representatives in a 12–0 triumph at Fenway Park. Despite the lopsided finale, this particular Midsummer Classic remained special, as the first postwar All-Star Game. Many players later stated that they had never seen a more festive occasion, and many of them had not seen their major league rivals in several years. "Home field" slugger Ted Williams of the Boston Red Sox led the charge with two home runs, two singles, a walk, four runs scored, and four runs batted in.

1948

On March 29, 1948, in St. Petersburg ,Florida, the New York Yankees and rival Boston Red Sox went head-to-head for 17 grueling innings only to have the contest called at a 2–2 tie after four hours and two minutes of play. It was the longest, and perhaps the most frustrating, spring training game in major league history.

At the end of the 1948 season, the Brooklyn Dodgers traded the extremely talented, but even more accident prone Pete Reiser to the Boston Braves for Mike McCormick. Reiser was one of the top outfielders of his time, but had damaged his reputation after being carried off the field on a stretcher 11 times throughout the season after crashing into the outfield walls.

Major league baseball Commissioner Happy Chandler fined the 1948 New York Yankees, Chicago Cubs, and Philadelphia Phillies $500 each after he learned that they were attempting to sign high school players for the upcoming season.

1949

A pharmacist from Cleveland named Charley Lupica climbed a 20-foot platform atop a flagpole on May 31, 1949, and announced that he would remain perched there until the Indians won another pennant. Unfortunately, the seventh-place Tribe was only able to manage fourth place by the time Lupica descended on September 25.

A riot literally broke out in the Philadelphia Phillies stands on August 21,

1949, after fans threw bottles in protest of umpire George Barr's call over a trapped fly ball. The unruly crowd behavior resulted in the first forfeiture in the major league in seven years. Ironically, the visiting New York Giants were forced into the same situation in 1942 after hundreds of youngsters rushed their field.

On September 15, 1949, Pittsburgh pitcher Ernie Bonham died following an emergency appendectomy and stomach surgery. His untimely death shocked the Pirates organization, as Bonham had just beaten the Philadelphia Phillies 8–2 only 18 days earlier. Mrs. Bonham later became the first spouse to receive benefits under the major league players' pension plan, which provided the widow with a check for $90 a month over the next 10 years.

1950

On June 8, 1950, the Red Sox recorded the most lopsided victory in baseball history by crushing the visiting St. Louis Browns 29–4. Boston also set several other major league records, including most extra bases on long hits (32) in a game and the most extra bases on long hits in consecutive games (51). Leadoff batter Clyde Vollmer set a major league mark of his own as the only batter to go to the plate eight times in eight innings.

In an effort to discourage the continued major league signing of black ball players, Dr. J. B. Martin, the president of the Chicago Giants of the Negro American League, ordered manager Ted "Double Duty" Radcliffe to sign several white players. Radcliffe obliged his employer by signing three white teenagers immediately and then by adding at least two others later in the 1950 season.

1952

American League umpire Bill Summers turned in seven players, including members of the 1952 Chicago White Sox and Cleveland Indians, for apparently "fraternizing" before a game. Although the players remained nameless, they were fined $5 each for violating a 1951 rule that strictly prohibited socializing between players from two competing teams.

The 1952 Celler Congressional Committee announced that legislation for government control of major league baseball was unnecessary. The committee stated that the sport was obviously "competent and trustworthy" enough to solve its own problems. The committee also opposed all legislation exempting the reserve clause from Federal antitrust laws.

In 1952, the Soviet Union openly criticized the American game of base-ball by citing its own version of the game, called *lapka,* as being the original concept for the sport. The State Department quickly came to the national pastime's defense by accusing this claim by the Soviets to be the founders of baseball to be part of its "Hate America" Cold War campaign.

Major league attendance plummeted in 1952 (for the second season in a row) as National League ticket sales dropped a staggering 904,854 and American League sales decreased by 588,788.

1953

The 1953 St. Louis Browns set the major league mark for most consecutive home defeats by losing their 20th game in succession, 6–3, to the visiting Cleveland Indians.

A U.S. Court of Appeals affirmed the dismissal of a lawsuit filed by for-mer Chicago Cubs pitcher Boyd Tepler against major league baseball and owner William Wrigley. The lawsuit, filed in 1951, accused the Cubs' coach-ing staff of negligence that led to a premature career-ending arm injury for Tepler in 1944.

1954

On August 30, 1954, the Cleveland Indians—on their way to a 111-win sea-son—completed an embarrassing 11-home-game sweep of the visiting Bos-ton Red Sox. It was the first such sweep since the New York Yankees, led by "Murderers Row," blanked the laughable St. Louis Browns back in 1927.

On July 31, 1954, Milwaukee Brave Joe Adcock hit four home runs and added a double for a total of 18 total bases during a 15–7 massacre over the Brooklyn Dodgers at Ebbets Field. Adcock's 18 total bases set a major league record, and when combined with his seven total bases from the day before, gave him a two-day tally of 25, which tied the Braves' slugger with the immortal Ty Cobb for the record for the most total bases in two consecutive games.

In 1954, the major league owners association voted down the sale of the Athletics to a syndicate representing the city of Philadelphia. One week later, Arnold Johnson emerged to buy a controlling interest in the fran-chise from the Mack family for a reported $3.5 million. He later decided to move the team to Kansas City amid mixed emotions on the part of the rest of the league.

1955

In his first major league start, Pittsburgh Pirates' pitcher Al Grunwald threw "for the cycle" by surrendering a single, a double, a triple, and a home run (for four runs) all in a single inning during a 12–3 loss to the New York Giants.

1957

On August 17, 1957, future Hall of Fame centerfielder Richie Ashburn of the Phillies proved that lightning could indeed strike twice after hitting spectator Alice Roth with foul balls twice during the same at bat. The first foul struck the wife of Earl Roth, sports editor at the *Philadelphia Bulletin*, in the face and the second hit her body while she was being removed from her seat on a stretcher. Mrs. Roth went to the hospital to be treated for a broken nose as Philadelphia beat the New York Giants, 3–1.

1959

The 1959 Boston Red Sox remained the only major league team not to include minority players in its lineup. The National Association for the Advancement of Colored People filed a grievance against the franchise, charging it with racial discrimination and calling for an official investigation into the team's signing policies.

In 1959, controversy erupted over the American League batting title as the Cleveland Indians' Tito Francona finished the season with a league-leading .363 average, but fell one at bat short (399) of the required total (400). As a result, Harvey Kuenn of the Detroit Tigers was crowned the American League batting champion.

Political tensions between the United States and Cuba in 1959 initially prevented all Cuban players, including Minnie Minoso of the Chicago White Sox and Camilo Pascual and Pedro Ramos of the Minnesota Twins, from returning to the U.S. for the 1961 season. After negotiations, a high-ranking Cuban foreign ministry official finally permitted their unconditional return.

Few events in the game of baseball are more thrilling to witness than watching a pitcher twirl a no-hitter. The drama is intense, and both players and crowd hang onto each pitch as the hurler closes in on a slice of immortality. There is, however, no glory in being the team that fails to get a hit in such games. The Philadelphia Phillies have been on the receiving end of 17 no-hitters in the course of their long history, probably more than any other major league team. Two of those are of special interest. Lew Burdette was a talented right-handed pitcher who toiled for the Milwaukee Braves. In 1959, Burdette won the game against the Pittsburgh Pirates when Harvey Haddix pitched 13 perfect innings before finally losing the game. Burdette won, 1–0, scattering 12 hits. He joked, "I'm the greatest pitcher that ever lived. The greatest game that was ever pitched in baseball wasn't good enough to beat me, so I've got to be the greatest!" The next season, he took the hill against the Phillies on August 18, 1960, and threw a no-hitter, winning 1–0, and facing the minimum 27 batters. Tony Gonzalez, the only Phillie to reach base, was retired on a double play. Burdette scored the only run of the game. Twenty-eight days later, the great Warren Spahn took the mound against the Phillies. Spahn, the ace of the Braves' pitching staff, was probably the greatest left-handed pitcher to toe the rubber. He won 363 games in his long career, including 23 at the age of 42. Spahn faced the Phillies, who were on their way to a 59–95 record and a last-place finish, on September 16, 1960, and hurled a 4–0 no-hitter. Spahn faced only 29 hitters, walking 2, and had 15 strikeouts in winning his 20th game of the season and earning his first no-hitter. Thus, the 1960 Phillies were no-hit twice in 28 days by two different hurlers of the same pitching staff. That was the first time that such a rare feat happened, and it has not been repeated since.

1961

After nine innings, the 1961 season's second All-Star Game was called at a 1–1 tie due to heavy rain at Boston's Fenway Park.

1963

On September 27, 1963, Houston Colt 45s (Astros) manager Harry Craft shocked the New York Mets after starting an all-rookie lineup. Fifteen rookies appeared in all, but were bested by the older and wiser Mets, who "mentored" them with a 10–3 lesson in experience.

1964

Decades before the "Roberto Alomar incident," Golden Glove first baseman Vic Power of the California Angels was suspended for 10 days and fined $250 after spitting on umpire Jim Honochick during a 1964 doubleheader loss to the Chicago White Sox.

1966

The infield at Houston's Astrodome became the first to be replaced by the new experimental surface known as "Astroturf." In the first game ever to be played on the artificial grass, the visiting 1966 Los Angeles Dodgers prevailed over the home team, 6–3. It took baseball several decades to recover when classic outdoor ballparks finally returned to playing in fresh air and on real grass.

Dan Topping sold his remaining interest in the New York Yankees to the Columbia Broadcasting System (CBS) for a reported $1.4 million dollars. In the end, the television dynasty paid a total of $14 million for total control of the franchise. Topping initially looked to get the best of the deal when three days later, only 413 fans showed up at Yankee Stadium for a game against the Chicago White Sox.

1969

On May 13, Ernie Banks of the Chicago Cubs had seven RBIs (including his 1,500th) with a pair of three-run home runs and a double during a 19–0 massacre of the San Diego Padres. The blowout tied the mark for the largest shutout margin in the history of the modern National League.

In 1969, both leagues agreed to try the new "designated pinch hitter" (DPH) rule during spring training, but under two different variations. The American League allowed the optional use of a DPH only for the home team while the National League required home managers to obtain the visiting skipper's approval for the experimental substitution.

1970

On August 3, 1970, the Kansas City Royals set an unwanted major league mark by falling to the Baltimore Orioles 10–8, marking their 23rd loss to the Orioles in just two seasons.

In 1970, St. Louis Cardinals' Golden Glove outfielder Curt Flood filed a civil lawsuit against major league baseball in an effort to challenge the contract reserve clause. Flood refused to report to the Philadelphia Phillies after being traded, and contended that the rule violated federal antitrust laws. Flood eventually lost his $4.1 million suit when Federal Judge Irving Ben Cooper upheld the legality of the reserve clause. However, Cooper did recommend changes to the reserve system to be achieved through negotiation between both players and owners.

"X-5" baseballs, a new experimental brand claiming to travel faster and farther than traditional balls, were field-tested during all 1970 major league spring training games in both Arizona and Florida. Commissioner Bowie Kuhn ordered a halt to their use after a three-week trial period that ended with inconclusive results.

1971

On New Year's Day in 1971, the Baseball Writers Association of America (BBWAA) failed to elect anyone during the annual Baseball Hall of Fame voting. With 270 votes required for induction into the Hall of Fame, the closest nominees were Yogi Berra with 242 and Early Wynn with 240.

1972

Eighty-six games had been cancelled due to the first general players' strike, which was eventually resolved on April 13, 1972. Concessions came after both the owners and players agreed on a $500,000 increase in pension fund payments. In an effort to prevent paying the players for the work stoppage, the league decided not to make up the missed contests. As a result, some teams only played 153 total games.

1973

In 1973, the American Leagues' two premiere catchers, Carlton Fisk of the Boston Red Sox and Thurman Munson of the New York Yankees, squared off after the Bombers' captain barreled into Fisk while trying to score from third on a missed bunt by teammate Gene Michael. The legendary rivalry between the two teams combined with genuine dislike between the two players fueled the fight. Although the winner of the brawl remained undetermined, the winner of the game went to the Red Sox, 3–2.

Pitcher Wilbur Wood attempted to set a record during the 1973 season by starting both games of a doubleheader between his Chicago White Sox and the New York Yankees, but it backfired completely as the "Iron Man wannabe" took 12–2 and 7–0 losses.

At a joint meeting in 1973 of all 24 major league owners, the owners unanimously decided to allow the use of the "Designated Hitter" in the American League for a three-season probationary period. The experiment marked the first time since 1901 that the National and American Leagues played under different rules. The concept of interleague play was also submitted for committee review.

1974

In 1974, "Ten-Cent Beer Night" in Cleveland backfired after drunken and disorderly fans stumbled onto the field of play, causing the Indians to forfeit the game to the Texas Rangers. With a five-all score in the ninth, Tribe fans poured onto the field and surrounded outfielder Jeff Burroughs, trying to take his hat and glove for souvenirs. After players from both sides rushed to his aid, the umpires wisely called the game in favor of the visitors.

Commissioner Bowie Kuhn suspended principal New York Yankees owner George Steinbrenner for two years after he was convicted in federal court of making illegal contributions to the reelection campaign of President Richard Nixon.

On September 11, 1974, the Mets lost 4–3 to the Cardinals during a "long-distance" marathon night game. After 7 hours and 25 innings, the outing became the longest game in major league history. In the end, New York batted 103 times and St. Louis was not far behind with 99 plate appearances, for a record 175 total official at bats. Both sides set another major league record by stranding 45 runners on base. Despite the historic moment, only a thousand fans were still on hand when the game finally ended at 3:13 A.M.

1975

On September 22, 1975, a near-impossible statistical oddity occurred when brothers Gaylord Perry of the Texas Rangers and Jim Perry of the Oakland Athletics matched identical career win-loss records of 215–174.

Joe Torre of the New York Mets tied a major league record by hitting into four consecutive double plays during a 6–2 loss to the Houston Astros. The future Yankee manager joined the company of Hall of Famer Leon "Goose" Goslin, who first set the record in 1934 and Mike Kreevich who matched Goslin's dubious feat in 1939.

Charles Finley's experimental position known as the "designated runner" ended after the Oakland Athletics owner released the prototype, Herb Washington. The worldclass sprinter appeared in 105 games while never batting, scored 33 runs, and stole 31 bases in 48 attempts.

A pregame ceremony honoring the United States Army's 200 birthday "backfired" at Shea Stadium after two 75mm artillery batteries from nearby Fort Hamilton fired a 21-gun salute. After the smoke cleared, there was a large hole in the center field fence and broken windows throughout the box seat areas. The New York Yankees defeated Nolan Ryan and the California Angels, 6–4, after a quick cleanup and repairs.

1976

On September 11, 1976, Minnie Minoso of the Chicago White Sox joined the "four-decade player club" after entering a contest against the California Angels as a designated hitter. The 53-year-old went 0–3 as his team fell 7–3 to the "Halos." Four years later Minoso became only the second member of the five-decade player club in major league history.

1977

Major league baseball's first black manager hired became the first also fired when the struggling Cleveland Indians, who were 26–31 and in fourth place in the American League East, let Frank Robinson go in June. Jeff Torborg was named as his replacement.

As part of a promotional night to debut the new "Reggie Bar," a candy bar named after Reggie Jackson, fans at Yankee Stadium received free samples. The marketing scheme backfired when fans threw hundreds of them onto the field, halting the game until the ground crew cleared them away.

Despite a miserable 54–107 record, the Toronto Blue Jays boasted a home attendance of 1,701,052 during their debut season.

Prior to the start of the season, the Toronto Blue Jays had agreed to a trade that would send veteran left-handed pitcher Bill Singer to the New York Yankees for little-used, left-hander Ron Guidry. Management canceled the deal once the front office realized that Singer was on the cover of the new team's printed media guide. By the end of the season, Singer went 2–8 and then retired, while Guidry compiled a 16–7 record and an impressive 2.82 ERA.

1978

On September 23, 1978, after going two-for-four against the Chicago White Sox earlier in the day, fourth year Angels' outfielder Lyman Bostock was killed in a bizarre shooting accident. During a domestic dispute, the 27-year-old budding star took a .410 gauge shotgun blast fired by his uncle in the head. Bostock intercepted his uncle, who was on his way to shoot his wife and paid for it with his life. Bostock was a .311 hitter and his father, Lyman Sr. had been a star player in the Negro Leagues.

The *New York Times* reported that the renovations to the "House That Ruth Built" would cost a staggering $95.6 million dollars and that it would have cost only $48.8 million to build a brand new Yankee Stadium.

Don Sutton threatened to sue umpire Doug Harvey after the official claimed to find three "doctored" balls belonging to the Dodger righty during a game against the St. Louis Cardinals. After an investigation, Sutton received a warning from National League president Charles Feeney.

In a sign of things to come, major league umpires went on strike in August 1978, attempting to get better benefits. Amateur officiating crews called 13 games before a judge issued a formal restraining order sending the disgruntled picketers back to work.

1981

On May 29, 1981, the executive board of the Players' Association voted unanimously to strike on May 29, 1981, due to the unresolved issue of free-agent compensation. The deadline was extended briefly, however, after the National Labor Relations Board heard the Players' Association's unfair labor complaint was heard by the National Labor Relations Board. At 12:30 A.M. on June 12, union chief Marvin Miller announced the player's strike, beginning the longest labor action to date in American sports history. By the time the season finally resumed on August 10, 706 games (38 percent of the major league schedule) had been canceled. Due to the two-month strike, major league owners elected to split the 1981 season into two halves, with the first-place teams from each half in each division meeting in a best-of-five divisional playoff series. As a result, the Oakland A's, New York Yankees, Philadelphia Phillies, and Los Angeles Dodgers were guaranteed playoff spots as first-half league champions.

Seattle Mariners manager Maury Wills was suspended for two games after ordering the grounds crew to enlarge the batter's boxes by one foot prior to a game with the Oakland Athletics. Wills' request was in response to an A's complaint that Seattle's Tom Paciorek frequently stepped out of the box while hitting.

1983

The revolving door at the New York Yankees clubhouse continued to spin when Billy Martin was fired in 1983 as the skipper of the Bronx Bombers and was replaced by teammate Yogi Berra. Both were hired, fired, and re-hired repeatedly by George Steinbrenner.

Baseball Commissioner Bowie Kuhn ordered Hall of Famer Mickey Mantle to end all associations with major league baseball, after the "Mick" became involved in a sports promotion capacity with a casino in Atlantic City, New Jersey. Willie Mays was also targeted with a similar action due to his associations with legalized gambling.

New York Yankees owner George Steinbrenner received a $50,000 fine and a one-week suspension after making derogatory remarks about major league umpires. White Sox President Jerry Reinsdorf also paid a $500 fine after making remarks of his own about the outspoken Yankees owner at the All-Star Game.

Los Angeles Dodger reliever Steve Howe was banned for an entire season as a result of his ongoing battles with drug addiction by the Commissioner's Office. Bowie Kuhn refused to allow the troubled pitcher to return to major league baseball until he was proven to be drug-free. Earlier that 1983 season, Howe was fined $53,867 in salary for missed games after completing 30 days of rehabilitation in what was the largest fine levied to date.

1984

At Fulton County Stadium, the Atlanta Braves and San Diego Padres erupted in a 10-minute brawl over a pitching duel that resulted in 16 ejections by the officials. Several major league umpires stated that it was the worst disgrace ever witnessed on a baseball diamond and that it clearly set the game back 50 years in the minds of many fans.

Due to a strike by major league umpires, college replacement officials called the first game of the National League Championship Series. The labor dispute was predominately over a pool of $340,000 that the regulars wanted distributed to all umps, including those who were not working the postseason.

1985

Sports Illustrated pulled off a major April Fool's Day joke in 1985 by publishing a story about a Tibetan Buddhist monk named Sidd Finch with a 168 mph fastball who was the New York Mets latest rookie phenomenon.

Despite the April 1 date on the article and the byline by George Plimpton, many fans believed the story was real and were disappointed after discovering that Finch was a fake.

1986

In an effort to set an example, Commissioner Peter Ueberroth suspended seven players for drug abuse. All seven decided to contribute 10 percent of their seasonal salary to drug abuse programs, to serve 100 hours of community service, and to be subjected to random drug testing. The seven included Keith Hernandez of the New York Mets, Dale Berra of the New York Yankees, Joaquin Andujar of the Oakland Athletics, Jeffrey Leonard of the San Francisco Giants, Lonnie Smith of the Kansas City Royals, Enos Cabell of the Los Angeles Dodgers, and Dave Parker of the Cincinnati Reds.

Bret Saberhagen sued Rawlings over a misrepresented endorsement deal. Many other players were paid more than $50,000 as part of their compensation, but the Kansas City Royals pitcher received two free gloves per season as his compensation.

A free baseball promotion night at Arlington Stadium backfired when hundreds of fans targeted the Texas Rangers and umpires after the visiting Milwaukee Brewers rallied for a 10–2 win.

The Chicago Cubs fired their 28-year-old ball girl, Marla Collins, after she posed nude for *Playboy*. Despite fan support, the young lady was terminated for "behavior unbecoming an employee" of the franchise.

1987

Dwight "Doc" Gooden of the New York Mets entered a 28-day drug rehabilitation program at the Smithers Alcoholism Treatment Center. The '85 Cy Young Award winner tested positive for cocaine use and did not start the season until June 5 as a result of his rehab stint.

1988

Major league baseball's rules and regulations committee dropped the game-winning RBI as an official statistic.

Left-handed pitcher Dave Dravecky of the San Francisco Giants snapped his own arm while delivering a pitch in the sixth-inning against the Montreal Expos. He suffered a stress fracture of the humerus, which resulted from cancer surgery on that arm. Dravecky was pitching a shutout at the time of his injury and received the win for the final 3–2 decision. The next year, he tried to return, but a recurrence of the cancer caused the arm to fracture again and he retired with a 64–57 win-loss record. The arm and shoulder had to be amputated in 1991 to prevent further spread of the cancer.

1989

Sports Illustrated published details of Pete Rose's rumored gambling activities, including allegations of hand signaling to several betting associates from the dugout in Riverfront Stadium. A few months later, the FBI reported possessing several betting sheets with the Reds manager's handwriting and fingerprints on them. In August, after a thorough investigation, the baseball commissioner's office found him guilty of betting on games and forced Rose to sign an agreement banning him entirely from major league baseball for life.

1991

On June 6, 1991, the Kansas City Royals and Texas Rangers combined played an 18-inning game and tied a major league mark by leaving 45 runners stranded on base. The Royals also set an American League record by contributing 25 of the "castaways."

Darryl Strawberry tied a National League record by striking out five times in a single game as his Los Angeles Dodgers fell to the Montreal Expos, 9–3. The struggling slugger also stumbled in the outfield and dropped a fly ball for a three-base error.

The major league's Umpires Union voted to sit out Opening Day, resulting in amateur officials reporting as replacements. The arbiters, whose contract had expired on December 31, returned to work the following day with better benefits and an increased starting salary.

1993

The Reverend Jesse Jackson accused baseball owners of discriminatory practices and threatened to start a selective boycott unless a plan to hire more minorities for front office jobs was put in place by April 5, 1993. Ironically, Marge Schott, the Cincinnati Reds owner, was fined $25,000 by the commissioner's office and was banned for an entire season after several complaints accused her of using of ethnic and racial slurs.

The Major League Players Association rejected an owner's salary cap proposal and a request that players split all revenues 50–50. In addition, the owners proposed the elimination of salary arbitration, in return for which players could be eligible to file for free agency after four years in the major leagues instead of six. As negotiations heated up, the owners withheld $7.8 million that they were obligated to pay into the players' pension and benefit plans. The final straw came when the Senate Judiciary Committee failed to approve antitrust legislation, leaving players with little choice but to strike. Thirty-four days into the strike, the Commissioner canceled the remainder of the baseball season on September 14, 1994. As a result, the World Series was also canceled for the first time since 1904. Three months later, the owners unilaterally implemented a salary cap when negotiations remained at a standstill.

1995

On August 10, 1995, the St. Louis Cardinals were awarded the first forfeit victory in the major leagues since July 12, 1979, after fans bombarded the field with more than 200 souvenir balls that they had received on "Ball Day" at Dodger Stadium. The near-riot resulted from the ejections of Dodgers outfielder Raul Mondesi and manager Tommy Lasorda in the bottom of the ninth inning.

The 1994 strike continued into the 1995 season when players' union chief Donald Fehr declared all 835 unsigned major league players to be free agents in response to unilateral contract changes made by the owners. Five bills aimed at ending the baseball strike were introduced in Congress, and President Bill Clinton ordered both players and owners to resume bargaining and reach an agreement by February 6. After the deadline passed with no compromises, baseball's executive council approved the use of replacement players for spring training and regular season games. Finally, on April 25, the 234-day strike ended, although the opening games were played with replacement umpires. The regular officials continued to be locked out until May 3.

1996

On May 2, 1996, as the Seattle Mariners hosted the Cleveland Indians, an earthquake, measuring 4.8 on the Richter scale, rattled the Kingdome, causing officials to suspend the game with the Indians leading 6–3 in the seventh inning. Once the stadium's structure was thoroughly inspected, play resumed the following day.

Popular umpire John McSherry died of a massive heart attack after calling time from behind home plate seven pitches into a Reds-Expos game at Riverfront Stadium. The 21-year veteran suffered from a series of medical problems that were aggravated by his obesity.

Second baseman Roberto Alomar of the Baltimore Orioles set off a national debate after spitting in the face of umpire John Hirschbeck following an argument. Alomar was ejected over a called strike in the first inning of a game against the Toronto Blue Jays. U.S. District Judge Edmund W. Ludwig later prevented other umpires from sitting out the playoffs in protest of the incident, citing a no-strike clause in their contract.

1997

National League Vice President Katy Feeney reprimanded Deion Sanders of the Cincinnati Reds for altering his uniform as a tribute to Jackie Robinson. Sanders wore his pants at knee length and trimmed the sleeves off his jersey after seeing a photograph of the late Brooklyn Dodger on a Wheaties box. The following day, his teammates mimicked his alterations, thereby circumventing the league official's decree by promoting team uniformity.

1999

The Baltimore Orioles traveled to Havana, Cuba, to play the National Team in an exhibition game, witnessed in person by Fidel Castro. The Birds defeated the Cubans 3–2 in an 11-inning affair. Two months later, the tables were turned though, when the National Team traveled to Camden Yard and crushed the home team 12–6 in the first game ever played on American soil between the two countries.

2000

On September 1, 2000, the Cleveland Indians became the American League's fifth triple-play victim of the season at the hands of the Baltimore Orioles. With runners at first and second and no outs, shortstop Melvin Mora intentionally dropped catcher Sandy Alomar Jr.'s pop fly, threw to second baseman Jerry Hairston, who tagged both the runner at second as well as the runner coming from first. A confused Alomar retreated to the dugout, believing the infield fly rule was in effect and was called out for leaving the base path.

Following a May 16, 2000, incident in which 16 Los Angeles Dodger players and 3 coaches entered the stands during a fight with fans at Wrigley Field, 19 suspensions were handed out, resulting in the loss of 60 games for the players and 24 for the coaches.

A state court jury awarded $1.05 million to Andrew Klein, a boy who was struck in the head and suffered permanent brain damage while attending batting practice before a Florida Marlins game in 1997. The decision set the stage for limiting children's access to players on the field and required stricter safety guidelines for pregame ballpark programs for children.

2001

A new era of baseball in Pittsburgh began with the opening of PNC Park, which resembled the classic stadiums of old. The park served as the fifth home for the Buccos, replacing Three Rivers Stadium, which had replaced the sacred grounds of Forbes Field.[1] Unfortunately, Pirate legend and Hall of Famer Willie Stargell died the evening before its Opening Day, casting a dark shadow over the debut festivities.

The New York Yankees weren't the only baseball team from the Bronx that played well only to come up short in the end. The little league team from the South Bronx stole the show at the Little League World Series in Williamsport, Pennsylvania, but was later disqualified after officials discovered that star pitcher Danny Almonte was actually a 15-year-old ringer.

2002

For only the second time in the history of the Midsummer Classic, the 2002 All-Star Game was called at a 7–7 tie after 11 innings due to both teams running out of available pitchers. Following an outcry of disappointment from both the sports media and fans, MLB commissioner Bud Selig announced that "This will never happen again."

2003

The ongoing rivalry between the Boston Red Sox and New York Yankees came to a head during Game 3 of the 2003 American League Championship Series after both dugouts emptied twice as a consequence to what some felt was "overly aggressive" pitching. The infield melee was instigated after Boston ace Pedro Martinez struck Yankees' designated hitter Karim Garcia in the back and was fueled by Manny Ramirez who took offense to a high pitch thrown by Roger Clemens. As both dugouts cleared, New York's bench coach Don Zimmer charged at Martinez, who promptly reacted by throwing the 72-year-old to the ground. After several minutes of suspended play, both teams got back to business until a second brawl erupted in the Yankees bull pen between Jeff Nelson, Garcia and a member of Fenway Park's grounds crew. Following the 4–3 Yankees victory, major league baseball issued fines to Martinez, Ramirez, Garcia, and Zimmer while the Boston Police pressed additional charges against Garcia and Nelson for their involvement in the bull pen altercation.

The entire baseball world was shocked after one of its most beloved athletes, Sammy Sosa, was ejected in the first inning of a game between the Chicago Cubs and the Tampa Bay Devil Rays after umpires found cork in his shattered bat. Sosa, who had recently joined the 500 home run club and who had gained national prominence during his epic 1998 home run battle with Mark McGwire, apologized to fans, his teammates, and the commissioner of major league baseball. Stating that the corked bat had been strictly used for batting practice and had been mistakenly taken to the plate, Sosa received a seven-game suspension following an appeal. Sosa's other bats, which had been confiscated by security personnel and turned over to major league baseball, showed no signs of tampering. Still, many doubted the integrity of Sammy's previous accomplishments and it took time for him to return to fan favor.

On February 16, 2003, Baltimore Orioles pitcher Steve Bechler collapsed at the team's spring training complex in Fort Lauderdale, Florida, and died the next day. An autopsy determined that the 23-year-old had suffered a "heart attack-like event" after taking a dietary supplement containing ephedra. His widow later filed a $600 million lawsuit against the manufacturers, focusing national attention on the dangers of using potentially harmful weight loss aids. The lawsuit, filed in U.S. District Court in Fort Lauderdale, called the product Xcnadrinc RFA-1 a "poisonous cocktail" unsafe for human consumption.

2004

On August 31, 2004, the Cleveland Indians scalped the New York Yankees in a record-setting 22–0 massacre. The defeat marked the fifth consecutive loss for the Bronx Bombers in Yankee Stadium for the first time since May

2003. The 22 runs allowed were the most ever given up by the Yankees in their home ballpark, and the most runs allowed since 1928, when the Indians took a 24–6 decision (one of only two 18-run defeats in Yankees' history). The loss also tied the largest margin of defeat in a shutout since 1900, equaling a mark set by the Pittsburgh Pirates in a 1975 22–0 win over the Chicago Cubs at Wrigley Field.

America's "National Pastime" returned to the nation's capital for the first time in 33 years after major league baseball approved the relocation of the Montreal Expos to Washington, DC. Ironically, the announcement came one day before the anniversary of the 1971 final game of the Washington Senators before moving to Texas. The relocation of the Expos was subject to certain contingencies, including a vote by team owners in November and passage of legislation by Washington's City Council to build a ballpark on the Anacostia River waterfront.

2005

In a year filled with parity and mediocrity, the San Diego Padres finished the season with an 82–80 record and avoided becoming the first playoff team to ever finish the season at .500 or under. The Padres actually won more games in 2004 (87) and recorded back-to-back winning seasons for the first time since 1991 and 1992. Overcoming a seemingly never ending string of injuries and ailments, the Padres won the National League West, but were later swept 3–0 by the defending National League Champion St. Louis Cardinals in the National League Divisional Series.

Fed up with the lack of substantive response by major league baseball to the latest steroid scandals, the U.S. House of Representatives' Government's Reform Committee took its first step toward intervention in 2005, by holding a hearing focusing on the problems of doping in baseball. Following a criminal ongoing investigation into the Bay Area Laboratory Co-Operative ("BALCO," a California nutritional supplements company accused of distributing human growth hormones and steroids), the committee called several past and present players to testify regarding their knowledge and/or experience with performance-enhancing drugs. The publication of former star outfielder Jose Conseco's controversial memoir entitled *Juiced: Wild Times, Rampant 'Roids, Smash Hits, and How Baseball Got Big* helped to trigger the Congressional investigation. Former all-time, single-season homerun champion Mark McGwire, Baltimore Orioles stars Rafael Palmeiro and Sammy Sosa, and Boston Red Sox pitcher Curt Schilling testified before the Congressional committee. Schilling and the Chicago White Sox' Frank Thomas, who testified via videoconference, were invited because of their outspoken views against steroid use. Ultimately hurting the cause more than helping it, Sosa crafted an opening statement in which he denied ever using illegal performance-enhancing drugs. McGwire refused to answer any questions directly, assuming a Fifth Amendment–like stance that ultimately tarnished his legacy in the eyes of many fans. And Palmeiro vehemently denied having used steroids. Unfortunately, "Raffy" later became one of the first players to test positive and receive a multiple game suspension. In retrospect, it appeared that the most unpopular member of the panel, Canseco, was apparently the most (if not the only) honest witness.

2006

When legendary Hall of Famer Buck O'Neill passed away on October 6, 2006, major league baseball Commissioner Bud Selig's press release reflected the baseball world's feelings. He stated, "Major League Baseball is saddened by the passing of Buck O'Neil. Buck was a pioneer, a legend and will be missed for as long as the game is played. I had the good fortune of spending some time with him in Cooperstown a couple of months ago and I will miss his wisdom and counsel. I have asked all clubs to observe a moment of silence before today's games."

2008

The Tampa Bay Devil Rays finished four games shy of a 100-loss season and finished last in the American League Eastern Division. 2008 was truly their Cinderella season, as they changed their name to the Tampa Bay Rays and then took a payroll that was $160-plus million less than the New York Yankees to a first place finish in the AL East. Every current major league franchise has now been to the playoffs at least once.

The end of Yankee Stadium: it almost does not seem possible to imagine baseball without "the House That Ruth Built," but 2008 marked the final season in what can arguably be considered the single most historic stadium in the entire baseball sporting world.

2009

Harry Kalas, play-by-play announcer for the Philadelphia Phillies, passed away on April 13 after collapsing in the press box at National Park.

2010

The Pittsburgh Pirates extended a dubious record in 2010. It was their 18th consecutive losing season, setting a record for North American major professional sports teams. The team also matched the 1963 New York Mets for the worst road record in a 162-game season at 17–64.

There were two milestones and two heartbreakers. The Chicago Cubs played the 20,000th game in team history on June 26, 2010, but lost to their crosstown rivals, the Chicago White Sox, with a score of 3–2 at U.S. Cellular Field. Their record was 10,197–9,643 (with 160 tied games). The Atlanta Braves played the 20,000th game in their team history on August 6, 2010, having started in 1876 in Boston, then transferring operations to Milwaukee in 1953, and finally coming to Atlanta in 1966. They lost the game in 11 innings with a score of 3–2 to the San Francisco Giants at Turner Field. Their record was 9,916–9,930 (with 154 tied games).

The financially foundering Texas Rangers were purchased from former owner Tom Hicks, at an auction in U.S. Bankruptcy Court on August 5, 2010 by a group led by Chuck Greenberg and Hall of Famer Nolan Ryan. The ownership change was approved by the Major League Baseball owners on August 12, 2010. Ironically, just one year later, the team made it to the 2011 World Series.

2011

In June of the 2011 season, the Los Angeles Dodgers filed for bankruptcy protection in a Delaware court, adding to the off-the-field troubles that hobbled one of baseball's most storied franchises. Team owner Frank McCourt had upset Commissioner Bud Selig the week before by summarily rejecting a multibillion-dollar TV deal. This led to a public feud that played out in the papers. In a statement following the filing, Frank McCourt stated, "(Bud Selig has) turned his back on the Dodgers, treated us differently, and forced us to the point we find ourselves in today. I simply cannot allow the commissioner to knowingly and intentionally be in a position to expose the Dodgers to financial risk any longer." The bankruptcy filing listed Dodgers' assets of up to $1 billion and debts up to $500 million.

The Boston Red Sox and Atlanta Braves each experienced the worst collapses in MLB history. On the morning of Aug. 26, the Braves were up 9½ games in the National League wild card race and 10½ games on the Cardinals. Experts calculated Atlanta's odds of making the playoffs at that point by simulating the remainder of the season a million times and gave them a 98.99 percent chance. On the morning of September 4th, the Red Sox had a nine-game lead in the American League wild card race with 24 games left to play. Experts figured their chance of making the playoffs at 99.78 percent, giving them less than a quarter of a one percent chance of missing out on October play. And then it happened. . . . Boston went on to finish in third place in the AL East with a 90–72 record. Atlanta ended the season with an 89–73 record in second place in the NL East. Neither team made it to the post-season.

The biggest disappointment to their fans, without a doubt, were the 2011 Pittsburgh Pirates, who looked to finally break their record-streak of 18 consecutive losing seasons early on. A year after finishing with a big-league-worst 57–105 record, the Pirates were 51–44 and had a half-game lead in the NL Central standings before play on July 20. Unfortunately, it was all downhill from there, as they resumed their perennial ineptitude, finishing the season with a dismal 72–90 record and consequently securing their 19th losing campaign.

Notable Quotables

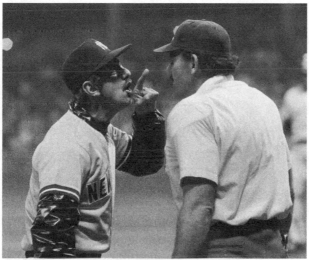

Yankees manager Billy Martin has a few words with home plate umpire Nick Bremigan (AP Photo/Mark Duncan)

★ | Lines About Losing . . .

No American sport has been responsible for more memorable quotes than baseball. From amusingly brilliant sayings from players like Yogi Berra, to raunchy belittlements from stingy skippers like Miller Huggins, and from romantic film dialogue from *Bull Durham, Field of Dreams* and *A League of Their Own,* to top-10 songs like *Centerfield,* baseball has a language and a lore that is all its own. Here are just a few of the game's best sayings:

"If a tie is like kissing your sister, losing is like kissing your grandmother with her teeth out."
   —*George Brett*

"I managed a team that was so bad, we considered a 2–0 count on the batter a rally."
   —*Rich Donnelly*

"Baseball is like a poker game, nobody wants to quit when he's losing: nobody wants you to quit when you're ahead."
   —*Jackie Robinson*

"We made too many wrong mistakes."
   —*Yogi Berra*

"We didn't lose. We just didn't play good enough to win."
   —*Nomar Garciaparra*

"The best possible thing in baseball is winning the World Series. The second best thing is losing the World Series."
—*Tommy Lasorda*

"Show me a good loser, and I'll show you an idiot."
—*Charlie Gehringer*

"There is no crying in baseball."
—*Tom Hanks in* A League of Their Own

"Losing streaks are funny. If you lose at the beginning, you got off to a bad start. If you lose in the middle of the season, you're in a slump. If you lose at the end, you're choking."
—*Gene Mauch*

"I lost it in the sun!"
—*Billy Loes, after fumbling a grounder*

"Winning is never final—losing is never fatal."
—*Vincent M. Fortanasce*

"The only thing worse than a Mets game is a Mets double header."
—*Casey Stengel*

"I learned a lot, but I don't want to learn it again."
—*Pitcher Matt Keough, after 18 straight losses*

"There are peaks and valleys in this game. We're in a valley—Death Valley."
—*Kirby Puckett*

"How can a guy win a game if you don't give him any runs?"
—*Robert "Bo" Belinsky, after losing a game 15–0*

"You can't sweep if you don't win the first game, and it's tougher to win two out of three if you lose the first one."
—*Todd Helton*

"It's hard to win a pennant, but it's harder losing one."
—*Chuck Tanner*

"You can't tell how much spirit a team has until it starts losing."
—*Rocky Colavito*

"The Mets have found ways of losing that I never knew existed."
—*Casey Stengel*

"Your chances of winning, I've got to believe are really, really small when you score one run in 18 innings."
—*Clint Hurdle*

"They (the Rockies) don't look like a major-league baseball team, but more like a Wednesday night Industrial Softball League team with every player supplying his own uniform."
—*Woody Paige*

"I'm tired of it. I don't want to hear about it anymore."
—*Bill Buckner*

"A baseball game is simply a nervous breakdown divided into nine innings."
—*Earl Wilson*

"When you're in a slump, it's almost as if you look out at the field and it's one big glove."
—*Vance Law*

"Strikeouts are boring. Besides that, they're fascist. Throw some ground balls. They're more democratic."
—*Kevin Costner in* Bull Durham

"Poets are like baseball pitchers. Both have their moments. The intervals are the tough things."
—*Robert Frost*

"It breaks your heart. It is designed to break your heart. The game begins in spring, when everything else begins again, and it blossoms in the summer, filling the afternoons and evenings, and then as soon as the chill rains come, it stops and leaves you to face the fall alone."
—*A. Bartlett Giamatti, "The Green Fields of the Mind," Yale Alumni Magazine, November 1977*

"The designated hitter rule is like letting someone else take Wilt Chamberlain's free throws."
—*Rick Wise, 1974*

"If a horse can't eat it, I don't want to play on it."
—*Dick Allen on artificial turf, 1970*

"Baseball is almost the only orderly thing in a very unorderly world. If you get three strikes, even the best lawyer in the world can't get you off."
—*Bill Veeck*

"No matter how good you are, you're going to lose one-third of your games. No matter how bad you are you're going to win one-third of your games. It's the other third that makes the difference."
—*Tommy Lasorda*

"During my 18 years I came to bat almost 10,000 times. I struck out about 1,700 times and walked maybe 1,800 times. You figure a ball-player will average about 500 at bats a season. That means I played seven years without ever hitting the ball."
—*Mickey Mantle, 1970*

"A critic once characterized baseball as six minutes of action crammed into two-and-one-half hours."
—*Ray Fitzgerald, in* Boston Globe, *1970*

"Things could be worse. Suppose your errors were counted and published every day, like those of a baseball player."
—*Author Unknown*

"There are two theories on hitting the knuckleball. Unfortunately, neither of them work."
—*Charlie Lau, 1982*

"To a pitcher, a base hit is the perfect example of negative feedback."
—*Steve Hovley, 1969*

"Hating the New York Yankees is as American as apple pie, unwed mothers and cheating on your income tax."
—*Mike Royko, 1981*

"Baseball is too much of a sport to be called a business, and too much of a business to be called a sport."
—*Philip Wrigley*

"Baseball isn't a business, it's more like a disease."
—*Walter F. O'Malley*

★ | Acknowledgments

ERIC: As always, I could not do what I do without the support of my wife Susan, who tolerates my need to suffer watching my Philadelphia sports teams. I thank my father for introducing me to the game of baseball, and for being my favorite buddy to watch a game with all these many years later. I owe a debt of gratitude to my high school baseball coach, Bob Wolfrum, for teaching me what it was like to be a member of a truly terrible team. I also owe a great debt of gratitude to my co-author, Michael Aubrecht, for giving me the chance to bring my childhood dream to fruition in the form of this book. Finally, I am incredibly grateful to the terrible teams and pathetic players who made this book possible.

MICHAEL: I would like to thank my beautiful wife Tracy and my wonderful children Dylan, Madison, Kierstyn, and Jackson, my parents Thomas and Linda Aubrecht, as well as all of my family, friends, associates, and former tee-ball, minor league, little league, and softball coaches. I would also like to thank my childhood heroes of the baseball diamond, who grabbed my attention at an early age and have yet to let go. Finally, I want to express my sincere thanks to my co-author Eric Wittenberg, who trusted me with his wonderful concept and invited me along for the ride, despite his hatred of my beloved Bronx Bombers.

We would both like to thank Dave Raymond for being willing to pen the excellent foreword to this book that helped to set the tone for what follows. We also want to thank Will Underwood, Joyce Harrison, Carol Heller, Mary

Young, Darryl Crosby, and Jonathan Knight from the Kent State University Press. Pat Kelly, John Horne, and Freddy Berowski from the National Baseball Hall of Fame & Museum's A. Bartlett Giamatti Research Library. Sean Holtz from *Baseball-Almanac,* noted baseball author Harvey Frommer, and the Society for American Baseball Research (SABR).

★ | Notes

#1. Not Louisville Sluggers

1. The fledgling Louisville Colonels were managed by four skippers: Dude Esterbrook, Jimmy Wolf, Dan Shannon, and Jack Chapman.

#2. Bad News Brownies

1. Until the late 1890s the St. Louis team was still called the "Browns," as they had been during their heyday in the then-major American Association. Around 1899 the team abandoned the brown motif and switched to cardinal red. Thus, a new and lasting nickname was born.

#3. Squashed Like a Bug

1. On July 15, 1899, the Spiders accomplished the rare feat of playing a doubleheader against the Orioles without scoring a single run, losing 10–0 and 5–0. The Spiders allowed more than eight runs per game while scoring only three per game themselves. This was par for the course as Cleveland had gone 0–30 at the start of the season and only won 12 of their remaining 116 games. The Spiders wound up the season losing a record 87 percent of their games.

#4. "Et Tu, Brute?"

1. After a brief stint with Washington's NL entry in 1892, Patsy Donovan starred with the Pirates for eight seasons while serving as player-manager in 1897 and 1899. Dealt to the Cardinals in 1900, Donovan was their player-manager in 1901–1903. Being traded to, and later leading the Washington club of the American League in 1904 gave him the distinction of playing for three Washington clubs in three major leagues.

#5. The Curse Continues

1. Collins was a good ballplayer in his own right. He once hit three bases-loaded triples in a single game, a record he held alone for more than a quarter of a century until Elmer Valo tied the record in 1949. His grandson, Bob Gallagher, played first base for the Mets and Astros in the 1970s.

2. McManus retired with an excellent career batting average of .289, 120 homers, and 999 RBIs. He had 1,926 hits in his 15-year career.

#6. Even the Babe Couldn't Save This One

1. The business partner to whom Fuchs owed the money was Charles Francis Adams III, the great-great-grandson of Pres. John Adams and great-great-grandson of Pres. John Quincy Adams. Charles Francis Adams Jr., the father of Charles III, was a decorated hero of the Civil War. Charles Francis Adams III served as Secretary of the Navy during the administration of Franklin Delano Roosevelt, and his son, Charles Francis Adams IV, served as the first president and chairman of the board of Raytheon Corporation. The Adams family dynasty left its mark in many diverse ways.

2. Adams was involved in horse racing, a venture deemed inappropriate by Commissioner Kennesaw Mountain Landis, who remained extremely concerned about avoiding any possible links between baseball and organized gambling in the wake of the 1919 World Series scandal that nearly destroyed major league baseball.

#8. Tie: '42 and '61 Phillies

1. It is worth noting that the Philadelphia Athletics also finished last in 1942, posting a wretched record of 55–99, meaning that the City of Brotherly Love's two major league franchises posted a combined record of 97 wins and 208 losses in 1942, for a combined winning percentage of .318 for the season.

#9. Tie: '50-'51-'52-'53-'54 Buccos

1. Kiner led the National League in home runs for seven consecutive seasons (1946 through 1952). But the team around Kiner placed in the first division only one time— in 1948—and in 1952 compiled one of the worst records in major league history.

#10. The Worst Record of the Modern Era

1. Bell is noteworthy for a variety of reasons. First, and foremost, he was a fine player in his own right. Second, his son, Buddy Bell, was an all-star third baseman with the Cleveland Indians and Texas Rangers for 18 years. Buddy Bell also managed in the major leagues for several years. Buddy's son David Bell also had an 11-year major career as a third baseman before a bad back ended it prematurely. David Bell is now a minor manager in the Cincinnati Reds' system. The Bells are one of only two families to place three generations of players in the major leagues.

2. The "Miracle Mets," as they became known, won the World Series in 1969, seven years after their first season. They did so on the talented young arms of pitchers Tom Seaver and Jerry Koosman. Seaver had a Hall of Fame career, winning 311 games, National League Rookie of the Year, and three Cy Young Awards. Koosman won 222 games in a 19-year career. Both made their major league debuts in 1967, and both were products of the Mets' farm system.

3. In 1995, Ashburn was elected to the Hall of Fame. He died in 1997 while still a much beloved broadcaster for the Phillies.

4. Believe it or not, Craig had an even worse year in 1963, going 5–22, with an 18-game losing streak. He retired in 1965. Ironically, Craig became an extremely effective pitching coach, teaching Jack Morris and Mike Scott the split-fingered fastball. He was the pitching coach for the 1984 World Series champion Detroit Tigers. He won a National League pennant as the manager of the 1989 San Francisco Giants and also managed the San Diego Padres for several years.

5. Not surprisingly, the last team to have two 20-game losers was the 1936 Phillies, mired in their long run of miserable seasons. Bucky Walters and Joe Bowman both lost 20 games for the Phillies that year.

#11. One Year of Wretchedness

1. O'Brien's twin brother was an official in the Seattle city government, so it's not much of a stretch to imagine that his brother Eddie was hired by the Pilots to curry favor with the city administrators.

2. The designated hitter rule was not adopted until 1972, with Ron Blomberg of the New York Yankees serving as the first regular season Designated Hitter (DH) in the spring 1973.

3. Fortunately for Bouton, the Astros were in the heat of a pennant race, and finished well above the Pilots in the standings. The Astros cut Bouton in the summer of 1970, ending his season. He had just published his book, *Ball Four,* which flew off the shelves and infuriated most of Bouton's teammates, who felt that Bouton had invaded their privacy by relating stories that had traditionally been kept private under baseball's version of the code of silence. However, *Ball Four* remains one of the most influential and important books on baseball ever published. Nearly 40 years later, the book is still in print.

#12. In Need of Forgiveness

1. The San Diego Chargers of the National Football League still play in this stadium today.

#13. Fundamentally Flawed

1. Schilling finally retired in March 2009 after 20 years. He retired with a career record of 216–146, a career ERA of 3.46, and 3,116 strikeouts in 3,261 innings. Perhaps most importantly, he was one of the most effective postseason pitchers to

ever toe the rubber. Schilling went 4–1 with a 2.06 ERA in seven World Series starts and will undoubtedly receive consideration for election to the Hall of Fame. Luckily for him, he overcame his atrocious major league debut with one of the worst teams in the history of major league baseball.

15. Scaredy Cats

1. The other three are the Boston Red Sox, Chicago White Sox, and Cleveland Indians.

#1. Worst Season.

1. Although the Union Association is conventionally listed as a major league, its status as such has been questioned by a number of modern baseball historians, most notably Bill James in *The Bill James Historical Baseball Abstract*. The lopsided competition of its franchises and schedules was a continual problem and the association was derisively dubbed "The Onion League" by its critics.

#3. Worst Collapse

1. Many said that the main catalyst for the Mets' "collapse" was their pitching, or lack thereof. In a 10-game sequence from September 16 to 25, the Mets lost six games. In four of these six games, the Mets scored six, eight, seven, and nine runs. These losses were directly related to the weak pitching from the Mets' starters and even their bull pen.

2. The epic collapse of the Mets finally allowed the Phillies to exorcise the demons of their own epic collapse in 1964, when they had a 6½-game lead with 12 to play and promptly lost 10 in a row to finish tied for second. That collapse would have been featured in this book, but for the collapse of the Mets.

#4. Worst Pitching Staff

1. In fact, in 1939, pitcher Walter Beck earned the derisive nickname "Boom Boom." The first boom was the sound of the bat hitting the ball, and the second boom was the sound of the ball slamming into the tin-covered outfield walls of Baker Bowl.

2. Interestingly, Klein's 170 RBIs weren't even close to leading the league. Chicago Cub outfielder Hack Wilson set the major league record for RBIs in a single season that year with 191.

#6. Worst Call

1. At an early age, Maris is said to have exhibited a woefully independent, no-nonsense personality. Originally recruited to play football at the University of Oklahoma, he arrived by bus in Norman and found no one from the university there to

greet him. He turned around and went back home to Fargo. Stories like this were used by the press to paint Roger as a simpleton.

Disappointment on the Diamond: A Timeline of Terribleness

1. Author Eric Wittenberg attended the University of Pittsburgh School of Law, which was built on the site of the former Forbes Field. Thus, although the old stadium itself no longer existed, Wittenberg spent a great deal of time on its hallowed grounds. Author Michael Aubrecht was born and raised in Pittsburgh, but he spent his years watching the Buccos in Three Rivers Stadium, also no longer in existence.

★ Bibliography

Internet Web Sites

Baseball Hall of Fame: www.baseballhalloffame.org
Baseball Library: www.baseballlibrary.com
Baseball-Almanac: www.baseball-almanac.com
Baseball-Reference: www.baseball-reference.com
FORBES: www.forbes.com
Jay Jaffe's Baseball Journal: www.futilityinfielder.com/home.php
Major League Baseball: www.mlb.com (plus misc. team pages)
The Pinstripe Press: www.pinstripepress.nct
SABR (Society for American Baseball Research): www.sabr.org
The Sporting News (Vault): www.sportingnews.com
USA Today (Sports): www.usatoday.com

Print

Anderson, Dave, ed. *The New York Yankees Illustrated History.* St. Martin's Press, 2002.
Angell, Roger. *Late Innings: A Baseball Companion.* Simon & Schuster, 1982.
Angus, Jeff. *Management by Baseball.* Harper Business, 2006.
Aubrecht, Michael. "All-Star Game, Commissioner Bios, Divisional Playoffs, Pinstripe Press, World Series, Year In Review." *Baseball-Almanac* 2000–2006.
Bouton, Jim. *Ball Four: The Final Pitch.* Bulldog Publishing, 2000.
Bowman, John S., and Zoss, Joel. *Pictorial History of Baseball.* Smithmark Publishers, 1987.
Boyer, Mary Schmitt. *The Good, the Bad, & the Ugly: Heart-Pounding, Jaw-Dropping, and Gut-Wrenching Moments from Cleveland Indians History.* Triumph Books, 2008.
Breslin, Jimmy. *Can't Anybody Here Play This Game? The Improbable Saga of the New York Mets' First Year.* Viking, 1963.
Cantor, George. *The Good, the Bad, & the Ugly: Heart-Pounding, Jaw-Dropping,*

and Gut-Wrenching Moments from Detroit Tigers History. Triumph Books, 2008.

Caren, Eric C. *Baseball Extra: A Newspaper History of the Game from Its Beginnings to the Present.* Book Sales, 2000.

Center, Bill. *Padres Essential: Everything You Need to Know to be a Real Fan.* Triumph Books, 2007.

Chandler, Bob, and Bill Swank. *Tales from the San Diego Padres.* Sports Publishing, 2006.

Cook, William A. *The Summer of '64: A Pennant Lost.* McFarland, 2002.

Dawidoff, Nicholas. *Baseball: A Literary Anthology.* Library of America, 2002.

Deveaux, Tom. *The Washington Senators. 1901–1971.* McFarland, 2001.

DK Publishing. *The Baseball Timeline.* DK Adult, 2001.

Editors of *Sports Illustrated. The Baseball Book.* Sports Illustrated, 2006.

Eisenberg, John. *From 33rd Street to Camden Yard: An Oral History of the Baltimore Orioles.* Contemporary Books, 2001.

Finoli, David, and Rainer, Bill. *The Pittsburgh Pirates Encyclopedia.* Sports Publishing, 2003.

Frommer, Harvey. *A Yankee Century: A Celebration of the First Hundred Years of Baseball's Greatest Team.* Berkley Hardcover, 2002.

———. *Five O'Clock Lightning: Babe Ruth, Lou Gehrig and the Greatest Baseball Team in History, The 1927 New York Yankees.* Wiley, 2007.

——— and Frederic J. Frommer. *Red Sox vs. Yankees: The Great Rivalry.* Sports Publishing, 2004.

———. *New York City Baseball: The Last Golden Age.* Harvest Books, 1992.

———. *Primitive Baseball: The First Quarter Century of the National Pastime.* Athenium, 1988.

———, ed. *The New York Yankee Encyclopedia.* Macmillan, 1997.

Fuchs, Robert S., and Wayne Soini. *Judge Fuchs and the Boston Braves.* McFarland, 1998.

Garagiola, Joe. *It's Anybody's Ball Game.* Contemporary Books, 1988.

Golenbock, Peter. *Red Sox Nation: An Unexpurgated History of the Boston Red Sox.* Triumph Books, 1992.

———. *Red Sox Nation: An Unexpurgated History of the Boston Red Sox.* Triumph Books, 2005.

Gummer, Scott, and Larry Shenk. *Phillies: An Extraordinary Tradition.* Insight Editions, 2010.

Gutman, Dan. *Baseball's Biggest Bloopers: The Games That Got Away.* Penguin Young Readers, 1995.

Hanks, Stephen, Dick Johnson, David Raskin, and David Nemec. *The Baseball Chronicle* (Illustrated). Publications International, 2003.

Hogan, Kenneth. *The 1969 Seattle Pilots: Major League Baseball's One-Year Team.* McFarland, 2007.

Honig, Donald. *Baseball America: The Heroes of the Game and the Times of Their Glory.* Touchstone, 2001.

Jaffe, Jay. "The Futility Infielder Tony Suck: The Man Who Lived Up To His Name," *Jay Jaffe's Baseball Journal,* www.futilityinfielder.com/home.php.

James, Bill. *The New Bill James Historical Baseball Abstract.* Free Press, 2003.

Jenson, Don. *The Timeline History of Baseball.* Palgrave Macmillan, 2005.

Jordan, David M. *Occasional Glory: A History of the Philadelphia Phillies.* McFarland, 2003.

———. *The Athletics of Philadelphia: Connie Mack's White Elephants, 1901–1954.* McFarland, 1999.

Kaese, Harold. *The Boston Braves, 1871–1953.* Putnam's Sons, 1954.

Kahn, Roger. *The Boys of Summer.* Harper Perennial Modern Classics, 2006.

Kashatus, William C. *September Swoon: Richie Allen, the '64 Phillies, and Racial Integration.* Pennsylvania State University, 2004.

Kurkjian, Tim. *America's Game.* Crown, 2000.

Mantle, Mickey, and Gluck, H. *The Mick.* Jove, 1986.

Mosedale, John. *The Greatest of All: The 1927 New York Yankees.* Doubleday, 1983.

Nathanson. Mitchell. *The Fall of the 1977 Phillies: How a Baseball Team's Collapse Sank a City's Spirit.* McFarland, 2008.

National Baseball Hall of Fame. *Baseball as America: Seeing Ourselves Through Our National Game.* National Geographic, 2005.

Nemec, David, and Saul Wisnia. *100 Years of Major League Baseball: American and National Leagues, 1901–2000.* Publications International, 2000.

——— and Dave Zeman. *The Baseball Rookies Encyclopedia.* Brassey's, 2004.

Paskin, Janet. *Tales from the 1962 New York Mets.* Sports Publishing, 2004.

Pluto, Terry. *The Curse of Rocky Colavito: A Loving Look at a Thirty-Year Slump.* Gray, 2007.

Robinson, George, and Charles Salzberg. *On a Clear Day They Could See Seventh Place: Baseball's Worst Teams.* Dell, 1991.

Rossi, John P. *The 1964 Phillies: The Story of Baseball's Most Memorable Collapse.* McFarland, 2005.

Ryczek, William J. *The Amazin' Mets 1962–1969.* McFarland, 2008.

Shecter, Leonard. *Once Upon the Polo Grounds: The Mets That Were.* Dial Press, 1970.

Silverman, Matt, Michael Gershman, and David Pietrusza. *Baseball: The Biographical Encyclopedia.* Total Sports, 2000.

Smith, Ron, ed. "Baseball's 100 Greatest Players: Second Edition." *Sporting News,* 2005.

———. "The Ballpark Book: A Journey Through the Fields of Baseball Magic." *Sporting News,* 2003.

Smith, Ron, and Billy Crystal. Sporting News. *61*: The Story of Roger Maris, Mickey Mantle.* McGraw-Hill/Contemporary, 2003.

Stargell, Willie, and Tom Bird. *Willie Stargell: An Autobiography.* HarperCollins, 1984.

Stout, Glenn, and Richard A. Johnson. *Yankees Century: 100 Years of New York Yankees Baseball.* Houghton Mifflin, 2002.

Tan, Cecilia, and Bill Nowlin. *The 50 Greatest Red Sox Games.* Wiley, 2006.

———. *The 50 Greatest Yankee Games.* Wiley, 2005.

Thorn, John, ed. *The Complete Armchair Book of Baseball: An All-Star Lineup Celebrates America's National Pastime.* Galahad, 2004.

———, Phil Birnbaum, Bill Deane, Rob Neyer, Alan Schwarz, Donald Dewey, Nicholas Acocella, and Peter Wayner. *Total Baseball, Completely Revised and Updated: The Ultimate Baseball Encyclopedia* (8th ed.). Sport Classic Books, 2004.

Trucks, Virgil, and Ronnie Joyner. *Throwing Heat: The Life and Times of Virgil "Fire" Trucks.* Pepperpot, 2004.

Vancil, Mark, and Mark Mandrake. *The New York Yankees: New York Yankees—100 Years—The Official Retrospective.* Ballantine Books, 2005.

Worth, Fred. *Baseball's Worst Team (Academic Forum 21 2003–04).* Henderson State University (Department of Mathematics and Computer Science), 2004.

Zolecki, Todd. *The Good, the Bad, & the Ugly: Heart-Pounding, Jaw-Dropping, and Gut-Wrenching Moments from Philadelphia Phillies.* Triumph Books, 2010.

Index